Books

Augustinian Heritage Institute, Inc.

www.augustinianheritage.org

THE WORKS OF SAINT AUGUSTINE

A Translation for the 21st Century

Part I – Books

Volume 8:

On Christian Belief

THE WORKS OF SAINT AUGUSTINE
A Translation for the 21st Century

On Christian Belief

True Religion (*De vera religione*)
translated by Edmund Hill, O.P.
The Advantage of Believing *(De utilitate credendi)*
translated by Ray Kearney
Faith and the Creed (*De fide et symbolo*)
translated by Michael G. Campbell, O.S.A.
Faith in the Unseen (*De fide rerum invisibilium*)
translated by Michael G. Campbell, O.S.A.
Demonic Divination (*De divinatione daemonum*)
translated by Edmund Hill, O.P.
Faith and Works (*De fide et operibus*)
translated by Ray Kearney
Enchiridion (*Enchiridion de fide et spe et caritate*)
translated by Bruce Harbert

I/8

general introduction and other introductions
by
Michael Fiedrowicz
(translated by Matthew O'Connell)

editor
Boniface Ramsey

New City Press
Hyde Park, New York

Published in the United States by New City Press
202 Cardinal Rd., Hyde Park, New York 12538
©2005 Augustinian Heritage Institute

Cover art (paperback):
Jan van Scorel, *Episcopal Consecration of Augustine*. Oil painting.
The Dominican Church of St. Stephen, Jerusalem.

Library of Congress Cataloging-in-Publication Data:

Augustine, Saint, Bishop of Hippo.
    The works of Saint Augustine.

    "Augustinian Heritage Institute"
    Includes bibliographical references and indexes.
    Contents: — pt. 3, v .15. Expositions of the Psalms, 1-32
—pt. 3, v. 1. Sermons on the Old Testament, 1-19.
— pt. 3, v. 2. Sermons on the Old Testament, 20-50 — [et al.] — pt. 3,
v. 10 Sermons on various subjects, 341-400.
    1.   Theology — Early church, ca. 30-600.   I. Hill,
Edmund.   II. Rotelle, John E.   III. Augustinian
Heritage Institute.   IV. Title.
BR65.A5E53   1990   270.2   89-28878
ISBN 1-56548-055-4 (series)
ISBN 1-56548-233-6 (pt. 1, v. 8)
ISBN 1-56548-234-4 (pt. 1, v. 8, pbk.)

Printed in the United States of America

Table of Contents

The Advantage of Believing

Faith and the Creed

Faith in the Unseen

Demonic Divination

Divine the Future — 207; Comparison with the Marvels even Bad Human Beings Perform, Which nonetheless Do not Entitle Them to Greater Respect than the Good and Just. — 209; How Demons Succeed in Forecasting Future Events — 210; Demonic Predictions, unlike Genuine Prophecy, Can Be both Mistaken and Deliberately Misleading — 211; Reasons why Demons Are Allowed to Predict What Had already Been Foretold by the Prophets — 213; The One True God of Israel Has never Been Attacked or Denied by the Oracles of Pagan Gods — 214; The Conversion of the Gentiles Foretold by the Prophets — 215; The Mockery of the Few Remaining Educated Pagans May Be safely Ignored — 216

Faith and Works

The Enchiridion on Faith, Hope, and Charity

General Introduction

The works in this volume of Augustine's writings cover a lengthy period of his life. Between 390 (*True Religion*) and about 421 (*Enchiridion*), first as a layman, then as a priest, and finally as a bishop, he composed a number of works that shed light on the phenomenon of Christian faith from different perspectives and deal with different aspects of it.

The earliest work, *True Religion,* sought to determine in principle the relationship between Platonic philosophy and Christianity, between rational thought and belief based on authority, and to draw up a first synthesis of Augustine's views at the time. Later works were meant to show that the act of faith (*The Advantage of Believing, Faith in the Unseen*) and the content of the faith (*Faith and the Creed, Enchiridion on Faith, Hope, and Charity*) are in accord with reason.

The existential dimension of faith, or its exercise in a concrete way of life, also had to be brought out in contrast to a narrow, reductive concept of faith (*Faith and Works*). Finally, the work entitled *Demonic Divination* shows how Augustine the bishop felt obliged to counteract uncertainties in matters of faith that were stirred up in contemporary Christians by the last rearguard actions of paganism.

Augustine's reflections on faith display an unmistakable autobiographical element. According to the testimony of *The Advantage of Believing*,[1] he himself had in his earlier years been attracted by the critical rationality of the Manicheans, whose rejection of a faith based on ecclesial authority he accepted as his own. With the insight of later years he judged the Manichean claim to rationality to be an empty promise, a lure, a deceitful claim that could not be fulfilled. In response to this rationalist view Augustine defended the thesis that faith precedes every kind of understanding and that human beings cannot live without faith. But Manichean rationalism was only one front on which faith had to be defended as a legitimate way of knowing. The same defense had to be made in response to ancient philosophy, especially that of the Platonic school, which defined faith, in contrast to true knowledge (*epistémé*), as having the cognitive status of mere opinion (*doxa*) and therefore as a defective form of knowledge.

It is true that in his early writings Augustine himself cultivated an optimism about knowledge and expressed his confidence that such Christian truths as the

---

1. *The Advantage of Believing* 1, 2; 9. 21.

Trinity and the resurrection could be philosophically demonstrated by reason.[2] But he knew that reason alone could not bring the human race, dependent as it is on what is sensible and transient, to the invisible world of the eternal God (*mundus intelligibilis*). Reason is able to disclose truth only to a very few human beings who are trained in philosophy. The great mass of people, however, receive this truth through faith that is based on the history of salvation and is mediated by ecclesial authority. The access to truth which ancient philosophy made possible for an elite was thus made universal in Christianity. Alongside the way of reason (*via rationis*), the way of authority (*via auctoritatis*) was now open to all human beings, provided they were prepared to believe.

When Augustine showed that many of life's activities were based on an act of faith,[3] he was using a familiar topos of early Christian apologetics.[4] But he shifted the emphasis to a new argument when he based the necessity of faith on the historical nature of Christianity. Since knowledge of history always depends on witnesses who speak from their own experience, the only form of knowledge possible in this area is faith (*credere*) and not insight (*intellegere*).[5] In addition, Augustine went back to the theories of knowledge of the Hellenistic philosophcal schools in order to prove the importance of faith in the acquisition of knowledge.[6]

But Augustine's thinking was not limited simply to proving that the act of faith is reasonable. It was also a constant concern of his to gain a deeper understanding of the content of the faith (*intellectus fidei*). The creed provided a summary of the basic truths of faith, and it was due to Augustine's theological reflection that this very ancient formula of faith acquired new vitality.[7] In his view the Church's creed contains the biblical message in a compressed form. The theologian of Hippo knew how to relate the creed, or symbol, to all the problems that exercised him and his age. His intellectual efforts to plumb the contents of the creed, his speculative elucidation of its individual articles, and his demonstration of the coherent character of the whole kept it from becoming a mere liturgical "formula."

His works titled *Faith and the Creed* and *Enchiridion on Faith, Hope, and Charity* are two precious witnesses to his several explanations of the baptismal

---

2. See J. J. O'Meara, "St. Augustine's View of Authority and Reason in A.D. 386," *Irish Theological Quarterly* 18 (1951) 338-46.
3. *The Advantage of Believing* 12, 26; *Faith in the Unseen* 1, 2-2, 4.
4. See Theophilus, *To Autolycus* I, 8, 2; Arnobius, *Against the Nations* II, 3; Eusebius, *Preparation for the Gospel* I, 5, 7-8.
5. *True Religion* 25, 40.
6. See T. Führer, "Zum wahrnehmungstheoretischen Hintergrund von Augustins Glaubensbegriff," in T. Führer and M. Erler, eds., *Zur Rezeption der hellenistischen Philosophie in der Spätantike* (Stuttgart 1999) 191-212.
7. F. Kattenbusch, *Das Apostolische Symbol* II (Leipzig 1900; repr. Hildesheim 1962) 403-10.

profession of faith. The first of these is a succinct explanation of the Church's faith by the young priest (393) who admittedly has not yet developed the speculative powers of his later years but does already project a clear theological image. The *Enchiridion*, just thirty years later (c. 421), is a comprehensive treatise on the faith and is at the same time often regarded as the best compendium of Augustinian thought.

As the title *Enchiridion on Faith, Hope, and Charity* already hints, Augustine was unwilling to look upon faith as an isolated entity. Instead he located it in the larger context of the entire Christian life. The same concern is operative in the book *Faith and Works*. It is possible to speak of authentic, living faith only when this faith shows itself in the works of love. A faith that prescinds from its practical demonstration in one's concrete life is but a "dead" faith.

Augustine's work *Demonic Divination* makes it clear that Christians who in their baptismal profession of faith had renounced the *pompa diaboli*, the diabolical splendors of ancient paganism, were nonetheless shaken in their faith by continuing spectacular manifestations of that paganism. This little treatise is an excellent example of how the Bishop of Hippo endeavored to accept responsibility for the faith in the oneness of God which Christians professed at their baptism; this was necessary because the old gods seemed not yet to have been silenced for good.

Augustine embodies the sum total and high point of reflection on the faith in the early Church.[8] His religious genius and speculative mind, his philosophical impulse and personal experience produced an understanding of the faith that is supremely authentic and exemplary. The legitimation of faith (*credere*) as an independent form of knowledge alongside direct knowing (*scire*), as well as its differentiation from defective forms such as false knowledge (*opinio*) and gullibility (*credulitas*),[9] the basing of faith on an authority, the establishment of criteria for its credibility,[10] and, finally, the beginning of a systematic differentiation between the content of faith (*fides quae creditur*) and the act of faith (*fides qua creditur*):[11] all these decisively marked later reflection on faith not only in the Middle Ages but in western Christianity as a whole.

---

8. For a survey see D. Lührmann, "Glaube," *Reallexikon für Antike und Christentum* 11, 64-122; on Augustine, see E. TeSelle, "Credere," *Augustinus-Lexikon* 2, fasc. 1/2, 119-31.
9. See *The Advantage of Believing* 9, 21-14, 32; *Faith in the Unseen* 1, 2-3, 4.
10. See *True Religion* 24, 45-25, 47; *The Advantage of Believing* 15, 33-17, 35; *Faith in the Unseen* 3, 5-7, 10.
11. See *The Trinity* XIII, 2, 5; XIV, 8, 11.

True Religion

Translation by Edmund Hill, O.P.

Notes by Michael Fiedrowicz and Edmund Hill, O.P.

Introduction

1. Genesis

"Every approach to a good and blessed life is to be found in the true reli-gion."[1] Ever since Augustine began to think about the meaning of life, he was preoccupied with the question of how human beings might reach the satisfaction of their deepest desire, that is, how they might find happiness. Writing shortly after his baptism, he agreed with the Neoplatonists that only a life devoted to philosophy could ensure happiness.[2] After returning from Italy to Thagaste, the city of his birth, in 388, he had the opportunity to put this ideal of a philosophical life into practice together with some friends. In this quasi-monastic common life "he lived for almost three years, fasting, praying, and doing good works for God the Lord, far removed from all worldly cares and in the company of like-minded friends, and meditating day and night on the law of God."[3] Here Augustine found the intellectual and spiritual atmosphere in which he could deepen his own reli-gious experience and philosophical insights and then organize them within a broader framework. These three years were probably the happiest of his life. In 390, shortly before his ordination to the priesthood and before "it pleased God to tear him away suddenly and for ever from this secure nest, in which almost all his dreams had been fulfilled,"[4] Augustine composed his work *True Religion*.

In doing so he was fulfilling a promise he had made in the autumn of 386,[5] before his baptism, to his fatherly friend and benefactor Romanianus.[6] The latter had not only generously financed Augustine's studies; he had also made it possible for Augustine to open his own school of rhetoric in Carthage; in addi-tion, he had entrusted to Augustine the education of his two sons. Since Romanianus had, in addition, "given him a place in his heart,"[7] as Augustine

---

1. *True Religion* 1, 1.
2. *Answer to the Skeptics* II, 2, 4.
3. Possidius, *Life of Augustine* 3, 2.
4. F. van der Meer, *Augustine the Bishop: Church and Society at the Dawn of the Middle Ages*, trans. B. Battershaw and G. R. Lamb (New York: Harper & Row, 1965) 209.
5. *True Religion* 7, 12. In Letter 15, 1, written in 390, Augustine told Romanianus that he had completed and was sending on a book on the Christian religion.
6. On Romanianus see F. Decret, *L'Afrique manichéene (IV-Ve siècles)* (Paris: Études Augustiniennes, 1978) 66-72, 373-374; A. Gabillon, "Romanianus, alias Cornelius," *Revue des études augustiniennes* 24 (1978) 58-70.
7. *Answer to the Skeptics* II, 2, 3.

gratefully attests, he allowed himself to be so far influenced by the persuasive Augustine as to follow him into the Manichean sect and to become a more confirmed follower of Mani than did the much younger man who had led him astray. Social obligations later took the big landowner from North Africa to Milan, where he witnessed the religious crisis of his protégé. Since Romanianus was unable, after Augustine's conversion to the Christian faith (386), to take part in the philosophical discussions of Augustine's friends at Cassiciacum, not far from Milan, Augustine promised to send him a discussion on religion (*disputatio de religione*)[8] and to let him know his own views on the true religion (*quid de vera religione sentirem*).[9]

Although the completion of this project came only several years later, these thoughts "on the true religion" should be regarded as mirroring the intellectual and spiritual outlook of Augustine only a few months after his conversion in the garden at Milan.[10] Despite the delayed publication, then, the content and method of this work reflect the early phase of Augustine's philosophical and religious thought. But since the work takes up various subjects which Augustine developed in greater detail in his later work *The City of God*,[11] the early date of *True Religion* is all the more significant for the continuity-amid-development of Augustine's thought.

But the present work was intended as something more than a token of friendship for Romanianus. Since Augustine had formerly taken his friend with him into the sect of the Manicheans, he now wanted to rescue him from the influence of their teachings by opening up to him the Christian religion which he himself had discovered and in which he had moved beyond his former errors. His own personal experiences were to show the path by which Romanianus, too, could make his way to the true religion.[12]

Unfortunately, traces of this friend soon vanished from Augustine's biography, so that we do not know whether the reading of the work led to his conversion. But we do find a relevant indication in the correspondence of Paulinus of Nola, who seems to address Romanianus as a Christian in 395.[13] In any case, Romanianus was not simply a follower of Manicheanism. Rather he was a pagan by birth, a philosopher in his interests, and someone who was led astray in his way of life, a doubter, and a seeker. These many sides of the man played a part in the conception of the present book.

---

8. Ibid. II, 8, 3.
9. *True Religion* 7, 12.
10. See A. Mandouze, *Saint Augustin. L'aventure de la raison et de la grâce* (Paris: Études Augustiniennes, 1968) 491-492.
11. See G. Madec, "Le *De civitate Dei* comme *De vera religione*," in idem, *Petites études augustiniennes* (Paris: Études Augustiniennes, 1994) 189-213.
12. See *True Religion* 10, 20.
13. See Letter 7, 1.

2. Subject

The unity of the work is due not to a thesis that is supported by arguments but to a subject that is seen in various perspectives, and the author constantly varies his treatment of it. Initially, indeed, Augustine's remarks have to do with Manichean dualism,[14] but they are at the same time intended to rebut all forms of religious error (*omnes pravas et falsas opiniones*).[15] On the positive side, the work is concerned to make known the true religion.

In the Christian tradition the concept of *vera religio* occurs for the first time in Tertullian (*Apol.* 24, 2) and Minucius Felix (*Oct.* 1, 5). Inasmuch as the Christian apologists took the nonbiblical term *religio* from the vocabulary of the pagans, their aim, on the one hand, was to locate Christianity within a non-Christian intellectual horizon.[16] But, when they simultaneously modified "religion" with the adjective "true," they were avoiding an identification of Christianity with elements of a pagan religious outlook.[17] When described as *vera religio*, Christianity was claiming to overcome the defects of all pre-Christian and non-Christian religions and to ensure the fulfillment of their deepest aspirations.

What meaning did the concept of "religion" have for Augustine? At the end of the present work he derives *religio* etymologically from *religare*: "Directing ourselves with their [i.e., the holy angels'] help towards the one God and . . . binding (*religantes*) ourselves tightly to him alone (which is what religion is said to get its name from), [we are] quit of every superstition."[18] "So let our religion, then, bind us tightly to the one almighty God (*religet ergo nos religio uni omnipotenti Deo*)."[19] In contrast, in his *City of God* Augustine adopts a different etymology that comes from Cicero, although he also modifies its meaning: "When we choose him or, rather, choose him again, in order not to fail to regain what we lost—when, then, we choose him again (*religentes*, from which the word 'religion' must be derived), we strive toward him through love in order to find rest in him and be happy, for the goal of fulfillment beckons to us from him."[20] In the *Revisions* Augustine expressly justifies the derivation from *religare*, which he had chosen in *True Religion*. This choice was not due to igno-

---

14. See *Revisions* I, 13, 1.
15. See *True Religion* 9, 16. See the typology of errors in religion ibid. 6, 10; 10, 18; 37, 68; 55, 107-11.
16. See M. Sachot, "Comment le Christianisme est-il devenu *religio*?" *Revue des sciences religieuses* 59 (1985) 95-118; idem, "<Religio/superstitio>. Historique d'une subversion et d'un retournement," *Revue de l'histoire des religions* 208 (1991) 355-95.
17. See M. Fiedrowicz, *Apologie im frühen Christentum. Die Kontroverse um den christlichen Wahrheitsanspruch in den ersten Jahrhunderten* (Paderborn 2000) 160, 240-43.
18. *True Religion* 55, 111.
19. Ibid. 55, 113.
20. *The City of God* X, 3.

rance of Cicero's etymology but represented a deliberate preference.[21] Thus Augustine is convinced that religion is concerned with the union of human beings with God. The ascent to God by way of true religion can therefore be regarded as the central theme of *True Religion*.[22] References to this ascent recur throughout the work.[23]

3. Structure

In order to refute Manicheanism Augustine used Neoplatonic arguments. The latter philosophy of being, especially as developed by Porphyry,[24] was well suited for invalidating Manichean dualism, according to which evil was an independently existing substance. But Augustine was not satisfied with a simple denial of this view. Rather he wanted to win over Romanianus to a kind of "intellectual Catholicism," and therefore in the second part of the work he developed the idea of an ascent of the soul. There is no doubt that in the background, once again, was Porphyry and his work *The Return of the Soul*.[25] In consciously appealing to this Neoplatonic conception, even while modifying it along Christian lines, Augustine must have been looking beyond his immediate addressee to followers of Porphyry in the Milanese world. Anti-Manichean apologetics and the differentiation of his own views from those of the Neoplatonists and Porphyry in particular are thus clearly distinguishable aspects of this work.[26]

These distinguishable but not always separable aims[27] produce the complex structure of the treatise:[28]

---

21. *Revisions* I, 13, 9.
22. See F. van Fleteren, "Augustine's *De vera religione*: A New Approach," *Augustinianum* 16 (1976) 475-97.
23. See *True Religion* 11, 21-12, 25; 12, 26-17, 34; 18, 35-23, 44; 26, 49; 29, 52-31, 58; 32, 59-36, 66; 29, 72-45, 83; 45, 84-48, 93; 49, 94-51, 100; 55, 107-113.
24. See W. Theiler, *Porphyrios und Augustin* (Halle, 1933) = idem, *Forschungen zum Neoplatonismus* (Berlin 1966).
25. See B. R. Voss, "Spuren von Porphyrios *De regressu animae* bei Augustins *De vera religione*," *Museum Helveticum* 20 (1963) 237-39.
26. See F. van Fleteren, "Background and Commentary on Augustine's *De vera religione*," in *"De vera religione," "De utilitate credendi," "De fide rerum quae non videntur" di Agostino d'Ippona* (Rome 1994) 33-74, esp. 46-47.
27. See J. J. O'Meara, review of Du Roy, *L'intelligence...*, in *Augustinian Studies* 1 (1970) 266ff.
28. I. Bochet, "*Animae Medicina*: La libération de la triple convoitise selon le *De vera religione*," in L. Alici, ed., *Il mistero del male e la libertà possibile (IV): Ripensare Agostino* (Rome 1997) 143-75, esp. 145; W. Desch, "Aufbau und Gliederung von Augustins Schrift *De vera religione*," *Vigiliae Christianae* 35 (1980) 263-77; F. van Fleteren, "Background and Commentary" (note 26, above) 48.

Prologue (1, 1-10, 20)
  Christianity as the fulfillment of Platonism (1, 1-6, 11)
  Religious errors, Manicheanism in particular (7, 12-10, 20)

Part I. The problem of evil (11, 21-23, 44)
  A1. Ontology: Being and nothingness; evil as perversion of the will
      (11, 21-15, 29)
  B1. Soteriology: Christ, the incarnate Wisdom of God, is the fulfillment
      of the three areas of philosophy (16, 30-17, 34)
  A2. Ontology: Evil does not compromise the harmony of the universe
      (18, 35-23, 44)

Part II. Ascent of the soul to God (24, 45-54, 106)
  B2. Soteriology: The function of authority; the *dispensatio temporalis* as the
      healing of mankind (24, 45-28, 51)
  A3. Ontology: Ascent of the mind from things visible to God (29, 52-36, 67)
  B3. Soteriology: Christ as victor over the three temptations, and the healing
      of the three desires (37, 68-54, 106):
  pleasure (39, 72-45,83)
  pride (45, 84-48, 93)
  curiosity (49, 94-51, 100)

Concluding appeal (55, 107-13)
  Breakaway from every kind of false religion (55, 107-11)
  Union with the only God by way of the true religion (55, 112-13)

As the outline shows, interlocking constructions play an important role in the structure of the work. The second main section corresponds to the first part of the prologue, and the first main section to the second part of the prologue. Each main part in turn has its own interlocking construction. While the first main part is dogmatic and anti-Manichean in content, the second is more philosophical and speculative. It is in light of this artfully complex structure that Augustine's own judgment on his work, as formulated in the *Revisions*, makes known its main emphases and intentions: "At that time I also wrote my book on true religion, in which I explain from various points of view and in great detail that in true religion the one true God, who is the Trinity of Father, Son, and Holy Spirit, must be worshiped. In addition, I show what a great mercy is manifested in the fact that in the form of a temporal institution God communicated to humankind the Christian religion, which is the true religion, and showed how human beings are to be made fit for this worship of God by means of a gentle divine guidance. Above all, however, this work opposes the two-nature teaching of the Manicheans."[29] The four basic features of the work that are listed in this summary will now be considered one by one.

4. True Religion as Worship of the One True God

In Augustine's understanding of it, true religion is characterized by an inseparable combination of worship, doctrine, and morality.[30] Paganism did not succeed in achieving this religious ideal. Philosophical enlightenment admittedly brought myths into increasing discredit, but it continued to accept the old forms of divine worship. The philosophers had long since taken the ground out from under the traditional forms of worship by regarding temples, sacrifices, processions, and prayers as unnecessary in light of a higher conception of God. And yet, contradicting their philosophical convictions, they spoke up for the preservation of the official practice of worship. Thus Seneca, a Stoic, was of the opinion that "the wise man will observe all this because it is commanded by the laws, not as though it pleased the gods."[31] The growing gap between reason and piety, between philosophy and mythico-political theology led to an inner breakdown of the ancient religion. It was to this open discrepancy between worship and doctrine, religious practice and philosophical conviction, that Augustine objected in pre-Christian antiquity and especially in the sages. In their religious practice the Platonists did not reach the level of their philosophical theory. Even Socrates was untrue to himself when he practiced idolatry.[32] The later criticism, made in detail in *The City of God*, of the inconsistency of the philosophers as well as of the falsity of the official Roman religion[33] was thus present in germ twenty years earlier in the work *True Religion*.

A further focus of criticism was the inability of the philosophers to convince the broad masses of the knowledge they were providing. In an "imaginary interview"[34] with Plato Augustine sketches both the grandeur and the limitations of his philosophy.[35] Plato (Augustine says) indeed reached a true knowledge of God, but he was unsuccessful in winning the masses over to this truth which he grasped at the purely intellectual level. Plato was even convinced that the only being who could achieve that goal was one filled to an extraordinary degree with

---

29. *Revisions* I, 13, 1.
30. See T. Kobusch, "Das Christentum als Religion der Wahrheit: Überlegungen zu Augustins Begriff des Kultus," *Revue des études augustiniennes* 29 (1983) 97-128.
31. See Augustine, *The City of God* VI, 10. See G. Bardy in Bibliothèque Augustinienne 34, 572-574, note complémentaire 23.
32. *True Religion* 2, 2.
33. See *The City of God* IV, 27.29-31; VI, 5-6,10; X, 1.3.
34. See Mandouze, *Saint Augustin* (note 10, above) 495 and, in general, 488-508.
35. *True Religion* 3, 3.

divine power and wisdom. Over against this admission Augustine sets the picture of the Christian era, in which even the broad masses believed in that world-transcending reality of which Plato had a rough knowledge accessible only to himself and a small group of disciples.[36] Augustine urged contemporary Neoplatonists to "perceive the distinction between the feeble guesses of the few and the obvious well-being and correction of whole peoples" and to follow Christ who brought about this state.[37] This exhortation is emphasized by means of an impressive fiction: Were Plato living today with his disciples and were he to catch sight of the filled churches and the empty temples and see how human beings have their eyes on the other world, he would admit that Christianity has brought to pass what he himself had sought in vain.[38]

In light of this vision Augustine was able to describe Christianity as the fulfillment of Platonism.[39] He adopted the optimistic view that the Platonists "with a few changes here and there in their words and assertions . . . would have become Christians."[40] It is noteworthy that in his *Revisions* he did not retract or modify these statements. Even twenty years later (410) he stated this position in almost the same words in his letter to Dioscurus.[41] To his mind Platonism and Christianity were in agreement inasmuch as they called men and women to a spiritual world (*mundus intelligibilis*). In his early writings he identified Christian redemption with the Neoplatonic ascent of the soul to the vision of God.[42]

At this time in his life Augustine saw the decisive difference between the Neoplatonic system and the Christian religion as lying in the area of competence in communicating the truth. Only Christianity had the ability to disclose the highest truths even to simple people. This position is, of course, by no means unproblematic. Nietzsche's objection comes to mind, that Christianity is Platonism for the people.[43] But elsewhere Augustine expresses himself in a more differentiated way.[44]

In the present context, however, there is another important statement. Augustine emphasizes the identity in principle of *philosophia* and *religio*: "Our faith and teaching have demonstrated (and this is the fundamental principle of human salvation) that there is not one thing called philosophy, that is devotion to

---

36. Ibid. 3, 4-5.
37. Ibid. 4, 6. See also *Order* II, 5, 16; Letter 118, 20.32-33; *The City of God* X, 29.
38. *True Religion* 4, 6.
39. See G. Madec, " 'Si Plato viveret...' (Augustin, *De vera religione* 3, 3)," in *Néoplatonisme. Mélanges offerts à Jean Trouillard* (Fontenay aux Roses 1981) 231-47.
40. *True Religion* 4, 7.
41. See Letter 118, 21; Mandouze, *Saint Augustin* 506.
42. But see Augustine's critical revision in *Revisions* I, 3, 2.
43. See P. Alfaric, *L'évolution intellectuelle de saint Augustin* I. *Du manichéisme au néoplatonisme* (Paris 1918) 525: "In his [Augustine's] view, Christ is the Plato of the masses."
44. See G. Madec, *Saint Augustin et la philosophie* (Paris, 1996) 22-23, 115-120.

wisdom, and another called religion."[45] The same idea is voiced again in other words: "Repudiate all those who neither philosophize about sacred matters nor attach sacred rites to philosophy."[46]

In keeping with this criterion Augustine could describe Christianity as a successful synthesis of philosophy and religion, of doctrine and worship. At the same time, he could assert the superiority of Christianity over all other religio-philosophical manifestations, since the defect of the latter consisted, in every case, precisely in the separation of *religio* and *philosophia*.

In adopting this approach Augustine placed himself in the line of the early Christian apologists who insisted first on the reasonableness of religion in contrast to the ancients' understanding of religion. In comparison with traditional mythology, political theology, and the mystery cults, Christianity submitted to the requirements of plausibility and rationality (see 1 Pt 3:15). Among all the religions of late antiquity Christians alone made their teaching the object of a proof of credibility and reasonableness. Christianity rejected the retreat of ancient religion from the presence of the Logos, its withdrawal into tradition and convention. By its uncompromising choice of the truth Christianity distinguished itself as the only rational religion of late antiquity, a period marked by an increasing collapse into the vortex of the irrational.[47] In contrast to ancient philosophy, which increasingly took on religious traits but, being the product of human thought, could lead human beings only to an abstract concept of God, Christians were able to show the personal character of truth by pointing to the person of the incarnate Logos. Christianity was thus able to see itself as a synthesis of *religio* and *philosophia*. Until that time there had been either a religious practice without any relation to truth or a philosophical theory without any deep religious spirit. As "true worship of the true God,"[48] Christianity overcame both the weakness of ancient religion, which did not attain to philosophical truth about God, and the inadequacy of ancient philosophy, which did, however, uncover the beginnings of a religious relationship with God.

Augustine thought extensively about the conditions needed for the possibility of such a synthesis of religion and philosophy.

---

45. *True Religion* 5, 8. See I, Bochet, *"Non aliam esse philosophiam...et aliam religionen* (Augustin, *De vera rel.* 5, 8)," in B. Pouderon and J. Doré, eds., *Les apologistes chrétiens et la culture grecque* (Paris 1998) 333-53; Mandouze, *Saint Augustin* 499-503.
46. *True Religion* 7, 12.
47. See A.-M. Festugière, *La Révélation d'Hermès Trismégiste* I (Paris 1950) 1-18.
48. *True Religion* 2, 2.

5. The Economy of Salvation as the Basis of True Religion

According to the *Revisions*, the basic thesis of the present work is that "through the economy of salvation (*dispensatio temporalis*) God has communicated to humankind the Christian religion, which is the true religion."[49] This statement shows us the innermost essence of the Augustinian concept of religion. God himself has made it possible for the soul to travel the way of ascent and return because in his providence he opened a path for it in the history of salvation. By its faith in a divine initiative that operated in history to the advantage of the human race, Christianity differed both from Manicheanism, which rejected the Old Testament and did not take the incarnation of Christ seriously, and from Neoplatonism, which attributed to the soul the ability to redeem itself. According to that philosophy, if the soul detaches itself from everything corporeal and material, it can by its own powers ascend to the divine. Over against this idea of redemption, as represented especially by Porphyry, Augustine emphatically asserts the basic principle of the true religion. The latter is based on "the history and prophecy of what divine providence has arranged to be enacted in the course of time (*dispensatio temporalis*) for the salvation of the human race, that is for its refashioning and preparation once more for eternal life."[50]

Augustine nonetheless did try to locate Christian belief in redemption within the horizon of philosophical intelligibility. He was convinced that the salvation for which Christians hope could be expressed fully in the terminology of the Platonists: "This [salvation] is the return from the temporal to the eternal and the refashioning of the new man from the life of the old."[51] In his view there was no doubt about the equivalence of the Platonic and Pauline formulations. The Platonic idea of a "turning away from the temporal to the eternal" allowed him to make it plausible that the specifically Christian element—the action of God in history (*dispensatio temporalis*)—should be the necessary starting point of soteriology. The intervention of God in history and his bodily manifestation in the form of the incarnate Logos were the only way suited to the concrete situation of humanity. God chose to meet human beings in the place in which they found themselves as a result of their sin: "Thus it was that the man was expelled from Paradise into this age, that is from eternal to time-bound things."[52] God determined to come himself into this world in order to make it possible for human beings to arise: "In the spot where a person has fallen, there one has to stoop down to him, so that he may get up again."[53]

---

49. *Revisions* I, 13, 1.
50. *True Religion* 7, 13.
51. Ibid. 52, 101.
52. Ibid. 20, 38.
53. Ibid. 25, 45.

In adopting this idea Augustine gained, first of all, an interior insight of faith (*intellectus fidei*) into the meaning of the divine economy of salvation, a reality which the Manicheans and Platonists rejected. The *dispensatio divina* was the sufficient means of salvation which humanity needed after falling under the control of the temporal and the material. In this dispensation Christ, as mediator between time and eternity, formed, as it were, the "intermediate step . . . in the human situation for grasping divine things, by which human beings could stride up to a likeness of God from their earthly life."[54] In view of the weakness of human knowing, which could be viewed by Platonists as an incapacity for the vision of truth or by Christians as a consequence of sin, Augustine interpreted the economy of salvation, and the incarnation of Christ in particular, as an authority (*auctoritas*), a way of knowledge different from the way of reason (*ratio*), by which even the uneducated could attain to the truth.[55] *Ratio* is the power to discover and ground truth, while *auctoritas* is the ability of the known truth to convey itself or, if you prefer, its power to convince.

This *auctoritas*, the ability to "convince ordinary people to believe all this, even if they were not capable of grasping it,"[56] was what made Christianity superior to Platonism, which reserved knowledge of truth to an intellectual elite.[57] Nietzsche disparagingly described Christianity as Platonism for the people; Augustine might well have subscribed to this saying, but he would have taken the derogatory judgment as an honorable description. According to Augustine's summary of his imaginary dialogue with the ancient thinker, Plato himself would admit that the broad circulation of truth, which he himself was able to make accessible to only a small group of people, was possible only for a divine human being who would lead humanity to belief through a supreme love and authority (*summo amore atque auctoritate*).[58]

The remarks on the relationship between *auctoritas* and *ratio* show how Augustine dealt critically with the philosophy of Porphyry and set over against it a Christian conception of redemption.[59] As he explained later in *The City of God*,[60] the Neoplatonist philosopher in his *The Return of the Soul* (*De regressu animae*)[61] searched in vain for a universal way of liberating the soul. As a result,

---

54. Ibid. 10, 19.
55. Ibid. 24, 45-28, 51. See F. van Fleteren, "Authority and Reason, Faith and Understanding in the Works of St. Augustine," *Augustinian Studies* 6 (1973) 33-71, esp. 61-63.
56. *True Religion* 3, 3.
57. See ibid. 3, 4-5; Letter 118, 16-21.32.
58. *True Religion* 3, 3.
59. See J. J. O'Meara, *Porphyry's Philosophy from Oracles in Eusebius' Praeparatio evangelica and Augustine's Dialogues at Cassiciacum* (Paris 1969) 31.
60. See *The City of God* X, 32.
61. From 386 on Augustine probably knew of this work from his own reading of it. See M. Cutino, "I *Dialogi* di Agostino dinanzi al *De regressu animae* di Porfirio," *Recherches Augustiniennes* 27 (1994) 41-74.

he was forced to think up a two-class system of redemption. The complete ascent of the soul remained the preserve of only a few philosophers, while the broad masses had to be satisfied with a lesser form of redemption. They could only draw closer to the realm of the divine, and this by means of magical practices. No more was possible for them. Augustine, indeed, also distinguished two ways, but the salvation which the majority of human beings reached by way of *auctoritas* was not different from the salvation which some few could find by way of reason. Thus the divine economy of salvation opened to all human beings the way of universal salvation which Porphyry had sought in vain: "That, in our times, is the Christian religion; it is in knowing and following this that salvation is most surely and certainly to be found."[62]

There was a further way in which Christianity showed itself to be the fulfillment of philosophy.

6. The Healing of the Soul by the True Religion

Another main focus of the work, according to Augustine's summary of it in the *Revisions*, is the question of "how human beings are to be made fit for this worship of God by means of the life they live."[63] This concern sheds light on extensive sections of the work, especially the detailed chapter on the three main desires.[64] The aim, once again, is to show Christianity to be the completion of Platonism.

The ideal of ancient philosophy was the healing of the soul.[65] A sentence of Epicurus, which Porphyry cites in his *Letter to Marcella* 31, makes this clear in exemplary fashion: "Empty is the talk of any philosopher whose words do not heal any passion of the soul; for just as the art of healing is utterly worthless if it does not expel the sicknesses of the body, so also is philosophy worthless if it does not expel the passion of the soul."[66] By proving that Christianity made possible the healing of the soul, Augustine intended to show how the Christian religion brings completion to philosophy.

In his analysis of the three basic desires (*voluptas, curiositas, superbia*) Augustine effected a synthesis of Neoplatonic philosophy and Johannine theology (see 1 Jn 2:16: *All that is in the world—the desire of the flesh, the desire of the eyes, the pride in riches...*). These three desires are disordered tendencies

---

62. *True Religion* 10, 19.
63. *Revisions* I, 13, 1.
64. *True Religion* 39, 72-51, 100. See Bochet, "*Animae Medicina*" (note 38, above); N. Cipriani, "Lo schema dei *tria vitia* (*voluptas, superbia, curiositas*) nel *De vera religione*. Antropologia soggiacente e fonti," *Augustinianum* 38 (1998) 157-195.
65. See A. J. Voelke, *La philosophie comme thérapie de l'âme. Études de philosophie hellénistique* (Paris 1993).
66. Epicurus, frag. 221, ed. H. Usener (Stuttgart 1966).

of human beings, who seek fulfillment where it cannot be found. *Voluptas* seeks fulfillment in the beauty of material things; *superbia* seeks fulfillment in power over material things; *curiositas* seeks fulfillment in the knowledge of things transitory. Human beings need, then, to become clear about the true goal of these tendencies: "What after all is curiosity aiming at but knowledge, which is only to be had with certainty about things that are eternal and always maintain themselves in the same way? What is pride aiming at but power, which goes with ease of action, which the perfect soul only finds when it submits to God and has its eyes turned towards his kingdom with total charity? What is bodily self-indulgence aiming at but satisfaction, which is only to be found where there are no needs and no decay?"[67]

Philosophy played an important part in this process. Ever since his reading of Cicero's protreptic work, *Hortensius*, Augustine thought of philosophy not simply as theoretical discourse but also as a choice of a manner of life, a spiritual exercise.[68] The classical three parts of philosophy—physics, ethics, and logic— had for their goal a new way of seeing and therefore a transformation of existence in its entirety. By making it possible to discover the order which the creator gave the world, physics enables human beings to adapt themselves to this order and, as far as possible, to subordinate the body to the soul. By making it possible for them to discern in other human beings human nature in its completeness as it corresponds to God's plan, ethics enables them truly to love the other. By making it possible for them to discern the truth, logic enables them not to let themselves be captivated by what is transitory but to seek what is important. By means, then, of the three parts of philosophy, human beings discover the true meaning of the longing that is within them and has gone astray through seeking bodily pleasure (*voluptas*), power (*superbia*), and amusement (*curiositas*).

Augustine wanted to prove that the healing of the soul from the three desires was achieved only through Christ. Being wisdom incarnate, Christ lived as a wise man and put the Platonic ideal into practice. Not only did he conquer these desires in his three temptations in the wilderness[69] and not only did he teach humanity, which had become enslaved to the senses, to contemn false goods.[70] He also brought philosophy to completion in all three of its parts.[71] He completed physics inasmuch as his resurrection showed that bodily desire has for its goal not fleshly pleasure (*voluptas*) but the health and peace of the body.[72] He brought ethics to its completion by teaching his commandment of love and showing how

---

67. *True Religion* 52, 101.
68. See *Confessions* III, 4, 7-8.
69. *True Religion* 38, 71.
70. Ibid. 16, 31.
71. Ibid. 16, 32-17, 34; 52, 101-54, 106; see also Letter 137, 17.
72. *True Religion* 39, 72-45, 83.

the striving for freedom has its true goal not in control over other human beings (*superbia*) but in true love.[73] Finally, Christ brought logic to its completion inasmuch as his teaching in word and deed instructed human beings that their striving for knowledge has its true goal not in things of sight and the other senses (*curiositas*) but in spiritual and divine realities.[74] The victory over the threefold desire shows the Christian religion to be philosophy in its perfect form.

Augustine's line of argument here was not solely apologetical in intention. It was also an effort to achieve an insight of faith (*intellectus fidei*). During this period of his life Augustine was concerned primarily with the question of the meaning of the economy of salvation. Insofar as the *dispensatio temporalis* was understood as a healing of the soul, it not only had to be believed (*credere*) but could also be understood (*intellegere*). This was also a refutation of the Manicheans, who ridiculed the credulity of Christians and made an exclusive claim to knowledge.[75] According to what Augustine himself says, the disagreement with the Manicheans was the final main focus of his work.[76]

7. True Religion as a Surmounting of Manichean Dualism

The fascination exercised by Manicheanism in Augustine's time was due not least to the answer which this system had found to the problem of evil. In Manichean dualism, evil was understood as an independent substance that was in continual conflict with the principle or source of good. Consequently, individual human beings were not personally responsible for their sins, since they were only the battlefield on which that eternal conflict was being carried on. Once Augustine had, with the help of Neoplatonic philosophy, found release from the influence of Manichean thought, he endeavored with the help of that same philosophy to refute dualism and give a different answer to the problem of evil.[77]

Augustine challenged the idea that evil is a substance.[78] He defined evil metaphysically as *omnino nullum* or "nothing at all,"[79] as a turning from being and a turning to nothing. At the level of morality he explained evil as being a corruption of the will.[80] In contrast to the Manichean identification of evil with matter he defended the value of creation and human nature.[81] Against Manichean deter-

---

73. Ibid. 45, 84-48, 93; 52, 101-54, 106.
74. Ibid. 49, 94-51, 100.
75. See ibid. 8, 14; *Confessions* VI, 5, 7.
76. See *Revisions* I, 13, 1.
77. See *True Religion* 11, 21-23, 44. See also Fleteren, "Background and Commentary" (note 26, above) 56-64.
78. *True Religion* 20, 39.
79. Ibid. 11, 21.
80. Ibid. 14, 27.
81. Ibid. 23, 44.

minism he defended the freedom of the human will.[82] Since the Christian religion set human beings free to serve not what is created but the creator himself,[83] it proved itself once again to be "the true religion" in contrast to Manicheanism.

8. The Importance of the Work

This work, which was the fulfillment of an earlier promise, gives a representative survey of Augustine's thinking during the period from 386 to 390. It manifests his intention of summarizing his present philosophical and theological thought, effecting a synthesis of Platonism and Christianity and linking together reason, speculation, and belief based on authority.

Augustine knew that he could achieve his apologetical and exhortatory purpose only on the basis of a deepened understanding of his own faith. In reaching this *intellectus fidei* he made use especially of Neoplatonic philosophy. He thought its terminology suitable for shedding light on the human condition and the meaning of human life. At the same time, however, he broke through the limits of that philosophical system by recognizing the incarnation of Christ to be the only way to union with God.

These ideas unmistakably reflect Augustine's own experiences during the period of his conversion. As he had freed himself from the Manichean deterministic theory of evil by means of Neoplatonic philosophy and had discovered in the latter the doctrine of the soul's ascent to God, so the present work also advances from an explanation of the problem of evil to the ascent to God. Again, as he had made his way from the philosophical notion of ascent to Christian faith in the incarnation, so too the present work culminates in a clarification of this mystery. Augustine was able to universalize his personal experience and to see in this personal experience the situation of all humankind.[84]

---

82. Ibid. 14, 27.
83. Ibid. 10, 19.
84. See J. J. O'Meara, *The Young Augustine. The Growth of St. Augustine's Mind up to His Conversion* (London 1954) 12, 18.

New City Press
202 Cardinal Rd.
Hyde Park, NY 12538

Place
Stamp
Here

NEW CITY PRESS
www.newcitypress.com
1-800-462-5980

Thank you for choosing this book.
If you would like to receive regular information
about New City Press titles, please fill in this card.

Title purchased: _____

Please check the subjects that are of particular interest to you:

- ☐ **FATHERS OF THE CHURCH**
- ☐ **CLASSICS IN SPIRITUALITY**
- ☐ **CONTEMPORARY SPIRITUALITY**
- ☐ **THEOLOGY**
- ☐ **SCRIPTURE AND COMMENTARIES**
- ☐ **FAMILY LIFE**
- ☐ **BIOGRAPHY / HISTORY**
- ☐ **INSPIRATION / GIFT**

Other subjects of interest: _____

(please print)

Name: _____

Address: _____

_____

Telephone:

True Religion

The Inconsistency between the Private Teaching of Philosophers and their Public Observance of Religious Rites

1, 1. Every approach to a good and blessed life is to be found in the true religion, which is the worship of the one God, who is acknowledged by the sincerest piety to be the source of all kinds of being, from which the universe derives its origin, in which it finds its completion, by which it is held together. That being so, the error of those peoples, who have preferred to worship many gods rather than the one true God, is shown up most clearly by the fact that the wise men among them, whom they call philosophers, used to maintain rival schools and share common temples. It could not, after all, have escaped the notice of either the masses or the priests that, while these philosophers held quite different opinions about the nature of the gods themselves, they had not the least hesitation in each publicly proclaiming his views and putting every effort into persuading the public that he was right; and yet all of them, with their followers holding variant and contrary opinions, used to frequent the common rites of worship, without anyone's protesting.

Our concern now is not which of them came closer to the truth. But what certainly seems obvious to me is that they upheld one thing publicly in religion with the people at large and defended quite a different position privately with the same people as their audience.

2, 2. Socrates, however, is said to have been more daring than the rest, in that he used to swear by any old dog and any old stone and anything else that came immediately to hand when he was about to take an oath. I believe he was expressing his awareness that any works of nature whatsoever, which are brought into being under the guiding hand of divine providence, are better, and therefore more worthy of divine honors,[1] than the things that were worshiped in temples. Not of course that stones and dogs were really to be worshiped by the wise but that in this way a demonstration might be given of how gross was the superstition in which the masses were sunk, and those who were beginning to emerge from it might be shown, if they were capable of getting the point, that, if they were ashamed to step onto such a shocking grade of superstition as this, how much more shameful it must be to continue standing on a more shocking one still.[2] At the same time he was admonishing those who were of the opinion

---

1. When one swears by anything, one thereby accords it divine status.
2. I.e., on the grade of worshiping man-made idols—like the great image of the goddess Athena in the Parthenon on the Acropolis at Athens.

that this visible world is the supreme God and teaching them that a consequence of their infamous notion was that any stone should rightly be worshiped as a part of the supreme God and that, if they abominated the idea of such a practice, they should change their opinion and seek the one God.

That it is he alone who is above our minds, the one by whom every soul and the whole of this world has been fashioned, was later put by Plato into writing which was more agreeably, if not more effectively, persuasive. These men, you see, were not of the caliber[3] to turn the minds of their fellow citizens to the true worship of the true God, away from their superstitious regard for idols and from the vanity of this world. In fact Socrates himself used to venerate idols together with the *hoi polloi*, and after his condemnation and death nobody dared to swear by a dog, or call any old stone Jupiter, but only to commit these actions to memory and writing. Whether they so acted out of fear or out of some awareness of the times[4] is not for me to judge.

Had Socrates and Plato Been Alive in Augustine's Day, They Would Have Recognized Christ for what He Really Was

3, 3. This, however, I will say with complete confidence, *pace* all those who have an obstinate love for their books—that in these Christian times there can be no doubt about which religion should be embraced, and which is the way to truth and bliss. Let's suppose, after all, that Plato were still alive and would not object to my asking him some questions. Or rather, let's imagine that some disciple of his at the time he lived was convinced by him that truth is not to be seen by the eyes in our heads but by uncluttered minds[5] and that any soul that has clung to it is thereby made blessed and perfect. Nothing hinders a soul from grasping it, this teaching would have continued, more than a life given over to greed and lust and the deceitful images of material things, which are stamped on our minds from this material world through the body and give rise to a whole variety of false opinions and errors. The spirit, accordingly, requires healing, if it is ever to behold the unchanging form of things and the beauty that is likewise always the same and everywhere consistent with itself, not stretched out in space, nor varying in time, but preserving the same identity in every respect. "All other

---

3. *Non sic nati sunt*: literally, "were not so born." At the back of Augustine's mind there is the unspoken comparison of these pagan philosophers with the Hebrew prophets; so the phrase could be cumbrously translated, "Were not born in such a time and place," or "among God's chosen people." But I prefer my rendering, because Augustine did in fact think that these men were not in themselves a patch on men like Isaiah.
4. That they were, in Greece, the times of the pagan gentiles.
5. *Pura mente* in the Latin, but to translate by "pure minds" or even by "purified minds" would give far too narrow an idea of what he is thinking about.

things come to birth, know their setting, flow along, slip away,"[6] and yet, insofar as they are, they exist as fashioned by that eternal God through his Truth. Among them it is given only to the rational and intellectual soul to enjoy and be influenced by the contemplation of his eternity and to have the ability to earn eternal life. But it is wounded by love and by grief for things coming to birth and passing away, and, being given to familiarity with this life and to the senses of the body, it is fading away among empty images; and therefore it mocks those who say there is something which can neither be seen with these eyes nor be given imaginative form in thought but can be perceived by mind and intellect alone.

So now, suppose that this disciple is convinced about all this by the master and asks him for his judgment on the following case. Suppose, he says, some great and divine man should come on the scene who would convince ordinary people to believe all this, even if they were not capable of grasping it; or, if they were able to grasp it, would convince them not to smother it with vulgar errors through their involvement in the crass opinions of the multitude. Would he be worthy of divine honors? I believe the master would answer that this could not be done by any human being, unless the power and wisdom of God[7] were to except him from the ordinary course of nature and from any human teaching and, by enlightening him from the cradle with some inner illumination, were to adorn him with such grace, strengthen him with such firmness of purpose, and finally bear him up with such majesty, that he would shun everything that depraved humanity sets its heart on, endure everything that horrifies it, do everything that amazes it, and in this way by his sovereign love and authority would convert the human race to such a healthy, saving faith.

As for honors, the master would conclude, it was pointless to consult him about them, since it was simple enough to work out what infinite honors were due to the Wisdom of God, with whose support and under whose direction such a man would deserve, for the true salvation of the human race, to be something above all mankind and quite special in himself.

4. If all this has happened;[8] if it is being celebrated in writings and monuments;[9] if from one small corner of the earth, in which the one God used to be worshiped and where it was fitting for such a man to be born, men outstanding in virtue and eloquence were sent to kindle conflagrations of divine love; if they left to posterity whole countries enlightened by the doctrine of salvation they had established; and if—not to go on talking about past events which anyone may be free to disbelieve—if today there is proclaimed throughout nations and

---

6. Cicero, *De oratore* 10.
7. See 1 Cor 1:24.
8. It's only fair to warn the reader that the apodosis to this conditional, and the innumerable conditions that follow it, will only be found in the question at the end of section 5.
9. That is, churches and the tombs of the martyrs.

peoples: *In the beginning was the Word, and the Word was with God, and the Word was God. This was in the beginning with God. All things were made through it, and without it was made nothing* (Jn 1:1-3); if for the grasping, the loving and enjoying of this Truth, so that the soul might be healed and the fine point, the pupil, of the mind might grow strong enough to drink in such a brilliant light, the miserly are told: *Do not store up treasures for yourselves on earth, where moth and rust disfigure them and where thieves dig them up and steal, but treasure up treasures for yourselves in heaven, where neither moth nor rust disfigure nor thieves dig up. For where your treasure is, there also is your heart* (Mt 6:19-21); the lecherous are told: *Whoever sows in the flesh, from the flesh will reap corruption, whoever sows in the spirit, from the spirit will reap eternal life* (Gal 6:8); the proud are told: *Whoever exalts himself will be humbled, and whoever humbles himself will be exalted* (Lk 14:11; 18:14); the quick-tempered are told: *You have received a slap in the face, offer your other cheek* (Mt 5:39); the quarrelsome are told: *Love your enemies* (Mt 5:44); the superstitious are told: *The kingdom of God is within you* (Lk 17:21); the inquisitive are told: *Do not look for the things that can be seen, but for those that cannot. For the things that can be seen last only for a time, while those that cannot be seen last for ever* (2 Cor 4:18); and, finally, everybody is told: *Do not love the world, since what is in the world is nothing but the lust of the flesh and the lust of the eyes and worldly ambition* (1 Jn 2:15-16)—

5. If these things are now being read to ordinary people throughout the world and are being listened to with reverence and the greatest pleasure; if, after the martyrs have shed so much blood, endured so many fires, so many crucifixions, churches have blossomed and spread all the more fruitfully, all the more abundantly right out to alien[10] nations; if nobody is any longer surprised at so many thousands of young men and maidens[11] turning their backs on marriage and living chastely (when Plato did this, he was so afraid of the perverse public opinion of his times that he is said to have sacrificed to Nature for the fact to be atoned for as a sin); if this practice is so taken for granted that, whereas it was previously the subject of controversy, nowadays it would be regarded as monstrous to argue against it; if to those making such a promise and commitment throughout all parts of the earth the Christian sacraments are entrusted;[12] if accounts of these things are read out daily in the churches and expounded by the priests; if there is a beating of breasts by those who would dearly like to under-

---

10. Augustine's word is *barbaras*; but "barbarous" in English has harsher and at the same time more limited connotations than the Latin word.
11. See Ps 148:12.
12. In 390, as Augustine was writing the present work, the Synod of Carthage forbade married bishops, priests and deacons to have sexual relations with their wives.

take such things;[13] if so countless are the numbers entering upon this way that the once uninhabited islands and lonely deserts of many countries are being filled with men and women of all kinds and conditions who, forsaking the riches and honors of this world, wish to dedicate their whole lives to the one supreme God; if, finally, throughout cities and towns, camps, villages, hamlets and even private estates, the turning away from earthly affairs and conversion to the one true God is so openly advertised and sought after that every day, throughout the whole wide world, the human race answers with practically a single voice that "we have lifted up our hearts to the Lord"[14]—

Why do we still gape open-mouthed over the dregs of yesterday's drinking bout[15] and scrutinize the entrails of dead beasts for divine oracles, while, if ever it comes to discussion, we are at greater pains to have Plato's name rattling around in our mouths than our bosoms filled with truth?[16]

Invitation to Serious Platonists to Become Christians

4, 6. As for people, then, who think that it is vain, not to say evil, to set this world at naught and to submit the soul for cleansing with virtue to the most high God and to attach it to him, they are to be rebutted on other grounds, if indeed they are worth arguing with at all. As for those, however, who agree that it is good and to be sought after, let them take cognizance of God and yield themselves to God, by whose influence all peoples have been persuaded to believe these things. This is something they would certainly do if only they were up to it; or, if they did not do it, they could not avoid the charge of envy. Let them therefore yield to him and not allow themselves to be prevented by an itch for questioning[17] or by empty boastfulness from acknowledging what a difference there

---

13. *Qui haec implere conantur* in the Latin, which literally means "who are striving to fulfill these things." If that is what Augustine meant, it would follow that the beating of breasts was being done by the "servants of God" who had committed themselves to such a life. No doubt they did beat their breasts with the best of them; but I fancy what he was really wishing to say was that good Christians—who for one reason or another did not live such a life because of their worldly responsibilities, people like his friend and patron Romanianus, to whom this work on true religion was addressed—were beating their breasts at not being able to lead such a life. This is admittedly stretching the meaning of *conor* almost to the limits; but when dogs are "straining at the leash" they may genuinely be said to be striving.

14. To Augustine, the exhortation to "lift up your hearts" expressed a basic attitude of Christian life. Compare Paul's exhortation in Col 3:1: *Seek the things that are above.*

15. The modern equivalent would be fortune-telling by tea leaves.

16. This is a very curious finale to such a tremendous bout of rousing rhetoric. It was aimed at the followers of Porphyry, who as part of their Neoplatonist philosophy/religion did indeed practice this kind of divination; so the lapse into such bathos is indeed a deliberate piece of ridicule. It was such practices that constituted for Augustine the sin of *curiositas*, for which we really have no suitable equivalent in English.

17. *Curiositas*; thus the itch for questioning oracles, consulting fortune-tellers.

is between a few timid conjectures and the manifest salvation and reform of whole populations.

For if those men, whose names these people glory in, were to come back to life and find churches crammed, temples deserted, the human race being called away from greed for the abundant good things of the times to the hope of eternal life and to the goods of the spirit and the mind, and racing to obey the summons, they would probably say, if they were such as they are recorded to have been: "All this is what we never dared to put across to the common herd, and we gave in to what they were accustomed to, instead of attempting to bring them across to the object of our faith and will."

7. Thus, if those men had been able to live this life again with us, they would have seen immediately to whose authority people could more easily turn for such advice, and, with a few changes here and there in their words and assertions,[18] they would have become Christians, as indeed several Platonists have done in recent times and our own days. Or, if they didn't agree to all this and act accordingly but remained in the grip of pride and envy, I don't know how they could ever fly up to those things which they had said were so much to be desired and sought after, with their feet trapped in the birdlime of such foul vices.

As for the third instance of the vice of curiosity in consulting demons,[19] by which these pagans above all, with whom we are now engaged, are held back from Christian salvation, it is so excessively childish that I cannot imagine men such as those ancients being chained by its fetters.

The Church's Sacramental Discipline Bears Testimony to the Coherence of its Doctrine

5, 8. But whatever the classical philosophers may have been able to brag about, something it's very easy to understand is that there's no point in asking them about religion, seeing that they were initiated into the same sacred mysteries[20] as the people at large and in their schools trumpeted out varying and mutually contradictory opinions about the nature of their gods and the supreme good, as the same ordinary folk could testify. Now, if we were to see this single vice alone cured by Christian teaching and discipline, nobody could reasonably deny that this teaching and discipline should be lauded to the skies.

Now, the innumerable heresies that have deviated from the rule of Christianity can testify that none are admitted to communion in the sacraments who

---

18. See Letter 118, 3, 21.
19. I.e., the third after divination by the dregs in wine cups and by the entrails of sacrificial victims; see section 5.
20. Received the same *sacra*: the allusion is without doubt primarily to the Eleusinian mysteries, the great mystery cult of Attica and the Athenians.

have ideas about God the Father and his Wisdom and the divine Gift that differ from what truth requires and who attempt to persuade people to share them. In this way, you see, our faith and teaching have demonstrated (and this is the fundamental principle of human salvation) that there is not one thing called philosophy, that is devotion to wisdom, and another called religion, when those whose teaching we do not approve of are not even admitted to share the mysteries[21] with us.

9. This is less surprising in the case of those who also wished to differ from us in their rites and sacraments, like the ones, whoever they are, called Serpentines,[22] like the Manicheans,[23] like several others. But the ones we have to take more notice of and be more on our guard against are those who celebrate the same kind of sacraments as we do and yet differ widely in doctrine and prefer brazenly to defend their errors rather than carefully to correct them. They have therefore been excluded from Catholic communion and participation in our sacraments (though they are of the same kind as theirs) and have acquired the distinction not only of having their proper names and their own conventicles but also of qualifying as distinct religions,[24] such as the Photinians[25] and the Arians[26] and many others.

As for those who have made schisms, it's a different matter altogether.[27] The Lord's threshing floor, you see, could have kept them on it like chaff until the final winnowing, if they hadn't been so lightweight that they were swept off by the wind of pride and separated from us of their own accord. The Jews on the other hand do indeed make their supplication to the one God Almighty; but still

---

21. *Nec sacramenta nobiscum communicant.* Augustine is of course talking about the sacraments, in fact about the eucharist; but I translate the word here as mysteries, since that is how I had to render *sacra* in the previous paragraph.
22. This is just the Latin form for the Gnostic sect called the Ophites.
23. The Manicheans were followers of Mani, who lived in Persia in the third century A.D. and who regarded himself as the emissary of the Paraclete, claiming to be the last and the greatest of the prophets. The core of his teaching was a dualism of two eternal principles: light-darkness, good-evil, God-matter. The Manicheans explained events in the world as resulting from the struggle of these two principles. See *Heresies* 46.
24. My interpretation of a most puzzling sentence: *propria vocabula propriosque conventus non in sermone tantum, sed etiam in superstitione meruerunt.*
25. The Photinians derived their name from Photinus, Bishop of Sirmium in Pannonia. No writings of his have survived, but he appears to have compromised the full doctrine of the divinity of Christ, whom he regarded as a mere man whom the Word ensouled; see *Confessions* VII, 19, 25. The sect died out after being condemned at the Councils of Antioch (344), Sirmium (348, 351) and Rome (382).
26. Of all the heresies that Augustine mentions here, Arianism was the most significant and the most tenacious, persisting well into the fifth century as a force to be reckoned with. Essentially it denied the divinity of Christ, regarding him as God's first and highest creation. Its chief opponent was Athanasius of Alexandria. It was condemned at the Council of Nicea in 325. See *Heresies* 49.
27. Augustine is referring to the Donatists.

they are only looking for the visible good things of time from him, and they have been so sure of themselves that they have refused to take any notice of the first hints in their very own scriptures of the new people rising up from humble beginnings, and thus they have stuck fast in the "old man."

All this being so, religion is not to be sought in either the confusions of the pagan philosophers or the sweepings of the heretics or the sickness of the schismatics or the blindness of the Jews but among those alone who are called Catholic or Orthodox Christians, that is, keepers of the whole tradition unimpaired and followers of the right path.

Divine Providence Uses All Kinds of Men to Further the Work of the Catholic Church

6, 10. This Catholic Church, you see, spread firmly far and wide throughout the whole world, makes use, for the advancement of her members and for their own correction, of all who go astray, when they are prepared to wake up. I mean, the pagan gentiles provide her with the material for her work, the heretics help her to refine and test her doctrine, the schismatics enable her to demonstrate her stability, the Jews provide her with a contrast to her beauty. So then, some she invites into her house,[28] others she turns away from the door, others she leaves alone, others she excels; to all, however, she offers the possibility of sharing in the grace of God, whether they are still to be formed in it, or in it to be reformed, or to be gathered in again, or to be admitted for the first time.

Her own carnal members, though, that is those who live and think in terms of the flesh, she tolerates like chaff, which it is safer for the grains of wheat to have with them on the threshing floor, until the threshing and winnowing strips them of these husks. But because on this threshing floor people are chaff or grains of wheat by their own choice, she puts up all the time with whatever their sin or error is until they are openly charged with it or continue to defend their perverse opinion with obstinate pertinacity. When they are excluded, though, from communion, they either come in again by repenting, or else they trickle down with an evil kind of freedom into some sink of iniquity by ignoring our loving admonitions, or else again they start a schism to test and try our patience, or else they give birth to some heresy to weigh our intelligence in the balance and give it some work to do. These are the ways fleshly-minded Christians end up, when it hasn't been possible either to correct them or to tolerate them.

11. Sometimes, too, divine providence will allow even good men to be expelled from the Christian community through some outbreak of turbulence and discord on the part of fleshly-minded folk. When they show inexhaustible

---

28. See Prv 9:1-6: Wisdom building herself a house, and inviting her guests to the feast.

patience in putting up with such an insult or injury for the sake of the peace of the Church and do not undertake any novelties in the way of schism or heresy, they will teach us all with what heartfelt loyalty and what genuine charity we should serve God. The intention therefore of such men is certainly to find their way back once the tornado has subsided. But if this is not permitted them—because the same hurricane persists, or an even more savage one would start if they came back—they will continue willingly to consider the interests even of those to whose agitations and trouble-making they have given way, without ever setting up their own separate conventicles, and to defend and assist with their testimony the same faith that they know is being proclaimed in the Catholic Church. *The Father who sees in secret* (Mt 6:4) will in secret award these men their crown.

This kind is rarely to be seen, but, all the same, instances of them are not lacking; indeed there are more of them than you could imagine. Thus it is that divine providence makes use of all kinds of men and women and their examples for healing souls and establishing a spiritual people.

The True Religion Is Catholic Christianity, the Mystery of the Trinity Revealed in Sacred History

7, 12. Accordingly, my dearest friend Romanianus, since I promised you a few years ago that I would commit to writing what my thoughts are on true religion, I have decided that now is the time, because I have reached the stage where, bound to you as I am by the bonds of charity, I cannot allow the flood of your acute and persistent questions to continue unanswered.

So, then, we must repudiate all those who neither philosophize about sacred matters nor attach sacred rites to philosophy,[29] as well as those who by their distorted ideas or by their proud and jealous rivalry have deviated from the rule and communion of the Catholic Church; that group also which has refused to accept what illuminates their scriptures and accords grace to a new people, which is called the New Testament; all of these I have summarized above as briefly as I could. Instead, we must hold on to the Christian religion and to communion with that Church which is Catholic and is called Catholic not only by its members but also by all its enemies. Willy-nilly, after all, heretics them-

---

29. As admitted by its own representatives—Scaevola, Varro, Seneca—Rome's state religion was based on custom (*consuetudo*), not on truth; see *The City of God* IV, 27.29-31; VI, 5-10. The "natural theology" of ancient philosophy reached only a divinity that was not responsive to religious individuals, since the supreme principle was understood to be "nature" or a "world soul" or was identified with fire, numbers or atoms; see ibid. VI, 5. Augustine was convinced that only in Christianity was a harmony of faith and reason possible. The God whom philosophical thought reached without being able to pray to him entered history and drew near to human beings, so that religious people could now also turn to the God of philosophy.

selves, and the alumni of schisms, when talking not among themselves but with outsiders, have no other name for the Catholic Church but "Catholic." I mean, they would not be understood unless they distinguished it by the name which is given it by the whole world.

13. The source of this religion for its followers is the history and prophecy of what divine providence has arranged to be enacted in the course of time for the salvation of the human race, that is, for its refashioning and preparation once more for eternal life.[30] When this is believed, a way of life accommodated to the divine commandments will purge the mind and make it capable of grasping spiritual realities, which have neither past nor future but always remain the same, with no liability or tendency whatsoever to change—of grasping, that is, the one God, Father and Son and Holy Spirit. When this Trinity is known, as far as that is given to us in this life, then it is perceived without the slightest doubt that every creature, intelligent, animated, material, gets its being, to the extent that it is, from the same creator Trinity and derives from that source its own specific nature and is governed by it in the most beautiful order conceivable.

Not that the Father should be understood to have made one part of the whole creation and the Son another and the Holy Spirit yet another, but that each and every nature has been made simultaneously by the Father through the Son in the Gift of the Holy Spirit. Every particular thing, you see, or substance or essence or nature, or whatever else you like to call it, has simultaneously about it these three aspects: that it is one something, and that it is distinguished by its own proper look or species from other things, and that it does not overstep the order of things.

The Need to Progress from Faith to Understanding; the Value of Heresies in this Regard

8, 14. Once we have realized this, it will be quite apparent, within the bounds of human comprehension, how all things have been subjected, by laws that are necessary, irrefutable and just, to their God and Lord. This will mean that things we first of all believed purely and simply on authority can now be understood, being seen partly as absolutely certain and partly as perfectly feasible and fitting,[31] so that we feel sorry for those who still do not believe and who have preferred to laugh at us for previously believing rather than to believe together with us.

---

30. "Refashioning and preparation once more" because the first fashioning and preparation was the work of creation before the fall, of which the perfection was symbolized by the first man and woman being placed in paradise, in the garden of delights, that is of Eden.
31. Augustine is here giving programmatic expression to his theological concern with the *intellectus fidei*.

What I mean is that it is now not just a question of believing in that most holy taking on of a man[32] and his birth of the Virgin, and in the death of God's Son for us, and his resurrection from the dead, and his ascension into heaven, and his being seated at the right hand of the Father, and in the abolition of sins and the day of judgment and the resurrection of bodies, cognizance being taken of the eternity of the Trinity and the mutability of created things: now all this is also assessed as belonging to the loving mercy of the most high God, which he shows to the whole human race.

15. But it has been most truly said: *There needs must be many heresies, so that the tried and tested ones among you may stand out* (1 Cor 11:19). So let's make use of this favor of divine providence too. It's people, you see, who, even while they were within the Church, would nevertheless go astray that become heretics; when they are outside it, however, they are of the greatest value, not of course in teaching the truth they don't know but in prodding fleshly-minded Catholics into seeking the truth and spiritual ones into opening up its riches. After all, there are countless tried and tested men in the holy Church, but they don't stand out among us as long as we prefer to sleep on, enjoying the darkness of our ignorance, rather than to wake up and gaze at the light of truth.

Accordingly it's through heretics that many people, in order to get them seeing and rejoicing in God's daylight, are roused from their slumbers. Let's then make use even of heretics, not by way of giving approval to their errors but by way of upholding Catholic teaching against their wiles and being more wide awake and careful, even if we cannot call them back to the way of salvation.

The Purpose of this Work, as Regards the Manicheans

9, 16. I believe, however, that with God's help this text of scripture can avail good-hearted readers, given due piety in their approach, against all twisted and false opinions, not just against one in particular. Nonetheless it is set there most effectively against those who maintain that there are two natures or substances, each with its prime source, which are constantly at war with each other.[33] There are some things, you see, that offend them, and again others that delight them, and they want God to be the author of those that delight them, not of those that offend them. And since they cannot now break out of the nets of the bad habits they are caught in, they reckon that there are two souls in one body, one from God, which is by nature what he is, the other from the race of darkness, which

---

32. What we usually call the incarnation. No doubt, as he was aiming this work principally at pagans, Augustine was at some pains to avoid technical terms of Christian theology.

33. Augustine is referring to the Manicheans. Romanianus, to whom this work is addressed, Augustine's wealthy patron in Thagaste, was probably still a member of this sect; he had certainly been a Manichean together with Augustine in previous years.

God neither begot nor made nor produced nor discarded but which had its own life, its own territory, its own brood and animated beings, and finally its own kingdom and unbegotten prime source. They dream up the idea that this race of darkness declared war on God, who had nothing else he could do about it and could find no other way of withstanding the enemy, so that, under the pressure of necessity, he sent good soul hither and a certain particle of his own substance, and that the enemy was tempered by this admixture, and the world as we know it was thus fashioned.

17. I am not now concerned to refute their opinions, which I have partly done and will partly do in the future, as God may permit.[34] But in this work I am setting out to demonstrate as best I can, with such rational arguments as the Lord may be pleased to grant, how secure against them is the Catholic faith and thus how the mind should not be troubled by the things which bother people so much that they give in to their line of thought. The first thing I want you to grasp firmly, thoroughly familiar as you are with my mind, is that it is not just to avoid the charge of arrogance that I solemnly make the following declaration: anything erroneous that can be found in these writings is the only thing that is to be attributed to me, while anything that is true and aptly expressed comes from the one God, the one and only distributor of all good gifts.

The Basic Principle of True Religion; This to Be Found in Christ and Christianity

10, 18. Accordingly, it should be obvious to you, a basic principle, that no error could have arisen in religion if the soul had not worshiped soul[35] or body or its own fancies as God, or two of these jointly, or indeed all three together; if, adjusting itself frankly in this life to membership of the human race in a temporal manner,[36] it had instead meditated on eternal things in its worship of the one God. If he, after all, did not abide unchanging, no changeable nature would remain in existence at all. That the soul can be changed, not indeed in space but

---

34. *True Religion* was written between 389 and 391; in 388 Augustine had written *The Catholic Way of Life and the Manichean Way of Life*, which he finished in 390, and *On Genesis: A Refutation of the Manicheans*, completed in 389. All these while he was still a layman, and hoping to spend the rest of his life as a "servant of God" with a group of like-minded friends in his home town of Thagaste. In 391, after being kidnapped and ordained priest in Hippo, he wrote *The Two Souls*, and in 391-395 he wrote *Free Will*.
35. See *Revisions* I, 13,2 where Augustine says: "Here I put *soul* for the whole incorporeal creation, not following the custom of the scriptures...." He goes on to make further comments on what he says in this section, which do not affect our understanding of it.
36. Augustine is here evidently presupposing the pre-existence of the soul before it is dispatched into this world to animate a body.

nonetheless in time by its affects, is something everybody experiences. That the body is changeable both in time and in space is something anyone can easily observe.

As for the fancies, lastly, of the imagination, they are nothing but its figments, drawn in by the bodily senses from the appearances or looks of bodies. It is the easiest thing in the world to commit them to memory as they are received, or to divide or multiply them, or contract or extend them, or arrange or shuffle them or mould them in any way you like in thought, but, when what you are seeking is the truth, it is difficult to be on your guard against and altogether avoid such distortions.

19. Let us then but avoid *serving the creature rather than the creator*, and *becoming vain in our thoughts* (Rom 1:25.21), and religion is all it should be. If we cling to the eternal creator, we too are bound to be affected by eternity. But the soul, being overwhelmed and bundled up in its sins, would be quite unable to see this and hold onto it by itself; and there is no intermediate step, what's more, in the human situation for grasping divine things, by which human beings could stride up to a likeness of God from their earthly life. Accordingly, God's inexpressible mercy comes to the rescue[37] both of individuals and of the whole human race by means of a creature subject to change and yet obedient to divine laws,[38] to remind the soul of its primal and perfect nature. That, in our times, is the Christian religion;[39] it is in knowing and following this that salvation is most surely and certainly to be found.[40]

20. There are many ways, however, that it can be defended against chatterboxes and opened up to genuine seekers, with almighty God himself demonstrating its truths and helping persons of good will to behold and grasp them through the ministry of good angels and of human beings of all sorts. Each of these, naturally, employs the method which he sees is most suited to the people

---

37. Here we have, in its essence, the Augustinian teaching on grace that will later be used to refute the views of the Pelagians.

38. I.e., Christ, of course, with whom in effect the Christian religion is simply being identified.

39. See *Revisions* I, 13, 3, where Augustine says: "This is said with reference to the term 'Christian religion,' not with reference to the actual thing. The thing itself, after all, which is now called the Christian religion, existed also among the ancients, and was not lacking from the beginning of the human race, until Christ himself came in the flesh, from which point the true religion, which already existed, began to be called Christian. When, you see, the apostles had begun to preach after his resurrection and ascension, and great numbers were coming to believe, it was first at Antioch, as it is written, that the disciples were called Christians (see Acts 11:26). That's why I said, 'That, in our times, is the Christian religion,' not because it wasn't there in previous times but because it was in later times that it acquired this name."

40. Later on, Augustine emphasized even more strongly the claim of the Christian religion to exclusivity; see *The City of God* X, 32: "This way has never been withheld from mankind.... And apart from this way, no one has been set free, no one is being set free, no one will be set free." (Trans. Bettenson)

he is dealing with. I have accordingly given long and serious thought to what sort of people in my experience have been barking against it, and what sort have been genuine seekers; also to what I was like myself when I was doing the barking, or when I was doing the seeking; and I have decided in consequence that this is the method for me to follow:

Everything you perceive to be true, hold fast to it and attribute it to the Catholic Church; spit out whatever you perceive to be false, and make excuses for me, who am only a man; whatever is doubtful believe, until either reason teaches you or authority instructs you that it is to be spat out, or that it is true, or that it is always to be believed. Pay pious and diligent attention, therefore, to what follows, as best you can. People like that, after all, are the ones to whom God gives a helping hand.[41]

Life, Death, Nothingness and Wickedness

11, 21. There is no life which is not from God, because God of course is supremely life and is himself *the fountain of life* (Ps 36:9); nor is any life, precisely as life, something evil, but only insofar as it tilts towards death. Now, the death of life is nothing but wickedness, which is so called from a word meaning worthless, and that's why the most wicked people are called worthless fellows or nihilists.[42] So then, life, by a willful defection from the one who made it and whose very being it was enjoying, wishes against the law of God to enjoy bodies, which God put it in charge of, and so tilts towards nothingness. And that is wickedness, but not because the body is already nothing, since it too has a certain harmony of its parts without which it could not be at all.

So the body too, then, was made by him who is the source of all harmony. The body gets a kind of peace from its shape, without which it would certainly be nothing. He therefore is the fashioner of the body also, from whom all peace is derived and who is shape unforged, and of all shapes the most shapely. The body has a certain look about it, without which a body isn't a body. If therefore you are inquiring about who instituted body, you should make your inquiries about the

---

41. See *Revisions* I,13, 4, where Augustine writes: "This is not to be understood as if he only helps people like that, since he also helps those who aren't like that to become like that, namely to seek with pious and diligent attention; while those who are like that he helps to find."

42. None of this makes much sense in English, since Augustine is indulging in some Latin etymology, and dubious etymology at that. The only death of life, he says, is *nequitia*, wickedness; and this word, he goes on, comes from *nequiquam*, an adverb meaning fruitlessly, worthlessly; and that's why the most wicked of men are called *nihili homines*, worthless fellows, indeed nihilists! The sentence, anyway, has been lifted straight from Cicero's *Tusculan Disputations* III,8,18.

most good-looking of them all.[43] The good looks of all things, I mean, come from him.

Now, who can this be but the one God, the one Truth, the one salvation of all things and the first and supreme Being, from which is everything whatever that exists, insofar as it exists, because insofar as it exists, whatever exists is good?

22. And that is why death is not from God, because *God did not make death, nor does he delight in the destruction of the living* (Wis 1:13), since the supreme Being makes everything to be that is, which is why he is also called Being. Death on the other hand forces whatever dies not to be, insofar as it dies. You see, if things that die were to die totally, they would without a doubt be reduced to nothing, but they only die to the extent that they participate less in being, which can be put more briefly like this: They die the more the less they are.

Now, body is less than any kind of life, because, when it keeps its specific appearance even to the slightest extent, it does so through life, whether that by which every animal or that by which the whole nature of the world is governed.[44] Body therefore is more prone to death and thus nearer to nothing. Accordingly, the life which by taking delight in the enjoyment of body is neglectful of God thereby makes a bow towards nothingness, and that is wickedness.

Sin and its Punishment, Constituting Evil; the Overcoming of Evil by the Abolition of Death

12, 23. Now, it's on these terms that life is made fleshly and earthly and for this reason is also called flesh and earth, and, as long as this is the case, it will not gain possession of the kingdom of God and is being snatched away to what it loves. What it loves, after all, is what is also less than life, because it is body. And because of the actual sin, what is loved becomes perishable, and thus by trickling away it forsakes its lover,[45] because he in turn by loving it has forsaken God. He

---

43. Calling God first shapely and then good-looking is, I admit, scarcely permissible in English; but it is in fact what Augustine is doing in the Latin. He speaks first of bodies having their own *forma*, which I translate, quite correctly, as "shape"; then in relation to this noun he says that of all things God is *formosissima*—"the most shapely" is all I can do, though *formosus* is just one of several Latin synonyms for "beautiful." Next he says that body, the body, has some *species*. This in technical philosophical language is practically synonymous with *forma*. But here Augustine is taking philosophical language back to its literal, everyday roots, where this word does mean the look of things; that being so, the only adjective going along with "look," as *speciosissimus* of course goes along with *species*, is "good-looking." English needs sometimes to be taken beyond the permissible back into the raw.

44. It looks as if Augustine is subscribing to the notion of a world soul; but it would be fairer to say that he is allowing for such a theory at this point, not committing himself to it.

45. Here life, which has been equivalent to soul, suddenly turns into Adam, committing the first sin in paradise.

ignored his commands, you see, his telling him: "Eat this, don't eat that."[46] So then he is dragged off to punishment, because by loving low things he is assigned his place among the lowest,[47] lacking all his pleasures, enduring all his pains.

What, after all, is the pain of the body but the sudden perishing of health and salvation in that very thing which the soul has rendered liable to perish by loving it badly? And what is the pain of the spirit but the lack of those changeable things it used to enjoy or had hoped it would be able to enjoy? And that is the sum total of what we call evil, namely sin and the punishment of sin.[48]

24. If the soul, however, while engaged in the stadium of human life,[49] beats those greedy desires it has been cherishing in itself by mortal enjoyments and believes with mind and good will that it has been assisted in beating them by the grace of God, then without a shadow of doubt it will be restored to health and will turn back from the many things that change to the one unchanging good,[50] being reshaped by the Wisdom that was never shaped but gives its shape to all things, and will come to enjoy God through the Holy Spirit, which is the gift of God.

In this way you become spiritual, judging all things, being judged by none,[51] loving the Lord your God with all your heart, with all your soul, with all your mind, and loving your neighbor not in a fleshly manner but as yourself. On these two commandments, after all, hang the whole law and the prophets.[52]

25. The consequence of all this will be that, after the bodily death which we owe to the first sin, this body will be restored in its own time and its own order to its original stable condition,[53] which it will not have directly through itself but through the soul made stable in God. This in turn is not made stable through itself but through God, whom it is enjoying, and for that reason it will be flourishing more vigorously than the body. The body, you see, will flourish through the soul,

---

46. See Gn 2:16-17.

47. I.e., the dead in the underworld, *apud inferos*, which is here echoing the *inferiora*, the low things he has been loving.

48. Augustine is referring mainly to the pains of hell but also to the ills endured in this life.

49. Taking part in a foot race, rather a long one presumably, of several *stadia* or furlongs. See 1 Cor 9:24.

50. See *Confessions* XIII, 3, 4-4, 5.

51. See 1 Cor 2:15.

52. See Mt 22:37.39-40.

53. See *Revisions* I,13,4 where Augustine writes again: "This is to be taken in the sense that even the body's original condition of stability, which we lost by sinning, enjoyed such vigor that it would not slip down into the defects of old age. So it is to that original condition of stability that this body will be restored in the resurrection of the dead. But it will have something much more, so that it will not need to be sustained by bodily nourishment but will be kept alive by the spirit alone, when it has risen again into *a life-giving spirit* (1 Cor 15:45), for which reason the body too will be an embodiment of spirit. As for what it was at first, even though it wasn't going to die if the man didn't sin, it was nonetheless made an embodiment of soul, that is, *into a living soul* (Gn 2:7)."

and the soul through the unchanging Truth, which is the only Son of God; and thus the body too will flourish through the Son of God himself, because *through him are all things* (Jn 1:3).

By his gift also which is given to the soul, that is by the Holy Spirit, it is not only its recipient, the soul, that is rendered safe and peaceable and holy but the body too that will be quickened and in its own order will be of the utmost purity. For he is the one who says: *Purify the things that are inside, and the things that are outside will be pure* (Mt 23:26). The apostle too has this to say: *He will also give life to your mortal bodies on account of the Spirit abiding in you* (Rom 8:11). So, with sin removed, the punishment of sin will be removed, and where is evil then? *Where, Death, is your striving? Where, Death, is your sting?* Being, after all, overcomes nothingness, and thus *death shall be swallowed up in victory.* (1 Cor 15:55.54)

The Devil

13, 26. Nor will the bad angel who is called the devil do any harm to those who have been sanctified,[54] because he too is not bad insofar as he is an angel but insofar as he has been perverted by his own will. One has to admit, you see, that angels too are changeable by nature, if God alone is unchanging. But, by that act of will by which they love God more than themselves, they remain firm and steady in him, and, in being most willingly subject to him alone, they enjoy his greatness. That angel, however, by loving himself more than God, refused to be subject to him, and thus swollen with pride he deserted the supreme Being and fell. And because of this he is less than he was, since he wished to enjoy what was less, when he wished to enjoy his own power more than God's.

Although he did not have being in the supreme degree, still he had it to a fuller extent when he was enjoying that which is in the supreme degree, since God alone supremely is. But anything that is less than it was is evil, not insofar as it is but insofar as it is less. For, to the extent that it is less than it was, it is tilted towards death. What wonder then if from desertion comes want, and from want comes envy, which is of course what makes the devil a devil?[55]

---

54. This chapter sounds like an unexpected excursus on the angels, but it serves as a transition to the succeeding reflection on the concept of sin, which in turn is an element in the controversy with the Manicheans.

55. Because the Latin *diabolus* (of which the English "devil" is just a very ancient anglicization) is in fact a Greek word meaning "false accuser"—one who brings his accusations out of envy or jealousy of those he accuses.

The Reality of Sin Implies the Reality of Free Will

14, 27. Now, if this defection which is called sin were, like a fever, to grab an unwilling victim, then quite rightly would the punishment that follows on the sinner's heels and that is labeled damnation be seen as unjust. As it is, however, so much is voluntary and deliberate sin an evil that in no way at all would it be sin were it not voluntary and deliberate.[56] This indeed is so obvious that neither the small band of the learned nor the great crowd of the unlearned would disagree. Accordingly, one either has to deny that a sin has been committed or to confess that it has been committed willingly. Now, you have no right to deny that the soul has sinned if you admit that it is put straight by repentance and that, while the penitent is granted pardon, the one who perseveres in sinning is damned by a just law of God. Finally, if we only do evil involuntarily, there is no place either for reprimanding people or for giving them fair warning. Eliminate these, and you have to eliminate Christian law and the discipline of every religion.

So then, committing a sin is an act of will, and since there is no doubt that sins are committed, I do not see how there can be any doubt about this either, that souls enjoy freedom of will.[57] God, you see, decided that his servants would be all the better for serving him freely, which could not possibly be done if they served out of necessity instead of freedom of choice.

28. Angels therefore serve God freely,[58] and this not to God's advantage but to theirs. God, after all, is in no need of anyone else's good, since it is from himself that he is. And what is begotten of him likewise is, because it is not made but begotten.[59] Those things, however, that have been made stand in need of his good, that is, of the highest good, that is, of the highest being. Now, they are something less than they were when, thanks to the sin of the soul, they move less towards that highest good; still, they are not thereby utterly cut off from it, because in that case they would be nothing. What happens to the soul in its affects happens to the body in space, seeing that the soul is moved by the will, the body through space. The man, though he is said to have been persuaded to sin by

---

56. In *Revisions* I, 13, 5 Augustine has a long comment on this sentence, beginning: "This definition can look as if it is false, but if it is carefully examined, it will be found to be the very truth." But it does not affect our understanding of this passage and can be read in the text of *Revisions*.
57. In English we talk about free will and the freedom of the will. Latin uses a more accurate phrase, *liberum voluntatis arbitrium*, the free decision or judgment of the will, thus making it clear that what we are concerned with is an *act* of will, not just the will as a faculty or power of the soul.
58. The service of freedom is based on love; see *Commentary on the Letter to the Galatians* 43: "One who serves out of love serves freely, doing what he is told with love and not being forced with fear."
59. I.e., the Word of God, the only begotten Son of the Father.

the crooked angel, consented to this too by an act of will. If he had committed it out of necessity, he would not have been liable in any way for a criminal sin.

God's Justice, in Harmony with his Benevolence, Gives Us Good Training in the Cardinal Virtues

15, 29. That the human body, while before sin it was the best of its kind, has become feeble after sin and destined to die is indeed a just punishment for sin; all the same it is a greater manifestation of the Lord's clemency than of his severity. This, you see, is the way to convince us how right it is to turn our love away from the pleasures of the body to the eternal reality of Truth. And the beauty of justice proves to be in harmony with the graceful quality of benevolence when, after we have been deceived by the sweetness of lesser goods, we are taught a lesson by the bitterness of the penalties. In this way, you see, divine providence has so tempered our pains and penalties that we are allowed to tend towards justice even in this perishable body and also, putting down our load of pride, to submit our necks to the one true God, to put no confidence in ourselves, and to commit the task of ruling and directing our lives to him alone.

Thus it is that under his guidance people of good will turn the vexations of this life to the service of courage and fortitude. On the other hand, when they have pleasures in plenty and do very well in their temporal affairs, they test and strengthen their temperance and moderation and sharpen their prudence in temptations, so that they are not only not led into them[60] but even become more vigilant and more ardent in their love of Truth, which is the only thing that is not deceptive.

What Was Achieved by the Incarnation of the Word

16, 30. God of course makes use of all appropriate means for healing spirits, as may be required in different epochs, which are marshaled by his marvelous Wisdom (these times and his control of them are not for discussion now, and in any case should only be discussed with the devout and the perfect). But he found no better way of conferring benefits on the human race and of consulting its interests than when this very Wisdom of God, that is his only-begotten Son, consubstantial with the Father and coeternal with him, was good enough to take to himself the whole man, when *the Word was made flesh and took up residence among us* (Jn 1:14).

---

60. See Mt 6:13.

This was the way by which he demonstrated to the fleshly-minded, incapable of gazing directly at Truth with the mind and given over to the sensations of the body, what a lofty place is held among creatures by human nature, this Truth being manifested not just visibly—after all, this could have been done in some ethereal body,[61] adjusted to what our sense of sight could bear—but in a real human being to human beings. For the same nature had to be taken on as needed to be set free. And lest either sex should imagine it was being ignored by its creator, he took to himself a male and was born of a female.

31. He did nothing by force, everything by persuasion and admonition.[62] Once, that is to say, the old penal servitude had run its course, the time of freedom dawned, and now he was reminding man in a seasonable and wholesome way how he had been created with free will. By miracles he linked faith to the God he was by suffering to the man he bore. Thus, while speaking to the crowds as God, he renounced the mother whose presence was announced to him; and yet, as the gospel tells us, he was subject to his parents as a boy.[63] He presented himself, you see, as God by his teaching, as a human being by the age he was. Again, when he is on the point of turning water into wine as God, he says: *Get away from me, woman, what is there between you and me? My hour has not yet come.*(Jn 2:4) When his hour had come for him to die as a man, though, he acknowledged his mother from the cross and entrusted her to the disciple whom he loved above the rest.[64]

Whole peoples, to their own ruin, were setting their hearts on riches, the escort required by pleasures of all sorts; he made up his mind to be poor. They were greedy for honors and political power; he refused to be made a king.[65] They thought having children in the flesh was a great good; he turned his back on marriage and children of his own. They in their pride and self-esteem couldn't stand insults; he put up with insults of every kind. They considered it intolerable to be treated unjustly; what greater injustice than for a just and innocent man to be condemned? They shrank from physical pain; he was scourged and crucified.[66]

---

61. *In aliquo aethereo corpore*; the "ether" was thought of as a region of the purest light, even above the visible heavens. Quite how an ethereal body could reveal to us the superiority of human nature, it's hard to see; Augustine probably had in mind some Manichean concept here, which he is allowing, as we would say, for the sake of argument.

62. See *Revisions*, I, 13,6, where Augustine writes: "It had not occurred to me that he cast those who were buying and selling out of the temple with a whip (see Jn 2:14-15; Mk 11:15). But what did this really amount to? Though he also cast unwilling demons out of human beings not with a word of persuasion but with the force of his authority."

63. See Lk 8:19-21; 2:51.

64. See Jn 19:26-27.

65. See 2 Cor 8:9; Jn 6:15.

66. See Mt 27:26.

All the things we longed to have while we were not living decent lives, *he* treated as trash by doing without them. All the things we were so anxious to avoid while we were deviating from concern for the truth, *he* suffered and dethroned. No sin, indeed, can be committed except while things which he shunned are being eagerly sought, or things are being shunned which he endured.

32. So the whole of his life on earth, then, as lived by the man he had the goodness to take to himself, was a lesson in morals.[67] His resurrection from the dead, however, was a sufficient indication that no part of human nature is lost, since they are all safe in God's keeping; it also shows how all things serve their creator, whether for the punishment of sins or for the liberation of mankind, and how easily the body serves the soul when this submits to God. When all this has been achieved, not only is no substance evil,[68] which can never be the case, but none—what's more—can be touched by any evil, something that was possible previously through sin and its punishment. And this is the lesson that calls for unqualified faith from Christians of limited understanding, while, for those who can understand well, it is a lesson purged of all error.

The Difference between the two Testaments; Analogies in Ordinary Life

17, 33. Now the way this teaching is presented is partly in a completely straightforward manner and partly by comparisons in words, in deeds, in sacraments, which are well adapted to both instructing and training the soul. So what else has it kept to but the rational rules governing every learning process?[69] For the explanation of mysteries too is directed to things that are said quite openly; and, if these were only things that are easy to understand, there would be no eagerness in seeking the Truth nor delight in finding it; while, if pointers to the Truth were there in the scriptures and not in the sacraments, there would not be sufficient coordination of action with knowledge.

As it is, however, since piety begins in fear and is perfected in charity, the people that was restrained by fear in the time of slavery was burdened in the old law with many sacraments. This, you see, was of use to such as they to make

---

67. This statement is characteristic of Augustine's understanding, at this time, of Christ's redemptive act. This act does not yet mean for him, first and foremost, a liberation from the guilt of sin but consists rather in the ethical example which Christ gave through his teaching and his person, all of which was to be imitated.

68. For the Manicheans all matter, as such, was evil.

69. Adopting the threefold division of ancient philosophy, Augustine sees ethics as being brought to completion in the model given by Christ's earthly life (see sections 30-31), physics in the Christian doctrine of creation, sin and resurrection (see section 32), and logic in the linguistic form of biblical preaching.

them long for the grace of God, about whose future coming the prophets used to sing. When it came through the very Wisdom of God taking to itself the man by whom we have been summoned into freedom, just a few sacraments of the most salutary kind were instituted, which would hold together the fellowship of the Christian people, that is, of a vast multitude of the free under the one God. Many things, on the other hand, which had been imposed upon the Hebrew people, that is, the multitude chained together under the same one God, were withdrawn from actual observance and left on record for faith and interpretation. Thus, without binding the soul to slavish observance, they provide the mind and spirit with the liberal training of the free.[70]

34. Anyone though who denies that both Testaments can be from one and the same God, on the grounds that our people is not being held to the same sacraments as the Jews were or still are, can just as well say that it is impossible for one and the same fair-minded head of a household to impose one set of tasks on those slaves who in his judgment will profit by a harder kind of servitude and another on those whom he proposes to adopt into the rank of his sons.[71] If, on the other hand, they are bothered by the fact that in the Old Testament the precepts of life are less demanding and in the New Testament more so,[72] and that's why they think that both cannot derive from one and the same God, then those who think like this could be worried by one and the same doctor's administering some remedies through his attendants to his weaker patients and others by his own hand to the stronger ones, for restoring or obtaining health.

Just as the science of medicine, after all, while remaining the same and in no way undergoing change in itself,[73] still varies its prescriptions for the sick, because our state of health is variable, so too divine providence, while being in itself absolutely unchanging, nonetheless comes to the aid of changeable creatures in various ways, and in accordance with the diversity of diseases commads or forbids different regimes—this in order to bring back from the malady which is the beginning of death, and from death itself, to their proper condition and state of being, and to strengthen them in it, the creatures that are failing, slipping, that is to say, into nothingness.

---

70. A very dense paragraph indeed, which it would take a whole essay to unpack; and essays have no place in footnotes.
71. All the ritual requirements of the law, as expounded by the scribes and Pharisees, constituting the slavery of the law, as compared with the simplicity of Christian sacramental rituals and worship, exemplifying the freedom of the gospel.
72. The precepts of the Sermon on the Mount in Mt 5, culminating in the command: *You therefore be perfect as your heavenly Father is perfect*, are more demanding, more total than the ten commandments of the Mosaic law.
73. This is untrue, of course, of modern medicine, but in Augustine's time it was universally assumed that the last word in the art and science of medicine had been said by Galen, the doyen of medical studies, in the second century A.D.

God, the Author of Everything Good, even of What Is only Potentially Good, Has Made Everything out of Nothing

18, 35. But you say to me: "Why are they failing?"
Because they are subject to change.[74]
"Why are they subject to change?"
Because they do not have being in the supreme degree.
"Why not?"
Because they are inferior to the one by whom they were made.
"Who is it that made them"?
The one who *is* in the supreme degree.
"Who is that?"
God, the unchanging Trinity, since he both made them through his supreme Wisdom and preserves them through his supreme Kindness.
"Why did he make them?"
So that they might be. Just being, after all, in whatever degree, is good, because the supreme Good is being in the supreme degree.
"What did he make them out of?"
From nothing, since whatever is must have some kind of specific look, however minimal.

Thus even the minimal good will still be good and will be from God, for, since the supreme specific look is the supreme good, the minimal specific look is the minimal good. Now, every good is either God or from God; therefore even the minimal specific look is from God. What is said about specific looks can naturally also be said about specific shapes; nor is it pointless, after all, that both the most good-looking as well as the most shapely are the object of praise.[75] Accordingly, what God made all things out of is that which has no specific look and no shape, which is nothing else than nothing.[76] I mean that what is said, in comparison with complete things, to be shapeless or formless, if it has any form or shape at all, however meager, however inchoate, is not yet anything; and thereby it too, insofar as it is, is from none but God.

---

74. In order to reach the concept of being, Augustine here raises a series of questions that flow logically each from the preceding. His aim is to show matter as something good. This is an element in the refutation of the Manichean error, which identified matter outright with evil.
75. See section 21.
76. Augustine derives the concept of creation out of nothing from the Old Testament; see 2 Mc 7:28. But he is also able to justify it philosophically. It was entirely foreign to contemporary pagan thought. Moreover, his neat argument here as to the goodness of all matter, however small, however seemingly insignificant, contradicts Manichean thought on the subject. See *Music* VI, 17, 57; *Unfinished Literal Commentary on Genesis* I, 2; *Answer to Felix, a Manichean* II, 19.

36. For this reason, even if the world was made out of some unshaped, form-less matter, this was itself made out of absolutely nothing. You see, even that which has not yet been given any shape or form, but has all the same been somehow or other begun with the potentiality of being formed, can be given a form by God's good act. For the good is that which has been formed; even the potentiality, therefore, of being formed is a good of some sort, and that is why the author of all good things, who has bestowed form on them, has himself also made the potentiality of being formed.

Thus everything that is, insofar as it is, and everything that is not yet, insofar as it potentially is, has this from God—which can be put in other words as follows: Everything formed or shaped, insofar as it *is* formed or shaped, and everything which has not yet been formed or shaped, insofar as it *can be* formed or shaped, has this from God. Now no particular thing attains to the integral completeness of its nature unless it is preserved safe and sound in its own kind of being. But all safety and soundness comes from the one from whom comes all good, and all good comes from God. Therefore all safety and soundness comes from God.[77]

On Faultiness in General in its Relation to the Good

19, 37. Hence anyone who has his mental eyes open and not befogged and turned dizzy by any pernicious zeal for winning empty victories will readily understand that everything which develops a fault and dies is good, although the actual fault and the actual death are bad.[78] After all, unless they were deprived of some sound well-being, no fault or death would injure them, but if a fault did not injure them, in no way would it be a fault. If then a fault is opposed to well-being, and well-being beyond any doubt is a good, all things are good to which a fault is opposed, but it is the very things to which a fault is opposed that are rendered faulty. Therefore the things that are rendered faulty are good, but the reason they are rendered faulty is that they are not good in the supreme degree.

Therefore, because they are good, they are from God; because they are not good in the supreme degree, they are not God. The good, therefore, which cannot be rendered faulty, is God. All other goods are from him, which by themselves can be rendered faulty, because by themselves they are nothing. By him, however, they are on the one hand not rendered faulty, and on the other, once they have developed faults, they are put right.

---

77. This language of potentiality and being and form, of *posse* and *esse* and *forma*, suggests the influence of some works of Aristotle on Augustine.
78. In a further step in this line of thought, evil, decay and death are explained as deprivations and diminutions. Evil always presumes good.

More Illustrations of the Non-subsistent Nature of Evil

20, 38. Now, the first fault or vice of the soul is the will to do things which are forbidden by the highest and deepest[79] Truth. Thus it was that the man was expelled from Paradise into this age,[80] that is, from eternal to time-bound things, from plenty to poverty, from firmness and strength to weakness. It was not then from subsistent good to subsistent evil, because nothing subsistent is evil, but from eternal good to time-bound good, from spiritual good to flesh-bound good, from intelligible good to sensuous good, from the highest good to the lowest good. There is therefore a certain good by loving[81] which the soul sins, because it is a good that has been placed under the soul in due order. That's why the sin is evil, not the substance which it is a sin to love.

So it's not the case, then, that that tree was something evil, which is described as having been planted in the middle of Paradise, but the transgression of the divine command. The condemnation that follows upon this is appropriately just, because from that tree which was disobediently touched arises the power to distinguish good and evil.[82] Thus the soul, being entirely wrapped up in its sin, learns by paying the penalty what the difference is between the command which it refused to keep and the sin which it committed; and in this way it learns by experience the evil it did not learn by avoidance; and the good, which while obedient it used to love the less, it now on obtaining it loves the more ardently.

39. So the fault of the soul, then, is what it has done, and the distress ensuing from the fault is the punishment it suffers.[83] And that is the sum total of evil. Now, doing and suffering are not subsistent realities, and for this reason evil is not a subsistent reality either. Thus, you see, water is not an evil, nor is the living creature which lives in the air; these, after all, are substances. But its willful plunge into the water and the drowning it suffers on being submerged: these

---

79. Most deeply impressed upon the soul.
80. *In hoc saeculum. Saeculum* primarily means "age," secondarily "world," but always signifies time rather than space. It rather looks, therefore, that in Augustine's view Paradise was in the same space frame as this world we know, geographically located somewhere, but in a different time frame; he is indeed suggesting that it was in the same time frame as eternity. I doubt if he retained this idea in his more mature thought.
81. The word Augustine uses for "loving" is *diligere*, which is the least emotion-bound Latin word for love. It really means to select or choose; in this case, as almost always, to choose one thing instead of another, thus the lowest good instead of the highest. Nonetheless, because of the poverty of English in this respect, we have, here at least, to retain "loving" as its English equivalent.
82. See Gn 2:9.17.
83. As is intimated in the next paragraph and explained in the approximately contemporary work *On Genesis: A Refutation of the Manicheans* II, 29-30, the "distress" consists in the fact that, after the fall into sin, human beings can only painfully overcome fleshly lusts and that they easily fall into error due to an overvaluing of earthly things. It was from this starting point that the doctrine of original sin could develop, which may already be seen, in its main outlines, in the final section of *Free Will.*

constitute evil. The metal stylus, which has one end we write with, the other we rub out with, has been most skillfully made and in its own way is beautiful and adjusted to our use. But, should anyone try to write with the end you are meant to rub out with or to rub out with the end you are meant to write with, he has not in the least made the stylus evil, while his misuse of it is rightly to be faulted. But if he corrects his mistake, where will the evil be?

If anyone looks suddenly at the midday sun, his eyes will be dazzled and hurt. Does that mean that either the sun or the eyes will be an evil? Certainly not: they are substances, after all. But the evil lies in the improper glance and the pain that is its consequence. This evil will not exist when the eyes have recovered and begun to look correctly at their own proper light. And when this light, which relates to the eyes, is worshiped in place of the light of Wisdom, which relates to the mind, it does not itself become an evil. But the evil lies in the superstition which has the creature being served instead of the creator. This evil will quite simply cease to be when the soul on acknowledging the creator submits itself to him, the one God, and realizes that everything else has been subjected to it by him.

40. Thus every bodily creature, if it is simply possessed by souls which love God, is a good of the lowest rank and beautiful of its kind, since it is defined by its shape and specific look. If, however, it is loved by souls which care nothing for God, not even thus does it become something evil; but, since the evil lies in the sin by which it is loved in this way, it turns into a punishment for its lovers, involving them in worries and feeding them on deceitful pleasures which neither abide nor satisfy and which end in painful torment. This is because the beautiful rhythms of time's changes make the specific look of a thing that such souls long for desert its lovers and withdraw from the senses to the anguish of the sentient souls. It then proceeds to play fast and loose with them, so that they begin to think that this is the primal specific look which is in fact the last and least, namely that of a bodily nature. The flesh, taking an evil delight in it, has regaled these souls with it through the slippery channels of the senses so that, when they reflect on it at all, they imagine they understand it, while in fact it is the shadowy fancies of their imaginations leading them up the garden path.

If ever, though, they fail to accept the lessons of divine providence in their entirety but reckon that self-control is all they need in their efforts to withstand the flesh, they get as far as the images of visible things, and in their imaginations they vainly fashion for this everyday light, which they can see is circumscribed within definite limits, some measureless space, and they promise themselves this fanciful picture as their future home. They don't realize that it is the lust of the eyes[84] dragging them along and that they are wanting to get outside the world

---

84. See 1 Jn 2:16.

together with this world, which they do not think will itself be there, simply because with their mistaken ideas they extend its more splendid part ad infinitum. This can be done with the greatest of ease, not only with this everyday light but also with water; finally, in fact, with wine, with honey, with gold, with silver, not to mention the flesh and blood and bones of any kind of animal you like and anything else of this sort. After all, there is no kind of body which, once you have seen one, you cannot think of times beyond number, or, once seen in a small space, you cannot with the same faculty of the imagination spread far and wide through infinite space. But it's the easiest thing in the world to forswear the flesh, one of the most difficult not to smack of the flesh in one's thoughts.

In What Sense Bodies Are "Vanity"

21, 41. By this waywardness of the soul, then, which goes along with sin and punishment, every bodily nature becomes what is said of it by Solomon: *Vanity of vanitators,*[85] *and all things are vanity. What abundance is there for a man in all his toil, with which he toils under the sun?* (Eccl 1:2-3) Nor is it pointless that he adds *of vanitators*, because if you remove the vanitators, who chase after the last and least things as if they were the first and foremost, body will not be vanity, but in its own class it will manifest beauty, though of the least and lowest degree, without any deception. So multitudinous are time-bound species and their looks, you see, that they have whipped fallen man away in all directions from the unity of God and have multiplied his emotional responses with their chopping and changing in their variety. Thus has been produced a toilsome abundance and, if one may say so, a plentiful poverty, while one thing follows another and nothing remains with him.

In this way he, fallen man, has been multiplied from the time of his corn, wine and oil,[86] so that he may not find the selfsame,[87] the unique unchanging nature, which would not lead him astray if he set his sights on it and would cause him no grief when he reached it. For then he will gain the consequent redemption of his body,[88] which will no more be subject to decay. Now, however, *the body, which is subject to decay, is a weight upon the soul, and the earthly dwelling is pressing*

---

85. This is the reading of Augustine's version: *vanitantium* instead of *vanitatum*. It does not follow the LXX in any of its variants; perhaps this verb, whose participle I render as "vanitators," was peculiar to the Latin spoken in Africa, whose inhabitants no doubt had the perspicacity to realize the need of a verb to express such generally common behavior.
86. See Ps 4:7.
87. In the expression *idipsum* ("the selfsame") of the Psalms (4:9; 121:3) Augustine sees a typical way of expressing the mystery of divine being, emphasizing its immutability; see *Confessions* IX, 4, 11; *The Trinity* III, 2, 8; *Expositions of the Psalms* 121, 5. See also J. Sweetman, "A Note on *in idipsum* in St. Augustine," *Modern Schoolman* 30 (1952/53) 328-331.
88. See Rom 8:23.

down upon the mind thinking many things (Wis 9:15), because the least and lowest beauty of bodies is being carried along in a successive order. That, you see, is why it is the least and last, because it cannot have everything at once and all together; but, while some things give way and others take their place, they fill up the number of time-bound forms and shapes into one single beauty.

The Point Illustrated by Poetic Composition

22, 42. And the fact that all this is transitory does not make it evil. For this is the way in which a line of poetry is beautiful, even though two syllables of it cannot possibly in any way be spoken simultaneously. I mean that the second one cannot be pronounced unless the first one has passed away, and so in due course you reach the end, so that when the last syllable is heard, without the previous ones being heard simultaneously, it still completes the form and beauty of the meter by being woven in with the previous ones. Yet this does not mean that the art[89] by which verses are composed is equally dependent on time, so that its beauty has to be appreciated by rhythmic time.

But it has in itself simultaneously all the things with which it composes verse that does not have it all simultaneously, but which shuffles off what comes first to make room for what comes next yet is still beautiful because it displays the final stages of that beauty which the art itself preserves steadily and without any succession or change.

43. And so, just as some people perversely love the verse more than the art itself by which the verse is composed, because they have given themselves more to their ears than to their intelligence, in the same way many prefer time-bound things, while they give no thought to the divine providence which establishes and governs times, and in their preference for things of time they are unwilling to go beyond what they love and are in fact behaving as absurdly as if someone in the recitation of some well-known poem wanted to listen to just one single syllable all the time.

But while you won't find anybody listening to poems in that way, the world is full of people who make judgments on things in that way. This is so because, while there is nobody who cannot easily listen to a whole poem, let alone a whole verse, there is no human being who can grasp the whole range of time and its successive ages. It comes to this—that, while we do not play a part in a poem, we

---

89. Augustine is not referring to the poetic art in general but to the art which lies behind the composition of a particular poem or even of a particular line of verse.

have in fact been condemned[90] to play a part in the roll of the ages. So the recitation of the former, then, falls under our judgment, while the unrolling of the latter involves our hard labor.

Again, no loser enjoys the wrestling matches in the games, and yet his defeat contributes to their success. And this, after all, is a kind of copy of the Truth. The only reason, in fact, why we are forbidden to watch such spectacles is that we might be deluded by these shadows of reality and wander away from the reality of which they are the shadows.[91] In the same kind of way it is only godless and condemned souls who take no pleasure in the state and organization of this universe, while even their misfortune contributes to the enjoyment of those souls who are either winners on earth or spectators in no danger in heaven. For nothing that is just is displeasing to those who are just.

Since Evil Is not a Substance, its Presence in no Way Mars the Universal Creation

23, 44. So the position then is this: every rational soul is being rendered either miserable by its sins or blessed by its good deeds, while every non-rational soul either gives way to one that is stronger, or obeys one that is better, or is on a par with its equal; in any case they are there to provide training for persons still engaged in the struggle or injuries for those who have been condemned. Furthermore, bodies of every kind are at the service of their own souls, insofar as the natural order of things permits or their own souls deserve. It follows, then, that no evil is of a universal nature, but it is through people's own fault that things turn evil for them.

Accordingly, when souls have been born again through God's grace and rendered hale and hearty once more and have submitted to that one single being through whom they have been created anew, they will begin to possess the world together with their bodies now restored to their pristine firmness, instead of being possessed with the world.[92] At that point nothing will be evil for them, because this least and lowest sort of beauty of the changes and chances of this

---

90. Condemned, as a punishment for the first sin, which had the first man thrown out of the quasi-eternity of Paradise onto the roller coaster of time.

91. It is most unlikely that this consideration had anything to do with the Church's forbidding Christians to attend such games in the amphitheaters, just as it also forbade attendance at theaters to watch plays. The main reason was that both kinds of performance had pagan and idolatrous associations.

92. Being possessed, the implication seems to be, by the devil with the world. Augustine is not contrasting possessing the world with being possessed *by* the world; hence his deliberate use of the preposition "with" (*cum*).

fleeting world, which used to be enacted with them, will now be enacted under them, and there will be, as it is written, *a new heaven and a new earth* (Rv 21:1) for souls no longer toiling away in a part of the whole but reigning in and over the whole. *For all things,* says the apostle, *are yours, while you are Christ's and Christ is God's* (1 Cor 3:22), and, *Now the head of woman is the man, the head of man is Christ, while the head of Christ is God* (1 Cor 11:3).

The fault in the soul, therefore, is not its nature but against its nature and is nothing else but sin and the punishment of sin, from which it is to be understood that evil is not any kind of nature or, if this be a better way of putting it, not any kind of substance or being. Nor do the sins and punishments of the soul result in the universe's being defaced by any kind of deformity, because the rational substance which is clean of all sin,[93] having subjected itself to God, has every-thing else subjected to it as its lord and master. As for the substance which has sinned, it has been assigned to the place where it is fitting for such substances to be, so that, with God as their founder and ruler, all things in the universe fit neatly into place. Thus the beauty of the universe is not in the least marred by any of these three: the damnation of sinners, the exercising of the just, the perfection of the blessed.

God Heals the Human Race by a Gradual Process, Culminating in the Incarnation of the Word

24, 45. So it is that the very healing of the soul, which by God's providence and his inexpressible kindness is being applied step by distinct step, is also of the greatest beauty. It is divided, you see, between authority and reason.[94] Authority demands faith and paves the way for people to use reason. Reason leads on to understanding and knowledge, although reason is not entirely wanting in authority, when one considers who precisely has to be believed, and certainly the Truth itself, once perspicuously known, has supreme authority.

But because we have come down to the things of time and are being restrained by love of them from reaching the things of eternity, a certain time-bound method of healing, which is calling believers, not knowers, to salvation, comes first in the order of time, though not in natural excellence.[95] After all, in the spot where a person has fallen, there one has to stoop down to him, so that he may get

---

93. The reference here seems to be to the good angels, in contrast with the devil, obliquely alluded to at the beginning of this section.

94. See F. van Fleteren, "Authority and Reason. Faith and Understanding in the Works of St. Augustine," *Augustinian Studies* 6 (1973) 33-71.

95. I presume Augustine means that in theory, in the abstract, instant healing is better than a slow process.

up again.[96] So then, we have to try and make use of the flesh-bound shapes, by which we are being held back, to come to a knowledge of those which the flesh does not present us with. The ones, I mean, which I am calling flesh-bound are those which can be perceived through the flesh, that is through the eyes, the ears and the rest of the body's senses. So then, children are under the necessity of being glued to these bodily shapes by love of them, adolescents almost under the same necessity, while, as we grow up and out of these stages, this necessity no longer holds.

Which Authorities Are primarily to Be Trusted

25, 46. Now, divine providence, as well as caring for the interests of individuals, as it were privately, is also concerned publicly, so to say, with those of the whole human race. But, while God knows what he is doing with individuals, and they know what is being done with them, it was his will that what is being done with the human race should be brought to our attention through history and through prophecy. Now, faith is good for dealing with temporal matters, whether past or future, more by believing than by understanding, but it is our business to work out which human beings or books are to be trusted about the correct worship of God, in which lies the one salvation.

The first argument that arises here is whether we should rather trust those who bid us worship many gods or those who summon us to the worship of one God. Who can doubt that those are above all to be followed who summon us to the one, especially since those worshipers of many all agree about this one Lord and ruler of all the others? And numbering certainly begins with one.[97] So those then are first and foremost to be followed who say that the one supreme God is the only true God and is alone to be worshiped. If the truth has not shone out of what these are saying, then that's the time to be moving on to others.[98]

---

96. Here I have presumed that a word has dropped out of the Latin text, in which the last phrase reads: *ibi debet incumbere, ut surgat*: "There one has to stoop down, so that he may get up again." I have supposed that something like *medicus* or *adjutor*—or even *Samaritanus*—has dropped out in the copying process. An even more likely supposition is that *incumbere* originally read *incumbi*; literally: "There it has to be stooped down"—a mode of speech that perhaps struck Augustine's amanuensis, or a later copyist, as improbable.

97. Behind this statement lies a sense of the innate mystique of numbers, of what you could call mystical arithmetic, that is alien to us and not likely to be approved of by professional mathematicians nowadays.

98. See *Revisions* I, 13,6 again, where Augustine writes: "This could seem as if I had doubts about the truth of this religion. But I said it as applying to the man I was writing to [his old friend and patron Romanianus]. This, after all, is what I actually said: 'If the truth has not shone out of what these are saying,' having no doubts myself that it did shine out of what they said, in the way the apostle says: *If Christ has not risen* (1 Cor 15:14), without of course doubting that he had risen."

For just as in the very nature of things the authority of the number one, leading all things back to one, is the greater, and with the human race no power lies with the multitude unless they all agree, that is are all of one mind, so too in religion those who summon us to the one have an authority that should be the greater and more worthy of our trust.

47. The disagreement that has arisen among people about the worship of the one true God is another point that has to be considered. But what we have been told is that our ancestors reached the stage of rising up from temporal to eternal realities by taking note of miracles—there was no other way they could have done it, after all; and then they laid it down that such miracles would not be needed by their descendants. When the Catholic Church, you see, had spread and been established throughout the whole wide world, those miracles were not permitted to continue into our times for fear that the soul would always go on looking for visible signs and that, by getting used to things that had blazed up in their novelty, the human race might grow coldly indifferent.[99] Nor would it be right for us to have any doubts about believing these men, who have still been able to persuade whole populations to follow them, though they are proclaiming things which few can comprehend.

The point we are dealing with now, you see, is who the authorities to be believed are, before anyone is fit to exercise reason on divine and invisible matters. For in no way is merely human authority to be preferred to the reason of the uncluttered soul which has arrived at Truth in all its clarity; but no form of pride can be a guide to this Truth. If there were no such pride, there would not be any heretics or schismatics, or those circumcised in the flesh, or worshipers of the creature and of idols. While, if there were none of these around before God's people reaches the perfection it is promised, it would be much lazier in its quest for the Truth.

The Ages of Man, as Realized in the Old Man and the New

26, 48. So then, the remedial course through time laid down by divine providence for those who have earned mortality by sin goes something like this: Thought is first given to the nature and upbringing of any human beings that are born; their infancy is spent on material nourishments, due to be totally forgotten as they grow older. Childhood follows, from which point we begin to remember things. This is succeeded by adolescence, to which nature permits the propagation of offspring, thus making parents. Next youth takes over from adolescence,

---

99. See *Revisions* I, 13,7, where Augustine remarks that this is true, in that people no longer speak with tongues when hands are laid upon the newly baptized for them to receive the Holy Spirit; but he goes on to say that he must not be understood as denying that miracles still happen in his time, and he mentions ones that he had himself witnessed at the tombs of martyrs.

and now has to be trained in public duties and tamed under laws; at this stage the stricter prohibition of sins and punishment of sinners, by placing servile restraints on flesh-bound spirits, gives birth to the more savage impulses of lust and doubles the wrongness of all sins committed. Sin, after all, is not something simple, not just evil by itself, but involves giving free rein to what is forbidden.

After the laborious toils of youth, however, a certain amount of peace is granted to the elders. From there old age, with health deteriorating and fading, more liable to diseases and enfeebled, leads on up to death. Such is the life of human beings living from the body and wrapped up in greed and longings focused on time-bound things. With them we talk about the old man and the outward and the earthly man,[100] even if they achieve what the common crowd calls happiness in a well-established earthly city, whether under kings, or under emperors, or under a constitution, or under all of these together. There is no other way, after all, in which a people can be well-established, even one pursuing earthly goals, for such a one too has a certain style to its beauty.[101]

49. But take this man, whom we have described as the old or outward or earthly man, whether he be moderately so in his own kind, or whether he go beyond the limits even of servile justice.[102] Some people act him out from sunrise to sundown of this life, while some of necessity begin this life from him but break up and slay his other stages by their robustness of spirit and growth in wisdom and bind him to the keeping of heavenly laws until after this visible death he can be wholly refashioned. This one is called the new man, the inward and the heavenly man, and he too has certain equivalent spiritual ages of his own, distinguished by progress, not by years.

The first he spends at the paps of useful history, which nourishes him with good examples; the second is passed in forgetting things human and stretching out to things divine, no longer carried in the lap of human authority but struggling towards the supreme and unchanging law on the footsteps of reason. In the third the spirit is marrying with its manly strength the already more confident and flesh-bound appetite of reason and rejoicing inwardly in a kind of conjugal bliss, when the soul is coupled with the mind[103] and veils itself with the veil of modesty, so that now there is no question of his being compelled to live an upright life; rather, he takes no pleasure in sinning, even if everyone gives him permission. In the fourth he continues on the same lines much more firmly and systematically, and thus he blossoms out into the perfect man, fit and ready to

---

100. For the "old man" see Rom 6:6; Eph 4:22-24 gives us the "old man" and also the "new man" in contrast.
101. We already have the seeds here of Augustine's thought about the two cities, or two societies, which will be fully worked out in *The City of God*.
102. That is, I presume, if his justice is even less than that of the scribes and Pharisees.
103. The soul is the life, the vital force, which humans have in common with animals. The mind works as understanding; the soul perceives what the senses show to it.

endure and defeat all the persecutions of this world and also its tempests and its stormy waves.

In the fifth age he is living at peace amid the wealth and abundance of the unchanging kingdom of supreme and inexpressible Wisdom. In the sixth he passes from every kind of change into eternal life, to the extent of forgetting the life of time, now that he has been perfected in the form and shape which was made to the image and likeness of God.[104] The seventh age, after all, is now eternal rest and everlasting bliss, not to be divided into any ages. For just as the end of the old man is death, so the end of the new man is eternal life. That one, you see, is the man of sin, this one the man of justice.[105]

More about the Old Man and the New

27, 50. About these, however, there is no doubt at all that one person can act out one of them, that is the old and earthly man, throughout the whole of this life, while nobody can act out the new and heavenly man in this life except together with the old man. This is because he is not only bound to start from him but also has to continue with him until this visible death, though with the old man wearing out along the way, the new getting fitter every day. Well, in the same way by analogy the whole human race, whose life lasts like that of one man from Adam up to the end of this age, is so regulated under the laws of divine providence that it is manifestly divided into two kinds. One of these consists of the whole gang of the godless, who bear the image of the earthly man from the beginning of the age to the end. The other consists of the series of the people which is devoted to the one God, but which bears the life of the earthly man from

---

104. See Gn 1:26.27.
105. In this section we have a slightly baffling, but nonetheless typical, mixture of themes. Augustine begins with the theme of ways in which the Bible can be read. The first way, corresponding to childhood, is by reading it just as history, which gives the pious Christian reader good examples to follow—and, I suppose, bad examples to avoid. He will elsewhere refer to this as the literal sense of the Bible; and it was in accordance with this sense that he went on to write his *Literal Meaning of Genesis*. The second way is that of trying to work out the spiritual sense, the way, that is, in which historical events or characters are figures of a deeper, "divine" sense, sacraments of the mystery of Christ, and ultimately indeed of the Trinity.

But then Augustine moves on to the moral theme when we come to the third age, that of youth, in which the Christian, the new man, is enabled to resist the trials of persecution and also the temptations of the passions. However, this theme is still mixed up with the earlier one, because it represents the spirit, the mind, the *animus*, marrying the rational *anima* or soul, which covers itself with the veil of modesty. There is an allusion here to what St. Paul says about Moses having to veil his face, so that the Israelites might not see the glory with which it shone after he had spoken to the Lord; while Christians do not need to veil their faces when looking on the glory of Christ (see 2 Cor 3:3-18). And it is Christ who is revealed through the "sacramental" understanding of scripture Christ also who marries the Church and its members, as the spirit or mind here marries the soul (see Eph 5:32; 2 Cor 11:2).

Adam right up to John the Baptist by a kind of servile justice,[106] of which the history is called the Old Testament, promising a sort of earthly kingdom, which is nothing but the image of the new people and the New Testament promising the kingdom of heaven.

Meanwhile the temporal life of this people starts from the advent of the Lord in humility and goes on until the day of judgment, when he is going to come in glory. After this judgment and the elimination of the old man, there will take place that change with its promise of the angelic life.[107] *For we shall all rise again, but we shall not all be changed* (1 Cor 15:51).[108] So then, the godly people will rise again in such a way as to transform the remnants it has of the old man into the new, while the godless people, which has been bearing the old man from the beginning to the end, will rise again in such a way as to be hurled into the second death. Those, however, who take care in passing through the successive ages one by one, stage by stage, neither find the tares any problem nor feel horrified by the husks.[109] The godless person, after all, lives for the godly, and the sinner for the just, so that, in contrast with them, these may grow more briskly until they are ripe.

From the Plain History of Scripture to its Hidden Meanings

28, 51. Anyone, however, who has deserved in the times of the earthly people to attain to the enlightenment of the inward man has helped the human race by presenting it with what that age required and by prophetically hinting at what it was not opportune to present it with unambiguously. Such are the patriarchs and prophets discovered to be by those who, instead of jumping in like children, treat such good, such great hidden meanings of things human and divine with due piety and care.

---

106. The allusion is to the contrast between law and grace which runs through most of Paul's epistles; see in particular Rom 7 and Gal 3-4. What may have been more in Augustine's thoughts, however, is what he says in his own rule, written for his community of "servants of God": he exhorts them to follow the rule, *not like slaves under the law, but like free men under grace.*
107. See section 110; *The City of God* XXII, 29.
108. This seems a slightly inappropriate text to quote here; one would have expected Augustine, rather, to quote Lk 20:36: *For they will not be able to die any more; for they are equal to the angels and are sons of God, since they are sons of the resurrection.*
109. See Mt 13:30.38-43; 3:12. The Latin says that those who have been careful in passing through the *aetatum articulos*, the links of the six or seven ages set out in the previous chapter, "neither find the tares nor feel..."—*inveniunt nec zizania nec paleas perhorrescunt.* But this really makes no sense, and certainly does not harmonize with the next sentence where the godless man, the tares, and the sinner, the husks, are said to be of use to the godly and the just. So I have presumed that a word has dropped out, through the oversight of an early copyist, after *zizania;* which word, I suggest, was *perturbantia*, "troublesome," "a problem."

Even in these times of the new people I observe that these hidden meanings are probed and offered to the alumni of the Catholic Church with the greatest caution by outstanding spiritual men, to avoid dealing in a popular fashion with anything, which they are aware the time is not yet ripe for discussing with the people. They are generous and urgent in suckling with milk foods the avid majority, while they themselves feed on more solid foods with the few who are wise.[110] *For they speak wisdom among the perfect* (1 Cor 2:6), but for the flesh-bound and "soulish"[111] and those who are still little ones, even though they are new men and women, they keep some things covered up but do not lie about anything.

They are not concerned, after all, for vain honors and empty praise for themselves but for the profit of those in whose company they have been found worthy to share this life. This, you see, is the law of divine providence, that none should be helped by those above them to the knowledge and reception of God's grace, who have not given the same assistance out of the purest affection to those below them. Thus as a result of our sin, which our nature committed in the man who was a sinner, not only has the human race been made into the glory of the earth and its greatest adornment but it is still being so fittingly guided under the supervision of divine providence that the inexpressible art of the divine healer changes the very ugliness of human vices into I know not what special beauty of its own kind.[112]

The Life of Reason

29, 52. And since we have been talking what seems quite long enough for the moment about the beneficent work of authority, let us now see how far reason can make progress in climbing up from the visible to the invisible and from the temporal to the eternal. It should not, after all, be pointless and vain to observe the beauty of the sky, the order of the constellations, the brilliance of light, the succession of nights and days, the monthly cycles of the moon, the fourfold arrangement of the seasons of the year, corresponding to the four elements;[113] then there is the energy in seeds, begetting species and numbers,[114] and the way all things in their own kind keep their proper measure and nature.

---

110. See 1 Cor 3:1-3; Heb 5:12.
111. The *carnales et animales*, this last word being the literal translation of the Greek *psychikoi*. These are people whose life is only under the direction of the *anima*, the soul, not yet of the *pneuma*, the *spiritus,* the spirit. Augustine, following St. Paul, is here at least not identifying soul with spirit but rather yoking it to flesh, in contrast to spirit.
112. Augustine is at his most opaque and incomprehensible in this whole paragraph.
113. The four elements of ancient chemistry, earth, water, air and fire.
114. Number, in this context, is practically synonymous with species. The text governing Augustine's use of it in this way is Wis 11:20: *You have arranged all things in measure and number and weight.*

It is not a matter of indulging idle curiosity, here today and gone tomorrow, in reflecting on all this, but of setting up a ladder to things that are immortal and last for ever. So the next step is to pay attention to what the nature of this life may be that perceives all these things of time. Clearly, since this is what gives life to body, it must necessarily outclass body. No material mass, after all, of whatever kind, were it even to outshine this light of every day, is to be prized very highly if it lacks life. Any living substance whatsoever, I mean, is to be preferred by the law of nature to any non-living substance whatsoever.

53. But because non-rational animals are also alive, nobody doubts that the most excellent thing in the human spirit is not that by which it perceives the objects of sense but that by which it makes judgments on them. Many wild animals, after all, have a sharper sense of sight and are aware of bodies more keenly with the other bodily senses than is the case with human beings. But to make judgments about bodies is proper to a grade of life that is not only sentient but also capable of reasoning, a grade in which they are wanting, while we excel.

Now, it's the easiest thing in the world to see that the one making a judgment outclasses the thing on which the judgment is made. But the rational life, as well as making judgments about the objects of sense, also does so about the senses themselves. Why does an oar in the water have to look bent, though it is in fact straight, and why does it have to be perceived by the eyes like that?[115] I mean, the eyes can send back that message but cannot in any way make that judgment on it. Thus it is clear that, just as the sensitive life outclasses the body, so does the rational life outclass them both.

Above the Mind Is What It Judges Things by, and That is Truth

30, 54. And so, if the rational life makes judgments of its own accord, that now leaves no nature of a higher class. But because it is clear that it is changeable, when it is found to be now skilful, now wanting in skill, but is more reliable in its judgment the more skilful it is, and is more skilful the more it participates in some art or discipline or wisdom, then what we have to inquire about is the nature of that art. Here I do not wish you to understand the art which is marked by experience but that which is sought out by rational deliberation. Is it knowing anything very wonderful, after all, to know that the material made up of lime and sand is better for sticking stones together than mud, or that more elegant buildings are put up by an architect who knows that things which go in pairs should correspond to each other, while the place for solitary things is in the middle—though art in this sense is already closer to reason and to Truth?

---

115. See section 62.

But certainly what has to be asked is why it offends us if, of two windows, not placed above each other but next to each other, one of them is bigger or smaller, when they could be equal in size, while if one were above the other, and they differed in size but were both in the middle, their inequality would not now offend our sensibilities, and why we don't mind particularly how much bigger or smaller one of them is, because there are just two of them. If there are three of them, however, the sense of sight itself seems to require that either they should not differ in size or else that between the smallest and the biggest the middle one should be as much bigger than the smallest as it is smaller than the biggest. So it is, you see, that in the first place nature itself is consulted about what it approves of. And here the thing to be principally noted is that what does not displease when looked at by itself is brushed aside when compared with something better. Thus we find that common or garden art is nothing but the memory of taking pleasure in things experienced, joined to the practical application of it by some bodily skill and that, if you do not possess this, you can still make judgments about its artifacts, which, even though these are beyond your capacity, is something far and away more excellent.

55. But now what pleases in all matters of art is harmony, by which all things are rendered beautiful once it has been achieved, while harmony itself has an appetite for equality and unity, either through the similarity of comparable parts or the grading of non-comparable ones. Is there anyone therefore who will claim to find the acme of equality or similarity in bodies and will have the audacity to state after careful consideration that any particular body at all is truly and simply one, seeing that all bodies change by passing from look to look or from place to place and that all consist of parts occupying each its space and thus distributed into distinct places?

True equality, accordingly, and similarity and true and primary unity itself are not to be observed by the eyes in our heads, nor by any such sense, but only by the mind's understanding of them. How, after all, would any kind of equality be looked for and aimed at in bodies, or how would it be convicted of falling vastly short of perfection, unless the kind that *is* perfect were seen by the mind—if, that is to say, that which has not been made can be said to have been perfected?[116]

56. And while all things that appear beautiful to the senses, whether products of nature or works of art, are beautiful in space and time, as being bodies and bodily movements, that equality and unity which is known only to the mind, and which governs judgments made on the beauty of bodies through the mediation of

---

116. Augustine is here developing some of his ideas on aesthetics, e.g., order, harmony, and symmetry (*congruentia, convenientia, consonantia*). He also raises the question of the objective and subjective aspects of the beautiful and acknowledges the existence of a priori criteria in the human mind.

the senses, has no bulk in space nor want of stillness in time. Thus it cannot be said that it governs a judgment made on the roundness of a wheel and not on the roundness of a pot or made on the roundness of a pot and not on the roundness of a coin. Likewise, with times and bodily movements, it is ridiculous to say that it governs judgments made on the equality of years and not on the equality of months or on the equality of months and not on the equality of days. But whether something is being suitably moved through these spaces of time or through hours or through shorter intervals, it is judged according to the same one and unchanging equality.

Now, if smaller and bigger shapes and motions are judged according to the same law of equality or similarity or harmonious symmetry, the law itself is greater than all of them—but in virtue of its writ,[117] while in quantity of space or time it is neither greater nor lesser because, if it were greater in this way, we would not judge lesser things by it, while, if it were lesser, we would not judge what was greater by it. As it is, though, it is by the law of the square in its entirety that judgment is made on the squareness of the forum, and on the squareness of a paving stone, and on the squareness of a tablet and a gem, and it is by the law of equality in its entirety that judgment is made on the way a running ant's steps match each other and the way a plodding elephant's steps match each other. So who can doubt that this law is neither greater nor smaller by intervals of space and time, since its writ runs further than them all?

This law, though, governing all the arts, is altogether unchanging, while the human mind, to which has been granted a sight of it, can undergo the changes and chances of error; hence it is sufficiently clear that this law is above our minds and that its name is Truth.

It Is Unlawful to Pass Judgment on Eternal Truth, in Accordance with Which We Judge Everything Else

31, 57. Nor can there be any hesitation in identifying the unchanging nature which is above the rational soul with God and in asserting that primary life and primary being are one with primary Wisdom. This, you see, is that unchanging Truth which is rightly said to be the law of all arts and crafts, itself the art of the almighty craftsman. And so the soul, being well aware that it does not judge the looks[118] and motions of bodies by the standard of itself, must at the same time acknowledge that, just as its own nature excels the nature it makes judgments on,

---

117. Greater *potential*: I am assuming that Augustine is thinking in legal terms here—hence my rather odd rendering. But he is struggling for words to express his meaning.
118. *Species* in the Latin. See section 21 and the relevant note for an explanation of this translation of the word.

so too is it excelled itself by the nature according to which it makes such judgments and on which it is in no way competent to make judgments itself.

Thus I can say why the limbs of any particular body that resemble each other should correspond to one another on either side; it is because I take pleasure in that supreme equality which I behold with the mind, not the eyes. That is why I judge that those correspondences I perceive with the eyes are all the better the nearer they approach, within the limits of their nature, those I understand with the intellect. But why these should be as they are, nobody can say, nor would anyone not in his cups presume to say that that is how they ought to be, as if they could be any different.

58. Why, though, they give us pleasure, and why, when we savor them better, we are carried away with love of them, this too is something none will dare to say, if they have a right understanding of them. For just as we and all rational souls rightly make judgments about things beneath us in accordance with Truth, so does Truth herself alone make judgments about us when we adhere to her. On her, however, not even the Father makes judgments, for she is not less than he is, and that is why, whatever judgments the Father makes, he makes through her.[119] All things, you see, that have an appetite for unity find in her a rule or form or example or whatever else she lets herself be called. After all, she alone has fully realized the likeness of him from whom she has received being—if, at least, to say "has received" is not inappropriate for signifying why she is called Son, which is because he is not from himself but from the first and supreme Beginning, who is called the Father, *from whom all fatherhood in heaven and on earth takes its name* (Eph 3:15).

Accordingly, *the Father does not judge anyone, but has given all judgment to the Son* (Jn 5:22), and *the spiritual person judges all things, but is not himself judged by anyone* (1 Cor 2:15), that is, by any human being, but by that law alone by which he judges all things, since nothing could be truer than the words: *For all of us must be brought before the judgment seat of Christ* (2 Cor 5:10). So he judges all things, then, because he is above all things when he is with God. But he is with him when his understanding of things is totally uncluttered and when he loves what he understands with total charity. In this way, as far as he can, he himself also becomes the very law by which he judges all things and on which nobody can pass judgment.

It's the same with these temporal laws: although human beings make judgments about them when they are enacting them, nonetheless, once they have been enacted and confirmed, none will have the right to make judgments about them but only to judge in accordance with them. Still, the maker of temporal laws, if he is a good and wise man, will consult that eternal law itself, which no

---

119. See Jn 5:22, which is being echoed here and is quoted a few lines further on.

soul has been given the right to judge, so that in accordance with its immutable regulations he may discern what at this juncture in time is to be commanded and forbidden. Acquiring knowledge of the eternal law, therefore, is the sacred right of unspotted minds, while for passing judgments on it there is no such right. This, though, is the difference, that for acquiring knowledge we only need to see that something is or is not such-and-such, while for making a judgment we add something to signify that it could be otherwise, as when we say "it ought to be such-and-such," or "it ought to have been such-and-such," or "it will have to be such-and-such," the way craftsmen do with the things they make.

The Harmonious Unity of Bodies Is Judged in Terms of a Non-bodily Idea of Unity

32, 59. But for many people the end they have in mind is human delight, and they have no wish to aim at higher things, so that they can make a judgment about why these visible things give pleasure. And so if I inquire of an architect, who has just built one arch, why he is at pains to make the one on the other side its exact equivalent, he will answer, I believe, that it is to have the parts of the building corresponding in every way to their opposite numbers.[120] And if I press on with my questioning and ask why he is making that choice, he will say that this is how it should be, that this is beautiful, that this is what pleases the eye of the beholder. He won't presume to go any further. He leans back, you see, and closes his eyes[121] and does not understand what he is depending on for his answer.

But I will not give up prodding the man, who has eyes inside him and can see the invisible, to tell me why these things please the eye of the beholder, so that he may be bold enough to make a judgment about what delights human beings. In this way, you see, he is raised above it and not held by it, while he does not make judgments by, but upon, such delight. And my first question will be whether these things are beautiful because they delight, or delight because they are beautiful. Here he will undoubtedly answer that they delight because they are beautiful. So next I will go on to ask why they are beautiful, and, if he hesitates, then I will add a supplementary question: Is it because the parts are like each other and are being restored by being linked together in some way to one single harmony?

60. When he has satisfied himself that that is so, I will question him further, whether this very Unity, which these things are found to be reaching out to, is

---

120. *Ut paria paribus...respondeant*: a phrase taken from Cicero, *De deorum natura*, I,19,50.
121. A most peculiar phrase in the Latin: *inclinatus enim recumbit oculis*; it seems to be setting the scene, so to say, as a conversation at the dinner table, or rather among the dinner couches.

supremely realized by them or whether they lie prostrate far, far below her[122] and scarcely do more than caricature her. And if this is so—and who, after all, on having it pointed out, will fail to see that there is no look or appearance, no body whatsoever which does not have any trace of Unity at all, and that not even the most beautiful of bodies, necessarily occupying space with one part here, another there, can possibly attain her?—I will, if this is so, demand an answer from him to the question, where he himself sees her, or what he sees her with. And if he did not see her, how could he know both what the look of bodies was trying to imitate and why it could not fully realize her?

Now, however, he will say to bodies: "You would indeed be nothing unless some unity were holding you together; while again, if you yourselves were this very Unity, you would not be bodies." Then he needs to be told himself: "How have you come to know this Unity, in accordance with which you make a judgment on bodies? After all, if you could not see her, you would not be able to make the judgment that they do not fully realize her; while if you said you saw her with these eyes in the body, you would not be telling the truth, because, although they are fixed on her tracks, they are still a long way away from her, since with these eyes you only see bodily things."

So therefore it is with the mind that we see her. But where do we see her? If it were in this place where our bodies are, the person in the east, who is making judgments about bodies in this way, would not see her. So then, she is not contained in a place, and, when she is present anywhere to someone making a judgment, she is nowhere by space as in a place, and there is nowhere that her writ does not run.

Appearances never Lie, but if We Misjudge Them, We Become Vanitators and Prevent their Leading Us to the Contemplation of the Supreme Beauty, God

33, 61. But if bodies lie about her, then we must not believe liars in case we fall into *the vanities of vanitators,*[123] but (since the reason they lie is that they seem to present her to the eyes of flesh, while she is only to be seen by an uncluttered mind) we should rather inquire whether they are lying to the extent that they resemble her or to the extent that they do not attain her. Because, if they attained her, they would fully realize the Unity they imitate, while if they fully realized her they would be completely like her. If they were completely like her, there

---

122. I am treating "unity" as a feminine noun—which means of course in English according her feminity, personifying her—because it/she is in Augustine's mind to be identified with Truth, and so with Wisdom, which is personified in those great passages.

123. See Eccl 1:2; Augustine's text read *vanitas vanitantium*. See section 41 and the relevant note.

would be no difference between that nature and this one. Finally, if that were the case, they would not be lying about her; they would be just what she is.

In any case, they do not lie to those who pay more careful attention to them, because lying means wishing to seem to be what you are not. But if, without wishing it, you are thought to be other than you are, you are not lying, but all the same you are deceiving. I mean, this is how we distinguish the liar from the deceiver,[124] that every liar has the will to deceive, even if he is not believed, while you cannot be a deceiver if you do not deceive. So then, what a body looks like never lies, because it does not have any will. If, however, it is not even thought to be what it is not, it does not deceive either.

62. But the eyes themselves do not deceive either. For the only thing that they can report back to the spirit is how they are affected. And if not only they but all the senses of the body report back like that, I do not know what more we should require of them. And so take away the vanitators and there will not be any vanity. If anyone supposes that an oar is broken in the water and is put together again when it is taken out of it, it is not a bad messenger that he has but a bad judge that he is himself. The messenger, I mean, could not perceive otherwise in the water, nor should it have perceived otherwise. I mean, if air is one thing and water another, it is quite in order for perception in water to differ from perception in air.[125] So the eye has acted correctly; that is what it was made for, after all—to have just that capacity. But the spirit has acted perversely, considering that it has been endowed with a mind, not an eye, for contemplating the supreme beauty. But in this case it wishes to turn the mind to bodies, the eye to God. For it is trying to understand things of the flesh and see things of the spirit, which cannot be done.[126]

Multiplicity Has its Place in God's Plans, but We Must not Be Distracted by It from the One

34, 63. So this perversity has to be straightened out because, unless the spirit puts what is at the top of its list down at the bottom and what is down at the bottom up at the top, it will not be fit for the kingdom of heaven. Let us then not

---

124. Not a distinction we would make in English; I must simply ask the reader here to think in Latin, at least in Augustine's Latin, for a moment or two.
125. See section 53.
126. Augustine does seem to be leaping to a conclusion over the omission of at least half the argument! I think we have to realize that the business of the oar is no more than an illustration, and not a particularly apt one at that; it illustrates the perverse use of the mind, misjudging appearances, when it is only by a correct judgment of appearances that we can avoid being vanitators and can come to the contemplation of the supreme beauty, God. But then, as we have probably begun to realize already, Augustine was hardly at his best in this early work of his on *True Religion*.

seek the highest things among the lowest, and let us not look askance at the lowest either. Let us make a proper judgment of them, in order not to be judged with them; that is, let us attribute to them only as much as their outermost look deserves, or, while we are seeking the first things among the last, we may find ourselves numbered among the last, which will not harm the last things in the least but will harm us no end.

In any case, the arrangements of divine providence are not made any the less elegant because the unjust are set justly in their place and the ugly set beautifully in theirs. And if the reason we are deceived by the beauty of visible things is that it is constituted by unity and does not reflect unity to the full, we should understand, if we can, that we are not being deceived by that which is but by that which is not. Each single body, to be sure, is a true body but a deceptive unity. It is not, after all, supremely one, nor does it imitate that supreme One to the extent of fully reflecting it, and yet it would not even be a body unless it were in some sort one. What is more, it could not be even in some sort one unless it had this from that which is supremely One.

64. O obstinate souls, give me someone who can see, without imagining any flesh-bound things seen. Give me someone who can see that the origin of every unit can only be the One alone by which every unit is unified, whether it fully reflects the One or whether it does not. Give me not someone who argues, not someone who wishes to seem to see what he does not see. Give me someone who will stand up against the senses of the flesh and the blows with which the soul has been beaten by means of them, who will stand up against human custom, withstand human praise, who *will be sorry on his bed* (Ps 4:4), who *will rectify his spirit* (Ps 77:6), who will not *love vanities and go in search of lies* (Ps 4:2).[127]

O for someone who already knows how to say: "If there is one Rome, which some Romulus or other is said to have founded beside the Tiber, this other one is false, which I picture in my thoughts, since it is not the city itself, nor am I there in spirit, because in that case I would surely know what is going on there now. If the sun is one unit, this other one that I picture in my thoughts is false, because the real one is running its course through definite times and places, while I put this one where and when I wish. If that friend of mine is one unit, this one that I picture to myself is false, because I do not know where he may be, while I put this picture of him in whatever place I like. I myself am certainly one unit, and I am aware of my body in this place, and yet in the picture I have of myself I go anywhere at all, I talk to anyone at all. These images or pictures are all false, and yet nobody understands false things. So then, I am not understanding when I contemplate these things and believe them, because what I contemplate with the understanding has to be true. Can these things then be, perhaps, what are

---

127. In *Confessions* IX, 4, 8-11 Augustine uses the words of Ps 4 to describe his own conversion.

commonly called fancies? So from where does my soul get filled with illusions? Where is the truth that is observed by the mind?"

Someone thinking on these lines can already be told: "That light is true by which you come to realize that these things are not true. It is by this light that you see that One, by which you judge that whatever else you see is one and yet that whatever you see to be mutable is not what that One is."

Be Still from the Fancies of Place and Time, and Know that I Am God

35, 65. But if the mind's eye blinks and trembles at the prospect of gazing upon these things, set it at rest. Don't contend with anything but the habits of your bodies. Conquer those, and you will have conquered everything. We are certainly seeking the One, than which there is nothing more simple. So then, let us seek it in simplicity of heart. *Be still*, he says, *and acknowledge that I am the Lord* (Ps 46:10)—not with the stillness of sloth but with the stillness of reflection, so that you may be free of places and times. For their swollen and fleeting fancies do not allow us to see the unity that is constant. Places offer us things to love, times snatch away things we do love and leave behind in the soul a crowd of jostling fancies to stir up its greed for one thing after another. In this way the spirit is made restless and wretched, as it longs to lay hold of the things it is held by.

It is being summoned, accordingly, to stillness, that is, not to set its heart on things which you cannot set your heart on without hard labor. In this way, you see, it will master them, in this way it will not be held by them but will hold them down. *My yoke*, he says, *is light* (Mt 11:30). Those then who are subjected to this yoke have everything else subjected to them. So they will not endure hard labor, since what has been subjected to you, after all, does not resist you. But the friends of this world,[128] of which they will be the masters if they are willing to be sons of God, seeing that he gave them the right to become sons of God[129]—so the friends of this world, then, are so afraid of being torn from its embrace that they find nothing more laborious than not toiling away at hard labor.

Failure to Distinguish between Truth and the True, Likeness and the Like, Leads to Idolatry

36, 66. But at least those to whom this is clear—that it is falsehood which has people thinking that what is not is—can understand that it is Truth which shows us that which is. Now, if bodies are deceptive insofar as they do not fully realize

---

128. See Jas 4:4.
129. See Jn 1:12.

that One which it is agreed they imitate, the Beginning from which anything that is is one, the Beginning towards whose likeness we are inclined by nature to approve of things straining—because we are inclined by nature to disapprove of anything departing from its Unity and tending towards its unlikeness—then we are given to understand that there is something which is so like that one and only One (the Beginning from which anything is one that is a unit in any way at all) that it altogether perfectly realizes this likeness and is exactly the same. And this is Truth, and the Word in the Beginning, and the Word, God with God.[130]

For if falsehood derives from things which imitate the One, not insofar as they imitate him but insofar as they cannot fully realize him, then that is Truth which has been able to realize him fully and to be what he is. This is the Truth which shows him as he is, which is why she is most appropriately called his Word and his Light. Everything else can be said to be like that One to the extent that it is; to that extent it is also true. She, however, is his Likeness, and therefore Truth. Just as it is truth, after all, by which true things are true, so it is likeness by which anything like is like. So, just as truth is the form of things' being true, in the same way likeness is the form of things' being like. Accordingly, since things are true insofar as they are, while they are insofar as they are like the original One, she is the form of all things that are, who is the supreme Likeness of the Beginning and is Truth, because she is without any unlikeness at all.

67. Thus falsehood does not arise from things themselves' being deceptive, since all they show the senses is their proper looks, which they have received according to their own grade of beauty. Nor does it arise from the senses themselves' being deceptive, which according to the nature of their sensitive body only send on to the presiding spirit the message of their sensations. But it is sins that deceive souls, when they go seeking what is true after forsaking and neglecting Truth.

Since, after all, they have been setting their hearts on the works more than on the craftsman or the craft itself, they are punished by being led up the garden path as follows: they are hunting for the craftsman and the craft in the works, and when they have not been able to find them—for God does not fall under the senses of the body but soars above the mind itself—they conclude that the works themselves are both craft and craftsman.[131]

---

130. See Jn 1:1.
131. In this way Augustine explains the origins of idolatry.

From the Worship of God's Creatures to the Worship of Idols, the Work of Men's Hands

37, 68. This is the origin of all impiety, not just that of sinners but also that of those sentenced for their sins. They not only wish, you see, to investigate created things against the commandment of God and to enjoy them rather than the law itself and Truth, which we gather was the sin of the first man, making bad use of free will, but they go on to add this in the very sentence passed on them, so that, as well as loving, they also serve the creature rather than the creator and worship it through all its parts, going from the highest to the lowest.

But some of them check themselves at this point, so that instead of the supreme God they worship the soul[132] and the first intellectual creature, which the Father fashioned through the Truth for always gazing at Truth herself, and at itself through her, because she is as like him as can be, in every respect. Next they come to procreative life, the created mechanism by which the eternal and unchanging God effects the reproduction of things visible and time-bound. From here they slide down to worshiping animals and mere bodies, and among these they first pick on the more beautiful ones, among which the heavenly bodies are far and away the most excellent.

So then, it is first the body of the sun that comes to mind, and some of them stop with that. Some think that the brilliance of the moon is also worthy of religious devotion; after all, it is nearer to us, so they say, and is thus felt to have a more neighborly appearance. Others also add in the bodies of the other planets and the whole sky with its stars and constellations. Others couple the air to the ethereal heaven, and to these loftier corporeal elements they subject their own souls.

But among these, the ones who strike themselves as being the most religious are those who consider the whole created universe together, that is, the whole world with all the things that are in it and the life by which it is animated and draws breath, which some have believed to be corporeal, others incorporeal—who consider then this whole totality together to be one great god, whose parts are the other gods. They have no knowledge, you see, of the author and founder of the created universe. From here they were cast down headlong to the worship of images and plunged from the works of God into venerating their own works, which at least are still there to be seen.

---

132. I.e., the world soul; see section 22.

From Idolatry to Atheism; the Three Great Addictions and Temptations

38, 69. For there is another worse and lower cult of images, in which they worship their own fancies. And whatever their own erring spirits have imagined, by putting things together with pride and puffed-up vainglory, they honor in the name of religion, until finally the soul reaches the point that nothing at all is to be worshiped and that people greatly err who get involved with superstition and entangle themselves in such wretched slavery.

But it is in vain that they come to this conclusion.[133] For they do not succeed in releasing themselves from slavery; their vices remain, after all, by which they were drawn into supposing that those things are to be worshiped. I mean, they are the slaves of a threefold greedy longing—for pleasure or superiority or spectacles.[134] I maintain that there is not one of these men who have come to the conclusion that there is nothing to be worshiped who is not either addicted to the pleasures of the flesh, or does not cherish the prospect of some vain position of power, or does not go crazy with delight over some spectacle. In this way they ignorantly look for happiness from the things of time upon which they have set their hearts.

Now, anyone wishing to achieve happiness through such things is of necessity enslaved by them, willy-nilly. For he follows their lead and goes in dread of anybody who seems capable of depriving him of them. Now it only needs a spark from a fire or some tiny little beastie to deprive him of them. Finally, not to mention countless mishaps, time itself must of necessity deprive him of all things transient. And so, since all the things of time are included in this world, those who think nothing should be worshiped, in case they should be enslaved by it, find themselves enslaved by all parts of the world.[135]

70. Nonetheless, while they do indeed find themselves stuck miserably in this extremity, that they suffer themselves to be mastered by their vices, being sold into slavery either by lust or pride or curiosity, or by two of them, or by all three, it is still open to them in this stadium of human life to grapple with them and

---

133. How they come to the conclusion, genuinely atheistically, that nothing is to be worshiped from having sunk to the depth of worshiping the constructs of their own imaginations is something beyond the comprehension of Augustine's translator, who cannot see how else this strange passage might be translated.

134. In this threefold desire Augustine sees the basic cause of man's turning away from the worship of the true God. In the course of the ensuing argument he identifies those desires with the desires of the flesh, for admiration, and of the eyes, which are mentioned in 1 Jn 2:16. See *Confessions* X, 30, 41-39, 64. A similar trio of desires is found in Porphyry, on whom Augustine is probably dependent here; see W. Theiler, *Porphyrios und Augustin* (Halle 1933) 37-43.

135. Augustine here unmasks the rejection of religious worship as a subtle form of idolatry. In his view, even atheists have their own "pantheon."

conquer them,[136] if they first believe what they are not yet capable of understanding and stop setting their hearts on the world, *since everything that is in the world*, as we have it on divine authority, *is the lust of the flesh and the lust of the eyes and worldly ambition* (1 Jn 2:15-16). Here those three vices are signified, because by the lust of the flesh the lovers of the lowest kind of pleasure are signified, by the lust of the eyes the curious and inquisitive, by worldly ambition the proud.

71. That we must beware of this triple temptation has also been shown in the man whom Truth herself took up. *Tell these stones*, says the tempter, *to become loaves of bread.* But he, the one and only teacher, answered: *Not on bread alone does man live, but on every word of God.* (Mt 4:3-4) To this extent, you see, did he teach that the lust for pleasure has to be tamed, that one must not even give way to extreme hunger. But perhaps it would be possible to catch out, by pride's lure of temporal dominion, the one who could not be led astray by the pleasures of the flesh. So then, all the kingdoms of the world were shown him, and he was told: *All of them will I give you, if you prostrate yourself and worship me.* To which the answer came: *The Lord your God shall you worship, and him only shall you serve.* (Mt 4:8-10) Thus pride was trampled on. Now the final snare of curiosity was laid; he was only urged, after all, to hurl himself down from the pinnacle of the temple for the sake of experiencing such a great miracle. But not even here was he defeated, and the reason he answered as he did was that we might understand that for getting to know God there is no need of attempts to devise visible tests for the divine: *You shall not put*, says he, *the Lord your God to the test* (Mt 4:7).

Accordingly, those who feed inwardly on the word of God do not seek pleasure in this desert; those who submit to the one God alone do not seek things to boast about on the mountain, that is on earthly achievement; while those who cleave to the eternal spectacle of unchanging Truth do not hurl themselves down by means of the summit of this body, that is of these eyes, to acquire knowledge of the lower things of time.[137]

---

136. See 1 Cor 9:24.
137. See *The Catholic Way of Life* I, 21, 38: "There are those who have abandoned the virtues and have no idea of what God is and how majestic his nature is, which abides ever the same. They think that they are doing something great if they inquire very attentively and with much eagerness into the entire mass of this body that we call the world." See also Letter 11, 2. H-I. Marrou, in his *History of Education in Antiquity*, trans. by G. Lamb (Madison, Wis. 1982), writes that Augustine's philosophy is about the soul and about God and that it is not at all about this world.

Even Things of the Lowest Order Reflect the Supreme Concord and Harmony of the Truth

39. 72. Is there anything therefore left by which the soul cannot be reminded of its original beauty, seeing that it can be so by its very vices? This is why, after all, the Wisdom of God stretches out mightily to the end;[138] this is why the supreme craftsman has woven his works together through her into one final gracefulness and glory; this is why his goodness, reaching from the highest to the least of things, has been envious of no beauty (which could issue from him alone)—all this to ensure that nobody who was not excepted from being in some way a portrait of Truth[139] would be cast off from Truth herself.

Ask bodily pleasure what there is to it; you will find it is nothing else but concord. I mean, if things that resist you cause pain, then things that accord with you cause pleasure. Recognize therefore what the last word in concord might be. Do not go outside, come back into yourself. It is in the inner self that Truth dwells. And if you find your own nature to be subject to change, transcend even yourself.[140] But remember, when you are transcending yourself, that it is your reasoning soul transcending yourself. So then, direct your course to what the light of reason itself gets its light from. Where, after all, does every good reasoner arrive but at the truth? Since Truth herself, of course, does not reach herself by a process of reasoning but is herself what reasoners are aiming at, see there the concord which cannot be surpassed, and put yourself in accord with her. Confess that you are not what she is—if in fact she does not seek herself, while you have sought her, and come to her, not by walking from one place to another but by the desire of your mind, so that the inner self might find in accord with its lodger not a carnal pleasure of the lowest sort but a spiritual pleasure of the highest.

73. Or, if you are not sure what I am saying and have doubts about whether it is true, at least be sure that you have no doubt about your having doubts about this; and, if it is certain that you do have doubts, ask where this certainty comes from. What will not occur to you then, what will not occur to you in the slightest, is that it is from the light of this sun up there but that it is from *the true light, which enlightens every person coming into this world* (Jn 1:9), which cannot be seen by these eyes nor by those which think up the fancies that have been

---

138. See Wis 8:1; the writer has Wisdom stretching from end to end, i.e. from one end of the earth to the other; Augustine, by modifying the quotation, has her stretching as far as the end of time.

139. Satan and the wicked in hell excepted themselves from so being by their wickedness; they were not created as exceptions to the rule.

140. The Augustinian principle of interiority involves three kinds of movement: aversion, turning away from the world; introversion, looking into one's own mind; and a movement beyond creation and the self to God. See P. Cary, "Interiority," in A. D. Fitzgerald, ed., *Augustine Through the Ages* (Grand Rapids 1999) 454-456.

stamped on the soul through those outer ones. No, what it is seen by is the eyes which tell the fancies themselves: "*You* are not what I am looking for, nor are you that by which I juggle you around and disapprove of anything foul and ugly among you that occurs to me or approve of what is beautiful, since that in virtue of which I give both my approval and disapproval is more beautiful still. Accordingly, this is what I give my approval to most of all, and what I place not only before you but before all those bodies from which I have drunk you in."

Next, now that you see this rule, think of it in this way: Everyone who understands that he has doubts is understanding something true, and he is certain about this thing that he understands. He is certain therefore about something true. So then, everyone who has doubts whether there is such a thing as truth has something true in himself about which he cannot have any doubts, and there cannot be anything true except with truth. And so, one who has been able to have doubts about anything has no business to have doubts about truth.

Where these things are seen is where the light is that is independent of space and time and of any fancies or imaginings of such places and space. Can these things[141] in any degree perish, even though every reasoner should vanish or grow old among the carnal ones below?[142] Reasoning, after all, does not make such things but finds them. So then, before they are found they abide in themselves, and when they are found they make us new again.

God's Providence Directs All Creatures, from the Lowest to the Highest, to the Manifestation of the Supreme Beauty of Wisdom

40. 74. Thus the inner self is being reborn and the outer self is being broken down from day to day.[143] But the inner self pays attention to the outer and sees that, while compared with itself it is ugly and filthy, of its own kind nonetheless it is beautiful and enjoys the concordance of bodies and breaking them down for its own good, that is, things that nourish its flesh. These however, once broken down, on losing, that is, their own specific forms, travel into the fabric of these limbs and bodily parts. On being broken down they restore these by crossing over in virtue of bodily concordance into another specific form. Then through the vital processes they are somehow or other sorted out, so that those of them

---

141. Not of course the fancies of the imagination but the things Augustine was talking about in the previous paragraphs, all the qualities that form the escort of the Truth. Again, one has to state that he is writing very carelessly.

142. *Apud carnales inferos*: a most peculiar expression. *Inferi*, though a masculine plural, originally no doubt referring to the gods of the underworld, Pluto and Proserpine, nearly always meant simply the underworld, the realm of the dead. Here it presumably refers to the inhabitants of that realm.

143. See 2 Cor 4:16.

which are suitable may be taken over into the structure of this visible beauty, the body, while those which are not suitable are ejected through appropriate channels. So the most solid impurities are given back to the earth to take on other specific forms; some of the rest is sweated out through the whole body; some receives the latent formulae[144] of the whole animal and starts on its way to becoming offspring; whether by the concordant coupling of two bodies or by some similar stirring of the imagination, it is pumped through the genital tracts and flows down from the head itself to give pleasure at the lowest level.[145]

From then on in the mother it is adjusted through definite formulae of time to fit into the correct spatial formula so that every one of the limbs might occupy its proper place, and, if they have kept the measure of similarity, a body is born which, with the color of light added to it, is called beautiful, and, by those who have set their hearts on it, it is loved with the most vehement possible love. However, its form, its shape that moves about, does not please us more than the life which moves it about. You see, if that animal loves us, it attracts us all the more forcefully, while if it hates us we are furious and cannot bear it, even if it presents its form and shape to be enjoyed. This is the total kingdom of pleasure and the lowest kind of beauty; it is, after all, subject to decay. If it were not so, it would be considered the highest kind.

75. But divine providence is at hand to show us both that this lowest kind of beauty is not bad, considering that it presents such manifest traces of the primordial formulae, in which there is no limit to the Wisdom of God,[146] and yet to make clear that it is at the outermost edge of beauty by mixing in with it pains and diseases and distortion of limbs and dark coloring and rivalries and quarrels of spirits. All this is to warn us that there is something unchanging that we are to seek. And God does this through the lowest of his ministers, to whom carrying it out is a pleasure, whom the scriptures call destroyers and angels of divine wrath,[147] although they themselves are ignorant of the good that is being achieved through them.

Like them are the human beings who take pleasure in the miseries of others, and get a lot of fun out of the disasters and mistakes of other people, or want them

144. *Numeros* in the Latin, in the sense it has, for Augustine at least, in Wis 11:20. This is also the word rendered by "formulae," "formula" in the next paragraph. But as well as this text from Wisdom, the next section shows that he probably had in mind first and foremost Ps 147:5, where *numerus* can only mean "limit" or "measure." Here, however, I think "formulae" is the only possible translation.
145. From the head, I presume, because that is where the imagination is at work. But just as, according to Aristotle, when you pass water the urine is extracting impurities from the blood stream all over the body, so too here, perhaps, the idea is that the seminal fluid, bearing these vital "numbers" or formulae, is being draw from all over the body.
146. See Ps 147:5.
147. For "destroyers" see Jdt 8:25 in the Latin Vulgate, which here differs rather widely from the Greek original; see also Ex 12:23; 1 Cor 10:10; Rv 15:7.

turned into comic shows for their entertainment. But by such means the good are given warnings and training in all these circumstances, and they conquer and are honored with a triumph and reign as kings, while the wicked are cheated of their hopes, tormented, conquered, condemned, and become the slaves not of the one supreme Lord of all things but of the lowest rank of his slaves, namely those angels who feed on the pains and wretchedness of the damned and for this malevolence are racked by the freedom that is bestowed upon the good.

76. In this way all are directed by their functions, their duties and their ends towards the beauty of the whole universe, so that if what shocks us in the part is considered together with the whole, it gives us entire satisfaction. After all, in making a judgment on a building we ought not to consider just one single corner; or in assessing the beauty of human beings just their hair; or with good public speakers just the movements of their fingers; or with the course of the moon just its changes during three days.

These things, you see, which are at the lowest level precisely because, while complete in themselves, as parts they are incomplete, are to be considered with the wholes they are part of, if we wish to make a right judgment.[148] For our true judgment, whether it is made on the part or the whole, is something beautiful, since indeed it rises above the whole world; nor, insofar as we make a true judgment, do we cling to any one part of the world. The error we make, on the other hand, in clinging to a part, is *per se* ugly.

But, just as the color black in a picture becomes beautiful within the whole, so too the immutable providence of God puts on a worthy production of this whole contest by assigning one part to the vanquished, another to the contestants, another to the winners, another to the spectators, another to those quietly contemplating God alone, since among all these there is nothing evil but sin and the punishment of sin, that is to say the deliberate, voluntary falling away from the Supreme Being and the non-voluntary hard labor in the opposite grade of being. This evil can be stated in other words as follows: freedom from justice, slavery under sin.

The Preservation of the Right Order of Things

41. 77. Now the outer self is broken down by either the inner self's advancement or its failure.[149] But by the advancement of the inner self it is broken down in such a way that the whole self may be put together again in better shape and reconstituted in its entirety at the last trumpet, so that from then on it is neither

---

148. In this and the following sections Augustine is taking up thoughts that Plotinus had developed in his treatise on providence in *Enneads* III, 2, 3-4, 17.
149. Augustine neatly contrasts the *profectus* (advancement) of the inner self with the *defectus* (failure) of the outer.

broken down nor breaks down. By its own failure, however, it is tossed into more breakable beauties, that is into the order of pains and penalties. And let us not be surprised at my still calling them beauties. There is nothing, after all, that is in order which is not also beautiful. And as the apostle says: *All order is from God* (Rom 13:1).[150]

Now, we are bound to admit that a weeping man is better than a rejoicing worm,[151] and yet I am not lying when I say that I can say volumes in praise of the worm, having in mind its bright color, the smooth round shape of its body, the first sections fitting into the middle ones, the middle ones into those at the end, all observing the aim of unity according to the lowliness of their nature, nothing being formed from one part which does not correspond in parallel dimensions with another. What shall I say now about the soul which animates this tiny body, how it moves it rhythmically, section by section,[152] how it aims at what suits it, surmounts or avoids obstacles as best it can and, by referring all this to its one sense of safety, suggests much more clearly than does its body that founding unity of all natures?

I'm talking about any kind of animated worm.[153] Many have spoken most truly and eloquently in praise of ashes and dung.[154] So, what wonder if I say that the human soul, which is better than any kind of body, wherever it is and whatever it is like, is beautifully set in order, and that other beauties are brought into being from its pains and penalties, since it is not where it is fitting that the blessed should be, when it is wretched in misery, but is where it is fitting that the wretchedly miserable should be?

78. Accordingly, we should not let anyone deceive us. Whatever is rightly being disparaged is rejected in comparison with something better. Every nature, though, however far outside the pale, however low in the scale of things, in comparison with nothing is justly the object of praise. And only then are we not doing well, if we can do better. Thus, if we are able to do well with Truth itself, we are doing badly with any trace at all of Truth. Much worse, then, with the lowest kind of trace or vestige, when we are clinging to the pleasures of the flesh. So let us conquer either the blandishments or the vexations of this greedy desire. Let us subjugate this female to ourselves, if we are men. With us in the lead, she will become better and will no longer be given the name of greed but of modera-

---

150. Augustine slightly rephrases and rearranges this verse to suit his purpose.
151. The immediate reference here is to Ex 35:25, where the Vulgate and other Latin versions have *vermiculum* instead of what the Greek LXX has, *coccinum*, meaning scarlet. But either the Latin word had come by that time also to mean scarlet (hence ultimately our "vermilion"), or at any rate this little worm was thought of as producing or even being scarlet. Hence what Augustine goes on to say about its bright color.
152. *Numerose* in the Latin, that invaluable and untranslatable word again.
153. I.e., even those we find in our gardens, as well as the one found in Ex 35:25.
154. For example Cicero, *De senectute* 15,54.

tion or temperance. I mean, when she is the one in the lead and we are just following, she is labeled greed and lust, while we earn the labels of rashness and stupidity.

Let us follow Christ our head, so that we too may be followed by the one whose head we are. This is an injunction that can also be given to women not by marital but by fraternal right, by the right according to which *in Christ there is neither male nor female*.[155] Women too, after all, have something manly in them by which to subjugate the feminine pleasures, by which to serve Christ and be in command of greed. This is evident with many widows and virgins of God, with many married women too, those of them who are observing their conjugal rights and duties, but in a fraternal manner under the aegis of the Christian people.

But if by that part which God bids us master, encouraging us and giving a helping hand, so that we may be put in possession once more of what is ours—if then through negligence and ungodliness the man, that is, the mind and reason, is subdued by this part, the person will indeed be a shameful and miserable creature but will be destined in this life and ordered after this life to where that supreme ruler and lord sentences him to be destined and ordered. And thus it is not permitted that the universal creation should be blemished by any ugliness or filth.

The Unchanging Law of Numbers[156]

42, 79. Let us walk while we have the light of day, that is, while we can make use of reason, so that being converted and turned towards God by his Word, which is the true light, we may deserve to be enlightened, lest the dark overtake us.[157] Daylight, you see, means the presence of that light *which enlightens every man who is coming into this world* (Jn 1:9). By *man* he meant persons who can make use of reason and can apply themselves to rise from where they have fallen. So then, if the pleasures of the flesh are what they set their hearts on, let these be examined more diligently,[158] and when some traces have been recognized there of certain numbers or formulae, one must then go on to look for

---

155. See Gal 3:28; Eph 5:23. The "fraternal right" that Augustine has just mentioned, *fraterno jure*, makes married women the equal of their husbands in the context of the Christian people, while they are still obliged to observe the "marital right" which makes the man the head of the family—and which is, or was in those days, a matter of secular, not ecclesiastical, let alone divine, law.

156. In this section I really have to keep to Augustine's word "number," bearing something of the meaning "formula" I have been giving it, but still being closer to the numbers we count with than to whatever we nowadays mean by a formula.

157. See Jn 12:35.

158. "If the pleasure of the flesh *diligitur*, let this be examined *diligentius*"—a telling play on words, showing very clearly that *diligere* cannot properly be translated simply as "to love."

where these may be found without any kind of swelling or fermentation. That, after all, is where that which is, is more of a unity.

And if that is what those are like which function in the life force that is at work in seeds, they are more to be wondered at there than in bodies. For, if the numbers in seeds were to swell and ferment like the seeds themselves, then from half the pip of a fig half a fig-tree would be born; and, again, from incomplete seeds of animals only incomplete animals would be begotten; and just one tiny single seed of any species would not have the limitless force of its proper species. In fact, though, from just one seed, whatever its nature, of crops it is possible for crops be propagated, or of woods for woods to spring up, or of flocks for flocks to be multiplied, or of peoples for peoples to be born throughout the ages, so that there is not a single leaf, nor a single hair, all through such an endless succession of generations, whose number or formula was not in that first seed.

Then again we must reflect on how sweetly numbered are the beauties of the sounds the vibrations of the air bring to us when the nightingale sings, which the soul of that little bird would not fashion whenever it liked, unless it had those numbers impressed upon it in a non-bodily way by its life force. This sort of thing can also be observed in other animals which lack reason but do not lack sensation. There is none of these, you see, which, in the sound of its voice or in other movements and actions of its limbs, does not bring to bear something well numbered and regulated of its kind, not because it has the knowledge how to do so but rather because it acts within the innermost limits of its nature, which are regulated by that unchanging law of numbers.

About This and That, Ending up with God

43, 80. Let us come back to ourselves and leave aside those things which we have in common with bushes and beasts. I mean, swallows build nests, and birds of other kinds do the same, each in its own proper way. So what is it in us, then, by which we make judgments about all of them, what shapes they aim at, and to what extent they achieve them, and we ourselves in our buildings and other material works are masters of all such shapes and contrive an unlimited number of such things? What is it in us that understands inwardly how these visible masses of material are big or small only in relation to each other, and how every material body, whatever size it is, has a half and, if a half, then innumerable parts? And thus every grain of millet, in relation to that part of it which can be compared to us in this world, is as big as the whole world is in relation to us. And this entire world is beautiful by reason not of its mass but of all the shapes in it, while it seems big to us in virtue not of its quantity but of our littleness, that is, of the animals which fill it. And these again, being infinitely divisible, are not small *per se* but only in comparison with other things and, above all, with the universe.

The same goes for the divisions of time, because every length of time, like every length of space, has its half; even though it is as short as you wish, it both starts and proceeds and stops. And so it is bound to have a half, while it is being divided by the point through which it proceeds to its end. And so it is that the time a short syllable takes is short in comparison with a longer one, and a winter hour is short in comparison with a summer one.[159] Thus the time passed in an hour is short in comparison with a day, and so is a day compared with a month, and a month compared with a year, and a year compared with a century,[160] and a century compared with greater cycles of time, and these compared with the totality of time; while the very passage and, so to say, pacing out of spaces of time or place by numbers is judged as being beautiful not by the amount it expands or the length it takes but by its well-ordered symmetry.

81. The style of this order, however, lives in everlasting Truth and is neither vast in bulk nor rolling on and on off an endless wheel but is great by its dominance above all places and is motionless by its eternity over all times, yet without it no bulky vastness can be brought into unity, no rolling on of time be checked from straying off track and so be either some kind of body as body or some kind of movement as movement. It is itself the principal unity and is neither finitely nor infinitely massive, neither finitely nor infinitely subject to change. After all, it does not have some of it here, some of it there, or some of it now, some of it later on, because the Father of Truth is supremely the One, the Father of his own Wisdom, which is called his likeness, in no respect at all unlike him, and his image because it is from him.[161] And so the Son is rightly said to be *from* him, everything else to be *through* him.[162] He came forth, you see, as the form or shape of all things, supremely achieving the One, from whom he is, so that all other things that are, insofar as they are like the One, become so through that form or shape.

---

159. Hours were not yet artificially measured by clocks; these were an invention of monks in the Middle Ages. In Augustine's time, in any event, people thought of the day from sunrise to sunset as divided into twelve hours; consequently the hour had a different length in summer than in winter.
160. Augustine says "with a *lustrum*"; this was a sacred period of time, normally being five years, but then it could be extended to any long period of time.
161. Twins are very like one another, but they are not from each other; whereas they can properly be called the image of their father or mother, because they not only resemble them but are from them. An image in the literal sense, a statue or a picture, a portrait, is made by the artist according to what he observes the original to be like; it is in a real sense from the original as well as being its likeness.
162. Everything else is through the Son, through the Word, and only in that way from the Father.

The Effect of Man's Being Made to God's Image, fully Realized in the Resurrection of the Body

44, 82. Some of these are *through* this form in such a way as also to be *to* it,[163] such as all rational and intelligent creatures, among which man is so rightly said to have been made to the image and likeness of God.[164] In no other way, after all, would he be able to gaze with the mind upon unchanging Truth. Other things, however, are made *through* this form without being made *to* it.

And that is why, if the rational soul[165] serves her creator, by whom she has been made and through whom she has been made and to whom she has been made, all other things will serve her. These will include both the lowest life force, which is so close to her and is her assistant in ruling the body, and also the body itself, the lowest in the scale of nature and being, which gives in to her all along the line, and which she dominates at will, experiencing no trouble from it, because she will not now be looking for happiness from it or through it but will receive this directly from God through herself.

So then, the body being now refashioned, she will regulate it without its undergoing any wear and tear and without herself experiencing any burdensome difficulty. *For in the resurrection they shall neither marry nor be given in marriage, but they shall be like the angels in heaven* (Mt 22:30). On the other hand, *food for the stomach, and the stomach for food; God, though, will destroy both one and the other* (1 Cor 6:13), since *the kingdom of God does not consist in food and drink, but in justice and peace and joy* (Rom 14:17).

How even our Vices are Intimations of Eternal Blessedness; a Curious Comparison of the Charioteer Riding for a Fall

45, 83. Accordingly, even with these pleasures of the body we find that the reason for disdaining them is not that the nature of the body is something bad but that it is shameful to wallow in the love of this last and lowest of good things when you have been granted the privilege of cleaving to and enjoying the first and highest. When the charioteer is dragged along and pays the penalty for his foolhardy cutting of a corner, he blames whatever it is he was using. But what he ought to be doing is begging for help, imploring the patron of the races[166] to have

---

163. The formula *ut ad ipsam etiam sint* ("as also to be to it") is also a reminder of an inner movement toward the creator as confessed by Augustine in a programmatic statement in *Confessions* I, 1, 1: "Our heart is restless until it rests in you."
164. See Gn 1:27.
165. Which Augustine in effect just identifies with the man, the person.
166. The *dominus rerum*: the wealthy man who put on the games and the races and who presided over them.

someone stop the horses which are now making another spectacle of his tumble and are about to make one of his death if help does not come—to have him set back in his place, on top of the wheels, the reins put in his hands again, so that he can control more carefully the animals that are obedient and well trained. Then he will realize how well the chariot and the whole of that contraption has been constructed, though he had been badly hurt by its collapse when it had run off course for lack of appropriate, sensible control.

It was the greed of the soul making bad use of the body that gave birth to its feebleness, when she grabbed the forbidden fruit in Paradise against the regimen laid down by the physician,[167] the regimen which holds the key to everlasting health and salvation.

84. So then, if in this very feebleness of the visible flesh, in which the blessed life cannot be found, what you do find is a hint of the blessed life because of the idea's[168] coming down from the highest to the lowest, how much clearer a suggestion will you find in the appetite for celebrity and excellence and all the vain pomp and pride of this world? What else, after all, is man seeking in all this but to be the one and only, if that were possible, to whom all things are subject, in perverse imitation, that is to say, of almighty God?

And to think that he would only have submissively to imitate God by living according to his commandments, and he would have all other things made subject to him and would not sink to such baseness as to be afraid of that beastie[169] who wants to have humanity at his beck and call! So then, pride too has a kind of appetite for unity and omnipotence,[170] but in being prince over temporal affairs, which all pass away like a shadow.[171]

85. We certainly wish to be conquerors, and rightly so. After all, this goes with the very nature of our spirits, following God, by whom they were made to his image. But first his commandments were to be kept and, if they were, then nobody would conquer us. As it is, however, while she, to whose words we shamefully gave in, is being tamed by the pangs of childbirth, we too are toiling away at the earth and most shamefully being overcome by all the things that have been able to shake and disturb us.[172]

---

167. See Gn 3:6-7. "She" here is the soul—represented indeed by Eve.
168. The *species*, the Platonic idea.
169. The serpent; our thoughts should still be in Paradise with Adam and Eve, representing the entire human race.
170. In wanting to be like God, knowing good and evil, Gn 3:5.
171. See Pss 102:11; 109:23; Wis 5:9; Job 8:9; 1 Chr 29:15.
172. See Gn 3:16-19. Augustine was a male, writing unashamedly for other males. But there is a little more to this apparent male chauvinism than that. In the psychological analogy he always uses, the spirit or mind or intelligence, the *spiritus* or *animus*, in any human person is "male," the sensitive soul or *anima*, which includes the emotions, is "female." And what he has in mind here, and understands the Genesis story to mean at its deepest level, is the human intelligence being overcome by the seduction of the senses and passions.

And so we don't wish to be conquered by men, and we are unable to conquer our anger. Can anything more abominable be found than such infamy? We admit that this other is a man, which is what we are, who, while he indeed has vices, is nonetheless not himself a vice. How much more honorable therefore would it be for a man to conquer us than a vice? Can anyone doubt that envy is a terrible vice, by which you are bound to be tormented and defeated, if you are unwilling to be conquered and surpassed in temporal matters? So then, it's better that a man should surpass us than that envy or any sort of vice at all should overpower us.

The True Import of Loving your Neighbor as Yourself

46, 86. But if you have overcome your vices, you cannot even be overcome by a man. You are only overcome when what you love is snatched out of your hand by your opponent. So, if you only love what cannot be snatched out of its lover's hand, you undoubtedly remain unbeaten and are not tormented in any way by jealousy. You are loving something, after all, for which all the more abundant gratitude is felt, the greater the number of those who come to love and obtain it. What you are loving is God *with your whole heart and your whole soul and your whole mind, and your neighbor as yourself*.[173] So you are not jealous of his being what you are; on the contrary, you help him to be so just as much as you can. Nor can you lose the neighbor whom you love as yourself, because what you love in him is not what comes under the observation of your eyes or any of the senses of the body. Therefore you have with you the one you love as yourself.

87. Now, this is the rule of love, that the good things you want for yourself you also want to come his way, while you do not wish on him the bad things you do not want to happen to yourself. You adopt this attitude towards all people, because evil is not to be done to anyone, and love of neighbor does no evil.[174] So let us love then, as the commandment has it, even our enemies,[175] if we really wish to be unbeaten.

It is not, you see, through their own efforts that any human beings remain unbeaten but through that immutable law, being enslaved by which alone ensures anyone's freedom. This is how, after all, what they love cannot be taken from them, the one thing that makes them unbeaten and real men.[176] I mean to say, if one person loves another not as himself but as a mule or the baths or a peacock or a parrot,[177] that is, by way of getting out of him some temporal enjoy-

---

173. See Mt 22:37.39.
174. See Tb 4:16; Lk 6:31; Rom 13:10.
175. See Mt 5:44.
176. *Perfectos viros*: male chauvinism creeping in again, but with primary reference to that "manly" component of every human being, the spirit, the *animus*.
177. *Aviculam pictam vel garrulam*: more generally, "a colored or chattering bird."

ment or advantage, he is bound to be enslaved not to the other person, but—what is much more disgraceful—to the foul and detestable vice of not loving a human being as a human being ought to be loved. With this vice in the saddle, they are being ridden to the lowest kind of life, or rather death.

88. But loving your neighbor as yourself doesn't even mean loving in the way members of one's immediate family, brothers, sisters, children, wives and husbands are loved, or any other kith and kin, or one's next-door neighbors or fellow citizens. This too, I mean, is a love limited to time. After all, we would not have relationships of that sort, which are the result of being born and dying, if our nature had remained true to the precepts and the image of God and so had not been relegated to this perishable state.[178] And hence it is that Truth herself, in calling us back to our pristine and perfect nature, bids us stand up to the demands of family relationships, teaching us that nobody is fit for the kingdom of heaven who does not hate[179] these relatives, and that this is not to strike anyone as inhuman. I mean, it is more inhuman to love a man not for being a man but for being your son. For this means not loving in him what belongs to God but loving what belongs to you. Small wonder, then, if you don't get to the kingdom of heaven, seeing that you love what is personal and private to you and not what is common to all.

"Well then, for both reasons," says someone or other.

"Well then, for that single one," says God. For Truth says most truly: *Nobody can serve two masters* (Mt 6:24). Nobody, after all, can wholeheartedly love what he is being called to unless he hates what he is being called away from. Now we are being called to recover human nature in its perfection, such as God made it before our sin, while we are being called away from love of it in the state which we have earned by sinning. So we are obliged to hate what we are eager to be delivered from.

89. We hate time-related kinsfolk and connections, then, if we are on fire with charity, the love of eternity. Let a man love his neighbor as himself.[180] Assuredly

---

178. The reader will be relieved, I think, to know that about this indefensible statement Augustine himself writes in his *Revisions* I, 13, 8: "I utterly reject this idea, which I have already rejected above [10,9], when correcting the first book of *On Genesis: A Refutation of the Manicheans*. For what it leads to is that we would have to believe that the first couple were not going to produce any further human beings, as if it were necessary that any born of the intercourse of male and female would be born only to die. The fact is, I had not yet seen that from ones who were not going to die would be born children who were not going to die, if human nature were not changed for the worse by that great sin; and thus that, if in both parents and offspring there had remained both felicity and fecundity, human beings would go on being born until the definite number of saints was reached which God had predetermined, born not in order to succeed their parents on their deaths but to reign with them as they continued to live. So these relationships and connections would have existed, even if nobody trespassed and nobody died."
179. See Lk 9:62; 14:26.
180. See Lk 10:27.

no one is a father or a son or a relation or anything of that sort to himself, but just a man. So then, whoever loves someone as himself ought to love in that person what he is to himself. Bodies, however, are not what we are. Hence it is not the body in a person that is to be looked for or desired. This is also the bearing of that other commandment: *You shall not covet your neighbor's possessions* (Ex 20:17). Accordingly, whoever loves in his neighbor anything other than what he is for himself is not loving him as himself.

Human nature therefore is to be loved without any reference to the flesh, whether it is still to be perfected or has already been made perfect. We are all related to each other under one God the Father, all of us who love him and do his will, and we are both fathers to each other when we care for one another and sons when we submit to each other and, above all, brothers, because our one Father is summoning us to take possession of our inheritance by his will and testament.[181]

A Portrait of the truly Unbeaten Winner

47, 90. Accordingly, why may you not be unbeaten by loving a human being, when there is nothing you love in him but his being human—that is God's creation and one made, what is more, to his image—and when he cannot be lacking the perfect nature which you love, since you have been made perfect yourself? It is as if, for example, someone loves a good singer, not this or that particular one, but just any good singer, being himself an excellent singer, so that at least he does not go without what he loves, because he sings so well himself; still he wants all singers to be such as he is.[182] I mean, if he is jealous of anybody who sings well, it is not now good singing that he loves but praise, or something else which he aspires to reach by singing well, and he can get less of this, or have it snatched from his grasp, if someone else has sung well. So then, anyone who is jealous of someone who sings well does not love the good singer; but, on the other hand, anyone who stands in need of a good singer does not sing well.

This can all be put much more tellingly about someone who lives a good life, because he cannot be jealous of anybody; the goal reached by those who live

---

181. See Mt 12:48-50.
182. To get this sense, which seems to me to be the sense required, and the only one that makes good sense, I have had to re-arrange the Latin and add another *tamen*, the one rendered "still," while the one in the text as it stands is rendered "at least." I suggest it is the presence of this word twice, so close together, that caused some copyist to get the phrases in the wrong order. So what I am suggesting is that the original text ran thus: *cum sit ipse cantator perfectus, ut tamen non ei desit quod diligit, quia ipse bene cantat; ita tamen vult omnes tales esse.* The CCL text, and that of all the editors, has: *cum sit ipse cantator pefectus, ita vult omnes esse, ut tamen ei non desit quod diligit, quia ipse bene cantat.* This would mean: "Being himself an excellent singer, he thus wants all singers to be such as he is, so that at least he does not go without what he loves, because he sings so well himself."

good lives, after all, is the same for everyone and is in no way diminished the more of them there are who attain it. There can be times, too, when the good singer is unable to sing with propriety himself and when he needs the voice of another to offer him what he loves, as when he is dining out, where it would be unseemly for him to sing himself but entirely proper for him to listen to a singer. Living a good life, on the other hand, can always be done with propriety, which is why anyone who both loves this and does it is not only not jealous of people imitating him but even offers himself most willingly and affably as an example to the best of his ability, while still not standing in need of their example.

The only one he stands in need of is the one to whom it is happiness to cling. But nobody can snatch God from his grasp. He is therefore most assuredly and truly the unbeaten, unconquered man, who clings to God not in order to earn something extra from him but because nothing but clinging to God is for him worth anything at all.

91. As long as a man of this kind is in this life, he makes use of friends for practicing gratitude, makes use of enemies for practicing patience, makes use of whomever he can for showing kindness, makes use of everyone for showing good will.[183] And although he does not love time-bound things, he makes the right sort of use of them and makes sure that people get their share of them, even if he cannot do this equally for everyone. That is why, if he is readier to admonish a member of his own household than someone else, it is not because he loves him more but because he has greater responsibility for him and can devote more time to him.[184] I mean, he deals all the better with those given over to time the less he is tied down by time himself. Since then he cannot be of equal service to everybody, while he loves them all equally, he would be unjust if he did not prefer being of service to those with whom he has closer ties.

Now, ties of spirit are more important than those of time or place, with which we are born in this body, but the most important of these is the one which is superior to all the others.[185] So this man is not seriously upset by the death of anybody, because one who loves God with his whole being knows that he himself does not lose what God does not lose, and God is the Lord of both the living and the

---

183. Behind this rather repellent idea of using people lies one of the basic Augustinian distinctions, explained at length in *Teaching Christianity* I, the one between (in the Latin) *uti* and *frui*, "to use" and "to enjoy," and the inference it leads to, that it is wrong to enjoy what is meant for use, and to use what is meant for enjoyment. Now, the only "thing" that is meant for enjoyment without qualification is God; people, and things lower in the scale, may only be enjoyed in God or in connection with him; otherwise they are to be put to good use. So here, people in their different categories, and in relation simply to us, are to be put to good moral use, for us to practice virtues on (still a rather repellent idea, one must admit), but also to be enjoyed for their own sakes in and under God.

184. Because he has for him *apertiorem temporis januam*—a more open door of time. This is a rather striking metaphorical phrase, for which I cannot think of an English equivalent.

185. That with God, of course.

dead.[186] Nobody else's unhappiness makes him unhappy, because neither does anybody else's unjust behavior make him unjust. And in the same way that no one can take justice and God from him, so no one can take away his happiness. And if ever he is saddened by someone else's danger or error or grief, he turns this into a means of helping that person, of either comforting or correcting him, but does not allow it to turn to his own undoing.

92. None of the labors required of him by duty, however, can break his spirit, thanks to his sure expectation of the quiet rest to come. What will do him any harm, after all, if he can even make good use of an enemy? The one at whose bidding and by whose gift he loves his enemies is the one who guards and fortifies him against any dread of enmity and hostility. For this man it is little enough not to be cast down by tribulations, unless he can also rejoice in them, *knowing that tribulation gives rise to patience, patience to strength of character, this strength to hope, while hope does not disappoint us, since the love of God has been poured out in our hearts through the Holy Spirit, who has been given to us* (Rom 5:3-5).

Who will ever do this man any harm? Who will ever subdue him? The person who makes progress while things are going well with him learns what progress he has made when the going gets rough. When he has plenty of good things, you see, he does not put his trust in them, but, when they are snatched away from him, he finds out whether they had not really got a grip on him, since, usually when they are available to us, we think we do not love them, but, when they start not being to hand, we discover who we really are. For what we were not addicted to when it was available is what does not throw us by its withdrawal. So then, the person who, by dint of overcoming obstacles, attains to what it will pain him to lose seems to be a winner when in fact he is being beaten; while whoever, by giving way, attains to what he is not unwilling to lose seems to be beaten, while in fact he is a winner.

Even Vices Can Signify Virtues

48, 93. Those, then, whose delight is in freedom should seek to be free from love of changeable things, and those whose delight is in exercising authority should adhere submissively to God, the one author of all things, by loving him more than themselves (and this is perfect justice, to love better things more and lesser things less). Let them love wise and perfect souls for being such as they see them to be, foolish ones not for being such but because they are capable of being perfect and wise, since they should not even love themselves as being foolish. I mean, those who love themselves as being foolish will make no prog-

---

186. See Rom 14:9; 1 Thes 4:13.

ress towards wisdom, nor will any become what they long to be unless they hate what they are.

But, until they reach perfect wisdom, they should put up with the folly of their neighbors in the same spirit as they would put up with their own, if they were foolish and loved wisdom. And thus it is that, if even pride itself is a shadowy mimic of genuine freedom and genuine authority, divine providence is using even this to remind us what we signify with our vices and what we should be returning to when we have been straightened out.

Truth in Itself, and its Inferior Representations

49, 94. Then again, take all these shows and everything that goes by the name of a curiosity—what else are people looking for but enjoyment from the knowledge of things? So, what could be more wonderful, what more pleasing to the eye, than Truth itself, which every spectator admits he is longing to reach when he watches so keenly to see he is not taken in and goes on boasting about it if he observes something while he is watching and makes a sharper and livelier judgment on it than others do? Then there is the conjurer making it his business to deceive, whom they all watch attentively and take the greatest care in observing, and, if they are baffled, then, because they cannot take delight in their own knowledge, they are delighted by his in baffling them. I mean, if he too did not know how to take in the spectators, or was thought not to know, nobody would applaud him for sharing their ignorance. But if one of the audience catches him out, he thinks he deserves even greater applause than the performer for no other reason than that he could not be deceived and taken in. If however his act is obvious to many, then they do not applaud him but jeer at the rest who could not catch him out in such a performance. And thus the palm is always given to the knowledge of and the skillful juggling with and comprehension of Truth, who is in no way to be attained by those who seek her outside.[187]

95. And so it is that we have been plunged into disgraceful trifles of such power that, on being questioned which is better, the true or the false, we answer with one voice that the true is better. Nonetheless we are much readier to occupy ourselves with jests and performances, in which we enjoy not exactly untruths but make-believe, than to stick to the precepts of Truth herself. And so we are being punished out of our own mouths by our own judgment, giving our rational approval to one thing, frivolously chasing after another.

Now, a thing is a matter of laughter and joking as long as we know what true reality it is being compared with to raise a laugh. But by setting our hearts on such things we have fallen out of being interested in the real truth and do not now

---

187. Outside, that is, one's own mind.

find the things of which these are feeble imitations, which we are longing for as the primal beauties, and in drawing away from these we find ourselves embracing our own fanciful notions. As we come back to following the tracks of truth, you see, these fancies block our way and do not let us pass, try as we might, but catch us like bandits in one ambush after another,[188] because we fail to understand what a wide range of cases is covered by the saying: *Be on your guard against images* (1 Jn 5:21).

96. And so it is that some have gone rollicking around through innumerable worlds in their wandering thoughts,[189] others have supposed that God cannot be anything but a body of fire,[190] others have imagined the brilliance of immeasurable light spread out in every direction through infinite space and then produced the fable of its being split in one section by a kind of wedge of blackness into two hostile kingdoms, which their fertile imaginations then set up as the opposing principles of things.[191]

If I were to compel them to swear whether they knew this stuff to be true, they would probably not have the nerve to do so but would say in turn: "Well, you then, you show us what is true." If the only answer I gave them was that they should seek that light by which it was clear and certain to them that it is one thing to believe, another to understand, they too would swear that this light could not be seen with the eyes or thought of as being some vast space, and that there is nowhere that it is not at hand to those who are seeking it, and that nothing more sure or serene can be found.

97. Again, all these things that have been said by me from the light of my mind are manifest in virtue of nothing but this same light. It is through this light, after all, that I understand what has been said to be true, and by this light again that I understand that I understand all this. And the same again and again, when anyone understands he understands something and understands that again, I understand that it can go on and on ad infinitum, and I understand that there is no expansion or whirling around of spaces here. I also understand that I cannot understand unless I am alive, and even more surely do I understand that by understanding I become more alive still. Eternal life, after all, surpasses temporal life precisely by its intensity of life, nor do I observe what eternity is except by understanding.

It is, of course, by an observation of the mind that I eliminate every kind of change from eternity and perceive no intervals of time in eternity itself, because

---

188. I suggest the text should read: *sed magnis insidiis latrocinantur* instead of what we actually have: ... *latrocinantia*. This is syntactically unsound; but the translation remains the same either way.

189. I.e., the Epicureans.

190. I.e., the Stoics.

191. I.e., the Manicheans, Augustine's particular concern in this work, since his friend and patron, the landowner Romanianus, to whom it is addressed, was still a member of the sect.

intervals of time go with the past and future movements of things. But there is nothing past in the eternal and nothing future, because what is past has ceased to be, and what is future has not yet begun to be. Eternity, however, simply is, nor ever was as though it is not any longer, nor ever will be as though it is not yet. This is why it alone was able most truly to say to the human mind: *I am who I am* (Ex 3:14). And about it there could most truly be said: "He who is has sent me."[192]

Steps Leading to Ultimate Truth; Allegory

50, 98. If we are not yet able to cling to this Eternity, let us at least scold the fanciful products of our imaginations and turn the gaze of our minds away from the spectacle of such trifling and deceptive games. Let us make use of the steps which divine providence has been good enough to construct for us.[193] You see, by taking too much pleasure in such laughable fictions, the whole fabric of our thinking was growing threadbare, and we were turning the whole of our lives into nothing but empty dreams which had enslaved to their laws the reason that we were created with. But then, through sounds and letters, smoke, a column of fire and cloud, like visible words as it were, the inexpressible mercy of God did not disdain to play with us in our childhood[194] after a fashion with parables and similes, and to cure our inner eyes with this sort of mud.[195]

99. So let us then pinpoint and not confuse what trust we should place in historical narrative, what trust we should place in understanding,[196] what we should commit to memory without knowing that it is true, but still believing it is, and where the truth is that does not come and go but always remains in one and the same way, what the correct way is of interpreting an allegory[197] which is generally believed to have been uttered by Wisdom in the Holy Spirit; whether it is enough for it to lead us from ancient visible realities to more recent visible

---

192. See Ex 3:14.
193. Above all in the scriptures, primarily those of the Old Testament; and, as he is just about to mention dreams, Augustine may well have had in mind first and foremost Jacob's ladder, Gn 28:12-13, and the way in which that episode is recalled by Jesus in Jn 1:51.
194. The "childhood" of the people of Israel standing in for the childishness of us all.
195. See Jn 9:5.
196. What faith or trust we owe to *intelligentia*. As Augustine normally contrasts understanding with mere faith or trust or believing, like what we know for certain with what we only believe, it is odd that he should bring it in here as a kind of alternative to *historia*. What he seems to mean by it here is that special understanding of history, i.e., the historical narratives of scripture, which yields their inner, spiritual meaning.
197. In *Expositions of the Psalms* 103, sermon 1, 13, Augustine gives the following definition of allegory: "Allegory occurs when words seem to point to one thing, while they signify something else to the mind."

realities,[198] or on from there to the affects and the nature of the soul, or from there right up to unchanging Eternity; whether some allegories signify visible deeds, others the workings of minds, others the law of eternity; whether some are to be found in which these are all to be investigated; and what is the certainty to be had in historical and temporal interpretations or spiritual and eternal ones, which is what all authoritative interpretation should be aiming at; and what use faith in temporal realities is for understanding and obtaining eternal ones, in which is to be found the end of all good actions; and what the difference is between allegory in historical narrative, and allegory in something done, and allegory in sayings, and allegory in a sacrament; and then the actual language of the divine scriptures, the idioms of which must govern the way allegory is to be taken (every language, after all, has its own particular kinds of expression, which seem absurd when they are transferred to another language); what the value is of expressions so low and unexalted that we not only find there God's anger and sadness and waking from sleep and remembering and forgetting and several others which can apply to good men but also mention of his repentance, jealousy, drunkenness and other things of that sort in the sacred books; and whether God's eyes and hands and feet and other such parts of the body, which are mentioned in the scriptures, are to be referred to the visible shape of a human body or to the signification of intelligible and spiritual powers, like his helmet and shield and sword and belt and other such things.[199]

And there is the question that has above all to be asked: What advantage is it to the human race that divine providence should have spoken to us through creatures both rational and reproductive and merely material, which are at his service and disposal? Once this single matter is definitively cleared up, all childish impudence is excluded from our minds, and sacred and holy religion is allowed entry.

Scripture First and Last for Nourishing the Spirit

51, 100. Let us therefore leave aside and repudiate the trifles of poets and playwrights, and, to spirits that are worn out with the raging hunger and thirst of empty curiosity and are fruitlessly longing to find refreshment and satisfaction in the vain fancies of the imagination as if with pictures of banquets, let us offer the food and drink of the serious study of the scriptures. Let us learn how to play this truly liberal game, worthy of free men. If it is the marvels and the beauty of spectacles that delight us, let us yearn to see that Wisdom, *who stretches out mightily from end to end, and disposes all things sweetly* (Wis 8:1). What, after

---

198. From the Old Testament to the events, the history of the New Testament.
199. See Eph 6:14-17.

all, is a greater marvel than the immaterial force which constructs and regulates the material world? Or what more beautiful than its order and adornments?

So Many Reminders of Eternity, when even Vices Recall Virtues

52, 101. Now, if we all admit that these things are perceived through the body and that the spirit is better than the body, is the spirit not to observe things on its own, or can what it observes fail to be anything but more excellent and far and away more remarkable? No, the fact is that we are reminded by these things on which we make judgments to pay attention to what the standard is for making such judgments, and to turn from works of art to the law regulating the arts, and so to gaze with the mind on that sight and form, compared with which those things are ugly which only his kindness allows us to see as beautiful. *For the invisible things of God, from the creation of the world, being understood through the things that have been made, are clearly to be seen, as also his everlasting might and his divinity* (Rom 1:20). This is the return from the temporal to the eternal and the refashioning of the new man from the life of the old.

Is there anything, though, by which people cannot be reminded to get a grip on the virtues, when they can be so reminded by the very vices? What, after all, is curiosity aiming at but knowledge, which is only to be had with certainty about things that are eternal and always maintain themselves in the same way? What is pride aiming at but power, which goes with ease of action, which the perfect soul only finds when it submits to God and has its eyes turned towards his kingdom with total charity? What is bodily self-indulgence aiming at but satisfaction, which is only to be found where there are no needs and no decay?

So, what we have to beware of, then, are the lower regions, that is, the heavier pains and penalties among which there can be no reminder of the truth, because there is no use of reason, and there is no use of reason because there is not shed upon it *the true light which enlightens every person coming into this world* (Jn 1:9). Accordingly, let us make haste and walk while we still have the daylight, in case the dark should overtake us.[200] Let us make haste to be delivered from the second death,[201] in which there is no one who remembers God, and from hell, where nobody will confess to God.[202]

---

200. See Jn 12:35.
201. See Rv 20:14.
202. See Ps 6:5.

In this Life the Means to the End in the Next

53, 102. But we miserable human beings find things that we know well grow stale and novelties exciting, and so we are readier to learn than to know, when acquiring knowledge is the goal of learning. And those who find ease of action boring are readier to fight than to win, though the goal of fighting is winning. And those who find it dull just being in good health prefer eating to being satisfied and prefer getting enjoyment from their genitals to not undergoing such motions. You also find people who prefer sleeping to not being asleep, though the end to which all these pleasures point is not to be hungry and thirsty, and not to desire sexual intercourse, and not to be burdened with a weary body.

103. That is why those who desire the ends or goals in themselves lack curiosity in the first instance, because they know that the knowledge you can be sure about is within you, and this is what they enjoy, as far as they are able to in this life. In the second instance, they gain ease of action by laying aside self-assertion, since they know that a greater and easier victory is won by resisting anyone's animosity, and this they experience, as far as they are able to in this life. In the final instance, they also experience satisfaction by self-denial in these things, without which this life cannot be lived.

In this way they taste and see that the Lord is sweet.[203] Nor will there be any doubt what is in store for them after this life; and here their perfection consists in being nourished by faith, hope and charity.[204] After this life, though, knowledge too will be perfected, because *now we know in part, but when what is perfect has come* (1 Cor 9:9-10), there will be no *in part*, and every kind of peace will be enjoyed. For now there is another law in my members fighting back against the law of my mind, but the grace of God through Jesus Christ our Lord will set us free from the body of this death.[205]

For in large part we are reaching an agreement with our opponent while we are with him on the road,[206] and the body will have total health and no needs and no weariness, because this perishable thing will be clothed with imperishability in its own time and order, when the resurrection of the flesh is going to take place.[207] Small wonder, though, if this will be given to those who set their hearts on truth alone where knowledge is concerned, and on peace alone where action is involved, and on health alone where the body is concerned. What they set their hearts on more than anything in this life, you see, will be theirs after this life in full perfection.

---

203. See Ps 34:8.
204. See 1 Cor 13:13.
205. See Rom 7:23-25.
206. See Mt 5:25. The opponent in this case, of course, is understood to be Jesus Christ.
207. See 1 Cor 15:53.

The Parables of the Wedding Feast and of the Talents

54, 104. As for those then who make bad use of such a great good as the mind, so that they go chasing more readily after visible realities outside it, by which they ought to have been reminded to fix their attention and set their hearts on intelligible realities, to their lot will fall the outer darkness. The onset of this, in fact, is the prudence of the flesh[208] and the feebleness of the bodily senses. And those who delight in fighting their rivals will be strangers to peace and be involved in the greatest distress of all. This begins, you see, with warfare and quarreling. And I consider that this is signified by the man's being bound hand and foot, that is, being deprived of any possibility, let alone ease, of working. And as for those who actually choose to be hungry and thirsty, and to burn with lust, and to be weary, so that their pleasure is to eat and drink and fornicate and sleep, they are in love with need, which is the beginning of the most extreme pains, so that their lot in that place will be weeping and gnashing of teeth.[209]

105. There are a great many people, after all, who set their hearts on all these "beginnings" simultaneously and whose life consists of watching shows, guzzling, drinking, fornicating, sleeping. And all they do in their thoughts is embrace the fancies and images they pick up from this sort of life, and by them they are tricked into fixing rules of superstition or godlessness, by which they are deceived and to which they adhere, even if they make some attempt at abstaining from the allurements of the flesh. This is because they do not make good use of the talent committed to them, that is, their wits, in which all who have the name of being learned or cultured or witty seem to excel. But they have it tied up in a napkin or buried in the earth,[210] that is, rolled up in fancy or superfluous things, or else crushed under earthy lusts and desires.

So these too will be bound hand and foot and cast into the outer darkness. That is where there will be weeping and gnashing of teeth, not because they have set their hearts on this fate—who would, after all?—but because the things they did set their hearts on are the beginnings of this fate and of necessity lead their lovers to this fate. Those, you see, who prefer going and coming to arriving must be sent to more distant places than ever, *since they are flesh and wind that walks along and does not return* (Ps 79:39).

106. Those, however, who make good use either of the five senses of the body—for believing in and proclaiming the works of God and for nourishing the love of him—or of activity and knowledge—for bringing peace to their nature

---

208. See Rom 8:6.
209. See Mt 22:13, the fate of the man who came to the feast without a wedding garment, which gives the context for the whole of this section.
210. See the parable in Mt 25:14-30, with a glance at the parallel version, Lk 19:20.

and getting to know God—enter into the joy of their Lord.[211] That's why the talent which is taken away from the one who makes bad use of it is given to the one who has made good use of five talents—not that intellectual acumen can be transferred from one person to another, but what is thus signified is that clever people who are indifferent and godless can forfeit this gift and that those who are diligent and godly, even though slower in the uptake, can attain to it.[212]

That talent, you see, wasn't given to the one who had received two—he has already got this one as well, the person who is living a good life in action and in knowledge—but to the one who had received five. He, after all, does not yet have the mental acumen suited to contemplating eternal realities, the one who only believes in visible, that is, in temporal, realities; but he is capable of having it, since he praises God the artificer of all these sense objects, and prevails on him by faith,[213] and looks forward to him in hope, and seeks him by charity.[214]

Conclusion: Various Kinds of False Religion; an Exhortation to Bind Ourselves to the True Religion

55, 107. All that being so, I urge you, my dearest friends and neighbors, and along with you I urge myself, to run with all the speed we can manage towards the goal to which God is urging us on through his Wisdom. Let us not set our hearts on the world, since *everything that is in the world is the lust of the flesh and the lust of the eyes and worldly ambition* (1 Jn 2:16). Let us not set our hearts on corrupting and being corrupted through the pleasures of the flesh, lest we come to the more miserable corruption of pains and torments. Let us not set our hearts on fighting, lest we be given over to the power of those angels who enjoy such things, to be humiliated, to be bound, to be scourged. Let us not set our hearts on visible shows, lest by straying from the Truth and loving shadows we be cast into utter darkness.

108. Let our religion not consist in the fanciful products of our imaginations. Any true reality whatsoever, after all, is better than anything that can be fashioned at will; and yet, though the soul itself is something true, we ought not to

---

211. See Mt 25:21.23 and the whole parable, 25:14-28, for the background to this section.

212. An instance of how Augustine is being rather careless in his writing of this work, especially as he is drawing to the end of it and perhaps getting tired: he writes (dictates) *ad eam*, the feminine accusative pronoun, though its antecedent is the neuter noun *acumen*. Two MSS change this aberrant feminine to a correct neuter pronoun, *illud*; but, as all the others have the grammatically incorrect one, that is undoubtedly what Augustine dictated, no doubt assuming that its antecedent was the shorter form of *acumen*, which he nearly always uses, has just used, and will use again shortly, the feminine noun, *acies*.

213. The faith that moves mountains, that is persuades God to move mountains.

214. So, in Augustine's ingenious and surely somewhat perverse interpretation of the parable, the servant who received two talents got a better deal than the one who received five.

worship it when it is imagining falsehoods. A real, true straw is better than a light fashioned at will as a conjecture in a person's idle thoughts,[215] and yet you would be crazy to believe that a straw, which we can touch and feel, is to be worshiped.

Let our religion not consist in the worship of animals. For better than them are even the dregs of humanity, whom we are not, however, supposed to worship. Let our religion not consist in the cult of the dead because, if they lived godly lives, they are not to be thought of as seeking such honors, but they wish us to worship the one by whose enlightenment, they rejoice to think, we are made partners in their merits. So they are to be honored as examples to imitate, not worshiped as objects of a religious cult. If, however, they lived bad lives, wherever they may be, they are not to be worshiped.

Let our religion not consist in the worship of demons, because every superstition, being one of humanity's heavier punishments and a most perilous disgrace, is an honor for them and a triumph.

109. Let our religion not consist in the worship of lands and waters, because purer than these and brighter is the air, even when it is foggy, which nonetheless we ought not to worship either. Let our religion not consist in the worship even of the purer and calmer air, because in the absence of light it is darkened, and it is surpassed in purity by the flashing of even this fire, which we light and extinguish at will and so of course ought not to worship. Let our religion not consist in the worship of ethereal and heavenly bodies, which are indeed rightly given precedence over other bodies, and yet any kind of life is better than they are. So, even if they have souls, any sort of soul is in itself better than any kind of animated body, and yet nobody has entertained the idea that a vicious soul should be worshiped.

Let our religion not consist in the worship of that life by which trees are said to be alive, since there is no sensation in it, and it is of the same kind as that by which the basic rhythm[216] of our own bodies carries on, by which even hairs and bones live, which are cut without its being felt. Better than this, though, is sentient life, and yet we have no business to worship the life of dumb animals.

110. Let our religion not be directed even towards the perfect and wise rational soul, whether as established in the administration of the universe or in the administration of its parts, or whether in human beings at the top of the scale it is awaiting the change and refashioning of its allotted portion, since all rational life, if it is perfect, bows to the unchanging Truth speaking to it noiselessly within—and, if it does not do so, it is vitiated.

So then, what the highest angel worships is to be worshiped also by the lowest

---

215. The conjecture and idle thoughts of a Manichean.
216. The *numerositas* of our bodies—this important idea of "number" again.

human being, because it was by not worshiping this[217] that the very nature of man fell to the lowest place. For there is not one source of wisdom for an angel, another for a human being, one source of truth for the former, another for a human being, but for both one unchanging Wisdom and Truth. What was undertaken, you see, by an arrangement in time for our salvation—that the power of God and the Wisdom of God,[218] unchanging and consubstantial and co-eternal with the Father, should himself deign to take our human nature—was done to teach us thereby that humanity was to worship what is to be worshiped by every intellectual and rational creature. Let us believe that this is also what the very best angels wish, as also the most excellent ministerial agents of God, that together with them we should worship the one God, in whom they find, by contemplating him, their blessedness.

Neither are we blessed, after all, if we see an angel but when we see the Truth, in which we also love the angels themselves and receive their congratulations. Nor are we jealous of them because they are readier to enjoy this vision of God and do so without any troubles getting in the way, but we love them all the more, since we too have been commanded to hope for something of the same sort by our common Lord.[219] So it is that we honor them with charity, not with servility, nor do we set up temples for them, for they do not wish to be honored by us in that way, because they know that we too, when we are good, are temples of the most high God.[220] And so it is very properly written that a man was told by an angel to adore not him but the one Lord, under whom he too was his fellow slave.[221]

111. Those, however, who do call upon us to serve them and worship them like gods are like proud men who likewise would want to be worshiped, if the law permitted.[222] But having to put up with those men is less dangerous, as the domination of men over men ends with the death of either the masters or the servants, while slavery under the pride of evil angels is the more to be dreaded because of the time that comes after death. Then again, there is a point which it is easy to verify, that under a human master it is permissible to entertain thoughts of freedom, while we dread those other masters' controlling our very minds, our one and only eye for beholding and grasping Truth.

---

217. The reference of course is to the sin of Adam and Eve in Paradise—failure to worship the true God being seen, perhaps, in their hiding from him when they heard his voice in the garden, rather than in their "first disobedience" in eating of the tree of knowledge.
218. See 1 Cor 1:24.
219. Cf Lk 20:36.
220. See 1 Cor 3:16.
221. See Rv 22:8-9.
222. Of course the law did not permit, not in Augustine's time. But I presume he was thinking of the time of the pagan emperors before Constantine, when the law not only permitted but also required the formal worship of the emperors by burning a few grains of incense before their statues. It was precisely for refusing to do this that most Christian martyrs were martyred.

So our being bound by the chains of subjection to the powers that be and the authority given them for governing the state, being bound to pay back to Caesar what is Caesar's and to God what is God's,[223] is not to be feared as an exaction that may be levied after our death. And in any case, slavery of soul is one thing, slavery of body another.

Now the just and those who find all their joys in the one God happily accept the congratulations of those who praise them when it is God being blessed on account of their deeds, but when they are praised, as if in their own right, they correct this mistake where they can, and, where they cannot, they try not to accept such congratulations and hope to be cured of the vice of doing so where they do.[224] If the good angels and all the holy ministerial agents of God are like these men, and indeed purer and holier still, how can we be afraid of offending any of them by not being superstitious but instead directing ourselves with their help towards the one God, and by binding ourselves tightly to him alone (which is what religion is said to get its name from[225]), so that we are quit of every superstition?

112. So there you are: I worship one God, the one Source of all things, and the Wisdom by which is made wise any soul that is wise, and the very Gift by which is blessed any soul that is blessed. Whichever of the angels loves this God I am sure loves me as well. Whichever of them abides in him and is able to hear human prayers hears mine in him. Whichever of them holds him as his own good comes to my help in him and does not envy me my sharing in him.

So let those then who adore and flatter and fawn on parts of the universe[226] tell me if that man will not be winning the best advocate to his side, who worships that which all that are best in creation love, in the knowledge of which they rejoice, and by recourse to which as their origin they become the best. There are angels on the other hand who love their own deviations and are not willing to be subjects of the Truth and who, being eager to enjoy by themselves what is their own, have slipped away from the common and true blessedness of all the good. To their power and oppressive yoke all the bad are handed over, but none of the good, except for training purposes; angels such as these without a shadow of doubt are not to be worshiped, seeing that they find their weal in our woe and deem our recovery to be their loss.

---

223. See Mk 12:17.
224. A somewhat free rendering of a hopelessly dense original.
225. On this the author has this to say in his *Revisions* I,xiii,9: "The account given by these words of mine of where religion gets its name from was the one I favored the more. It did not escape me, I mean, that Latin authors had explained the origin of this word differently, saying that it was called religion because it had to do with binding (*religitur*). This word comes from *legendo*, that is *eligendo* (choosing), so that the Latin *religo* seems to be the same as *eligo*." The Latin word Augustine is deriving *religio* from is the verb *religare*, to bind tight or fasten. Modern etymologists are inclined to agree with him against Cicero.
226. The worshipers, that is, of the pagan gods of ancient Greece and Rome.

113. So let our religion, then, bind us tight to the one almighty God, because between our minds, by which we understand him to be the Father, and the Truth, that is, the inner light through which we understand him, there is set no intermediate creature. That is why we also venerate in him and with him this same Truth, which is unlike him in no way whatever, which is the form and shape of all things that have been made by the One and that direct themselves towards the One. From this it is apparent to spirit-filled intellects that all things were made through this shape and form, which alone fully matches what all of them are aiming at. All things nonetheless would not have been made by the Father through the Son unless God were supremely good, so good that he is not jealous of any nature's being able to derive its goodness from him and has given them all the ability to abide in this good, some as much as they wish, others as much as they can.

That is why it is incumbent on us to worship and confess the very Gift of God, together with the Father and the Son unchanging—a Trinity of one substance, one God from whom we are, through whom we are, in whom we are, from whom we have departed, whom we have become unlike, by whom we have not been allowed to perish; the Source to which we are retracing our steps, the Form or Shape which we are following, and the Grace by which we are being reconciled; the One, the author of our being, and his Likeness, through which we are being formed into unity, and his Peace, in which we cleave to unity; God, who said, *Let there be* (Gn 1:3.6, etc.), and the Word through which everything was made which was made as a substance and a nature, and the Gift of his kindness by which whatever was made by him through his Word pleased and proved acceptable to its author; one God, by whose creating us we live, by whose refashioning of us we live wisely, by loving and enjoying whom we live blessedly; one God, from whom, through whom, in whom are all things. To him be glory for ever. Amen.[227]

---

227. See Rom 11:36.

The Advantage of Believing

Translation by Ray Kearney

Notes by Michael Fiedrowicz

Introduction

1. Occasion and Addressee of the Work

"Immediately after they ordained me a priest in Hippo Regius, I wrote the book *The Advantage of Believing*. It was dedicated to a friend who had succumbed to the deceits of the Manicheans and, I knew, was still persevering in their error. He had only scorn for the teaching of the Catholic faith and justified himself by claiming that this teaching supposedly imposed faith on people instead of instructing them on how to reach the truth by means of pure reason."[1] Augustine's first publication after priestly ordination was written between the beginning of 391 and August 392.[2] An event of his own past still preoccupied him: together with his friends Alypius, Romanianus, and Honoratus he had endorsed Manicheanism. Since then, Alypius had followed him and converted to the Catholic faith. Meanwhile, Romanianus had in his hands the work entitled *True Religion*. Only Honoratus remained tied to Manicheanism.[3]

Initially, indeed, Honoratus had rejected that teaching but at Augustine's urging had looked into it more closely and had then joined the Manicheans. As is clear from the personal reminiscence in *The Advantage of Believing* 1, 2, the attraction of Manicheanism for the two student friends was its claim to give a scientific, rational explanation of all reality. Although Honoratus was not a Christian by birth, he made his own the rejection of the Catholic Church on the grounds that its call for faith and its subordination to authority did not meet the Manichean ideal. In addition, the Church held fast to the Old Testament, which in the Manichean view could not stand up to critical questioning. Honoratus was soon a convinced Manichean.

When Augustine went off to Rome the friends lost contact, but after his return to North Africa he felt obliged to repair, as best he could, the harm which he had formerly caused the soul of this friend of his youth. *The Advantage of Believing* is thus a work written in a very personal tone. "You, who are my special concern,"[4] is the way Augustine addresses the friend of his youth, and it is the intellectual abilities, rhetorical training, and critical mind of this friend that determine the line of argument, the themes, and the structure of the work. In

---

1. *Revisions* I, 14, 1.
2. On the work see A. Hoffmann, *Augustins Schrift "De utilitate credendi." Eine Analyse* (Münster 1997); O. Grassi, "Per una scoperta del *De utilitate credendi*," in *"De vera religione," "De utilitate credendi," "De fide rerum quae non videntur"* (Rome 1994) 11-30.
3. On Honoratus see F. Decret, *L'Afrique Manichéenne* I (Paris: Études Augustiniennes, 1978) 72-77, 378-379.
4. *The Advantage of Believing* 1, 3.

places the account turns into an implicit dialogue that is meant to overcome the reservations and resistances of a mentality that had once ruled Augustine himself.

But the work is not simply a purely personal conversation among friends. Augustine is also writing for a wider circle of readers. In the person of Honoratus the North African Manicheans are also being addressed, as are all who had come in contact with their propaganda against the Catholic Church.

2. Purpose of the Work

The Advantage of Believing has a strictly limited goal. In his final chapter Augustine says expressly that he intended neither a refutation of Manicheanism nor a comprehensive presentation of Catholic teaching. "I only wanted to weed out from you, if I could, the false opinions about Christian truths that were instilled in us through malice or ignorance and to raise your mind to learn certain great truths about God."[5] Augustine's concern was thus primarily protreptic or exhortatory. He wanted to "turn" his friend to the Catholic faith. But in order to win him over to that faith, he had first to overcome the negative prejudice of a Manichean against the views of the Church.

Honoratus was especially critical of the Catholic Church's demand for faith and its retention of the Old Testament. On the one hand, then, the issue was the method of appropriating truth; on the other, it was the valid method of interpreting texts. Before there could be any discussion of doctrinal content, fundamental questions of methodology had to be clarified. This requirement gave the work a further apologetical, anti-Manichean intention.

Augustine wanted to win Honoratus over to the Catholic Church by showing that the Church's position on both of these questions of method was the correct one. At the same time, these explanations would protect other Christians against Manichean propaganda. The entire set of arguments thus aims at a defense of the Catholic Church against Manichean attacks. Manicheanism as the opposing position is always in mind.

In addition, Augustine was pursuing a personal apologetical goal. About five years earlier, when still a supporter of the Manicheans, he himself had successfully defended their views in public debates with Catholic Christians.[6] He desired, therefore, to explain to his fellow believers the reasons for his change from Manicheanism to the Church. He also had to forestall an a priori condemnation of himself by Manicheans such as Honoratus, if he were to get any hearing at all from them. For the Manicheans rejected anyone who had turned

---

5. Ibid. 18, 36.
6. See *The Two Souls* 11.

away from them: their judgment was that "the light has passed through that person."[7] Augustine had therefore to make plausible his personal reasons for thus turning away. It is to this concern that we owe one of the first descriptions of the path Augustine followed in his conversion.[8]

Even here, however, there was no question solely of a personal justification of Augustine against Manichean criticism. Rather, using himself as an example, he sketches in *The Advantage of Believing* 8, 20 the process which he wishes to initiate in Honoratus by means of his book. In describing the path he himself followed, he is describing the path which the friend of his youth also followed to some extent. When he harks back to his journey through the Manichean error that led him away from the religion of his childhood,[9] he is beginning to describe his subsequent return to the Christian religion[10] and to justify it. His friend has plenty of opportunity to raise his objections; Augustine intends, step by step, to move his friend forward by argument and lead him to the same goal.[11]

3. Structure of the Work

Criteria both of content and of language and form reveal the following structure:

Introduction (1, 1-2, 4)

Part I. The problem being discussed (3, 5-6, 13)
 First line of argument: Possible methods of interpreting the Bible (3, 5-9)
 Second line of argument: Sources of possible error in interpreting the text
  (4, 10-5, 12)
 Conclusion: Arguments against Augustine's rejection of the Old Testament
  while he was a Manichean (6, 13)

Part II. The problem of belief (7, 14-17, 35)
 1) The search for truth in human life (7, 14-8, 20)
 2) Belief as an indispensable way of acquiring truth (9, 21-14, 32)
 3) The necessary acceptance of an authority (15, 33-17, 35)
 Conclusion (18, 36)

---

7. *The Advantage of Believing* 1, 3.
8. See P. Courcelle, *Recherches sur les Confessions de saint Augustin* (Paris 1968) 269-290.
9. *The Advantage of Believing* 7, 17.
10. Ibid. 8, 20.
11. See A. Hoffmann, " 'Ich will dir zeigen, welchen Weg ich genommen habe...' (Aug., *util cred* 20). Zur Funktionierung der eigenen Vita in Augustins Schrift *De utilitate credendi*," in B. Czapka, ed., *Vir bonus dicendi peritus. Festschrift A. Weische* (Wiesbaden 1997) 165-80.

4. *The Interpretation of Scripture*

The Manicheans accused the Catholic Church of dealing uncritically with the Bible. The accounts of creation (they said) were contradictory; the existence of evil (*malum*) could not be explained if only a single, good creator God were accepted; God did not in fact have anthropomorphic features or negative emotions; the so-called "just" of the Old Testament acted immorally; there was no connection between the Old Testament and the New, because the theological content and ethical directives of the two were compatible.

Augustine met these attacks with two arguments. First, he argued on the basis of the theory of the four methods of exegesis.[12] The Manichean critique of the Old Testament was improper because it presupposed that biblical statements had only a literal sense. Instead, Augustine says, there are four ways of interpreting scriptural passages. Historical exegesis aims at ascertaining the content of a text or story; etiological exegesis brings to light the basis of an event or saying; analogical exegesis establishes the agreement between the two Testaments; and allegorical exegesis looks for the figurative meaning of a text, whenever it becomes clear that the text is not to be understood literally. Augustine used this theory from the Greek tradition about two years later in *The Literal Meaning of Genesis*, but after that it is not used again in his writings. Consequently, Augustine's thoughts on the subject represent only a transitional phase. Only later on, in *Teaching Christianity,* will he develop his own self-contained theory of interpretation.

In a second argument he analyzed the various ways in which a text might be wrongly understood.[13] The purpose of this survey was to prove that none of the possible kinds of error applied to the Church's interpretation of the scriptures and that the Manichean criticism was unfounded.[14] Catholic Christians did not understand the texts of the Bible in the way which the Manicheans attributed to them, nor did the Old Testament writings have the meaning which the Manicheans assumed in their attacks. Instead, the Catholic interpretation of the Old Testament proves exemplary for the correct reading of a text that is given in *The Advantage of Believing* 5, 11; that is, a true text is rightly understood. Right understanding, however, presupposes a fundamental "sympathy" with the author.[15] Augustine and Honoratus had sinned against this hermeneutical principle in their youthful reading of the Old Testament by reading it with the negative outlook of the Manicheans or, in other words, by choosing Manichean

---

12. *The Advantage of Believing* 3, 5-9.
13. Ibid., 4, 10-5, 12.
14. See C. Schäublin, "Augustin, *De utilitate credendi*: Über das Verhältnis des Interpreten zum Text," *Vigiliae Christianae* 43 (1989) 53-68.
15. *The Advantage of Believing* 6, 13.

critics as interpreters of the Old Testament. In contrast, Augustine reminds his friend of the rule that holds for every kind of literature: to let an author's writings be explained by his disciple but not by his critic. A better and deeper understanding results from a connaturality with the text and its author.

5. The Problem of Belief

Honoratus' second prejudice against the Catholic Church was that it was hostile to reason. It is clear that in North Africa the Manicheans encountered Catholic Christians who had little schooling in the things of the mind and were unwilling or unable to defend their convictions with rational arguments. Instead, they demanded that doctrinal statements be believed, that is, accepted as true, without having any rational insight into them. The Manicheans, on the contrary, rejected belief as a rash acceptance of something as true on inadequate grounds; in fact, Faustus even attributed to his Catholic opponent scruples about using the natural gift of reason.[16] The Manicheans built upon rational insight and discussion, not on authorities and the obedience of faith. In their view, by reducing all events to the two principles of the Good and the Evil, the teaching of Mani offered a reasonable and even scientific explanation of all reality. According to *The Advantage of Believing* (14, 31), then, the Manichean position can be summed up in the statement: "It is wrong to believe anyone without proof."[17]

Augustine saw in these objections, too, a problem of methodology that had to be clarified before any discussion of content. Therefore the "belief" to which reference is made in the title of the work is not "belief" as the totality of contents and assertions, but rather "believing" as a personal act. The basic issue is the way in which the individual person achieves possession of truth. Against the Manicheans Augustine defended his conviction that rational knowledge alone cannot provide this access to truth. Instead, belief is the first, necessary step. For this reason he applies himself to giving a rational basis for belief as a method of appropriating truth.

First of all, he discusses the necessity of the quest for truth, as well as the best point of departure for the quest.[17] The claim that the soul finds itself in a state of error and ignorance is one that even Honoratus, a Manichean, can accept. Then, since the soul's salvation and at the same time its greatest happiness require knowledge of truth, the soul must look for a way to truth. The quest for truth is simultaneously a quest for God and also for the true religion as the "veneration and knowledge of God." Now, at what point shall the soul begin this quest? As they seek, human beings are faced with a multiplicity of incompatible offers of

---

16. See *Answer to Faustus, a Manichean* XVIII, 3.
17. *The Advantage of Believing* 7, 14-8, 20.

truth. Which shall seekers choose? What are the norms to guide their choice? The problem is that they themselves do not yet know the truth and therefore cannot judge whether or not the truth claims of a thinker or an institution are justified.

In response to this difficulty Augustine sets down as a criterion the outward success of a doctrine, that is, its reputation, the number of its followers, and its spread. This principle rests on the premise that truth, or, in this case, the true religion, has an inner power to win through. It is with this criterion in view that Augustine recommends the Catholic Church as the starting point of the quest (in *The Advantage of Believing* 7, 19). The choice among religions (Christian, Jewish, cults of pagan divinities) must fall on the Christian, because Christians are in the majority. Among Christian groups (Catholics, heretics) the Catholic Church must be given priority because it is numerically the largest group and therefore can alone be called "all-embracing," whereas heretics have each their special names. In keeping with Augustine's premise, the Catholic Church offers the best promise of success in the search for truth.

In *The Advantage of Believing* 8, 20, Augustine concludes the points made thus far by describing the course he himself had followed, and he deals next with the decisive problem: the method for appropriating the truth. The proof that the knowledge gained by reason alone is insufficient for finding the truth and that belief is indispensable makes it clear that the method of the Catholic Church is the only correct one. In 9, 21 Augustine formulates his principal thesis: In order to come to knowledge of the truth, it is necessary first to believe (that is, to accept as true statements which reason cannot yet grasp), to purify oneself morally, and, in both areas, to subject oneself to authentic authority.

Augustine gives both positive and negative arguments for the necessary temporal priority of belief before insight.[18] The first argument[19] vouches for believing by showing it to be rationally responsible and even necessary. Augustine uses the example of friendship to show how believing is indispensable in everyday life. An argument by analogy shows that belief is also necessary in the religious sphere. Belief is indispensable especially for the broad masses of human beings if they are to come to the knowledge of God. Since the majority of human beings do not have the needed philosophical training and since the salvation of the soul is involved when it comes to the knowledge of God, those without intellectual training must be led to the divine mysteries step by step along the way of belief.

The second, negative argument[20] is directed at non-belief, that is, in this anti-Manichean context, against the limitation of knowledge exclusively to rational insight. Using the relationship between parents and children as an

18. Ibid. 9, 22-14, 32.
19. Ibid. 10, 23-24.
20. Ibid. 12, 26-14, 32.

example, Augustine proves his thesis that human society is impossible without belief. No one can be certain from experience who his parents are. Renunciation of belief destroys the basic cohesion of human society. Augustine sums up his thoughts in the statement: "I do not know how it is possible at all for someone not to believe anything."[21] Once again, an argument by analogy shows non-belief to be impossible in the religious sphere as well. All religious seekers already believe that what is being sought (God or the true religion) exists and can be found. Finally, a rejection of belief is openly contradictory to the demands of Christ.

By means of this double argument Augustine proves his positive thesis: "It is not unreasonable to believe," and his negative thesis: "It is unreasonable not to believe." In a final step (15, 33-17, 35) he shows the necessity of following an authority. He had earlier shown (12, 27-13, 28) that an ignorant person striving to know the truth is unconditionally dependent on the help of a wise person. At the same time, however, being ignorant, he cannot recognize the truth even in other people. The result is a dilemma, for he is caught between the necessity of following someone who is wise and the impossibility of finding such a person. Augustine is convinced that divine authority alone can lead a human being out of this dilemma. God helped the ignorant when his Wisdom became a human being in Christ and acted with authority.

In Augustine's understanding of it, authority meant the ability to impress men and women and bind them to itself. Later on, this authority was transferred to the Church as Christ's representative in history. Looking back at his own conversion, Augustine once admitted: "I would certainly not have believed the gospel if the *auctoritas* of the Catholic Church had not moved me to do so."[22] In his eyes, it was chiefly miracles and worldwide success that won for Christ and the Church the authority, that is, the power, to prevail and to motivate human beings to change their behavior. Miracles and the throng of followers are not proofs of the possession of truth but they do lend credibility. It is this credibility that causes even the ignorant to follow the instructions of Christ and his Church and turn "from love of this world to the true God."[23]

6. The Importance of the Work

It is questionable whether Augustine's arguments moved Honoratus to convert to the Catholic Church. *The Advantage of Believing* was conceived as a work that would lead the addressee to take only the first step away from his

---

21. Ibid. 10, 25.
22. *Answer to the Letter of Mani* 5.
23. *The Advantage of Believing* 16, 34.

mistaken Manichean path and in the right direction. A more detailed refutation of his errors is lacking, as is a more comprehensive introduction to the truths of the Catholic faith. These indicators suggest that Augustine did not achieve the desired result and that Honoratus closed his ears to the appeal Augustine so passionately addressed to him.

Yet this work, as Augustine's attempt to get something going with a person of a different faith,[24] remains of interest in that it appeals to the universal foundations of thought and builds further argument on them. The author adapts his arguments to the addressee's present comprehension in order then to break down his prejudices, which block any approach to the faith of the Catholic Church. In the process, the work gives a great deal of information on North African Manicheanism in the fourth century.

To the extent that Augustine often uses his own career as part of the argument, the work is an informative source for his intellectual biography. The personal details serve as an important point of reference for the accounts in his other writings, especially the *Confessions*. Equally clear are the influences, considerations, and discoveries that distanced him from the Manicheans and led him finally to the Catholic Church.

Theologically significant is the treatment of questions of hermeneutical methodology, which is valid not only for biblical exegesis but for all forms of textual interpretation. But it is above all Augustine's thoughts on the problem of the acquisition of truth and on the concept of faith that became influential in the history of theology. Specifically, he worked out the alternatives of rational insight and belief that were to form the basis of medieval Scholastic thought and that have remained relevant down to our day in determining the relationship between believing (*credere*) and knowing (*scire*). The defense of faith in this work does not signify any rejection of reason. Augustine's concern is rather to show a broader way to wisdom and ultimately to God which all human beings can follow in their history.

Augustine's merit consists not least in having analyzed the act of belief and having thus brought to light this element in the theory of knowledge. The act of belief or faith, too, can be shown by reason to be a form of human knowledge. Belief is not an alternative to knowledge but is a way of knowing realities that are not the objects of immediate and evident perception (*perceptio*). Belief is an acceptance of a truth that cannot be reached in any other way. Differently than in his early dialogues and in *True Religion*, Augustine was not satisfied here to urge the way of belief.[25] Rather he sought to explain the nature of the act of belief by analyzing the cognitive value of this way in the larger context of human

---

24. The Manicheans understood themselves to be Christians, and indeed the true Christians in whom alone the teaching of Christ found its full embodiment.
25. See *The Advantage of Believing* 10, 24.

knowing in general and by carefully distinguishing believing (*credere*) from, on the one hand, knowing based on evidence (*scire*) and imagined knowing (*opinari*) and, on the other, from gullibility (*credulitas*).[26]

---

26. See ibid. 9, 22; 11, 25.

The Advantage of Believing

1, 1. If I thought, Honoratus, that believing heretics was just the same as being a heretic, I do not think I would need to say anything on this subject, either in speech or in writing. These two things, however, are not the same at all. As I see it, a heretic is someone who is either the author of false and novel views or upholds them for the sake of some temporal gain, especially fame and power, whereas the person who believes someone like that is seduced by a veneer of truth and devotion. For this reason I felt I should not keep from you my thoughts about finding and holding to the truth. This, as you know, has been my burning passion since early youth.[1] It is, however, a subject far removed from the thoughts of shallow-minded persons, who have gone to extremes with material considerations and fallen into thinking that nothing exists except what they perceive with those five well-known sources[2] of information of the body. Even when they try to detach themselves from their senses, they still want to keep the deceits and images[3] they have garnered from them and think they can best assess the inexpressible innermost recesses of truth by their fatal and deceptive standards.

There is nothing easier, dear friend, than to say one has discovered the truth, and even to think it, but from what I write here I am sure you will appreciate how difficult it really is. I have prayed to God, and I pray now, that it will be helpful, or at least not harmful, for you and anyone else at all into whose hands it chances to fall. This is what I hope for, knowing within myself that, in putting pen to paper now, I do so in a spirit of duty and devotion and not in pursuit of passing fame or shallow display.

2. My object then is to prove to you, if I can, that, when the Manicheans attack those who, before they are capable of gazing on that truth that is perceived by a pure mind, accept the authority of the Catholic faith and by believing are strengthened and prepared for the God who will bestow light, they are acting irrationally and sacrilegiously.

---

1. I.e., since Augustine read Cicero's *Hortensius*.
2. *Nuntiis*, literally "messengers." The senses are affected by things in the external world and "announce" this to the mind. See G. O'Daly, *Augustine's Philosophy of Mind* (London 1987) 80-105.
3. What seems to the senses to be true being is in fact only a weak reflection of the true, intelligible world.

You know, Honoratus, that the only reason we fell in with them is because they declared with awesome authority, quite removed from pure and simple reasoning, that if any persons chose to listen to them they would lead them to God and free them from all error. What was it that for almost nine years drove me to disdain the religion that had been instilled in me as a child by my parents[4] and to follow those people and listen attentively to them[5] except that they said that we were held in fear by superstition[6] and that faith was imposed on us before reason, whereas they did not put pressure on anyone to believe without first discussing and explaining the truth? Who would not be enticed by promises like that, especially if it was the mind of a young man yearning for the truth and made proud and outspoken by the debates in the classes of certain scholars? That is how they found me at that time, scornful of the "old wives tales" and keen to have and to imbibe the open, uncontaminated truth that they promised. What considerations held me back, and kept me from fully committing myself to them, and made me stay at the stage they called "listener,"[7] not yet putting aside the hopes and concerns of this world except that I noticed that they themselves were for the most part full and lengthy in their refutation of others rather than steadfast and assured in rational support of their own position? What can I say about myself, already a Christian and Catholic as I was at the time? That parched and almost overcome by prolonged thirst, crying and groaning I shook off those things and pushed them away, and that I have now returned avidly to that breast? That in the state I was in I would imbibe from it what I needed to restore me and bring me back to the hope of life and salvation?

So what need I say about myself? You on the other hand were not yet a Christian, and, even though you expressed contempt for them, at my insistence you were reluctantly persuaded to listen to them and examine what they had to say. What was it that attracted you, I wonder? Was it not, I beg you to remember, a certain grand assumption and promise of proofs? Because they went on at such length arguing passionately about the mistakes of the uneducated (and I learned too late that for anyone with an average education this is so easy to do), if they introduced anything of their own errors, for want of any acceptable alternative we concluded that that was what we had to hold. In this way they did to us what

---

4. See *Answer to the Skeptics* II, 2, 5; *The Two Souls* 1; *Confessions* I, 11, 17.
5. I.e., from his nineteenth to his twenty-eighth year (373-382). See *Confessions* IV, 1, 1: "nine years." More accurately it was not nine years but more than ten, since in 384 Augustine was thirty when he came in contact with the Manicheans in Rome, but with hardly any conviction left in him.
6. In *The Happy Life* 1, 4 Augustine tells of the superstition that kept him as a young man from the search for truth. By "superstition" he understood the simple popular piety such as his mother, for example, practiced.
7. The Manichean community was divided into the "elect" (*electi*), who were the officials and lived a strict ascetical life, and the "hearers" or "listeners" (*auditores*), who supported the elect but practiced renunciation only in a limited degree. See *Answer to Fortunatus, a Manichean* 3.

cunning trappers are accustomed to do, when they fix branches smeared with birdlime alongside the water to deceive the thirsty birds. They bury and in various ways cover up the other branches around the water, or even scare the birds away from them with contraptions to frighten them, and so the birds fall into their traps not through choice but by default.

3. Why do I not give myself my own answer—that these eloquent, witty analogies and criticisms like these can be poured out with elegant sarcasm by any opponent against anyone who teaches anything? I thought, however, that I should include something like this in my writing as a warning to them to abandon their use of these methods. Then, just as he said, putting aside the common trivia, fact may compete with fact, case with case, proof with proof.[8] So let them stop saying the thing that seems to force itself to their lips when anyone who has listened to them for a long time leaves them: "The light has passed through that person."[9] I am not too much worried about them, but you, who are my special concern, can see yourself how inane this is and how easy for anyone to answer. I leave its consideration, therefore, to your good sense. I have no fear that you will think that the light dwelled in me when I was caught up in the affairs of this world and pursued the ambitions of darkness, a beautiful wife, ostentatious wealth, empty honors and all the other dangerous and harmful pleasures. It is no secret to you that, when I was listening attentively to them, I did not cease to desire and hope for all this. It is not that I attribute this to their indoctrination; I even admit that they continually warned us to be on our guard against this. To say, however, that now, when I have turned away from all those shadows of reality[10] and have resolved to be content merely with the food and drink necessary for bodily health, the light has deserted me, whereas then, when I loved those shadows and was held ensnared by them, I was enlightened and shone with light—that, to put it as kindly as possible, is the statement of someone thinking too dimly about the subject but keen to talk about it. With your consent, however, let us move on to the topic.

2, 4. You are well aware that the Manicheans upset the uneducated by attacking the Catholic faith and especially by criticizing and tearing apart the Old Testament. They clearly do not appreciate how necessary it is to accept these and how beneficial it is for souls that are still crying babies, as it were, to drink from them and absorb them into the marrow of their bones.[11] There are certain things there that can be attacked in a popular way, on the grounds that they give

---

8. See Cicero, *Academica* II, 25, 80; idem, *Pro Caelio* 9, 22.
9. *Kephalaia* 99, 9-17 (H. J. Polotsky and A. Böhlig, eds., *Manichäische Handschriften der Staatlichen Museen Berlin* 1 [Stuttgart 1940]).
10. Another allusion to the nature of the world perceptible to the senses as being only a reflection of reality. In the background is Plato's allegory of the cave; see his *Republic* 514a-518b.
11. See 1 Cor 3:2.

offense to minds that are uninformed and unwary (which is the general majority). There are not many, however, who are able to defend them in a popular way through the symbolism they contain. The few who do have the knowledge to do this have no love for the publicity and particular competition for honor of debates, and for that reason they are not known at all except to those who deliberately go looking for them.

With regard to this blunder of the Manicheans, in criticizing the Old Testament and the Catholic faith, I beg you to listen to my response to it. It is my hope and wish that you will take what I say in the spirit in which I say it. God, who knows the secrets of my conscience, knows there is no malice in what I write now, but I believe it has to be accepted in order to establish the truth. I have long since resolved to live only for this. I do so with extreme concern that I may very easily lead you astray with me, but at best it is very difficult to stay on the right path with you. I am confident, however, that he to whom I am consecrated[12] will not desert me even in this hope, that you will arrive with me on the path of wisdom. Day and night I strive to look upon him, and with the eye of my soul ravaged by the wounds of old opinions[13] I realize, often in tears, that because of my sins and ingrained habits I do not have the power. It is like what happens after a long period of blindness and darkness. Our eyes are barely open and they still reject the light, blinking at it and turning away from it, even though it is what they want, and most of all if anyone tries to show them the sun itself. It is like this now with me. I do not deny that there is something words cannot describe, the soul's one and only good, that is visible to the mind, and sighing and lamenting I confess I am not yet fit to gaze on it. He will not desert me because of this, provided I make nothing up, I am led by duty, I have love for the truth, I value friendship, I have great fear of your being deceived.

3, 5. The whole of the scripture that we call the Old Testament is offered to those who seriously wish to understand it under four aspects: as history, as explanation, as analogy, and as allegory. You must not think it is inappropriate for me to use Greek words.[14] In the first place, that is how I received it, and I would not presume to convey it to you differently from the way I received it. Secondly, you will notice yourself that we have no commonly used names for these things, and it would surely be even less appropriate for me to make up names and define them. If, on the other hand, I employed circumlocutions, my

---

12. The term "consecrated" (*sacratus*) is not a conclusive indication of Augustine's ordination as a priest of Hippo. As section 18 shows, the term applies also to Christians in general.
13. For "opinion" in the sense of "imagined knowledge" see section 25.
14. The Latin text here uses the Greek-derived words *historia, aetiologia, analogia* and *allegoria.* Among the precepts of rhetoric was the demand for *latinitas*, that is, in particular, the use of exclusively Latin words, but Quintilian, *Institutio oratorica* I, 5, 58, had already allowed the use of Greek words, when the required words were lacking in Latin.

discussion would be too cumbersome. I only ask you to believe that, whatever my mistakes, I do nothing from pride or arrogance.

Accordingly, there is the aspect of history, when we are taught what was written or what happened, or what did not happen but was written only as a story. There is the aspect of explanation, when we are shown the reasons why something was said or done. There is the aspect of analogy, when we are shown how the two testaments, the Old and the New, do not contradict each other. There is the aspect of allegory, when we are taught that what was written is not to be taken literally but has to be understood in a figurative sense.

6. Our Lord Jesus Christ and the apostles used all these methods. It was quoted from as history when the criticism was made that the disciples picked the ears of wheat on the Sabbath. *Have you not read what David did,* he said, *when he and his companions were hungry; how he went into the house of God and ate the loaves that were offerings, which it was not lawful for him and his companions to eat, but only the priests?* (Mt 12:3-4)

It relates to explanation when Christ said that a wife was not to be divorced except for the case of adultery and was told by those interrogating him that Moses allowed this provided a document of dismissal was given. *Moses did this,* he said, *because of the hardness of your hearts* (Mt 19:8). Here the explanation is given of why it was right for Moses to allow that for the time being, so that the command that Christ gave could be seen as evidence that the times were now different. A detailed consideration of the differences between these two periods and the relation between them, designed and established in a wonderful plan of divine providence, would be very lengthy.

7. As for analogy, which enables the harmony between the two testaments to be perceived, what shall I say? It has been used by everyone whose authority those people recognize.[15] They can ponder for themselves how much they usually say has been inserted in the sacred scriptures by some or other perverters of the truth.[16] Even when I listened to them, this assertion always seemed very weak indeed, and not only to me but to you too, as I well remember, and to all of us who were striving to form our opinions somewhat more carefully than the general crowd of believers. Much was expounded and explained to me, and I was very impressed by it. They were questions on which most of them showed

---

15. Jesus and the apostles are meant.
16. The passages rejected as forgeries were those that contradicted the teaching of Mani. Among them were the infancy narratives with their story of Davidic descent, birth, circumcision, and then the baptism, all of which show Jesus to be a true human being with a fleshly body and connect him with Judaism. Also rejected were all positive references to the Old Testament in the discourses of Jesus and his disciples. Faustus the Manichean explained such texts thus: unknown authors who wrote the gospels long after the time of Jesus and the disciples were impelled on behalf of the Jews to insert false information into the accounts in question. See *Confessions* V, 11, 21.

off their skills, and the greater their assurance in the absence of any opposition the more effusive was their oratory. As I look back now, nothing they said seems so shameless or, to put it more gently, so uncritical and foolish as that the sacred scripture has been corrupted. They can offer no proof of this from any examples in recent memory. If they said they did not think they should accept those scriptures unreservedly because they were written by authors they do not believe wrote the truth, their rejection would at least be more direct and their error more human.

This is how they dealt with the book we call The Acts of the Apostles. When I reflect on this opinion of theirs, I cannot cease to be amazed. I am not looking for human wisdom here but only ordinary intelligence. That book has so much that is similar to things they do accept that it seems to me to be great stupidity not to accept this too, and, if there is anything there that upsets them, to say that that is untrue and an insertion. If this kind of talk is shameful, as it is, why do they think it has any validity in relation to Paul's epistles, and why do they think that it has any validity in relation to the four books of the gospel? I would venture to say that in these books there is proportionately much more that they would have us believe was inserted by corruptors of the text than there is in that book.

That is certainly how it seems to me. I ask you to think about this with me, assessing it calmly and without anxiety. You know that, in their attempt to count their founder Mani personally as one of the apostles,[17] they say that the Holy Spirit, whom the Lord promised to send to his disciples, came to us through him.[18] If they accepted those Acts of the Apostles, where the coming of the Holy Spirit is clearly preached,[19] there is no way they could maintain that was an interpolation. They would have it that certain corruptors of the sacred books existed before the time of Mani himself and that they corrupted those books because they wanted to associate the law of the Jews with the gospel. They cannot say this concerning the Holy Spirit, unless perhaps they say they foresaw what would be brought up against Mani at a future time, when he said that the Holy Spirit was sent through him, and they put that in their books. We shall have a fuller discussion of the Holy Spirit, however, on another occasion. For the present let us return to what I set out to do.

---

17. What is described here was not, however, a subordination but the relationship of a precursor to a successor who was greater than he. See the Cologne Mani Codex 66, 4-5 (L. Koenen and C. Römer, eds., *Papyrologica Coloniensia* 14 [Opladen 1988]); *Epistula fundamenti*, frag. 1 (E. Feldmann, ed. [Altenberge 1987]); L. Koenen, "Augustine and Manicheeism in Light of the Cologne Mani Codex, *Illinois Classical Studies* 3 (1978) 154-195, esp. 167-168.

18. See *Answer to Adimantus, a Disciple of Mani* 17; *Answer to Faustus, a Manichean* XIX, 31; *Answer to Felix, a Manichean* 1,2-5. See also Koenen, "Augustine and Manicheeism in Light of the Cologne Mani Codex" 168-176.

19. See Acts 2.

8. That the New Testament contains Old Testament history, explanation and analogy has been shown, I think, clearly enough. It remains to show what there is of allegory. In the gospel our redeemer himself makes use of allegory from the Old Testament when he says: *This generation asks for a sign; but they will not be given any sign except that of the prophet Jonah. Just as Jonah was in the belly of a whale for three days and three nights, so too the son of man will be in the heart of the earth for three days and three nights.* (Mt 12:39-40) And what shall I say about the apostle Paul? In the first epistle to the Corinthians he points out that even the actual history of the Exodus was symbolic of the future Christian people. *I would not have you unaware, brothers, that our ancestors were all under the cloud and all passed across the sea. In the cloud and the sea they were all baptized for Moses; all ate the same spiritual food, and all drank the same spiritual drink; for they drank from the spiritual rock that followed them; and that rock was Christ. With most of them, however, God was not well pleased, and they were struck down in the desert. These things were an image for us, to warn us not to yearn for evil as they yearned for it. We must not worship idols, as they did (as the Scripture says: The people sat down to eat and drink and got up to play). We must not commit adultery, as some of them committed adultery, and twenty-three thousand fell on one day. We must not put Christ to the test, as some of them put him to the test, and they were killed by snakes. We must not complain, as some of them complained and were wiped out by the Destroyer. All this happened to them as a sign; and it was written down as a warning for us, for whom the last age has arrived.* (1 Cor 10:1-11)

The apostle also has another allegory, although certainly relating mainly to causes. They themselves often referred to it and expounded it in their own arguments. It is what Paul says to the Galatians: *It is written that Abraham had two sons, one from a slave and one from a free woman; but the one from the slave was born by the flesh, whereas the one from the free woman was born as the result of a promise. These things are said as an allegory. The women are the two testaments. One is from Mount Sinai and her children are born into slavery; and that one is Agar, as Mount Sinai is a mountain in Arabia. She corresponds to the present Jerusalem, which is in slavery along with her children. The Jerusalem above is the free woman, and she is the mother of us all.* (Gal 4:22-26)

9. Those people do little harm by this. In trying to invalidate the law, they force us to justify that scripture. They note that it says that we are slaves, and they brandish above the rest the concluding words: *You who are justified in the law are emptied of Christ; you have fallen from grace* (Gal 5:4). We acknowledge the truth of all this, and we do not say the law is necessary except for those who still benefit from being slaves. It was good for the law to be in effect, because men and women who could not be persuaded from sinning by reason had to be constrained by a law like that, that is to say, by the threat and dread of those punishments, which even the foolish can apprehend. When Christ's grace sets us

free from this, it does not condemn that law, but the time comes when he invites us to submit to his love and not be slaves to the law from fear. This is the grace, in other words, the benefit, that those who still yearn to be in bondage to the law fail to perceive as coming from God. Paul rightly castigates them as unbelievers, because they do not believe that through our Lord Jesus Christ they have now been set free from the slavery in which, by God's most just plan, they were held subject for a set time. This explains that other text of the same apostle: *The law was our tutor in Christ* (Gal 3:24). So the one who later gave men and women a teacher to love first gave them a tutor to fear. Although it is wrong now for Christians to observe those precepts and commandments of the law, such as the Sabbath and circumcision and sacrifices and the like, there is still much symbolism in them. Any devout person, therefore, understands that there is nothing more harmful than to take everything there according to the literal meaning of the words but that there is nothing more beneficial than to have it unveiled by the Spirit. So it is that *the letter kills but the spirit gives life* (2 Cor 3:6);[20] and so it is that *in the reading of the Old Testament the veil itself remains, and the veil is not lifted, because it is taken away with Christ* (2 Cor 3:14). It is not the Old Testament that is taken away with Christ, but the veil over it. What is dark and hidden without Christ is understood, and as it were uncovered, through Christ. The same apostle immediately adds: *When, however, you go over to Christ, the veil will be taken away* (2 Cor 3:16). He does not say that the law or the Old Testament will be taken away. So it is not that they have been taken away through the Lord's grace, because there is nothing good hidden there, but rather the cover that hides the good things there has been taken away.

This is what happens for those who are earnest and devout in searching for the meaning of those writings, and not undisciplined and ill-intentioned. They are shown how things are related to each other, and the reasons behind what was said and done, and the harmony of the Old Testament and the New, which is so complete that there remains no point of disharmony, and the deep secrets of the figurative meaning. Everything the interpretation extracts forces us to recognize the wretchedness of those who choose to condemn these sources before learning about them.

4, 10. Leaving aside deep scholarship for the moment, let me deal with you in the way I think I should deal with someone close to me, and do what I am able to do rather than what I admired those scholars for being able to do. There are three kinds of error that lead people astray when they read anything, and I shall say something about each of them. The first is what occurs when something untrue is taken to be the truth, although it is not what the writer thought. The second is not

---

20. In *Revisions* I, 14, 1 Augustine says that he gave a better interpretation of this verse from Galatians in *The Spirit and the Letter* 4, 6-5, 8, but he does not retract the interpretation given here.

so widespread, but it is no less damaging: this occurs when something is taken to be the truth, and it is because it is also what the writer thought. The third kind of error occurs when something true is understood from the writings of others, although the authors did not have that understanding of it themselves. There is no small benefit to be gained from this. In fact, if you think carefully about it, that is the entire benefit of reading.

It would be an example of the first kind of error if someone said and believed, for instance, that in the underworld Rhadamanthus hears the cases of the dead and pronounces judgment on them, as that is what one reads in Virgil's poem.[21] Here there is a twofold error, because one believes something it is wrong to believe, and it is also wrong to think that the writer believed it.

The second kind of error is exemplified by someone who decides it is true and has to be believed that the soul is made up of atoms and that after death it breaks up into those atoms and passes away, because this is what Lucretius wrote.[22] This person is no less wretched for being convinced in a matter of such importance that something untrue is proven, even though that was the view of Lucretius, the writer of the books that caused the deception. What is gained from knowing for certain what the author thought, when one is choosing to be wrong with him rather than wrong because of him?

An example of the third kind of error would be the case of someone who reads a passage in Epicurus' writings, where he praises abstinence, and then asserts that Epicurus held virtue to be mankind's supreme good and that therefore he should not be criticized. If in fact Epicurus holds that bodily pleasure is mankind's supreme good, what harm comes from that person's mistake, since there is no acceptance of that immoral and dangerous doctrine and no approval of Epicurus on any other count? The only harm is in thinking he did not hold wrong views. This is not only human error but is often a very honorable human error. Why so? Suppose that it was reported to me about someone I loved that, even though he was a grown man, he said in the hearing of many people that he found childhood and infancy pleasant, even to the point of saying on oath that that is how he wanted to live; and suppose I was given such proof of this that I could not honorably deny it. Suppose, however, that I concluded that, when he said that, he only meant that he preferred innocence and a mind foreign to those desires that enmesh the human race, and because of this I loved him even more than I had before, even though perhaps he had also been foolishly infatuated with a certain freedom to play and eat and with the indolent idleness of childhood? Would anyone think I should be blamed for this? Suppose then that he died after I heard this report, and there was no one I could question to clarify

---

21. *Aeneid* VI, 566ff.
22. See *De rerum natura* III, 231-257; 323-349; 425-426; 437-712; 830-930.

what he thought. Would anyone be so shameless as to censure me for praising the intentions and desires I inferred from the actual words reported to me? Indeed, a fair judge of the matter would not hesitate perhaps even to praise my thinking and attitude because I not only approved of innocence but also, when there was doubt about the facts, preferred to think well of a fellow human being, even when it would not be wrong to think evil.

5, 11. This being the case, attend as well to the corresponding differences in the status of those writings. There has to be the same number of possibilities. Either someone wrote something worthwhile, but there is nothing worthwhile in someone's understanding of it; or there is nothing of value in either case; or there is benefit for a reader who understands it in a way contrary to what the author wrote. Of these three alternatives, I have nothing against the first, and I am not concerned about the last. I cannot criticize any writers who are misunderstood through no fault of their own. Nor can I take it badly that someone who fails to see the truth is read, when I see that no harm is done to the reader.

The one case that is fully approvable and as it were unblemished occurs when what is written is good and is also taken by readers to their advantage. Even this can still be distinguished as occurring in two ways, for the possibility of error is not entirely excluded. It usually happens that, when the writer has perceived well, the reader perceives well too, but the reader perceives differently from the author, often better, often worse, but always for good. When then we perceive what the author we are reading perceived—and it is something very relevant to leading a good life—truth is piled on truth and there is no opening left for falsehood. When the reading is about very obscure matters this case is entirely rare, and in my opinion it cannot be known for sure but can only be believed to occur. By what arguments can I conclude, so as to be able to swear to it, what the intentions were of persons who are dead or absent? Even if they were available for questioning, there could be much that good persons would have to conceal. For the purpose of discovering the truth, however, I do not think it matters what kind of person the author was. The honorable way is to assume that anyone whose writings serve the interests of the human race and future generations was a good person.

12. For these reasons I wish they would tell me which kind of error they think the Catholic Church makes. If it is the first, then it is a very serious allegation but not one that requires an extended defence. It is enough to say that we do not understand it in the way they ascribe to us in their attack. If it is the second kind of error, it is no less serious, but they are refuted with the same statement. If it is the third, there is nothing to answer.

Go ahead and look at the scriptures themselves. What is their objection with regard to the books that are called the Old Testament? Can it be that they are good but that we interpret them badly? But they themselves do not accept them. Or is it that they are not good and that the way we take them is bad? The answer above is enough to refute this. Or do they say this: "Although your response to them is good, they themselves are bad"? What else is this but to exonerate the living opponents with whom they are now dealing and to blame the dead with whom they have no argument?

I myself believe that those writers did well in putting everything on record, and that they were great and divinely inspired, and that that law was established and promulgated at God's command and according to his wishes. Although my knowledge of those books is very limited, I can easily prove this to anyone who listens to me with an open mind, free of obstinacy. Since we have the resources of your well-intentioned ears and mind, I shall do this, but I shall do it when I have the opportunity. Is it not enough for the present that, whatever the facts in that regard, I have not been deceived?

6, 13. My own conscience, Honoratus, and the God who dwells in pure souls are my witness that in my estimation there is nothing wiser or purer or more sacred than all those writings that the Catholic Church preserves under the name of the Old Testament. This, I know, surprises you. I cannot pretend that I was not once convinced quite to the contrary. But with any books there is nothing more full of that brashness that possessed us then as children than to abandon the instructors who claim they understand and accept them and can pass them on to their pupils and look to discover their meaning from those who, for whatever compelling reason, have declared bitter war on their authors and publishers. Who ever thought to have the learned and difficult works of Aristotle[23] expounded by his enemies, to speak of studies where the reader may well make a slip without committing sacrilege? Or who has ever chosen to read and learn the geometry of Archimedes with Epicurus as tutor? In many of his writings he opposed them tenaciously, although, in my opinion, without understanding them at all. Are those scriptures of the law, that they attack so foolishly and so ineffectually as though they were open to all, entirely transparent? They seem to me to be like that simple woman they themselves often hold up to ridicule, who became angry because a certain Manichean woman praised the sun and commended it to her for worship.[24] Religiously naive, she jumped up excitedly and repeatedly stamped on the spot that shone in the sunlight from the window. "See, I stamp on your sun and your god," she began to shout. It was her woman's way and quite foolish of her—who would say otherwise? But do you not think they too are just the same when with a massive onslaught of speeches and curses they tear at things they do not understand? They have no understanding of their

---

23. Augustine knew the *Categories* of Aristotle from having read it himself (see *Confessions* IV, 16, 28), probably in the translation of Marius Victorinus. Otherwise he had only a limited and mainly indirect knowledge of Aristotle's works.
24. The Manicheans venerated the sun as a "ship of light" that gathered up the portions of light that had been liberated from matter and carried them onward. See *Heresies* 46, 6.

nature or purpose, or how they are like ruins, although they are subtle and divine for those who understand them. Because the ignorant applaud them, they think they have achieved something.

Believe me, everything in that scripture is profound and from God. There is absolute truth there, and teaching finely adapted to the renewal and restoration of souls and clearly presented in such a way that there is no one who cannot draw from it. This is all anyone needs, provided he comes to draw from it in a spirit of devout respect, as true religion requires. To prove this for you would require considerable reasoning and a longer discourse. We must first do what we have to do for you. We must ensure that you do not despise the actual authors and then bring you to love them. How is this to be done other than by an exposition of their own statements and writings? If we had hated Virgil, before we understood him, or even if we did not love him because of the approval of our ancestors, we would never be satisfied with regard to those countless questions about him that keep grammarians busy and excited. We would not be content to listen to someone who explained them favorably to him, but we would prefer someone who tried to use them to show that he was wrong and deluded. As it is, however, many try to elucidate them, according to their own different interpretations, and the greatest applause is accorded to those whose commentary makes him the more excellent poet. Even those who do not understand him believe not only that he did nothing badly but also that he wrote no poetry that was not praiseworthy. Therefore, when our teachers fail us and do not have an answer on some questions of detail, rather than thinking their silence might be accounted for by some defect in Virgil, we become resentful. If in their own justification they choose to find fault with such a great author, hardly any of their pupils will stay with them, even if paid to.

How important was it for us to extend the same good will to those through whom, as such a long tradition assures us, the Holy Spirit spoke? We, however, brilliant young men and wonderful researchers of reason that we were, without even opening those writings, and without looking for teachers, and in no danger of being accused of tardiness, did not give even passing attention to those who throughout the whole world for so long have sought to have those documents read and preserved and handed on. Yet we concluded there was nothing in them worth believing. Excited by the speech of those who were enemies and hostile to them, we were persuaded by their false promise of proofs to accept and cultivate an incredible number of myths.[25]

7, 14. Now, if I can, let me complete what I began. My purpose with you is not just to reveal the Catholic faith in passing but to open up for those who have a care for their own souls the hope of a divine outcome and the discovery of truth.

---

25. The Manicheans demanded the very thing for which they criticized the Catholic Church.

No one doubts that anyone who is looking for the true religion either believes already that the soul is immortal and that that religion is for its good, or he at least wants to find that out in that religion. The soul, therefore, is the reason for all religion. Whatever the nature of the body, it excites no concern or anxiety, especially after death, for anyone who is intent on the soul and its happiness. If there is a true religion, it is either for the soul alone or principally for the soul that it was founded. As we know, however, this soul is foolish and makes mistakes (I shall look into the reason for this, and I admit it is very obscure), until it attains and apprehends wisdom, and perhaps that itself is the true religion.

Would I direct you to myths? Would I force you to believe something wrongly? I say that our soul is trapped and immersed in error and stupidity and is looking for the way of truth, if there is one. If that is not how it is with you, then forgive me and please share your wisdom with me. But if you do recognize the truth of what I am saying in yourself, then, I implore you, let us look for the truth together.

15. Suppose that we had not yet heard anyone preaching any religion. It is still something new to us, an activity just begun. If there is anything in it at all, I think we have to look for teachers in the subject. Suppose that we find there are different ones, each holding different views and all wanting to attract everyone to themselves with their different views. Among them, however, some stand out because of their greater present reputation and the almost universal attention they receive. The important question is whether they have the truth. But must we not investigate them first, so that if we do go wrong, human as we are, clearly we go wrong along with the whole human race?

16. Some few have the truth. If you know who has it, you already know what it is. Did I not just say to you that we would search as though we knew nothing? But if truth itself forces you to conclude that only a few have it, yet you do not know who those few are, what then? If those who know the truth, so as to be able to hold the masses by their authority, are so few in number, how is it that those few are able to extricate themselves, and be purified, as it were, to enter those secret places? Do we not see how few there are who attain perfect eloquence, even though throughout the whole world schools of oratory resound to the clatter of the flocks of young students? Does it happen that anyone who wants to become a good speaker is frightened away by the untalented masses and decides to concentrate on the speeches of Caecilius or Erucus[26] rather than those of Cicero? These are supported by the authority of our ancestors, and everyone looks to them. The untalented crowd set out to study the same speeches as the

---

26. The reference is to two opponents in famous trials. Q. Caecilius Niger claimed for himself, instead of Cicero, the right to prosecute Verres, but Cicero in his *Divinatio in Caecilium* eliminated him as unfit because he was an accomplice of Verres. C. Erucus was the prosecutor of Sextus Roscius from America, whom Cicero successfully defended.

few learned pupils are given to study. Very few get started, however; fewer still complete the task; and only a tiny number excel. What if the true religion is like that? What if great masses of the uneducated attend the churches, though beyond question this does not result in anyone's being made perfect by those rites?

If the number who studied oratory were as few as the number who are eloquent, our parents would never have thought to send us to those teachers. Since, therefore, we were attracted to those studies by the numbers of mostly uneducated persons, and as a result we grew to love something that few manage to attain, why do we not want it to be the same for us in the case of religion? Why do we perhaps hold it in contempt for being like that, to the great peril of our soul? It may be that true and genuine worship of God resides only with a few people, but it nevertheless does reside with them; and it may be that the masses agree with them, even though they are tied down by their desires and cut off from intellectual purity—and who has any doubt that this can happen? If, then, I ask you, anyone accuses us of being reckless and irrational because we do not carefully investigate the religion we are so concerned to discover in the works of its masters, what answer can we give? Have the masses frightened me away? Why is it that the masses have not frightened me away from the study of the liberal arts,[27] which scarcely contribute anything useful even to this present life? Why have they not frightened me away from the quest for money? Why have they not frightened me away from the pursuit of honor? Why have they not frightened me away from acquiring and maintaining good health? And finally, why have they not frightened me away even from the desire of a happy life? These are things everyone works for and in which few achieve excellence.

17. These would seem to be absurd things to say. Who would make such statements? Only enemies. Whatever the cause, and whatever the reason—and I am not investigating this now—they are enemies. I found this out for myself when I read them. Is that how it is? If you had no literary education you would not dare to open Terence Maurus[28] without a teacher. To learn to understand any poet, even one whose poetry is seen to win the applause of the theatre, Asper, Cornutus, Donatus[29] and countless others are consulted. So, do you rush in without a guide and dare to pass judgment without a teacher on those books that, whatever else there may be about them, are widely acknowledged by almost the

---

27. See *Order* II, 12, 35: grammar, rhetoric, dialectic, music, geometry, astronomy, and arithmetic. According to *Revisions* I, 3, this is the sequence of studies "whereby one can advance from corporeal realities to incorporeal ones."
28. A Latin grammarian from Africa in the second/third century A.D. He composed didactic poems, the content of which dealt with the theory of language.
29. Latin grammarians. Aemilius Asper lived in the second century A.D. "Cornutus" probably refers to L. Annaeus Cornutus (first century A.D.), who was a Stoic philosopher as well as a teacher of the poets Persius and Lucan. Donatus Aelius lived in the middle of the fourth century A.D. All three authors composed commentaries on Virgil.

entire human race as being holy and full of divine content? If you find something in them that seems absurd, do you not find fault with yourself for being slow and having a mind polluted by the poison of this world,[30] the same as all foolish people, rather than finding fault with those who perhaps cannot be understood by minds like that? Would you not look for someone both holy and learned, or at least having that reputation among many people, to instruct and teach you, in order to become both a better person and more learned? Would it be easy to find someone like that, even if you searched hard? Was there no one like that in the region where you lived? What better reason could you have to force you to travel? Was there no one like that, or you could find no one like that, on the continent? Then you would set sail. If you found no one like that in the nearest land across the sea, you would travel on, as far as the lands in which the events contained in those books are said to have occurred. Did we do anything like that, Honoratus? Yet, pitiful youngsters that we were, by our own judgment and assessment we condemned what was perhaps (I speak as though there were still some doubt about it) the most sacred religion, and one that was already respected throughout the whole world. What if certain things there seemed to be harmful for people who had no expertise in those scriptures? Could it be that they were put there so that, when we read things that were repulsive not only to the sensibility of the wise and holy but to the sensibilities of people generally, we would look much more carefully for the hidden meaning? Do you not notice how people try to interpret the Ganymedes of the Bucolics, when he turns out to be a cruel shepherd, and the boy Alexis,[31] to whom it is said that Plato also wrote a love song?[32] They interpret it as having some deep symbolic meaning,[33] which they say escapes the perception of the uneducated, even though it would be no sacrilege to think that the bountiful poet also composed some sensual verses.

18. What in fact drew us back and kept us from investigating it? Was it the threat of some law, or the strength of the opponents, or the foul character or evil reputation of the consecrated ministers, or the novelty of the teaching, or the secrecy of the membership? It was none of these things. Every divine and human law allows inquiry into the Catholic faith. Under human law it is certainly lawful to accept it and foster it,[34] even if, as long as we are in error about it, there may be

---

30. See *The Magnitude of the Soul* 33, 74.

31. See Virgil, *Eclogue* 2.

32. See Apuleius, *Apologia* 10; Diogenes Laertius, *Lives and Opinions of the Philosophers* III, 23, 31.

33. Augustine's knowledge of the allegorical interpretation of Virgil must have come from his study of rhetoric. Thus he was familiar with the method of allegorical interpretation before he learned from Ambrose how to apply it to the Bible. See J. Stroux, "Zur allegorischen Deutung Virgils," *Philologus* 86 (1931) 363-368.

34. After the edict *Cunctos populos* (380) of Emperor Theodosius the Catholic faith was even the legally prescribed religion of the Roman state.

some doubt about the divine law. There is no enemy striking fear into us in our frailty. (Even so, if truth and the soul's salvation are not found after careful inquiry where it is lawful and safe, it ought to be sought at any risk.) Every level of honor and authority is committed to the service of this divine worship. Religion has the highest standing and honor. What is there then to prevent examination and discussion, with a devout and careful investigation, as to whether we have here that thing which only a few need know and preserve with full understanding, even though it has the united approval and acceptance of all nations?

19. On this understanding let us proceed now in the way that I said. First we must ask what religion we shall commit our souls to for cleansing and renewal. Without question we must begin with the Catholic Church. There are now more Christians than even pagans and Jews combined. Although there are numerous heresies among those Christians, and all want to be seen as Catholics and they call those other than themselves heretics, everyone agrees that there is only one Church. Taking into account the whole world, it has the greatest numbers. Also, as those who know assert, it is more sincere about the truth than all the rest. Truth, however, is another question. For the one who is investigating that is enough. There is one Catholic Church, although different heresies give it different names, because each of them has its own name that it does not dare to reject. Consequently it is left to the judgment of those who assess it unhampered by any special interest to judge which one should be accorded the name of Catholic to which all aspire. In case anyone thinks there has to be a lengthy, wordy discussion on this point, there is no dispute that it is one Church only, and in a certain way even human laws are Christian in it.

I do not want any prejudgment to be drawn from this; but I think it is the most appropriate starting point for our inquiry. We must not have any fear that the true worship of God might seem to need propping up by those who in fact need it for their own support, rather than standing by its own strength. Undoubtedly the ideal is for the truth to be able to be discovered where it can be investigated and retained in perfect security; but, if this is not possible, then other sources must be approached and explored, whatever the perils.

8, 20. Having made these points, which in my opinion are so right that I ought to win your verdict against any opponent, I shall outline for you as best I can the path I followed when I was searching for the true religion, in the state of mind that I have just shown is the state of mind which that search requires.

When I left you to go across the sea,[35] I was already procrastinating and hesitating about what to hold and what to reject. This hesitancy grew stronger in me from the moment I heard that person who, as you know, we had been promised

---

35. The reference is to Augustine's leaving Carthage for Rome in 383; see *Confessions* V, 8, 14-15.

would come as though from heaven to explain everything that troubled us.[36] Apart from having a certain eloquence I found that he was just like the rest. I thought about it within myself, and, now settled in Italy, I struggled to decide not whether to stay in that sect that I regretted joining[37] but how to find the truth. No one knows my love and yearning for that better than yourself. Often it seemed to me that it could not be found, and I turned the great flood of my thoughts to the opinions of the academics.[38] Often, as best I could, I would look again at the human mind, so lively, so discerning, so perceptive, and I would think that the truth could not lie hidden unless the way to search for it lay hidden and that that way had itself to be obtained from some divine authority. It only remained to find out what authority that was, since among all their disagreements everyone promised to provide it.

So there was a bewildering forest, and it had finally become intolerable to be planted in it. At the same time the desire for truth continued to drive my mind on without respite. I had already decided to leave them, and I was becoming more and more convinced I should do so. In the midst of such great dangers there was nothing left for me except with tearful, piteous cries to implore divine providence to give me strength;[39] and I did that earnestly. Already some arguments of the Bishop of Milan had almost persuaded me it would not be unproductive if I chose to look at a large number of matters concerning the Old Testament that, as you know, we blasphemed against because they were misrepresented to us. I had also decided to be a catechumen in the Church to which I had been presented by my parents, for as long as it took either to find what I wanted or to become convinced it was not to be found.[40] At that time, therefore, anyone able to teach me would have found me ready and very receptive.

Your soul should be in a similar state of concern now. You too are aware that you have been unsettled for a long time. If you now think you have been tossed around enough and want to put an end to these struggles, then follow the path of the Catholic teaching, which has flowed down to us from Christ himself through his apostles and will continue to flow down to our descendants.

9, 21. "That is absurd," you say, "because this is what everyone claims to hold and teach." I cannot deny that all the heretics make this claim. They do so, however, by promising those they seduce that they will provide understanding of the most obscure matters, and by accusing the Catholic teaching especially for

---

36. The reference is to the Manichean bishop Faustus of Milevis; see *Confessions* V, 6, 10 – 7, 13.
37. But even in Rome Augustine had contacts with the Manicheans; see *Confessions* V, 10, 18 – 11, 21; 13, 23.
38. Augustine drew closer to philosophical skepticism. The so-called "New Academy" held the view that the mind could at best reach probable knowledge.
39. This came through Ambrose, who had a decisive influence on Augustine, especially through his sermons in the spring of 386.
40. See *Confessions* V, 14, 25.

its insistence that those who come to it must have belief. They themselves boast that they do not impose a yoke of belief but open up a fountain of doctrine.[41] "What can we say to this," you ask, "because it redounds so much to their credit?" That is not how it is. They do not do this because of any ability they have, but to attract numbers in the name of reason. The human spirit is naturally delighted by that promise, and without considering its own strength and state of health, but hungering after the food of the strong, harmful though it is for anyone unhealthy, it rushes on to the deceivers' poison. There is no right way of entering into the true religion without believing things that all who live rightly and become worthy of it will understand and see for themselves later on, and without some submission to a certain weight of authority.

22. Perhaps you want to be given some proof of this too, to convince you that you do not have to learn by reason before being taught by faith.[42] This is not hard to do, provided you keep an open mind. To make it easier, I want you to answer as though someone were questioning you. First of all, tell me why you think one should not believe. "Because," you say, "credulity itself, from which those who are called credulous get their name, seems to me to be a defect. Otherwise we would not commonly use this name as a criticism. If being suspicious is a fault, in that one suspects something not proven, how much more is it a fault to be credulous. The only difference between this and being suspicious is that the suspicious person has some doubt about things that are not known, whereas the credulous person has none."

I will accept this opinion and distinction for the present, but you also know that we do not usually call someone curious without some element of criticism, but we call someone studious even as a compliment. Consider, therefore, if you will, what you think is the difference between these two. You will answer for sure that, although both are motivated by a strong desire for knowledge, the curious ask about things that are none of their business, whereas the studious inquire about things relating to themselves. Yet we do not deny that one's own spouse and children and their well-being are important for everyone, and when those who are away from home question in detail everyone who comes to them as to how their spouses and children are keeping and what they are doing, they are driven by an intense desire to know; but we do not call them studious. It is true that anyone who is studious wants to know about things relating to themselves. It is not true, however, that everyone who does that should be called studious but only those who spend themselves inquiring about what relates to the finer nourishment and adornment of the mind.[43] At the same time it is correct to say they are keen to know, especially if we add what it is they are keen to know

---

41. See *Confessions* VI, 5, 7; Letter 118, 5, 32.
42. For the line of argument that follows see Letter 120, 1, 3.
43. The reference is to the liberal arts; see section 16.

about. We might even call them studious about their own family, if they only care about their own family, even if we do not think they deserve the general name of studious without qualification. We would not call those who wanted to hear about their own family studious, unless they enjoyed a good reputation and they wanted to hear it often; but we would call them keen to know, even if it was only once.

Now turn your attention again to the curious person and tell me: if someone listened willingly to stories that brought no benefit at all to himself, that is, about things not relating to himself, yet did not do so as a habit and maliciously but only rarely and with restraint, either at a dinner or in some meeting or gathering, would you say that person was curious? I do not think so. On the other hand you would certainly think that about someone who listened freely because he took such things seriously. So the definition of a curious person has to be qualified by the same restriction as that of the studious person. See, therefore, whether what was said previously has to be corrected. Why would it not be both that someone who sometimes suspects something does not deserve to be called suspicious and that someone who sometimes believes something does not deserve to be called credulous? Therefore, just as there is a great difference between being keen to know something and being simply studious, and between being interested in something and being curious, so too there is a great difference between believing and being credulous.

10, 23. "Just the same," you say, "see now whether we ought to believe in matters of religion. If we agree that believing something is not the same as being credulous, it does not follow that there is nothing wrong with believing something in matters of religion. What if believing and being credulous are both wrong, just as being drunk and being a drunkard are?" If anyone thinks this is beyond question, I do not think he can have any friends.[44] If it is wrong to believe anything, then either one does wrong by believing a friend or one never believes a friend, and then I do not see how one can call either oneself or the friend a friend. Perhaps you will say to this: "I grant that we should believe something sometimes, but show me now how it is not wrong to believe without knowing in matters of religion." I shall do that, if I can; and to that end I ask you, "Which do you think is the more serious fault, handing religion on to someone unworthy of it or believing what is said by those who hand it on?" If you do not understand what I mean by someone unworthy, it is someone who comes with a feigned interest. You will agree, I think, that one is more to be blamed for revealing holy secrets, if there are any, to someone like that than for believing the representatives of a religion when they make statements about that religion. It would be unworthy of you to answer otherwise. So, now imagine there is someone present

---

44. See *Faith in the Unseen* 1, 2.

who is going to hand that religion on to you. How will you assure that person that you come with a sincere mind and that you have no deceit or pretence in this respect? You will say in good conscience that you are not pretending anything and will assert this with the best words possible, but still only with words. You cannot reveal the hidden recesses of your mind to another human being, to be known from within. If the person then says: "Look, I believe you. So isn't it fair that you also should believe me, since, if I have any truth, it is you are going to receive the benefit and I who am going to bestow it?" What answer shall we give, other than that we should believe?

24. "But," you say, "would it not be better if you gave me proof, so that in following you wherever you lead me I would do nothing irrational?" Perhaps so, but since it is so important for you to know God by reason, do you think everyone is capable of grasping the arguments that lead the human mind to divine understanding? Or do you think most people are capable of it? Or only a few? "Only a few," I think you will say. Do you think you are one of these? "That is not for me to answer," you say. So you think it is for the other person to believe this about you too; and this is what happens. Remember then that the other person has now believed you on two occasions when you have said something unsubstantiated, although your religious advice is not to consent to believe even once. Let us grant, however, that you are sincere in your approach to accepting the religion and that you are one of the few who can understand the reasoning by which the divine faculty is brought to certain knowledge. What then? Do you think religion has to be denied to the rest of mankind, who are not endowed with such a clear intellect? Or do you think they have to be introduced to those deep secrets gradually and in stages? You can see clearly what is more truly religious. You cannot think that anyone who longs for something so important should be abandoned or rejected in any way. Do you not see, though, that, unless they believe they will achieve what they set out for and come to it with a suppliant mind, purified by a particular way of living in obedience to certain important, essential commandments, there is no other way for them to attain those perfect truths? You surely believe that.

So what about those, among whom I think you would be included, who are easily able to grasp the divine secrets with sure reasoning. If they receive them in the same way as those who at first only believe, do you think this will do them any harm? I do not think so. "Just the same," you say, "why do they need to wait?" Because, although it does them no harm at all to wait, their example would be harmful to others. There is hardly anyone who has a true opinion of himself. Those who underestimate themselves need to be encouraged; those who overestimate themselves need to be repressed, so that the former will not break with despair and the latter will not crash through overconfidence. This is easily effected if even those who can fly are made to proceed gradually, in a way that is safe for the others too, and so that no one is incited to take risks. This is the wisdom of the true religion. This is the divine command. This is the tradition of our holy ancestors. This has been the practice until now. To choose to disturb and distort this is nothing other than to look for the true religion along a path of sacrilege. Even if they are allowed to act as they wish, those who act in this way cannot reach their goal. They may be as brilliant as you like, but if God is not with them they crawl along on the ground. God, however, is with those who seek him with care for humanity. There cannot be found any more secure path to heaven than this.

I for my part certainly cannot oppose this argument, for who can say we should believe nothing that we do not know for certain? Even friendship cannot exist unless we believe some things that cannot be proved for certain. The servants in charge of expenditure are often believed without any fault on the part of their master. In religion what could be more wicked than for God's bishops to believe us when we avow our sincerity, while we refuse to believe them when they instruct us? Finally, what more salutary way can there be than first of all to be made fit to perceive the truth by accepting on faith the things that have been instituted by God to prepare and predispose the mind, or, if you are already perfectly prepared, to circle for a while where the approach is safest rather than to be a cause of danger to yourself and an example of recklessness to others?

11, 25. It remains now to consider the reasons why it is wrong to follow those who promise to lead us by reason. We have already shown how there is nothing wrong with following those who insist that we believe. There are some who think not only that they should not be blamed for turning to those patrons of reason but even that they should be praised for it. Not so. In relation to religion there are two kinds of persons who deserve to be praised. The first is those who have already found it, and they must be considered the most fortunate; the other is those who are dedicated to the proper search for it. The first have already arrived, while the others are on the path by which they will surely arrive.[45]

There are three other kinds of persons who undoubtedly deserve blame and contempt. The first is the opinionated ones, that is, those who think they know what they do not know. The second is those who are aware that they do not know but do not use the right methods to find out. The third is those who do not think they know nor want to find out. In the human mind too there are three very closely related things that it is very important to distinguish: understanding, believing, and being opinionated. Considered in themselves, the first is always good; the second is sometimes wrong, and the third is never without fault. To understand things that are important and good, or even divine, is the greatest

---

45. In his later years Augustine was convinced that complete happiness could only be found in the life after death, because only then would the truth, that is, God, be fully known; see *Revisions* I, 14, 2.

blessing.[46] To understand inessential things does no harm, although learning about them could be harmful by taking up the time needed for essential things. To understand things that are bad for us is no misfortune, but to do them or endure them is. If someone understands how to kill an enemy without risk, the actual understanding does not have the guilt of the desire to do it. If that is not there, what could be more innocent? Believing, however, is at fault on those occasions when something unfitting is believed about God or too easily believed about another person. In other matters there is nothing wrong with believing, provided one understands it is something one does not know. I believe that criminal conspirators were once executed through the influence of Cicero,[47] but not only do I not know that, but I know for certain that there is no way I can know it. To be opinionated, however, is bad for two reasons. Those who are already convinced they know something are not able to learn about it, if learning about it becomes possible, and being hasty is in itself a sign of an ill-adjusted mind. If anyone thinks that he has knowledge about the subject I mentioned concerning Cicero, this is no hindrance at all to his acquiring knowledge of it, since it is not a matter about which it is possible to have knowledge. Nevertheless they do not understand that it matters a great deal whether something is ascertained by the secure mental reasoning that we call understanding, or whether for good reasons it is entrusted to oral tradition and writing for the belief of future generations. In this they are certainly making a mistake, and there is no mistake that does not have something bad about it.

Therefore, we must hold what we understand as coming from reason, what we believe as coming from authority,[48] and what we are opinionated about as coming from error. Anyone who understands also believes, and anyone who is opinionated also believes, but someone who believes does not always understand, and someone who is opinionated never understands.[49]

We can relate these three things to those five types of persons that we mentioned previously, namely, the two commendable ones that we mentioned first, and the other three that are reprehensible. We find that the first kind of person, the blessed, believes the truth itself, whereas the second, the keen lover of truth, believes authority; and in both these cases believing is commendable. With the first of the reprehensible ones, those who think they know what they do not know, there is certainly the fault of credulity. The other two reprehensible ones, those who seek the truth with no hope that they will find it[50] and those who

---

46. In *Revisions* I, 14, 2 Augustine again stresses the point that this statement must be referred to happiness in the life to come.
47. This is an allusion to the Catiline plot of 63 B.C.
48. In *Revisions* I, 14, 3 Augustine points out that in everyday language, of which the Bible too makes use, "believe" and "know" are not so sharply distinguished from one another.
49. See *The Teacher* 11, 37, 2.
50. The supporters of philosophical skepticism must be meant.

do not seek it at all, do not believe anything. This moreover is in matters where there exists appropriate teaching. In other aspects of life I do not know how it is possible at all for someone not to believe anything. Even those who say they act according to probabilities[51] want to be seen as not able to know anything rather than as not believing anything. Does anyone test something without a belief about it? And how is the course he follows probable if it is not tested? Hence enemies of the truth can be of two kinds. There are those who only attack knowledge but do not attack belief; and there are those who condemn both. Whether people like this are actually to be found in human life once again I do not know.

I have said these things so that we might appreciate that in maintaining our belief in those things that we do not yet understand we are exonerated from the rashness of being opinionated. Anyone who says we should believe nothing that we do not know is only warning against what is called "being opinionated," and this admittedly is a miserable defect. If, however, he considers carefully the great difference there is between thinking one knows something and believing on authority something one is aware that one does not know, then he will surely avoid mistakes and escape the charge of being proud and lacking in humanity.

12, 26. If it is wrong to believe something we do not know, I should like to know how children can obey their parents and return their love and respect without believing they are their parents. There is no way this can be known by reason. We have a belief about our father based on the word of our mother. For our belief about our mother herself we usually depend not on our mother but on midwives, nurses and servants. Is it not possible for a mother to have her child stolen and another substituted for it and so, being deceived herself, to cause others to be deceived? We do believe, however, and believe without any hesitation, things that we admit we cannot know. Can anyone fail to see that, if this were not so, filial love, humanity's most sacred bond, would be the victim of criminal arrogance? Is there anyone even so insane as to blame those who carried out all the usual duties towards those they believed to be their parents, although they were not? Is there anyone on the other hand who would not condemn, as not fit to live, persons who failed to love their true parents for fear of loving impostors? There are many examples we could give to show that absolutely nothing in human society would be safe if we decided not to believe anything that we cannot hold as evident.[52]

27. Listen now to something about which I confess it will now be easier for me to persuade you. When we are dealing with religion, that is, worship and

---

51. Once again the reference is to the skeptics; see *Answer to the Skeptics* III, 1; *Confessions* VI, 11, 18.

52. See *Confessions* VI, 5, 7; *Faith in the Unseen* 2, 4. A similar view is expressed earlier in Cicero, *Laelius on Friendship* 7, 23.

understanding of God, even less should we be guided by those who forbid us to believe and so freely promise us proofs.

No one will question that everyone is either foolish or wise.[53] By wise here I do not mean those who are wily and ingenious but those who have, as much as is possible for a human being, a strong perception and understanding both of human nature itself and of God and a way of life that conforms to this. All others, whatever their skills or lack of skills, and whatever their conquests in proving and disproving, I count among the foolish. If this is so, is there anyone of ordinary intelligence who does not see clearly that it is more effective and safer for the foolish to accept the guidance of the wise than to live according to their own judgment? Anything we do that is not done rightly is a sin, and nothing can be done rightly if it does not proceed from right reasoning. So right reasoning itself is a virtue. But where is this virtue present in humanity except in the minds of the wise? Only the wise, therefore, do not sin. All the foolish sin, except when they obey the wise. In that case what they do does proceed from right reasoning, and the foolish, so to speak, are not to be considered the owners of their own deeds, since they are like tools and agents of the wise. Therefore, if for everyone not sinning is better than sinning, the foolish would surely all live better lives if they could be the slaves of the wise. If no one questions the value of this in less important matters, such as commerce and farming, marrying, having and raising children, and the general management of the household, it is even more expedient in the case of religion. Not only are human affairs easier to assess than those that relate to God, but also, with anything of greater sanctity and excellence, the greater the respect and reverence due to it, the more wicked and perilous it is to sin.

It is clear that as long as we remain foolish, if we have our hearts set on leading a good and truly religious life, we have no alternative but to seek out the wise and be obedient to them. In this way, while the foolishness remains in us, we shall feel its domination less and one day be delivered from it.

13, 28. Here again there arises a very difficult question. How can the foolish find someone who is wise? Although hardly anyone would dare claim this title openly, most people would claim it for themselves indirectly. Because they disagree among themselves so much about the very things whose knowledge constitutes wisdom, it must be either that none of them is wise or that at the most one of them is. But who is that one? Since it is the foolish who are trying to find out, I do not see at all how they can distinguish clearly and discern who that one is. They cannot recognize something by any of its signs, if they have no knowl-

---

53. In *Revisions* I, 14, 4 Augustine notes a seeming contradiction here to *Free Will* III, 24, 71, where a middle state between wisdom and ignorance is mentioned. But in that passage the reference is to two special cases—Adam before the Fall, and very little children.

edge of the thing itself whose presence they indicate.[54] It is not that someone who does not have it can discern wisdom with the mind's eye, in the way you are able to recognize gold and silver and things like that when you see them, even though you do not own any. Anything we apprehend with our bodily senses is presented to us externally, and so we can detect with our eyes things that belong to others, even when we ourselves have nothing the same or similar. What the intellect apprehends, however, is within the mind, and perceiving it is the same as having it. Since then the foolish do not have wisdom, and it is not possible for them to see it with their eyes, they do not know wisdom. It is not possible for them to perceive it without having it, and it is not possible for them to have it and be foolish. Therefore they do not know it, and as long as they do not know it they cannot recognize it anywhere else. So as long as one is foolish one cannot find with certainty the wise person to submit to in order to be delivered from that great evil of being foolish.

29. As our inquiry has to do with religion, the cure for this immense problem can only come from God, and, unless we believe both that he exists and that he can be invoked by the human mind, we should not even look for the true religion. What are we trying to investigate with such great effort? What are we hoping to achieve? Where do we want to arrive? At some place that we do not believe exists or do not believe has any relevance for ourselves? Nothing could be more perverse than a mentality like that. You yourself would not venture to ask a favor from me, or would certainly be very stupid to do so, if you did not believe I would grant it. Do you come then asking to find out about religion, even though you think that God does not exist, or, if God does exist, that he does not care about us?

So then, what if it is something of such great importance but it cannot be discovered except by untiring investigation with all our resources? What if the extreme difficulty of the investigation itself trains the mind of the investigator to grasp and display the object it uncovers?[55] Is there anything more pleasant for our eyes or anything they are more at home with than our light? Yet after a long period of darkness they cannot bear to endure it. For a body exhausted by illness is there anything more appropriate than food and drink? Yet we see people recovering from illness restrained and prevented from risking harm to themselves by eating fully as healthy people do. They are held back from using the food itself in such a way as to bring about a relapse into the illness that caused them to reject it. I am speaking of persons who are convalescing. What of those who are actually ill? Do we not encourage them to eat or drink something? And

---

54. See *The Teacher* 10, 33; *The Trinity* X, 1, 2.
55. See *Teaching Christianity* I on the interpretation of the Bible.

surely they would not obey us, when it is such an effort for them, if they did not believe they would recover from the illness.

When, therefore, would you commit yourself to a difficult and demanding inquiry? Would you ever dare to undertake such a heavy task and responsibility, matching the importance of its subject matter, if you did not believe that the object of your search existed? Rightly, therefore, the high authority of the Catholic teaching has made it the rule that, before all else, those coming to religion must be persuaded to have faith.

14, 30. I ask you, what arguments do those heretics put to me (since these people we are discussing want to be known as Christians)? How would they persuade me to abandon belief as irrational? If they insist I should not believe anything, I do not believe that in human life there is any true religion like this, and, since I do not believe it exists, I do not search for it. He, however, as I believe, is going to show it to anyone who searches: *Whoever seeks, will find* (Mt 7:7).[56] Accordingly, I would not come to someone who forbids me to believe unless I did believe something. Could there be any greater insanity than this: they blame me only because I have belief that is not supported by knowledge, although it is only that which brought me to them?

31. What is this? The heretics all urge us not to believe Christ. Could there be any greater self-contradiction? They have to be pressed on this in two respects. First they must be asked where the rationality is that they promised, where the rejection of irrationality, where the expectation of knowledge: "If it is wrong to believe anyone without proof, why are you eager for me to believe someone without proof, in order for me to be more easily led on by your reasoning? Will your rationality build something solid on a foundation of irrationality?" I am speaking their language, as it is they who blame us for believing. I myself consider that, when you do not have the ability to appreciate the arguments, it is very healthy to believe without knowing the reasons and by that belief to cultivate the mind and allow the seeds of truth to be sown. Moreover, for minds that are ill this is absolutely essential, if they are to be restored to health. Their view that this is ridiculous and quite irrational, when in fact it is Christ in whom we believe, is insolent.

So I proclaim that I have already believed in Christ and instilled into my mind that what he said is true, even if this is not shored up by any proof. Are you, heretic, going to lead me on this basis? Let me ponder a little. I have not actually seen Christ in the way he chose to appear to the human race, although the teaching is that he was visible even to the eyes of ordinary people. Whose testimony about him is it that I have believed in order to come to you now on the basis

---

56. This verse of scripture was a favorite of the Manicheans; see *The Catholic Way of Life and the Manichean Way of Life* II, 17, 31.

of that belief? I see that what I have believed is only the accepted views and recognized traditions of communities and nations. Everywhere, however, these communities have been won over by the rites of the Catholic Church. Why, therefore, should I not look rather to them in my search for what Christ commanded, since it is already their testimony that has influenced me to believe that Christ commanded something of value? Are you going to give me a better account of what he said, even though I would not hold that he existed or exists if the advice to believe this had to come from you. As I said, I believed this because of the wide acceptance of the report, strong in its unanimity and antiquity.[57] No one doubts, however, that you, who are so few,[58] so new[59] and so confused, offer nothing worthy of credence. What insanity is this: "Believe them when they tell you that you should believe in Christ, but let us teach you what he said?" Why, I ask you? If they failed me and could not teach me anything, it would be easier to convince myself that I should not believe in Christ at all, rather than that I should learn anything about him other than from those through whom I had come to believe in him. What colossal confidence! Indeed, what colossal stupidity! "I shall teach you what Christ, in whom you believe, commanded," they say. "What? Would you be able to teach me about him, if I did not believe in him?" "But you should believe," they say. "Does that mean to believe in him because you commend him to us?" "No," they say, "because we guide by reason those who do believe in him." "Why, then, should I believe in him?" "Because it is reliably reported." "By you or by others?" "By others," they say. "Therefore I must believe them in order to be taught by you? Perhaps I should do that, except that they advise me particularly to have nothing to do with you, as they say your teachings are pernicious. You will answer that they are lying. But why then should I believe what they say about Christ, whom they have not seen, but not believe what they say about you, whom they do not want to see?" "Believe what is written," they say. "But any writing that is newly published and unknown, or is recommended by a few people with no supporting reasons, is not accepted on its own merits but because of those who publish it. Therefore, if it is you who publish those writings, as few and unknown as you are, I am not inclined to accept them. At the same time you even break your own promise by demanding belief rather than giving reasons. You will refer me again to the masses and to reputation.

"In the end contain your obstinacy, and whatever uncontrolled lust for glory it is, and direct me instead to search out the leaders of these masses, and to search long and hard, in order to learn something about these writings from them

---

57. See *True Religion* 3, 5; *Faith in the Unseen* 3, 5.
58. See *The Catholic Way of Life and the Manichean Way of Life* II, 20, 75; *Answer to Secundinus* 36; *Answer to Faustus, a Manichean* XIII, 5; XX, 23.
59. All the same, about 115 years had passed since the death of Mani.

instead. Without them I should not even know there was anything to learn. But you yourself go back to your lairs and do not lie in wait to snatch something in the name of the truth that you are trying to steal from those whose authority you yourself acknowledge."

32. If they say we should not even believe Christ without irrefutable proof, then they are not Christians. That is what some of the pagans say against us. It is certainly foolish of them, but at least they are not attacking or contradicting themselves. But who would allow these people to claim they belong to Christ, when they argue that nothing should be believed until they have provided the unintelligent with a clear understanding of God? As we see from the teaching of that historical record, which even they accept, his own first and greatest wish was to be believed, because those with whom he was dealing were not yet ready to comprehend the divine mysteries. What else are those many great miracles doing, when he himself said the only reason for them was to bring people to believe in him? He led the foolish by faith; you lead them by reason. He called on us to believe in him; you call us back. He praised those who believe; you blame them. If we could follow those who do nothing of that nature but only teach, then either he did not turn water into wine[60] (not to mention other miracles), or no weight should be given to that utterance, *Believe in God and believe me* (Jn 14:1), or the one who did not want him to come to his home because he believed his son would be cured by his mere command[61] is guilty of irrationality.

So he who brought the remedy that would heal corrupted morals established authority with miracles, won belief with authority, held the masses with belief, endured through the masses, and made religion strong by enduring. The crude novelties of the heretics have failed to dislodge it in any way with their deceits, any more than did the violent opposition of the ancient errors of the pagans.

15, 33. For these reasons, even though I am not empowered to teach, I do not cease to advise. Since many want to appear wise, and it is not easy for the unwise to tell whether they really are, if your heart is set on a happy life, then with total commitment and every kind of offering, with sighs and even in tears if possible, pray to God to deliver you from the evil of error.

This will be more readily accomplished if you give willing obedience to his commandments, which he chose to support with the great authority of the Catholic Church. The wise person is so united in mind to God that nothing can come between to separate them, for God is truth and it is not possible for anyone to be wise whose mind is not in contact with the truth. Hence we cannot deny that human wisdom is interposed as a kind of intermediary between human foolishness and God's absolute truth. The wise person imitates God, to the extent that

60. See Jn 2:7-9.
61. See Mt 8:8.

this is possible; the nearest thing the foolish can gainfully imitate is the wise person. Since, as we have said, it is not easy to discern this person by reason, certain miracles had to be presented for the eyes to see, which the foolish are better fitted to using than they are to using their mind. Then, by responding to authority, people would first have their lives and conduct purified and in that way grow capable of being given understanding.

Since, therefore, we had to model ourselves on a human being but not set our hopes on a human being, could God have done anything kinder or more generous than for the real, eternal, unchanging wisdom of God itself, to which we must cling, to condescend to take on human form? He would not only do the things that call us to God but would also suffer the things that turn us away from following God. No one can acquire the supreme and lasting good without loving it totally and unreservedly, and this is not possible as long as material evils and misfortunes inspire terror. By his miraculous birth and his deeds he won our love, but by his death and resurrection he drove out fear. In all the other things, which it would take a long time to go into, he showed himself for us to see how the divine mercy can reach out and human weakness be lifted up.

16, 34. Believe me, this authority is what saves us, this prior lifting of our mind from its earthly habitat, this turning from the love of this world to the true God. It is only authority that enables the foolish to move quickly to wisdom. As long as we are unable to understand reality, it is indeed a wretched thing to be misled by authority, but it is undoubtedly more wretched not to respond to it at all. If God's providence does not preside over human affairs, there is no need to be concerned at all about religion. If, however, the outward appearance of everything (which we surely must believe emanates from some source of true beauty[62]) and a certain inner consciousness combine, publicly and privately as it were, to urge all better minds to look for God and serve God, then we should not abandon hope that there is some authority established by that God himself to be like a fixed step on which we may stand to be lifted up to God.

Putting aside the reasoning that, as we have said repeatedly, is very hard for the foolish to understand in itself, this influences us in two ways: in part by the miracles, and in part because of its wide acceptance. No one denies that the wise person has no need for anything like this, but the present aim is to become capable of being wise, that is, able to be held by the truth. This is not possible for a mind that is defiled. What defiles the mind, if I may explain it briefly, is love of anything at all other than the mind itself and God. The more one is cleansed of this defilement, the more easily one discerns the truth. Since, therefore, your

---

62. In Neoplatonic thought, being is hierarchically ordered. Each next lower level proceeds from the higher by "emanation" ("overflow") without any diminution occurring thereby to the higher.

mind is purified in order for you to see the truth, it is obviously perverse and absurd to want to see the truth in order to purify your mind.

Hence authority is there for those who are incapable of gazing on the truth, so that they may become fit to do so by allowing themselves to be purified. No one doubts it has this power, partly because of the miracles and partly because of its wide acceptance, as I have just said. I call a miracle any event that is so difficult or extraordinary as to be beyond the expectation or power of those it astonishes. Under this heading nothing is more appropriate for people generally, and especially for foolish persons, than things that affect the senses. These in turn can be of two kinds. There are some that only inspire wonder, and some that also procure a great privilege and benefit. If we were to see someone flying,[63] that would bring no benefit to the spectator other than the actual spectacle, and we would merely be astonished. If, however, someone suffering from a serious and terminal illness recovers immediately when this is commanded, the charity of the person working the cure adds to the wonder at the cure.

This is what happened in those days when, as was required, God showed himself to the human race as a real human being. The sick were cured; lepers were cleansed; the lame were made to walk; sight was restored to the blind and hearing to the deaf.[64] The people of those times saw water changed into wine, five thousand people fed to fullness with five loaves, the seas crossed on foot, the dead restored to life.[65] Some of these things were more obviously for the good of the body, some were in more hidden fashion signs for the mind, but all were evidence to us of greatness. In this way the divine authority turned the straying souls of mortal men and women of those times towards itself.

Why, you say, do these things not happen now? Because they would not have any effect unless they caused wonder, and, if they were common occurrences, they would not cause wonder.[66] Think of the alternation of day and night and the undeviating pattern of the heavenly bodies, the four seasons of the year, the fall and return of the leaves of the trees, the infinite power of seeds, the beauty of light and colors and sounds and smells, and the variety of tastes. Imagine being able to talk to someone who saw and experienced these things for the first time. That person would be astonished and overwhelmed by the miracles. We, on the other hand, think little of all these things. It is certainly not because of any ease in understanding them, as nothing surely is more obscure than their explanation, but because it is a continual experience. These things were done, therefore, at the

---

63. Augustine may have been thinking of Medea in flight, on whom he wrote declamations during his study of rhetoric (see *Confessions* III, 6, 11), or of Daedalus and Icarus (see *Soliloquies* II, 20; *Order* II, 37).
64. See Mt 11:5; 15:31.
65. See Jn 2:1-11; Mt 14:13-23; Mt 14:22-33; Mt 9:18-26; Lk 7:11-17; Jn 11:1-46.
66. See *Revisions* I, 14, 5: "By this I meant to say that nowadays there are no longer so many and such great miracles, but not that there are no miracles anymore."

appropriate time, so that with the conversion and spread of so many believers authority would, because of them, become a beneficial influence on established morality.

17, 35. Any established morality holds such great power over people's minds that we are better able to condemn and detest any perversions in them, which happen because of the almost complete domination of sensuality, than to abandon them or change them. Do you think it matters little for humanity that so few scholars argue that nothing composed of earth or fire, in short nothing that the bodily senses can touch, should be worshiped as God, since God can only be apprehended by the intellect, yet the uneducated masses of men and women of many nations both believe this and preach it? Do you think it matters little that abstinence even from the tiniest morsel of bread and water, and not just fasting on single days but even fasting sustained over several successive days, is aspired to, and chastity even to the point of rejecting marriage and children, and endurance even to the point of ignoring crucifixion and fire, and generosity even to the point of distributing one's inheritance to the poor, in short, disdain for this world even to the point of desiring death? Few do these things, and even fewer do them well and wisely, but people everywhere approve of them, people everywhere praise them, people everywhere applaud them; in a word, people everywhere hold them in highest esteem. People blame their own frailty because they cannot do these things, but they do not do so without raising their minds towards God or without some spark of virtue.

This has been brought about by divine providence through the utterances of the prophets, through the humanity and teaching of Christ, through the journeys of the apostles, through the derision, crosses, blood and death of the martyrs, through the exemplary lives of the saints, and in all cases, as appropriate for the time, through miracles befitting such great deeds and virtues. When, therefore, we see such great help from God, so productive and so beneficial, shall we hesitate to hide in the bosom of his Church? From the apostolic throne,[67] through the chain of succession of the bishops, it occupies the pinnacle of authority, acknowledged by the whole human race. In vain do the heretics howl around her, condemned variously by the judgment of the ordinary people themselves, by the weight of authority of the councils, by the grandeur of miracles.

To refuse to acknowledge her primacy is assuredly either the height of sacrilege or the height of headstrong arrogance. If souls have no secure path to wisdom and salvation unless faith prepares the ground for understanding, is it anything but ingratitude for God's help and assistance if one chooses to resist such a strongly supported authority? If any subject, however lowly and easy to understand, requires a teacher or tutor, could there be anything more proud and reckless than to

---

67. See *Answer to the Letter of Mani Known as "The Foundation"* 4.

refuse to learn about the books of the divine mysteries from their interpreters and then to dare to condemn them without knowing anything about them?

18, 36. For these reasons, if either our reasoning or our pleading has any effect on you, and if, as I believe you do, you have any real concern for yourself, it is my wish that you will listen to me and commit yourself to the good teachings of Catholic Christianity, doing so with devout faith, lively hope and simple love, and that you will not cease to pray to God himself. It is only through his goodness that we were created, and only through his justice that we suffer punishment, and only through his mercy that we are set free. Then you will not lack either the guidance and commentary of great scholars who are also truly Christian, or the books, or the calm reflection itself, by means of which you will easily find what you are looking for.

Abandon completely those loquacious wretches—could I call them anything kinder? While they search too hard for the origin of evil,[68] they find nothing except evil. They often arouse their listeners to investigate this question, but, once aroused, what they teach them is such that it would even be better for them to sleep forever than to be awake like that. They change them from drowsy to delirious,[69] and between the two maladies, although both are usually fatal, there is the difference that the drowsy die without causing trouble to others, whereas the delirious are a danger to many healthy people, and especially to those trying to help them. God is not the author of evil, and he never regrets creating anything, and he does not become unsettled by any storm of mental tumult, and his kingdom is not some portion of the world, and he does not approve of any crime or atrocity, and he never lies. These and similar assertions influenced us, when they brandished them at us with great invective, claiming they were the teachings of the Old Testament, though that is entirely untrue.[70] I admit they were right to condemn those things. So what did I learn? What do you think? Only that when those assertions are condemned the Catholic Church is not condemned. So I retain the truth that I learned when I was with them, but I repudiate the false opinions I held.

The Catholic Church, however, has taught me many other things, to which these people with their feeble bodies[71] and gross minds cannot aspire: that God is not a material being and no part of him can be perceived by the eyes of the body, that nothing of his substance and nature is in any way corruptible or changeable or

---

68. *Malum*, used here, signifies both physical evil and moral wickedness.
69. This is possibly an allusion to the attacks on the name of Mani made in the Greek-speaking world. A play on words was often made between Manes, Mani's name in Greek, and *maneis*, i.e., "furious, raging, insane." See S. N. C. Lieu, "Some Themes in Later Roman Anti-manichean Polemics, 1," Bulletin of the John Rylands Library of Manchester 68 (1985-86) 440-441.
70. See *The Catholic Way of Life and the Manichean Way of Life* I, 10, 16.
71. "Feeble" because of the asceticism of the elect.

composite or created. If you agree with me about this—and God must not be thought of in any other way—all their machinations are overturned. As for that other matter, however, how it is that God did not generate or create evil, and also that there does not exist and there never has existed any nature or substance that God did not generate or create, and yet he delivers us from evil: that is established by such compelling arguments that there cannot be any doubt about it, especially for you and people like you. Along with a good intellect, however, there must be a devout attitude and a certain calmness of mind, without which it is not possible to understand anything at all about such profound matters. We are not dealing here with some story about smoke and a Persian myth[72] of some kind, where it is enough to give ear with a quite childlike mind rather than one of any subtlety. Truth is far, far different from this and is not as the Manicheans so foolishly perceive it.

As, however, our present discussion has lasted much longer than I thought it would, let us conclude the book here. I should like you to note that in it I have not yet begun to refute the Manicheans and have not yet started on that trivia, nor have I expanded on anything of substance about the actual Catholic teaching. I only wanted to weed out from you, if I could, the false opinions about Christian truths that were instilled in us through malice or ignorance and to raise your mind to learn certain great truths about God. That is why this volume is as it is. Now that your mind has been made more receptive, I shall perhaps move along more rapidly regarding other matters. Amen.[73]

---

72. Mani was of Persian origin; see *Answer to Faustus, a Manichean* XXIV, 4; *Answer to Secundinus* 2.
73. On this concluding section see *Revisions* I, 14, 6.

Faith and the Creed

Translation by Michael G. Campbell, O.S.A.

Notes by Michael Fiedrowicz

Introduction

1. Genesis

On October 8, 393, all the bishops of the Province of Africa gathered in Hippo Regius for a general synod (*concilium Hipponense*).[1] The assembly was not called simply to make disciplinary decisions in the form of canons. There were also basic pastoral questions to be raised. The bishops may have intended education in the faith to be the subject of their reflections.[2]

Augustine, who had been ordained a priest only two years earlier (391), was asked to read the bishops a paper (*disputatio*) on the Catholic faith. Looking back, he writes in his *Revisions*: "On the occasion of a general synod held by all the bishops of the Province of Africa, I was given the task, though I was then still a simple priest, of discoursing in their presence on faith and the confession of faith. At the urgent request of several of those close to me, I turned this address into a book."[3] The resultant work, *Faith and the Creed*, still shows some traces of the oral style,[4] but its form was revised and its content expanded for publication.

That a young priest should have been commissioned to speak on faith not only in the presence of bishops but directly to the bishops themselves was an exceptional occurrence in the history of the early Church. Not the least reason for assigning Augustine in particular was that his bishop, Valerius, had ordained this young priest primarily in order that he might take over the ministry of preaching in place of the bishop himself. As Possidius observed a half-century later in his biography of Augustine,[5] this action of the bishop caused a great sensation because it was so unusual; on the other hand, it caused many other bishops to follow Valerius' example and give priests the authority to preach, which had hitherto been an episcopal privilege.

This new direction taken in the area of preaching undoubtedly originated at the Council of Hippo. Augustine's address to the bishops was meant to prove that, although he was not a bishop, he was nonetheless worthy of belonging among the "spiritually-minded men [see 1 Cor 2:15], who have been found worthy not only to receive and believe the Catholic faith embodied in these few

---

1. See G. Bardy, "Conciles d'Hippone au temps de Saint Augustin," *Augustiniana* 5 (1955) 441-58.
2. Thus G. Madec, *La Patrie et la Voie. Le Christ dans la vie et la pensée de Saint Augustin* (Paris 1989) 189.
3. *Revisions* I, 17.
4. See *Faith and the Creed* 3, 3; 4, 10; 9, 17-18.
5. *Life of Augustine* 5.

words but also, with the Lord's enlightenment, to understand and possess a knowledge of it."[6] By describing the functions of a bishop in these words and by his explanation of the creed, Augustine was able to show that he himself could do justice to that high office.

It was apparently by a decision of the bishops that Augustine used the creed as a means of speaking about the faith.[7] But he did not base his remarks on the Creed of Nicea, the solemn recitation of which opened the Council of Hippo,[8] but rather on the confession of faith as Christians knew it from their baptism. But since he does not give verbatim the text of this creed, only with difficulty can we infer its concrete form. It is very likely that Augustine followed the Old Roman form (*Vetus Romanum*).[9] In any case, the young priest of Hippo reveals his pastoral concern when he chooses the baptismal faith of the Church as the basis for his theological reflection. Augustine regarded the creed as a comprehensive expression of the faith.[10]

2. Intention

The explanation of the creed was usually given as part of catechetical instruction. Well-known examples are the prebaptismal catecheses of Cyril of Jerusalem, the catechetical homilies of Theodore of Mopsuestia, the *Explanation of the Creed* of Ambrose, and the *Commentary on the Apostles' Creed* of Rufinus. Augustine, too, explained the creed to catechumens in a number of sermons in connection with the *traditio symboli* or the *redditio symboli* during Lent or immediately before Easter.[11]

The explanation in *Faith and the Creed*, however, has a different character. Augustine's address to the bishops is neither a homily nor a catechesis but a doctrinal lecture with its own specific terminology, theological analyses, speculative formulations, proofs, and abundant citations from scripture. His purpose is to convey a deeper understanding of the faith (*intellectus fidei*).[12] In the process he is able to introduce the results of his earlier philosophical reflections.

---

6. *Faith and the Creed* 1, 1.
7. Revisions I, 17 suggests this interpretation. F. Kattenbusch, however, in his *Das apostolische Symbol* II (Leipzig 1900; Hildesheim 1972) 407-408, sees the choice of the creed as Augustine's own.
8. See *Concilia Africae A. 354-A. 525* (CCL 149, 30).
9. See E. P. Meijering, *St. Augustine, De fide et symbolo. Introduction, Translation, Commentary* (Amsterdam 1987) 8-12.
10. See Kattenbusch, *Das apostolische Symbol* II, 406-407.
11. See *Sermon on the Creed to Catechumens*; Sermons 212-215. On the question of authenticity see P.-P. Verbraken, *Études critiques sur les sermons authentiques de saint Augustin* (Steenbrugge 1976) 104-105.
12. See *Faith and the Creed* 1, 1; 10, 25.

Augustine apparently wanted to show the bishops, by way of an example, how very suited the creed was not only for giving a short formulation of the faith to beginners and those not yet well established in their faith through the careful study of scripture but also and above all for giving, by means of judicious exegesis, a comprehensive and reliable orientation in all matters of faith to those making progress. In addition, Augustine was able to show that the creed not only addressed the intellect but also nourished spirituality.

3. Method and Structure

The explanation follows the creed article by article. More or less extensive commentaries serve, on the one hand, for theological exploration of the central dogmas and, on the other, for the refutation of various heresies, past and present, that tried to falsify these truths of faith.

Thus, against the Manicheans, Augustine defends the omnipotence of God;[13] against the Arians, the consubstantiality, undiminished by the incarnation, of the Logos and the Father;[14] against Apollinarism, Docetism, and Manicheanism the true human nature of Christ.[15] The defense of the bodily resurrection is directed, once again, against the depreciation of the human body in Manichean dualism.[16]

The structure of the work is as follows:[17]

Introduction: Purpose of the treatise (1, 1)

Body of the work:
    I. The omnipotence of the creator (2, 2-3, 3)
    II. The divine Logos (3, 4-4, 7)
    III. The incarnation of Christ, who is true God and true man (4, 8-8, 15)
    IV. The mystery of the Trinity (9, 16-20)
    V. The Church and the forgiveness of sins (9, 21-10, 22)
    VI. The resurrection of the flesh (10, 23-24)

Conclusion: A call to Christians to live in conformity with their faith (10, 25)

---

13. Ibid. 2, 2-3.
14. Ibid. 3, 3-4, 7.
15. Ibid. 4, 8-8, 15.
16. Ibid. 10, 23-24.
17. See J. Rivière in Bibliothèque Augustinienne 9, 13-14.

4. Importance of the Work

The explanation of the creed shows that at this time the young Augustine did not yet possess the conceptual equipment that would allow him, in his later works, to explain the truths of the Christian faith in all their depth. His thinking is still heavily philosophical, as can be seen in his remarks on the divine Word, in his cautious judgment on the consequences of the fall, and in the strong emphasis placed on the moral significance of the incarnation.[18]

Missing, too, are the clearly defined positions taken by the later Augustine on the damage done to human nature by original sin, on the working of grace, and on the mystery of predestination.

The work remains, nonetheless, a valuable proof that from his earliest years in ecclesiastical office Augustine felt bound to the service of the Church's faith. Even at this stage of his life he was able to speak with such depth of the Church's confession of faith that its structured articles opened up perspectives in all directions. At the same time, moreover, his interpretive skill made evident the cohesion of the whole and so kept the variety of the thoughts suggested from becoming a series of scattered themes. As a result, even in this early work of the young theologian of Hippo the Church's creed became once again a sure guide for every believer:[19] "This is the faith, consisting of a few short sentences and expressed in a creedal form to be firmly professed, which is given to those newly converted to the Christian faith. These brief articles have become well known to believers who, by putting their faith in them, become subject to God. By being subject to God they can live righteous lives and through such lives purify their hearts. Then, having purified their hearts, they may succeed in understanding what they believe."[20]

---

18. See *Faith and the Creed* 2, 2-3; 10, 23; 4, 6; 5, 11.
19. See Kattenbusch, *Das apostolische Symbol* II, 408.
20. *Faith and the Creed* 10, 25.

Faith and the Creed

An Explanation of the Creed

1, 1. In view of the scriptural text, that *the just person lives by faith* (Hb 2:4; Rom 1:17; Gal 3:11; Heb 10:38), which finds the strongest possible support in the teaching of the apostles, this faith makes demands both on our tongues and on our hearts. For, in the words of the apostle, *it is by believing with the heart that you are justified, and by making the declaration with your lips that you are saved* (Rom 10:10). We are, therefore, obliged to keep in mind both justification and salvation, since it will be impossible for us to reign in eternal justice and be saved from this corrupt age unless we endeavor to gain our neighbor's salvation by professing with our lips the faith that we carry in our hearts. This faith must also be guarded with devotion and care lest it be sullied within us in any way by the deceitful cleverness of heretics. This is the Catholic faith known as the creed and committed to memory by believers, a vast subject contained in such few words.[1] It is for the benefit of beginners and those still on milk food;[2] reborn in Christ, they have yet to be strengthened by a detailed spiritual study and knowledge of the divine scriptures and so are presented with the essentials of faith in a few sentences. However, for those who have advanced further and who, imbued with true humility and genuine charity, aspire to the divine teaching, the creed would of necessity have to be explained in much greater detail.

No small number of heretics have attempted to insinuate their poisonous doctrines into those brief sentences which constitute the creed. But the divine mercy has resisted and continues to resist such people through the influence of spiritually-minded men, who have been found worthy not only to receive and believe the Catholic faith embodied in these few words but also, with the Lord's enlightenment, to understand and possess a knowledge of it. For scripture says, *Unless you believe, you will not understand* (Is 7:9). Yet an exposition of the faith can help protect the creed—not, however, that it should be entrusted to those who are receiving the grace of God as something that is to be enjoined upon them and recited back.[3] Its purpose is to safeguard with full Catholic

---

1. See *Enchiridion* 2, 7.
2. See 1 Cor 3:2.
3. This is an allusion to the pre-baptismal ceremonies of the *traditio* and *redditio symboli*—the passing on of the creed to the catechumens and their reciting it back.

authority the truths expressed in the creed and to provide a more powerful defense against the heretics' onslaughts.[4]

God's Creation

2, 2. Some people have indeed tried to demonstrate that God the Father is not all-powerful: not that they dared to say as much, but it has been shown beyond doubt from their teachings that this is what they think and believe.[5] For when they postulate the existence of a nature which almighty God did not create and from which he constructed this world, a world which they admit is beautifully ordered, they are in this way denying the omnipotence of God. They consequently believe that he was unable to create the world unless he first had recourse to this other nature already in existence, and which he himself did not create. Accustomed in their worldly fashion to observing carpenters and house-builders and other kinds of workers who are unable to complete their work unless the materials are already at hand, they likewise infer that the creator of the world cannot be omnipotent, if it is beyond his power to create the world without the assistance of some kind of material nature which he himself did not make.

If they admit that almighty God is the creator of the world, they must also concede that, whatever he made, he necessarily did so from nothing. For no being can exist unless he made it, because he is omnipotent. And even though he made a thing from something else, like humankind from clay, it was not from some material which he himself had not made, since clay comes from the earth, and he created the earth from nothing. Also, if he made heaven itself and the earth, that is, the world and everything in it, out of some antecedent matter, as it is written, *You made the world from unseen matter* (Wis 11:18), or if he created them from matter that was formless, as some manuscripts hold, yet in no way are we to believe that the material of which we are speaking could by itself be coeternal and coeval with God.[6] We are referring here to the material of which the world was made, be it formless, unseen, or whatever else might constitute the

---

4. The role of theology as sketched out here is limited to the protection and defense of the faith. More comprehensive descriptions of the task of theology are given in *Enchiridion* 1, 4; *The Trinity* XIV, 1, 3 (it "breeds, feeds, defends, and strengthens the saving faith which leads to true happiness" [trans. E. Hill]).

5. This is an allusion to the Manicheans, whose dualism led to this conception of God.

6. The Manicheans understood Wis 11:18 as confirming their conception of a pre-existing eternal matter. Greek philosophy, too, held that matter was eternal. In contrast, Augustine insists that unformed matter is created by God; see *The Literal Meaning of Genesis* I, 14, 28ff. Unformed matter is the principle that receives a form, so that out of the combination creatures arise. See F. van Fleteren, "Matter," in A. D. Fitzgerald, ed., *Augustine through the Ages: An Encyclopedia* (Grand Rapids 1999) 547-549, esp. 548. On Wis 11:18 see A.-M. La Bonnardière, *Biblia Augustiniana. Le livre de Sagesse* (Paris: Études Augustiniennes, 1970) 87-90, 295.

mode of its existence. The mode of being that it possesses, one which enables it to receive the forms of different things, it owes to almighty God alone, by whose gracious disposition it not only has a form but becomes capable of receiving other forms as well. The difference between something already endowed with form and something that possesses form only potentially consists in this: what has been created already has form, while what is capable of receiving form has yet to receive it. The one who confers forms on things also confers the potential to receive form, because from him and in him is to be found that unchanging species of incomparable beauty. He is, therefore, one, conferring on each created entity not only the beauty it possesses but even the capacity to become beautiful. It is with absolute justification, then, that we believe God made everything out of nothing, for even if the world was created from some matter previously existing, that same material was itself created from nothing. Thus by the well-ordered design of God the original capacity for receiving forms[7] came into being, and what was subsequently destined to receive forms would do so. We have given this explanation lest anyone think that the teachings of the divine scriptures contradict one another, for they state both that God made everything from nothing and that the world was made from formless matter.

The Word

3. Since we profess our faith in God the Father almighty, we are therefore bound to acknowledge that there is no created thing that does not owe its existence to his almighty power. And because he created everything through the Word,[8] he alone was able to generate that Word, through whom all things were made and through whom he made all things. This particular Word is also described as *truth* (Jn 14:6) and *the power and wisdom of God* (1 Cor 1:24) and by many other terms and is presented for our belief as Jesus Christ the Lord, our redeemer and ruler, the Son of God.

3, 3. We also believe in Jesus Christ, the only-begotten Son of God the Father, that is, his only Son, our Lord. We must not equate this Word with our own words, which proceed from our voice and mouth, reverberate through the air, and remain only as long as they are heard. But that Word remains, beyond change. What was predicated of wisdom is applicable to the Word: *Herself unchanging, she renews all things* (Wis 7:27). He is called the Word of the Father, because through him the Father makes himself known. It is our intention,

---

7. According to the theory of *rationes seminales*, at the beginning of the world God inserted into the material world seminal energies that in the course of time would develop and unfold in a natural manner, as soon as conditions were favorable. See R. Williams, "Creation," in Fitzgerald 251-254, esp. 252.

8. See *Miscellany of Eighty-three Questions* 63.

when we use words to speak the truth, to reveal what is in our mind to the one who is listening to us and to disclose to that other person, through signs of this type, the secrets we carry within us. We can say precisely the same of that wisdom which God the Father has begotten, because it is through this wisdom that the Father, totally hidden, makes himself known to souls worthy of him, which is, most fittingly, called his Word.

The Expression of the Word

4. A vast gulf exists, however, between our mind and our word—those words we speak to reveal that same mind. In our case, we do not beget words which resound, rather we manufacture them. And the underlying material for making them is our body. A considerable difference indeed exists between the mind and the body. But when God begets the Word, he begets what he himself is; he begets it neither from nothing nor from any previously created matter, but he begets from himself what he himself is. We even attempt to do this ourselves whenever we speak, if we carefully consider the intention of our will, not when we are lying but when we speak the truth. For what else do we aim at if not to transfer our own mind to the mind of the person who is listening to us, so that it may be known and scrutinized? As a result, we remain within ourselves and do not go out of ourselves, yet the sign we give is such as to enable our communication to reach the other person, so that, as far as our intellectual faculty allows, we could almost say our mind was giving birth to a second mind, by means of which it makes itself known.

We endeavor to accomplish this both in words and by the very sound of our voice, through facial expression and bodily gestures, and our intention in deploying these various movements is to reveal what lies within us, for to bring forth such an entity exceeds our capabilities. This is precisely why we cannot fully know the mind of someone speaking, and hence the scope for telling lies. But God the Father, who both wills and can reveal himself most truly to souls who would know him, begot the Word in order to reveal himself, a Word which is what he himself, the begetter, is. It is also described as his power and wisdom,[9] for through the Word he is at work, governing all things. We further read: *It reaches powerfully from one end of the earth to the other, ordering all things harmoniously* (Wis 8:1).

---

9. See 1 Cor 1:24.

Through Him All Things Were Made

4, 5. The only-begotten Son of God, therefore, was not created by the Father, for, as the evangelist says, *All things were made through him* (Jn 1:3); nor was he begotten in time, because the God of wisdom has his eternal wisdom at his side eternally; nor is he inferior to the Father, that is, in any way less than him,[10] since the apostle declares, *Although he was in the form of God, he did not consider equality with God a thing to be grasped* (Phil 2:6). This means that those who claim that the Son is the same as the Father[11] find themselves outside the Catholic faith, for this Word could not be with God unless he were with God the Father, and he who is alone is equal to no one. Those people who assert that the Son is created, although different from the rest of creation,[12] also cut themselves off from the Catholic faith, for, however exalted a created status they may ascribe to him, if he is a creature, the fact remains that he has been fashioned and made. To fashion and to create mean one and the same thing, although sometimes in Latin usage "to fashion" takes the place of "to create," which means to beget. But the Greek language makes a distinction: what they term κτίσμα or κτίσις we simply refer to as a "creature" and, whenever we want to express ourselves without ambiguity, we do not use the word "create" but "fashion." Therefore if the Son is a creature, however exalted he may be, the fact remains that he has been made. Yet we profess our faith in him, through whom all things were made;[13] we do not profess faith in him, through whom all other things were made.[14] We cannot understand "all things" in this context to have any other meaning, except that they have been made.

God from God, Light from Light

6. However, because *the Word became flesh and lived among us* (Jn 1:14), that very same wisdom, which was begotten by God, condescended to take up a created dwelling place among humans as well. A text referring to this says, *The Lord created me in the beginning of his ways* (Prv 8:22). The beginning of his ways is the head of the Church, Christ, who became a man,[15] and who has been

---

10. See *Miscellany of Eighty-three Questions* 23; *Enchiridion* 10, 35.
11. Advocates of modalist monarchianism, such as Noetus and Sabellius (both of whom flourished in the early third century), regarded Father, Son and Holy Spirit as simply varied manifestations (*modi*) of one and the same God.
12. Augustine is referring here to the Arians.
13. See Jn 1:3.
14. In the Arian view, the Word, after having been created by God, became the demiurge or creator of the remaining creatures. Augustine holds that this position contradicts the Christian faith, according to which the uncreated Word is the source of all that is created.
15. Before the Nestorian controversy (428-431), this manner of speaking was current as a description of the incarnation. By *homo* ("man") Augustine means the concrete and unique human nature to which the Word united himself.

given to us as a model of behavior,[16] an infallible way on which we can travel to God. There can be no other way for us to return on except the way of humility, because pride was our downfall, exemplified in what was said to the first of our creation: *Taste the fruit, and you will become like gods* (Gen 3:5). Our redeemer, therefore, deigned to give us in himself this example of humility, the way by which we must return, *he who did not consider equality with God a thing to be grasped, but emptied himself to take the form of a slave* (Phil 2:6-7) and was created a man at the beginning of his ways, *the Word through whom all things were made* (Jn 1:3). Insofar as he is the only-begotten Son he has no brothers, but according to his status as the firstborn he graciously called everyone his brothers,[17] those who were to follow and, because of his firstborn status, are reborn into the grace of God through their adoption as sons,[18] as the teaching of the apostles informs us.

As a natural Son, he was born the only-begotten Son from the substance of the Father, sharing the same life as the Father, God from God, light from light. We cannot claim to be light by nature, but we are illumined from that light so that we can shine in wisdom. The evangelist says, *He was the true light which enlightens everyone who comes into this world* (Jn 1:9). We also include, therefore, together with those eternal realities of the faith, our Lord's ministry in time, a ministry which he graciously undertook and accomplished for our salvation. For in his status as the only-begotten Son of God we cannot say of him that he was and he will be but only that he is. The reason for this is that what has been no longer exists, and what will be has yet to come into existence. He therefore remains unchanging, neither bound to time nor subject to its vicissitudes. I have no doubt that herein lies the source of the divine name which he[19] revealed to his servant Moses. For when he asked, if those to whom he was to go despised him, who he would say sent him, he gave him this answer: *I am who I am*. Then he added: *This is what you are to say to the children of Israel, He who is has sent me to you.* (Ex 3:14)

7. Consequently, I trust it will be obvious to those who are spiritually minded[20] that no nature can possibly exist which is contrary to God.[21] For if the Word truly exists and is properly said to be from God, such a Word which indeed

---

16. Under the influence of his philosophical education, Augustine in his early writings emphasized chiefly the role of Christ as an exemplar; see *True Religion* 16, 32.
17. See Lk 8:21.
18. See Heb 2:11.
19. In early Christian theology a traditional exegesis attributed the theophanies of the Old Testament to the Word. Augustine regarded these theophanies as prefigurations of the incarnation.
20. On this term see R. J. Teske, "Spirituals and Spiritual Interpretation in St. Augustine," *Augustinian Studies* 15 (1984) 65-81.
21. Since God is Being itself, no being, but only non-being, can be set over against him.

exists and remains unchanging, God can in no way have a contrary. For whatever has undergone change was something other than it presently is and will be different from what it now is. If we were asked what the opposite of black was, we would reply white, and we would say that cold is the opposite of warm, slow the opposite of speedy, and so on. But when we are asked what the opposite of what exists is, we rightly respond: what does not exist.

Born of the Virgin Mary

8. But, as I have already said,[22] through a dispensation which took place in time, thanks to the goodness of God, the unchanging wisdom of God assumed our changeable nature so as to make possible our salvation and redemption. We give our assent of faith to those deeds which, for our salvation, were accomplished in time, and we profess our belief in him, the God of God, who was born of the virgin Mary through the Holy Spirit. For it was by God's gift, by the Holy Spirit, I mean, that such unbounded humility was granted to us by so great a God, in that he should condescend to assume man in his entirety in the womb of the virgin. He took up a dwelling-place in his mother's virginal body, and, when he came forth, her virginity remained intact.[23] This temporal order of salvation has been assailed by heretics on numerous occasions. Yet whoever holds fast to the Catholic faith, believing that the Word assumed man in his entirety, that is, body, soul, and spirit, possesses an adequate defense against such people.

However, when we predicate such an assumption on the part of the Word for our salvation, we must beware of thinking that, if a certain part of our nature is not included in that assumption, then that part is not saved.[24] It is commonly agreed that human beings, with the exception of their physical shape, which varies according to the different kinds of living things, only differ from beasts through the power of reason, also called the mind. How then can that faith be considered sound which maintains that what the wisdom of God assumed from us is what we have in common with the beasts but asserts that he did not assume that faculty which shines with the light of wisdom and is the distinguishing mark of human beings?[25]

---

22. See section 6.
23. See section 11.
24. In the background of the thought here is the axiom used in the christological controversies of the fourth century: *Quod non est assumptum non est sanatum* ("What is not assumed is not healed").
25. Apollinarianism denied the existence of the human soul in Christ; see *Miscellany of Eighty-three Questions* 80.

An Earthly Mother

9. Those who deny that our Lord Jesus Christ had an earthly mother, Mary, are also worthy of contempt.[26] For that divine saving economy conferred honor on both sexes, masculine and feminine, and demonstrated that, by being clothed in the nature of a man through his birth from a woman, God's love extends not only to what he assumed but also to the one through whom he assumed it. I refer to his manifestation as a man, through his birth from a woman. Nor should these words of Christ compel us to deny that he had a mother: *Woman, what is that to you and to me? My hour has not yet come.* (Jn 2:4) They should, rather, teach us to understand that he did not have a mother in his divine nature, a nature he was about to demonstrate by turning water into wine. As for his crucifixion, he was crucified in his humanity; and that was the hour which had not yet come, when he remarked, *What is that to you and to me? My hour has not yet come*—that is, the hour when I will acknowledge you.

It was at that moment, when he was crucified as a man, that he acknowledged his human mother and, with immense compassion, entrusted her to the care of the beloved disciple.[27] Moreover, we should not be unduly disturbed by his response, on being told of the arrival of his mother and brothers: *Who is my mother, and who are my brothers?* (Mt 12:48) and so on. Rather, our ministry, by which we proclaim the word of God to our brethren, should teach us that when parents become an obstacle we ought not to take notice of them. If, further, a person were to persist in thinking that Christ did not have an earthly mother because he said, *Who is my mother?* then by the same token an apostle must also be compelled to deny that we have earthly fathers, for the Lord gave his disciples this command: *Call no one on earth your father; for you have only one Father, who is in heaven* (Mt 23:9).

10. We must not allow the thought of a female womb to undermine our faith, leading us to recoil from such a birth on the part of our Lord, one which the foul-minded consider unclean,[28] for the apostle speaks with absolute truth when he says, *God's folly is wiser than human wisdom* (1 Cor 1:25) and, *To the clean, all things are clean* (Ti 1:15).The people who make such an assertion should consider the rays of the sun, which they indeed do not praise as part of God's

---

26. The Docetists regarded not only the passion of Jesus but also his birth as purely an appearance, because in their dualistic conception of things matter was evil and the body was to be scorned. The Manicheans shared that view, holding that the birth of Jesus from a woman was something inappropriate for God; see *Answer to Faustus, a Manichean* III, 6; XXIII, 10; *The Trinity* XII, 5. Other heretics maintained that Mary gave birth only to the man Jesus or only to his body but not to the Son of God.
27. See Jn 19:26-27.
28. In the ancient and Jewish view, the female body and the newborn child were thought to have been rendered unclean by the process of birth.

creation but worship as a god.[29] These rays penetrate even to the very stench of sewers and other such repulsive places, acting according to their nature without in any way suffering contamination as a result,[30] because by its nature visible light is closer to what is foul and what can be seen. How much less, therefore, could the Word of God, being neither corporeal nor visible, be contaminated through the body of a woman, when he assumed human flesh with soul and spirit, the means by which the majesty of the Word indwells, and in a manner hidden from the frailty of a human body! And so it becomes abundantly clear that the Word of God could not possibly suffer corruption through a human body, for not even the human soul itself is tainted by its union with the body. Whenever the soul rules and animates the body it does not become tainted from that fact, but only when it begins to lust after transitory things. If people who hold such opinions want to prevent their soul from being corrupted, they should rather recoil in horror from lies and profanations of this kind.

Humility in Dying

5, 11. But the degree of humility displayed by our Lord in his birth for us was small; he went even further when he condescended to die for human beings. For *he humbled himself, becoming obedient even to death, death on a cross* (Phil 2:8), lest any of us, for whom death held no terrors, might shudder at a manner of death which people generally consider most shameful.[31] Therefore, we believe in him, who was crucified under Pontius Pilate and was buried, for it was necessary to add the judge's name to indicate the period at which it took place. But when we profess our faith in his burial, we are reminded of a tomb that was new because it would witness to his resurrection to newness of life, as the womb of the virgin witnessed to his birth. For just as no one else was buried in that tomb,[32] either before or after, so in like manner no other mortal was ever conceived in the virgin's womb, either before or afterwards.[33]

---

29. This is an allusion to the Manichean cult of the sun. The sun was thought of as a "ship" which carried the elements of light that were mingled with matter back to their place of origin; see *Heresies* 46, 6-7.
30. This is a classical comparison that goes back probably to Diogenes the Cynic; see Diogenes Laertius, *The Lives and Opinions of the Philosophers* VI, 63. For its use in the context of the birth of Jesus see Origen, *Against Celsus* VI, 73; Athanasius, *The Incarnation of the Word* 17.
31. This point is discussed in greater detail in *Miscellany of Eighty-three Questions* 25.
32. See Jn 19:4.
33. When taken together with section 8, this text is a witness to belief in the complete virginity of Mary before, during and after giving birth (*ante partum, in partu,* and *post partum*).

Rose from the Dead and Ascended into Heaven

12. We believe that on the third day he rose from the dead, to be followed by many brothers, whom he called to become adopted sons of God,[34] making them worthy to be sharers with him and his co-heirs.

6, 13. We believe he ascended into heaven, an abode of blessedness that he also promised to us when he said, *They will be like the angels in heaven* (Mt 22:30), in the city which is the mother of us all, the eternal Jerusalem in heaven.[35] Our belief that a body of clay was taken up to heaven is a cause of scandal to some people, be they irreligious gentiles or heretics.[36] The gentiles, for their part, are usually keen to deploy philosophical arguments against us, asserting that it is impossible for anything earthly to be found in heaven. This is because they are unacquainted with our scriptures and the truth of the remark: *What is sown is a natural body, and what is raised is a spiritual body* (1 Cor 15:44). This does not imply that the body is changed into a spirit and becomes such, because our present body, which is described as natural, does not undergo transformation and become a soul. What is meant is a spiritual body, which because of its subjection to the spirit makes it compatible with its heavenly abode, changed and transformed from all frailty and earthly weakness to the purity and steadfastness of heaven.[37] This is the transformation of which the same apostle speaks: *We shall all rise, but we shall not all be changed* (1 Cor 15:51). He teaches that this will be a transformation not into something worse but into something better when he states: *And we shall be changed.* But any attempt to discover the place and position in heaven of the Lord's body represents both the height of curiosity and an exercise in folly; the only thing we are required to believe is that it is in heaven. It is not given to our human frailty to fathom the secrets of heaven, but it is in keeping with our faith, when reflecting on the dignity of the Lord's body, to think thoughts that are both sublime and free from error.

7, 14. We believe, also, that he is seated at the right hand of the Father. We should not take this to mean that some kind of human form is to be ascribed to God the Father,[38] so that a right and left side are envisaged in the minds of those

---

34. See Eph 1:5.
35. See Gal 4:26.
36. On pagans like Porphyry see *The City of God* XIII, 18; XXII, 4; *Sermon* 242, 3, 5. On the subject see J. Pépin, *Théologie cosmique et théologie chrétienne* (Paris 1964) 449-451. On the Manicheans see *The Christian Combat* 25, 27.
37. See section 23.
38. Augustine understood from the preaching of Ambrose that Gn 1:26 (*Let us make man according to our image*) by no means permitted the conclusion that God himself had a human form; see *Confessions* VI, 3, 4. It was precisely the difference between a spiritual and an anthropomorphic image of God that separated those who were "spiritual" and those who were "carnal" in the Church; see ibid. VI, 11, 18; *The Catholic Way of Life* I, 10, 17; *Answer to the Letter of Mani Known as "The Foundation"* 23, 25. See Teske, "Spirituals and Spiritual Interpretations in St. Augustine" 65-81, esp. 70-73.

who think about him. And when he is said to be seated at the right hand of the Father we are not to imagine this to mean a sedentary position, lest we incur the sacrilegious guilt of those whom the apostle excoriates, *who have exchanged the glory of the immortal God for the image of a mortal human being* (Rom 1:23). For a Christian to erect an image of this sort to God in a place of worship is forbidden; even more prohibited is the construction of one in our heart, which is the true dwelling place of God, provided it has been cleansed of this world's desires and fallacies. By "right hand," then, we are to understand a reference to the height of blessedness, where justice, peace, and joy are to be found, just as the goats are placed at the left hand,[39] which denotes a place of unhappiness, because of their evil and inhumane behavior. Consequently, when God is said to sit, what is meant is not the location of his members but his power to judge, a power which his divine person has never lacked, and one which confers their just deserts on those who deserve them. When the last judgment takes place, however, the undoubted glory of the only-begotten Son of God, judge of the living and the dead, is destined to be revealed with much greater clarity in the sight of the human race.

8, 15. We believe, too, that he will come from heaven to judge the living and the dead, at that time which he considers most appropriate. Whether the reference here is to the just and sinners or to those he will find on earth who have not yet died, they are described as the living, while the dead mentioned are those who will rise at his coming.[40] Not only may such a saving economy which took place in time not be compared with that divine generation which takes place in God but it also bears the character of past and future. For our Lord was once on earth, is now in heaven, and he will come again in glory as judge of the living and the dead. He will come in the same way as he ascended, as the Acts of the Apostles teaches.[41] And the Book of Revelation refers to that same temporal order in the text: *The One who is, who was, and who is to come, says these things* (Rv 1:8).

The Holy Spirit

9, 16. After the summary of our Lord's divine birth and of those deeds accomplished for our salvation, which are presented to us as articles of faith, our profession of faith, divine in origin, is rounded off and brought to completion by the Holy Spirit. The Holy Spirit is not to be regarded as inferior in nature to the Father and the Son but, as I will assert, is consubstantial and co-eternal with

---

39. See Mt 25:33.
40. See *Enchiridion* 14, 55.
41. See Acts 1:11.

them, because this Trinity is one God only. Not that the Father is to be under-stood as being identical with the Son and the Holy Spirit, but the Father remains the Father, the Son remains the Son, and the Holy Spirit remains the Holy Spirit, yet this Trinity is one God, as it is written: *Listen, Israel, the Lord your God is one God* (Dt 6:4). Should we be asked about each of them individually: Is the Father God? We would answer: The Father is God. Or: Is the Son God? We would give the same answer. And should the same question arise about the Holy Spirit, our reply must also be that the Holy Spirit too is God. Yet we must be very careful about how we understand the text addressed to human beings: *You are gods* (Ps 81:6). Those who have been created and formed by the Father, through the Son, by the gift of the Holy Spirit, are not gods by nature. The Trinity is explicitly referred to when the apostle says: *For everything comes from him, is through him, and is in him* (Rom 11:36).[42] Although, when we are questioned about the identity of any one of the three, we must respond that it is God, whether it be the Father, the Son, or the Holy Spirit, without, however, giving anyone the impression that we are worshiping three gods.

The Trinity

17. It should not surprise us that such statements are made about a nature that is ineffable, because something similar happens in the things we observe with our eyes and judge with our bodily senses. When we are asked about a fountain, we cannot say that it is a river; nor again can we say of a river that it is a fountain; nor can we call a drink, which comes from a fountain or a river, either a river or a fountain. Nevertheless, we use the name water when speaking of a trinity of this kind; and to the question as to what each is individually, we reply that it is water. For were I to ask if there was water in the fountain, the answer would be that there is water; and if I ask whether there is water in the river, the answer will be the same; and it would be no different in the case of the drink. Yet we do not speak of these as being three waters[43] but one. However, we must exercise great care lest anyone should imagine that the ineffable substance which constitutes the divine majesty resembles in any way that visible, tangible fountain, river, or drink. For in the case of these elements, the water which is now in the fountain flows into the river and does not remain within itself; and when it passes from the river or fountain and becomes a drink it no longer remains in the place where it is drunk. So it can happen, therefore, that the very same water which once pertains to the description of a fountain cannot belong to that of a river and then to a drink,

---

42. See section 19, where this text serves to distinguish the relations among the three persons of the Trinity.
43. For this analogy see Tertullian, *Against Praxeas* 8, 5-7; Marius Victorinus, *Hymn* 3; Marcellus of Ancyra, *Explanation of the Faith* 2.

although, where that other Trinity is concerned, it is not possible that the Father should at one time be the Son and at another the Holy Spirit.[44]

Take the case of the tree: the root remains the root only, and the trunk the trunk, and what are branches may not be called anything else but branches. For what is termed the root may not be called the trunk and the branches; nor does it happen by some process of transition that the wood, which presently constitutes the root, can now be found in the trunk and then in the branches, but it remains in the root only. The logic of the name requires that the root be wood, as well as the trunk and the branches, and yet we are not speaking of three woods but of only one. Even if these three differ sufficiently from one another so that it would not be unreasonable to speak of three woods, and if also because of their varying degrees of hardness they could possibly be described as three different woods, yet everyone will readily admit that, if we fill three cups from one fountain, we can only speak of three cups and not three waters, indeed of only a single water. Nonetheless, should you be asked about each of the cups, you would reply that there is water in each, despite no movement of water having taken place, as when we remarked about the flow from the fountain into the river. We cite these physical examples not because of their similarity to the divine nature but by reason of their visible unity, to enable us to understand how three objects can have, not only individually but even simultaneously, a single name. This is to prevent anyone from being amazed and believing it ridiculous that we speak of God the Father, God the Son, and God the Holy Spirit, as a Trinity not of three gods but of one and the same substance.[45]

18. Learned and spiritual men have discoursed extensively about the Father and the Son in numerous books.[46] Insofar as they were humanly capable, they endeavored to outline both how the Father was not the same as the Son, but that they were one, and also what was proper to the Father and what was proper to the Son. The Father is the begetter, the Son begotten; the Father is not from the Son, but rather the Son is from the Father; the Father is the origin of the Son, which is why he is also said to be the head of Christ (1 Cor 11:3), although Christ is also the origin,[47] but not of the Father; he is in truth his image,[48] but in no way dissimilar, and completely equal, without qualification. Such matters are treated in greater detail by these writers, whose intention is to provide an explanation of the whole Christian faith on a scale not as modest as ours. Consequently, inasmuch as he is the Son, he has received his being from the Father, whereas the

---

44. For a similar reserve toward this analogy see Gregory Nazianzen, *Oration* 31, 31.
45. The Latin word *substantia* is a synonym for *natura*, whereas the Greek equivalent, *hypostasis*, denotes the person.
46. Due to the Arian controversy the theology of the Trinity underwent an intense development in the fourth century.
47. See Jn 8:25.
48. See Col 1:15.

Father did not receive his being from the Son. And it was from the Father that he undertook to become a man, subject to change, in an act in time of unbounded mercy for our salvation, that is, a created being, destined to be transformed into something more perfect.[49] Scripture has many references to him, but they are expressed in such a way as to send those of evil disposition,[50] intent more on teaching than knowing, into the path of error, causing them to believe that he is neither equal to the Father nor of the same substance. Some examples are: *Because the Father is greater than I* (Jn 14:28); and, *The head of woman is man, the head of man is Christ, but the head of Christ is God* (1 Cor 11:3); and, *Then he himself will be made subject to the One who has subjected everything to him* (1 Cor 15:28); and again, *I am going to my God and your God* (Jn 20:17); and many other texts of this kind.

The reason behind these texts is not to show inequality of nature and substance on the part of the Son, lest the following texts be shown to be false: *The Father and I are one* (Jn 10:30); and, *Whoever sees me, also sees my Father* (Jn 14:9); and, *the Word was God*—for God was not made—*since all things were made through him* (Jn 1:1.3.7); and, *He did not consider equality with God a thing to be grasped* (Phil 2:6); and so on. These texts are found in scripture, partly because of the economy of the incarnation, of which it is said, *He emptied himself* (Phil 2:7)—not that the divine wisdom was changed, for it is altogether unchangeable, but because he wanted to reveal himself in such humble fashion to humankind. These truths, then, which the heretics distort, were put in writing partly because of this saving economy[51] and partly because of the fact that what the Son himself is he owes to the Father. Moreover, to the same Father he also owes his equality, whereas the Father is indebted to no one for what he is.

19. Those learned and eminent exponents of sacred scripture have not so far, in any extensive or detailed way, applied themselves to the subject of the Holy Spirit.[52] This would help us to understand what property is unique to him, what constitutes him as he is, so that we are able to state that he is neither the Father nor the Son but the Holy Spirit only. What they do postulate about him is that he is the gift of God, enabling us to believe that the gift God gives in no way ranks inferior to himself. However, they do insist that the Holy Spirit is not begotten, as they assert of the Son, from the Father, for Christ is the only-begotten Son, nor

---

49. This is probably an allusion to the restoration of human nature as a result of the glorification of Christ's assumed humanity.
50. The Arians are meant.
51. The Arians transferred to the Son of God the relative inferiority that resulted, they said, from his hypostatic union with the assumed human nature.
52. The controversy with the Pneumatomachians (as the deniers of the divinity of the Holy Spirit were called), which began in the mid-fourth century, became the stimulus to a deeper exploration of pneumatology. See, among Latin authors, Hilary, *The Trinity* I, 36; II, 4; XII, 55; Nicetas of Remesiana, *The Power of the Holy Spirit*; Ambrose, *The Holy Spirit*.

is he begotten from the Son, the grandson, as it were of the almighty Father, nor that he is indebted to no one for his existence. They maintain that the Holy Spirit owes his existence to the Father, from whom everything comes,[53] lest we should find ourselves postulating two principles of origin without an origin, an assertion which would be totally false, utterly absurd, and contrary to the Catholic faith, but an error characteristic of certain heretics.[54]

Some have ventured to believe of the Holy Spirit that he constitutes the very communion between the Father and the Son, which I may thus describe as the Godhead, and which the Greeks call the θεότητα. This means, therefore, that, because the Father is God and the Son is God, the divinity itself is equal to the Father, that is, the divinity by which they are joined to each other, both the Father by begetting the Son and the Son by being united to the Father, by whom the Son has been begotten. This divinity, which they also interpret as the mutual love and charity of each to the other, they say is called the Holy Spirit and that many scriptural texts exist to support their view, whether the following passage, *For the love of God has been poured into our hearts through the Holy Spirit who has been given to us* (Rom 5:5), or numerous other similar passages. They find support for their argument from the fact that it is through the Holy Spirit that we are reconciled to God. And so, whenever there is mention in scripture of the gift of God, they want to interpret it above all else as meaning that the charity of God is the Holy Spirit. For it is only through love that we are reconciled to God and through it that we are called children of God,[55] no longer like servants living in fear, *because perfect love drives out fear* (1 Jn 4:18), and that we have received the spirit of freedom, *in which we cry: Abba, Father* (Rom 8:15).

Because we have been reconciled and recalled to friendship with God, we are, through charity, in a position to know all the hidden things of God,[56] and so it is said of the Holy Spirit: *He will lead you into the whole truth* (Jn 16:13). This was the reason that the confidence which filled the apostles at his coming and enabled them to preach the truth[57] is, with justification, attributed to love, for the lack of confidence which accompanies fear is only cast out by the perfection of love. It is, therefore, called the gift of God,[58] for a person does not enjoy what he knows unless he loves it. The enjoyment of God's wisdom means nothing other than to be united with him in love, and no one can remain firmly in what he

---

53. The doctrine of the procession of the Holy Spirit *ex utroque*, that is, from both Father and Son, had not yet matured in Augustine's early thinking but is maintained later on as a result of careful reflection in his *Trinity* at IV, 20, 29; V, 14, 15; XV, 17, 29.
54. The Manicheans must have been meant, but Gnosticism and secular philosophy also fit the bill insofar as they taught the eternity of matter.
55. See 1 Jn 3:1.
56. See Rom 5:8-10.
57. See Acts 2:4.
58. See Eph 3:7.

apprehends except through love. The Spirit then is called holy, because to ensure permanence certain things are sanctioned or "made holy," and there is no doubt that "holiness" is derived from "sanction."[59] Those who hold this view make great use of the following scriptural proof: *What is born of the flesh is flesh, and what is born of the Spirit is spirit* (Jn 3:6), for *God is spirit* (Jn 4:24). This refers to our birth not according to Adam in the flesh but according to Christ in the Holy Spirit.

If, therefore, this text does refer to the Holy Spirit when it states that *God is spirit*, they say that note should be taken that it does not read "because a spirit is God" but *because God is spirit*, so that the very divinity of the Father and Son, spoken of in the passage, should be understood to be God, which is the Holy Spirit.[60] The apostle John provides us with further evidence when he declares: *God is love* (1 Jn 4:16). Also, John does not say that love is God but that *God is love*, so that the divinity itself is understood to be love. As for the particular text which lists a series of interconnected ideas: *Everything belongs to you, but you belong to Christ, and Christ belongs to God* (1 Cor 3:22-23), and elsewhere: *The head of woman is man, the head of man is Christ, but the head of Christ is God* (1 Cor 11:3), where no mention is made of the Holy Spirit, they offer as the explanation that it is not customary, when speaking of things which are interconnected, to mention the connection itself. So those who scrutinize closely the following passage appear to find a reference to the Trinity when it declares: *For everything is from him and through him, and in him is everything* (Rom 11:36) — *from him*, meaning from the One who is indebted to no one for his existence; *through him*, meaning through the mediator; *in him*, meaning in him who holds together, that is, joins together in unity.[61]

20. Those who would maintain that the communion of which we are speaking is not a substance, whether we call it divinity, love, or charity, contradict the preceding point of view. They attempt to explain the Holy Spirit to themselves in terms of substance and fail to grasp that the text, *God is love*, could not be expressed in any other way, unless love were actually a substance. They are influenced through their familiarity with physical bodies, for if two such bodies are united to each other and placed side by side, the union itself cannot be a body, for when the two bodies which had been joined are separated, nothing remains, nor does anyone believe that the unity has, as it were, departed and gone elsewhere, as did the two bodies. Let those who hold this opinion cleanse their hearts

---

59. *Nec dubium est a sanciendo sanctitatem vocari.*

60. A problem for pneumatology was the ambivalence of the word "Spirit," which described both the divine nature generally and the third person of the Trinity in particular.

61. Augustine was influenced chiefly by Marius Victorinus, who described the Holy Spirit as *copula* (*Hymn* 1, 4), *connexio* and *complexio* (*Hymn* 2,242-245)—all of which mean "joining" or "connection."

as best they can, in order to perceive that where the divine substance is concerned there cannot be anything of this kind, as if in this regard one thing could be the substance and something else could be accidental to the substance but not belonging to the substance. The fact is that whatever can be understood to be there necessarily belongs to the substance.

It is, assuredly, easy to say and believe such things, but only the clean of heart may see how they can be so. Consequently, whether that particular point of view is the truth or whether it is something else, we must maintain a faith which is unshakable, so that we call the Father God, the Son God, and the Holy Spirit God. Also, there are not three gods, but that Trinity is one God, not with different natures but of the same substance. Nor is the Father sometimes the Son and another time the Holy Spirit, but the Father is always the Father, the Son always the Son, and the Holy Spirit always the Holy Spirit. We should be restrained in what we affirm about things we cannot see, as if we were familiar with them; instead we should believe, because only by the clean of heart can they be seen. If, in this life, anyone glimpses them *partly*, as scripture says, and *in riddle-like fashion* (1 Cor 13:12), he cannot make his interlocutor see them, if that person is obstructed by a filthy heart. But *blessed are the clean of heart, for they shall see God* (Mt 5:8). This is what we believe about God, our creator and renewer.

21. Yet because we are commanded not only to love God, in accordance with what is prescribed: *You shall love the Lord your God with all your heart, with all your soul, and with all your mind* (Lk 10:27) but also our neighbor, for, the Lord goes on to say, *You shall love your neighbor as yourself* (Lk 10:27)—unless, therefore, our faith has its roots within a community and a human society, it will not attain full fruition.

10, 21. And so we believe in a Church which is holy but which is also Catholic. For heretics and schismatics also give the name of churches to their assemblies. But heretics, because of their erroneous doctrines about God, do harm to the faith, while schismatics, through their malicious divisiveness, abandon fraternal charity, despite believing what we believe. For this reason a heretic does not belong to the Church, because he loves God, nor does a schismatic, because he loves his neighbor. Therefore it finds it easy to forgive its neighbor's sins, because it prays to be forgiven[62] by the One who has reconciled us to himself, has wiped out all our past faults and continually calls us to a new life. Until we come to possess this life in its full perfection, it is not possible for us to remain without sin,[63] yet the kind of sins we commit makes a difference.

22. Now is not the time to discuss the different kinds of sins, but what we must steadfastly believe is that, if we adamantly refuse to forgive the sins of others,

---

62. In Sermon 181, 7 Augustine also links the request for forgiveness in the Lord's Prayer not only to the individual believer but also to the Church itself.
63. See *Enchiridion* 17, 64.

the sins we ourselves commit will assuredly not be forgiven.[64] We therefore also believe in the forgiveness of sins.

Forgiveness of Sins

23. Because a human being is constituted of three elements, spirit, soul, and body,[65] which at times are said to be two, since the soul is often included under spirit (for the reasonable part of that same entity, which animals lack, is called spirit), our principal element is the spirit.[66] Next, the life by which we are joined to the body is called the soul. Finally, the body itself, because of its visible nature, comprises our third element. This *whole creation has been groaning and giving birth until the present time* (Rom 8:22); however, he has conferred on it the first-fruits of the Spirit, because it has put its trust in God and is now well-intentioned. This spirit is at times called mind, and the apostle has this to say of it: *With my mind I obey the law of God* (Rom 7:25), while in similar fashion he says elsewhere: *God is my witness, whom I serve with my spirit* (Rom 1:9).[67]

Yet, because the soul still lusts after the desires of the flesh, it is called flesh and is opposed to the spirit not by nature[68] but through its sinful habits. Hence the statement: *With my mind I obey the law of God, but in my flesh I obey the law of sin* (Rom 7:25). Evil inclinations of this sort, contrary to nature, are in keeping with our mortal birth because of the sin of the first human being. It is therefore written: *At one time we also, by nature, were children of wrath* (Eph 2:3), that is, under punishment, which meant slavery to the law of sin. But that soul becomes perfect by nature whenever it obeys the spirit and closely follows God. *And so an unspiritual person fails to appreciate what belongs to the Spirit of God* (1 Cor 2:14).

Nevertheless, where true faith and good dispositions are concerned, the soul, for its part, cannot be brought into subjection to the spirit, thereby facilitating harmonious activity, as promptly as the spirit becomes subject to God. Instead, let its impulses, by which it dissipates itself in the direction of what is carnal and transitory, be restrained in gradual fashion. Yet, because the soul also undergoes purification, acquiring a natural stability through the dominance of the spirit, which is its head, and whose head in turn is Christ, we must not lose hope that the body, too, will be restored to its rightful state—not that this process will take

---

64. See Mt 6:15.
65. The Aristotelean triad of body-soul-spirit has a biblical parallel in the trichotomy of 1 Thes 5:23.
66. See *Miscellany of Eighty-three Questions* 7.
67. See ibid. 67, 6.
68. That is, not as the Manicheans understood.

place as quickly as that of the soul, nor that of the soul as quickly as that of the spirit, but at the appropriate time, *at the sound of the last trumpet, when the dead shall rise incorruptible, and we too shall be changed* (1 Cor 15:52). And therefore we believe in the resurrection of the flesh, not only because the soul is being made new, which at present bears the name "flesh" because of the desires of the flesh. We must also unwaveringly believe that even this visible flesh, which is truly such by nature and has received the name "soul" not from nature but because of the desires of the flesh—this visible flesh, properly so called, will rise again.

Resurrection of the Body

Paul the apostle almost appears to point this out with his finger when he says, *This corruptible body must put on incorruptibility* (1 Cor 15:53). When Paul says *this*, it is as if he is pointing his finger at it. He can point his finger toward what can be seen, because it can be described as the corruptible soul, since it is corrupted by bad habits. When we read, *And this mortal flesh must put on immortality*, the same visible flesh is meant, for it is as if a finger were pointed repeatedly at it. The soul also may be termed corruptible because of its bad habits and can even be called mortal in this regard. Apostasy from God brings death to the soul:[69] this, according to sacred scripture, was Adam's original sin in paradise.

24. According to the Christian faith, therefore, which cannot deceive, the body will rise again. And if this sounds incredible to anyone, it is because he understands flesh in its present condition, not as it is destined to be in the future, because at that moment of angelic transformation[70] it will no longer be flesh and blood but only a body.[71]Speaking about flesh, the apostle states: *There will be one kind of flesh for beasts, another for birds, another for fish, another for creeping things* (1 Cor 15:39,40). Paul did not add "and also heavenly flesh " but *both heavenly and earthly bodies.* For all flesh is of necessity corporeal, but not every body is flesh because, starting with those earthly bodies, a piece of wood is a body, but not flesh; humans and beasts are comprised both of body and flesh; but among the heavenly bodies no flesh is to be found, only bodies pure and simple, which the apostle calls spiritual, and others call ethereal. Paul's statement, therefore, that *flesh and blood will not inherit the kingdom of God* (1 Cor 15:50), does not contradict the doctrine of the resurrection of the flesh; rather, he is explaining what we now term flesh and blood will be like in the future.[72]

---

69. Eccl 10:14.
70. The reference is to the eschatological transformation of human beings, in which they will become like the angels in their nature; see Mt 22:30.
71. See *Enchiridion* 23, 91.
72. See Augustine's qualification of this statement in *Revisions* I, 17, where he rejects in detail the misconception that the risen body has neither limbs nor the substance of flesh.

Should someone imagine that it is impossible for our present flesh to be transformed into a nature of this kind, that person should be brought to faith by a gradual process of reasoning. For, if you were to ask him whether earth could be converted into water, he would not consider such a conversion an impossibility owing to the proximity of the two things. Again, if you should inquire about the possibility of water's being changed into air, the person would reply that it does not appear to be impossible because the two are adjacent to each other. Likewise, if you ask about air, whether it can be changed into an ethereal body, in other words, into a heavenly body, the answer would be yes, and again because of the extreme proximity of both. Since he concedes through this gradual demonstration that what is earthly can indeed be changed into a heavenly body, why then does he not believe it to be possible for this process to take place in an instant through the will of God, which enabled a human body to walk on the water,[73] and the way, without gradation, smoke sometimes turns into fire with remarkable speed, in accordance with the text, *in the twinkling of an eye* (1 Cor 15:52)? Our flesh does indeed come from the earth. Even the philosophers, whose reasonings are often marshaled against the doctrine of the resurrection of the flesh and who argue that no earthly body can be found in heaven,[74] admit that any body can be transformed and changed into any other. When that resurrection of the body does come to pass, we shall be freed from the constraints of time and enjoy unending life in a love and security beyond description. Then the words will come to pass: *Death is swallowed up in victory. Death, where is your sting? Death, where is your victory?* (1 Cor 15:54-55)

Conclusion

25. This is the faith, consisting of a few short sentences and expressed in a creedal form to be firmly professed, which is given to those newly converted to the Christian faith. These brief articles have become well known to believers who, by putting their faith in them, become subject to God. By being subject to God, they can live righteous lives and through such lives purify their hearts. Then, having purified their hearts, they may succeed in understanding what they believe.

---

73. See Mt 14:25.
74. See section 13.

Faith in the Unseen

Translation by Michael G. Campbell, O.S.A.

Notes by Michael Fiedrowicz

Introduction

1. Authenticity and Date

Since neither Augustine in the *Revisions* nor Possidius in the *Indiculus* mentions this work, Erasmus cast doubt on its authenticity in the edition of Augustine's works that he published in 1528.[1] In his view, Hugh of St. Victor composed it in the twelfth century by putting together statements of Augustine, especially from his letters. The editors of the critical Louvain edition (1577) adopted this position, as did Robert Bellarmine in his catalogue of Christian authors, *De scriptoribus ecclesiasticis* (1613). But soon thereafter scholars became convinced that Augustine was the author.

An important argument in favor of authenticity is Augustine's letter to his friend Darius, in which, along with other books, he mentions this work under the title *De fide rerum quae non videntur (liber)*.[2]

Many editors departed from the title given in all the manuscripts, *De fide rerum invisibilium (liber)*, and adopted instead the title attested by Augustine himself.[3]

The work must have been composed after 399. In sections 4, 7 and 7, 10 there are references to the destruction of the statues of the gods and of temples that occurred in North Africa after the promulgation of an antipagan law by Emperor Honorius in 399. It is more difficult to determine the *terminus ante quem*. Augustine's letter 231 was composed in 429/30. Material parallels to books 17 and 18 of *The City of God* suggest a date between 420 and 425.[4]

2. Literary Genre and Structure

Scholars disagree on the literary classification of *Faith in the Unseen*. Some consider it to be an apologetical treatise (*liber*), and indeed the logical sequence of arguments, the lack of spontaneity, and the scarcity of personal touches seem to confirm this characterization.[5] The Maurists were the first to classify the work as a *tractatus popularis*, that is, an address (*sermo*) to believers, either catechu-

---

1. See Erasmus, *Quartus tomus omnium operum divi Aurelii Augustini* (Basel 1528) 695.
2. Letter 231, 7.
3. See, for example, the Maurist edition in PL 40, 171.
4. See M. P. J. van den Hout, ed., "Praefatio," in Augustine, *De fide rerum invisibilium,* CCL 46, LXI.
5. According to M. F. McDonald, *Saint Augustine's De fide rerum quae non videntur. A Critical Text and Translation with Introduction and Commentary* (Washington 1950) 51-57.

mens or newly baptized, that sought to strengthen them in their faith so that they might also be able to defend it against attacks by nonbelievers.[6]

The address combines elements of apologetic and exhortation. The primary intention is an appeal (*suasio*) for faith, but the strengthening of faith is done by refuting opponents' arguments and by demonstrating the reasonableness and credibility of faith itself.

The classification of the work as an exhortatory address (*oratio suasoria*) is confirmed by a rhetorical analysis of the introduction, the conclusion, and the speech of the personified Church in the body of the work.

The structure of the work is simple and clear:

Introduction: Presentation of the subject and of the method of treatment (1, 1)
Main Section:
    Refutation of criticisms of religious faith; demonstration of the
        necessity of faith (1, 2-3, 4)
    Evidences for the credibility of the Catholic faith (3, 5-7, 10)
Concluding appeal to the faithful to nourish their faith and allow it to grow
    (8, 11)

3. The Line of Argument

The "unseen things" (*rerum invisibilium*) alluded to in the title as an object of faith are not only realities that are by their nature invisible, such as the divine Trinity. They also include all the events of salvation history, whether past, such as the incarnation, resurrection, and ascension of Christ, or eschatological, such as the resurrection of the dead and the universal judgment. The problem is this: May one believe in past or future events, of which one has neither direct experience nor rational proof? More concretely: Does what the Christian faith teaches have credibility? The answer to both questions forms the basic content of *Faith in the Unseen*.

a) The Necessity of Religious Faith

The point of departure of the argument is the refusal of the opponents of faith to accept realities of which they have no sense experience.[7] With his reference to human will-acts and thoughts, which can be grasped only intellectually, Augustine makes a first breach in his opponents' wall of defense. In a further step, he

---

6. See N. Cipriani, "De fide rerum quae non videntur," in *De vera religione; De utilitate credendi; De fide rerum quae non videntur* (Rome 1994) 95-109.
7. *Faith in the Unseen* 1, 1.

uses the example of feelings of friendship to prove that no immediate knowledge is possible here but only a belief based on outward signs: deeds, gestures, words. Faith can therefore be defined as a knowledge that is based not on direct sense experience nor on awareness of the self but on outward signs.[8]

In this analysis of faith, as in other works,[9] Augustine's primary purpose is to elucidate the epistemological value of faith. As he had already done in *The Advantage of Believing*, here too he emphasizes the indispensable need of faith in human social life: "If trust of this kind were to disappear from human affairs, how could anyone escape being aware of the confusion and appalling upheaval which would follow? Since the love of which we speak is unseen, who then could enjoy the mutual love of another?"[10] Without the invisible trust one places in his fellow human beings, his friends, his relatives, the social life of human-kind would become hopelessly confused. This argument now forms the basis for demonstrating the reasonableness of faith in the religious sphere as well.

Augustine is convinced that faith in things divine is even more necessary, because, if one rejects this faith, "not merely would certain human friendships suffer profanations, but it would extend even to the most supreme form of religion itself, with the direst possible consequences."[11] This argument is convincing, of course, only in the light of faith itself. Those who do not yet believe in a life after death will hardly be moved by the consequences against which Augustine warns those who refuse to believe.

This last point makes it clear that Augustine has chiefly in mind a circle of readers within the Church. In his apologetical treatise, *The Advantage of Believing,* he argued that faith is even more important in the religious sphere than in daily life because it is so difficult to know divine truths. Here, in *Faith in the Unseen*, he uses the practical argument from the greater risk that the refusal of faith entails in the religious sphere.

b) The Credibility of the Christian Faith

After this general proof of the necessity of religious faith, Augustine now explains the credibility of the Christian faith in particular.[12] His opponent has meanwhile changed his position: he no longer rejects faith in principle but accepts faith in the unseen as legitimate on the basis of certain evidences. But he now demands such evidences of credibility for the Christian faith. Augustine

---

8. Ibid. 1, 2-2, 3.
9. See *Confessions* VI, 5, 7; *The Advantage of Believing* 11, 25; *The Trinity* IX, 1.
10. *Faith in the Unseen* 2, 4.
11. Ibid. 3, 4.
12. Ibid. 3, 5-7, 10.

answers: "Those people who allege that our faith in Christ lacks any proof are greatly mistaken."[13]

He immediately turns his opponent's attention to the decisive point: "You, then, who think that no visible proofs exist which would enable you to believe in Christ, should pay attention to the things you can actually see."[14] In his argument Augustine is turning back to the proof from evidence in ancient rhetoric. According to Quintilian's definition, an *indicium* is "something by means of which one becomes aware of something else, just as, for example, one becomes aware of a murder through the presence of blood."[15] What evidences or signs can one adduce by means of which the credibility of the content of Christian faith can be known? Augustine points first of all to the fulfillment of Old Testament prophecies concerning the Church and then to the astonishing spread of Christianity throughout the world.

If the Old Testament promises of the conversion of the nations to Christ and to the only God have been fulfilled in the Church, then this visible Church is in turn a sign of things that are presently unseen. But just as the Church was shown forth in the scriptures, so these unseen things may now belong either to the past (the life of Christ, for example) or to the future (the universal judgment).[16] "Why is it then that we refuse to believe the first and the last things, which we do not see, although we have as witnesses of both the things midway between them, which we do see? I am referring to those prophetic writings in which we either hear or read how these first, middle and last things were foretold before they came to pass."[17] The evidence of present fulfillment guarantees the credibility also of biblical statements for which this evidence does not presently exist: "You did not see what was foretold and brought to pass regarding the human birth of Christ: *Behold, a virgin will conceive and bear a son* (Mt 1:23: Is 7:14), yet what you can see is how the promise made to Abraham has been fulfilled: *In your offspring all the nations of the earth will be blessed* (Gn 22:18)."[18]

With superb rhetoric Augustine develops this argument in a rather lengthy passage in which he places a hymn-like speech in the mouth of the personified Church:[19] With a motherly love she implores nonbelievers to attend to the signs that make the Christian faith credible: "Does it appear absurd and inconsequential to you, and the divine testimony of little or no worth at all in your estimation, that the whole human race flocks to the name of a single crucified man?"[20]

---

13. Ibid. 3, 5.
14. Ibid.
15. Quintilian, *Institutio oratoria* 5, 9, 8.
16. *Faith in the Unseen* 5, 8.
17. Ibid.
18. Ibid. 4, 7.
19. Ibid. 3, 5-4, 7.
20. Ibid. 4, 7.

But the apologetical value of the argument from prophecy seemed to be challenged by two objections. The first was: Were the prophecies about the Church
possibly only a Christian interpolation in the Old Testament texts, in order to
give its religion a higher authority? Augustine answers by pointing out that these
promises are also found in the manuscripts of the Jews, who were to be seen as
enemies of Christians. For this very reason they could be regarded as credible
witnesses. In addition, the scattering meant that the biblical prophecies
confirming the Christian claim were also in universal circulation and could
convince nonbelievers.[21]

There was, however, another more serious objection. If the Old Testament
really prophesied so much with utter clarity about the Church, why did the Jews
not understand these prophecies? Augustine skillfully counters with the argument that even the blindness of the Jews was foretold by the prophets as a just
punishment of their guilt.[22] Despite all this, the question arises of what persuasive power the argument from prophecy had for a non-Christian readership. As a
matter of fact, in his controversy with Faustus the Manichean, Augustine
expressly took the position that the fulfillment of many biblical prophecies,
especially about the Church, was so evident that it could convince even nonbelievers.[23] Nevertheless in the present work he seems to acknowledge the limited
apologetical value of this argument, since he now passes on to a different kind of
argument: "Even were we to suppose that no prior prophetic witnesses existed
pertaining to Christ and the Church, what person would not be immediately
impelled to believe that the divine splendor had indeed burst forth upon
humanity, when he sees how false gods are now abandoned and their images
smashed, their temples destroyed or put to another use, and the empty rituals for
so long part of human habit discontinued, while the one true God is invoked by
the whole human race?"[24] Instead of arguing from a typological interpretation of
biblical texts Augustine is here arguing from an objective fact that could be
empirically verified even by non-Christians.

Through further arguments Augustine attempts to make it plausible that this
undeniable spread of Christianity was due ultimately to a divine intervention.
This spread was due to a man whom others mocked, scourged, crucified, and
killed; uneducated fishermen and tax collectors proclaimed his message
throughout the world and attested to its truth by their deaths; human beings of
every age and social class believed the message; all the sects and heresies try to
win authority for themselves by using the name of Christ. "How could that cruci-

---

21. Ibid. 6, 9. On this Augustinian topos see B. Blumenkranz, *Die Judenpredigt Augustins* (Paris:
    Études Augustiniennes, 1973) 175-178.
22. *Faith in the Unseen* 6, 9.
23. See *Answer to Faustus* 13, 1-14.
24. *Faith in the Unseen* 7, 10.

fied one possibly have accomplished so much, if not for the fact that God had assumed human nature?"[25] As Augustine finishes his line of thought, he notches his argument up a degree by pointing out that all these facts are not only convincing in themselves but were in addition foretold by the prophets.

In his conclusion Augustine calls upon his primary addressees—both Christians who have long believed and those who have only recently become believers—to strengthen and deepen their faith and not to let themselves be deceived by anyone outside the Church (pagans, Jews, heretics) or within it (bad Christians).[26]

4. The Importance of the Work

Although *Faith in the Unseen*, by reason of its brevity, belongs among Augustine's minor works, it is marked by stylistic elegance, clarity of composition, lucid presentation of ideas, and beauty of expression. The rigorous refutation of a crass empiricism that accepts sense experience as the sole form of knowledge and the rational explanation of another way of knowing realities not directly and empirically verifiable give Augustine's plea for "faith in the unseen" an abiding topicality.

25. Ibid.
26. Ibid. 8, 11.

Faith in the Unseen

1, 1. There is a class of people who maintain that the Christian religion should be despised rather than embraced, because what it presents is not something tangible but something that demands faith in matters which lie beyond human vision.[1] In our efforts to refute such people, who consider themselves wise by refusing to believe what they cannot see, even if we are unable to demonstrate visibly the divine truths which we believe, we are nonetheless in a position to demonstrate that the human mind is duty-bound to believe those things which cannot be seen.

In the first place, those people stand rebuked who in their folly believe themselves answerable to what fleshly eyes alone can see and consequently maintain that they are not bound to believe what they cannot see. Yet in truth, many are the things which they not only believe, and indeed know to be true, but which they cannot see with eyes of that sort. Take this human mind of ours: it is the repository for such an immense number of things, a faculty whose nature remains unseen, to put it simply. Yet that very trust itself by which we believe, the act of thinking through which we know whether we believe or disbelieve something, which is far removed from the sight of those eyes—what else is so resplendent, so clear, and so certain before the interior gaze of our minds than this? How is it, therefore, that what we cannot see with our bodily eyes we are not bound to believe when, without any hesitation and without the assistance of our bodily eyes, we are able to see immediately whether we believe or not?

2. "But," they retort, "we have no need to see with the eyes of our body what is in the soul, since we can do that with our mind. You people assert that there are things we should believe, yet you are unable to let us see externally that we may verify them through the evidence of our bodily eyes, nor are such things to be found in our minds so that we may catch sight of them through reflection."

This is the way they argue, as if a person were only bound to believe once he was able to see for himself the object of his belief. Consequently, we must believe in many things pertaining to the temporal realm which we cannot see, so that we may also deserve to see those eternal things which we presently believe in.

But whoever you are,[2] you who refuse to believe what you cannot see: with the evidence of your bodily eyes you can assuredly see physical bodies all around you. With your mind you can also see the inclinations of your will and your thoughts. Tell me then, I beg you, with what manner of vision do you

---

1. See *True Religion* 3, 3.
2. The continual use of direct address shows that this work belongs to the genre of discourse.

observe the will of a friend in your regard? To actually see the will of any person is beyond the possibilities of the bodily eye. Or is it possible for you to glimpse with your mind what takes place in another person's mind? And if it is the case that you fail to see this, how can you possibly return mutual friendship if you refuse to believe what you cannot see? Or will you perhaps answer that you are indeed able to see the will of someone else manifested through his behavior? Therefore, because of the actions you are about to witness and the words you are going to hear, you intend to believe the intentions of a friend's will in your regard, something which it is impossible to see or hear. For the will we are referring to possesses neither color nor shape so as to be visible, nor has it sound or melody by which it can reach our ears, neither is it your own will of which you are conscious in your heart. The fact remains that what you cannot see or hear or glimpse within yourself you nevertheless believe, lest your life be totally devoid of that friendship and the affection shown you by your friend remains unacknowledged on your part.[3]

So, what about that statement of yours that you should not believe anything unless you see it either externally through the body or internally by the heart? For the truth is that from your heart you trust a heart other than your own and are prepared to believe what you are unable to see either with the eye of your flesh or with that of the mind. With your body you can see the face of a friend, with your mind you can see your own trust, but the trust of your friend cannot be the object of your love if no such mutual trust is found in you, a trust which enables you to believe something you cannot actually see in your friend. However, it is possible for a person to deceive by feigning goodwill and concealing his evil intentions; or, if the intention is not to harm, yet in the hope of gaining some advantage from you he may act deceitfully because he is lacking in love.

3. Yet you insist that you keep faith in your friend, whose heart you cannot see, because you have discovered his worth in time of trial and are aware how that friend feels towards you, since he refused to abandon you when you were in dire straits. Do you really think, therefore, that we should hope for adversity in order to prove the affection of our friends? And is no one to rest content in the certainty of his friends unless he has first experienced misery through adverse circumstances? In other words, is he not to enjoy the proven friendship of another without first passing through the crucible of suffering and fear? And, in the act of acquiring true friends, how can happiness be desired rather than feared, when happiness is a state which unhappiness alone can prove? Yet the truth of the matter is that in good times we can also have a friend, while bad times only serve to make that friendship even more assured.

---

3. On Augustine's ideal of friendship see J. T. Lienhard, "Friendship, Friends," in A. D. Fitzgerald, ed., *Augustine Through the Ages* (Grand Rapids 1999) 372-373.

2, 3. But, unless you believed in a friend, you would not entrust yourself to him in time of danger so as to prove the worth of his friendship. And so for this reason, when you do entrust yourself to a friend in order to prove his friendship, you are actually putting your faith in him before you have proof that he is your friend. For it remains true that if we are not to believe what we cannot see, yet, at those times when the dispositions of our friends remain somewhat uncertain and we do give them our trust, then, when we eventually ascertain proof of their intentions in adverse circumstances, it still comes down to a matter of believing rather than seeing their goodwill towards us. Unless, perhaps, the degree of trust is such that, through what we may not inappropriately refer to as a kind of eyes that it has, we judge ourselves to see the friendship we believe in when normally we ought to believe what we cannot see.

4. If trust of this kind were to disappear from human affairs, how could anyone escape being aware of the confusion and appalling upheaval which would follow? Since the love of which we speak is unseen, who then could enjoy the mutual love of another, if I don't feel bound to believe what I cannot see? Friendship as a whole would therefore disappear, because its essence is mutual love.[4] Who could ever receive anything from another if no visible, credible proof has first been given? Indeed, were friendship to disappear, there would be no way of preserving spiritually those bonds which exist between married couples, families and relatives, for the harmony characteristic of these relationships has its basis in friendship. It would therefore be impossible for a husband to show mutual love to his wife since, unable to see the love for himself, he would not believe she loves him. Likewise, they will cherish no desire to have children because they do not believe that they would return their love. If it should happen that they did beget and rear children, these in their turn will show even less love for their parents, because they will not see the love that they have for them in their hearts, since it is invisible. Such a state of affairs would result if those things which cannot be seen are not the object of a praiseworthy faith but instead are recklessly and rashly believed.

What am I to say about those other ties existing between brothers, sisters, sons-in-law, fathers-in-law, and any other kind of blood relationship and bonds between friends, if the love and goodwill of children for parents and of parents for their children remains unsure and dubious? And is a kindness which is obligatory to go unreciprocated or not to be considered obligatory, since what cannot be seen in another person is not believed to exist? Furthermore, caution of this kind is not clever but despicable, when we refuse to believe we are loved because we cannot see this love for ourselves, and we do not return it to those to whom we

---

4. In these two sentences Augustine uses three words for the one word translated here as "love"—*caritas*, *dilectio* and *amor*.

believe it is not due. The consequence of our refusal to believe what we cannot see is that human relationships are thrown into chaos, and foundations are utterly swept away by our failure to trust the goodwill of people, a goodwill which is impossible for us to actually see.

I refrain from mentioning how numerous is that particular class of people who find fault with us for believing things we cannot see, yet who themselves give credence to tradition and history and even to places they have never visited. Such people do not assert: "We withhold belief because we have not seen it for ourselves." Were they to make such a statement, they would be compelled to admit that the identity of their parents was a matter of doubt, for they have believed this on the basis of what others have told them, who were not in a position to demonstrate a fact which already belonged to the past. Of themselves, they retain no awareness of the period in question; nonetheless they are prepared to give their assent unhesitatingly to others who told them about it. For unless this were the case, and as long as we evade a bold act of faith in those things we cannot see, an upsurge of faithless impiety against parents would be the inevitable outcome.[5]

3, 4. If therefore human society itself could not endure because of our refusal to believe what we cannot see, and in view of the disappearance of mutual harmony, how much more credence ought to be given to those divine matters which remain unseen! And, if this credence were not forthcoming, not merely would certain human friendships suffer profanation but so would even the most supreme form of religion itself, with the direst possible consequences.[6]

5. "But," you will retort, "although I may be unable to see the goodwill of my friend, I can still discover this through numerous proofs; whereas, for your part, you who would have us believe things we cannot see fail to give us any proofs." However, it is no small concession for you to admit that there are certain things which, although not visible but because of certain clear proofs, must still be believed. Consequently, we are agreed on the fact that we are not to refrain from believing everything we cannot see, and that opinion, which maintains that we are in no way bound to believe what we cannot see, lies discredited and disproved.

Yet those people who allege that our faith in Christ lacks any proof are greatly mistaken. For what proofs could be clearer than the ones which were foretold and which we now see come true? You, then, who think that no visible proofs exist which would enable you to believe in Christ, should pay attention to the things you can actually see.

---

5. See *Confessions* VI, 5, 7.
6. This argument presupposes an initial faith in eternal life.

The Church herself addresses you with words of maternal love: "I, whose ongoing fruitfulness and growth throughout the whole world you admire, once did not exist as you see me now, but *in your offspring all the nations will be blessed* (Gn 22:18). By conferring a blessing on Abraham, God was at the same time promising me; in consequence of the blessing given to Christ, I am spread through all the nations. The sequence of generations testifies that Christ is the seed of Abraham. Let me recall briefly that Abraham was the father of Isaac, Isaac the father of Jacob, and Jacob the father of the twelve sons from whom arose the people of Israel. Jacob himself was also called Israel. One of his twelve sons was Judah, whence the name of the Jewish people, from whom was born the Virgin Mary, who bore Christ. And look: you see and are amazed at the fact that all nations are blessed in Christ, that is, in the seed of Abraham, and still you are afraid to believe in Christ, someone you ought to fear rather than believe in!

"Or could it be that you doubt or balk at the virgin birth, a truth that you ought to believe was appropriate to the birth of the God-man? Believe also what was foretold by the prophet: *Behold, a virgin shall conceive in her womb and bear a son, and he shall be called Emmanuel, which means God-with-us* (Is 7:14). Therefore have no doubts about the virgin giving birth, if you wish to have faith in the birth of God who, without abdicating his governance of the world, came in the flesh to humankind, bestowing fecundity on his mother, yet not taking away her integrity.

"If he was always God, it was entirely fitting that he should be born a man in this way and by such a birth become God for us. To this God the prophet speaks again: *Your throne, O God, shall last from age to age; a scepter of justice is the scepter of your kingdom. You have loved justice and hated evil; therefore, God, your God, has anointed you with the oil of gladness above your peers.* (Ps 44:7-8)[7] The anointing spoken of here, where God anointed God, is a spiritual one, referring to the Father's anointing of the Son. Consequently, we acknowledge that Christ is derived from chrism, which means anointing.

"I am the Church, about whom it is spoken to him in the same psalm and foretold as a deed to be accomplished: *The queen stands on your right hand, adorned in garments of gold and varied clothing* (Ps 44:10), that is, in the mystery of wisdom, clothed with a diversity of languages. There it is said to me: *Listen, daughter, and pay heed and give ear, forget your own people and your father's house, because the king has desired your beauty; for he is the Lord your God, and the daughters of Tyre shall worship him with gifts, all the richest of the land shall seek your presence. All the glory of the king's daughter is within; she is arrayed in cloth-of-gold. Virgins shall be led to the king after her, those who are*

---

7. See also the detailed christological and ecclesiological interpretation of Ps 44 in *The City of God* XVII, 16, and in *Expositions of the Psalms* 44.

her companions shall be brought to you; they shall be led amid joy and gladness, and brought into the king's temple. Sons have been born to you in place of your fathers; you shall establish them as princes throughout the whole earth. They shall make your name remembered from one generation to the next; therefore the nations shall praise you for ever and ever. (Ps 44:11-18)

6. "If you yourselves are unable to recognize even now this queen, fertile with royal offspring; if she fails to see fulfilled the promise made to her: *Listen, daughter, and pay heed;* if she, to whom it was said: *Forget your own people and your father's house,* has not willingly rejected those observances of this world which previously obtained; if she, to whom it was said: *The king has desired your beauty, for he is the Lord your God,* does not confess Christ as Lord in every part of the world; if she does not witness the nations of the world offering prayers to Christ and bringing him gifts, the one of whom it was said to her: *The daughters of Tyre shall worship him with gifts;* if it is not evident that the rich lay aside their pride and beg help from the Church, she whom the psalm addresses: *All the richest of the land shall seek your presence;* if the daughter of the queen, who has been commanded to pray: *Our Father, who art in heaven* (Mt 6:9), goes unrecognized and says this of her holy ones: *Our inner human nature is being renewed day by day* (2 Cor 4:16); if all the glory of the queen's daughter is within after his good odor is spread in every place[8] and consecrated virgins are not brought to Christ, and it is not she who is addressed and referred to as follows: *Virgins shall be led to the king after her, those who are her companions shall be brought to you;* and lest 'being led' might suggest captivity in some prison, the text continues: *They shall be led amid joy and gladness, and brought into the king's temple;* if she fails to bring forth sons, who shall be appointed rulers by her everywhere, like fathers, she to whom it has been said: *Sons shall be yours in place of your fathers; you shall establish them as princes throughout the whole earth,* and who, being a mother and both superior and subject, commends herself to their prayers, which explains what follows: *They shall make your name remembered from one generation to the next;* if, because of the preaching of these same fathers who make his name forever remembered, such great numbers of people do not gather and give praise ceaselessly to his grace, he to whom it is said: *Therefore the nations shall praise you for ever and ever—*

4, 6. "If these things are not clear beyond doubt, so that our opponents do not know where to look to avoid being overcome by the same force of argument and consequently find themselves forced to admit that they are obvious, you would in that case perhaps have good reason to retort that you see no proofs which would compel you to believe in what you cannot see. But were it to happen that the things you now can see, which have been long foretold and are now most

---

8. See 2 Cor 2:15.

clearly coming to pass; if truth itself resounds both through the word of ancient prophets and then with subsequent dramatic fulfillment—O vestiges of unbelief! blush at what you can clearly see, so that you may believe in those things you cannot see.[9]

7. "Pay heed to me," the Church is saying to you, "pay heed to me whom you can see, even if you don't want to see. Those faithful people who were present in Judea at that particular time learned directly of the virgin-birth, the miracles, the passion, resurrection and ascension of Christ, and of all those divine utterances and deeds of his. You did not witness these events and so refuse to believe them. Therefore consider these facts, weigh them up carefully, ponder on what you can see, for they are not narrated to you as past events, nor predicted as things yet to come, but are proved to be a present reality.

"Or does it appear absurd and inconsequential to you, and the divine testimony of little or no worth at all in your estimation, that the whole human race flocks to the name of a single crucified man?[10] You did not see what was foretold and brought to pass regarding the human birth of Christ: *Behold, a virgin shall conceive in her womb and bear a son* (Is 7:14), yet you do see how the promise made to Abraham has been fulfilled: *In your offspring all the nations of the earth shall be blessed* (Gen 22:18).

"You did not see what was foretold about the miracles of Christ and what has come to pass: *Come and consider the works of the Lord, the wonderful deeds he has done on the earth* (Ps 45:9), but you do see what was foretold: *The Lord said to me: You are my Son, today I have begotten you; ask me, and I will give you the nations for your inheritance, and the ends of the earth for your possession* (Ps 2:7-8).

"You did not see what was foretold and fulfilled about the passion of Christ:[11] *They have pierced my hands and my feet, and have numbered all my bones; they stared at me and fixed their gaze upon me; they divided my clothing among them and cast lots for my robe* (Ps 21:17-19), yet you do see what that same psalm foretold and what now clearly has reached fulfillment: *All the ends of the earth shall remember and return to the Lord, and all the nations of the world shall pay homage in his presence; for the kingdom belongs to the Lord and he shall rule over the nations* (Ps 21:28-29).

"You did not see what was foretold about the resurrection of Christ and is now fulfilled: *They went outside and began to speak; all my enemies whispered together about me and thought evil against me; they engaged in evil talk against me* (Ps 40:7-9). Showing that they achieved nothing by killing him who would rise again, the psalmist goes on to say: *Will the one who sleeps not succeed in*

---

9. See *Answer to Faustus, a Manichean* XIII, 1, 14.
10. See section 10; *The City of God* XXII, 5.
11. See *The City of God* XVII, 17.

rising again? (Ps 40:9) And further on in the same prophecy, having foretold the role of the traitor, which is also recorded in the gospel, as follows: *The person who ate at my table has raised his heel against me,* the psalmist immediately adds: *But you, Lord, have mercy on me and I will repay them* (Ps 40:11). This is precisely what has been fulfilled: Christ fell asleep but reawakened; in other words, he died and rose again. Speaking in the same prophetic way he says in another psalm: *I fell asleep and took my rest, but I arose because the Lord upheld me* (Ps 3:6).

"I concede that you may not have seen any of this, but you see his Church, about which the following prediction was both made and fulfilled: *To you, Lord my God, shall the nations come from the ends of the earth and declare: Our fathers did indeed worship false idols, and in them there was no profit* (Jer 16:19). Willing or unwilling, this you can certainly see, and if you still labor under the impression that there ever was profit in these idols, or still could be, then you can surely hear the exclamation of those countless nations of the world, which have abandoned, discarded or destroyed vanities of this kind: *Our fathers did indeed worship false idols, and in them there was no profit; if human beings devise their own gods, in truth they are not gods at all* (Jer 16:19-20).

"Because the text states: *To you shall the nations come from the ends of the earth,* you must not think this prophecy implies that the nations are to gather at the abode of some god. Grasp, as far as you can, that when the peoples of the world come to the God of Christians, the supreme and true God, they do so not by walking but by believing. Indeed, this very fact was foretold by another prophet when he said: *The Lord shall prevail against them and destroy all the gods of the nations; and each from his own place, the islands of the nations, shall worship him* (Zep 2:11). Jeremiah had expressed it this way: *To you shall the nations come,* while Zephaniah declared: *Each from his own place shall worship him.* They shall therefore come to him without leaving their own place, because by believing in him they will find him in their own heart.

"You have not seen what was foretold about Christ's ascension and then brought to fulfillment: *O God, be exalted above the heavens,* but you see what immediately follows: *And let your glory shine over the whole earth* (Ps 107:6).

"You have not seen all these prophecies which referred to Christ and have now been accomplished and completed, but you do not deny the present reality within his Church of all these other things. We have pointed out to you how both sets of events have been foretold, yet we are unable to show you visibly both sets of prophecies now fulfilled—because to recall the past for inspection is beyond our power."

5, 8. Yet, just as the good dispositions of our friends, though unseen, are considered trustworthy because of visible proofs, so in similar fashion the present visible reality of the Church is demonstrated in those writings where she is also foretold. Moreover, she is the proof of past prophecies and the herald of things yet to come, both of which are unseen. The reason for this is that past prophecies, which can no longer be seen, and those of the future, which still remain to be seen, as well as those of the present, which can now be seen—all of these lay in the future when they were first foretold, and not a single one of them at that time could be seen. When, therefore, these predictions began to be fulfilled, beginning from those which have already come to pass to those which, foretelling Christ and his Church, are at present being fulfilled—they unfolded in orderly sequence. Included in this same sequence are prophecies about the day of judgment, the resurrection of the dead, the eternal damnation of the wicked with the devil, and the eternal happiness of the just with Christ, which were similarly predicted and will come to pass.

Why is it then that we refuse to believe the first and the last things, which we do not see, although we have as witnesses of both the things midway between them, which we do see? I am referring to those prophetic writings in which we either hear or read how these first, middle and last things were foretold before they come to pass. Unless perhaps people of no faith are under the impression that matters of this kind were put into writing by Christians, in order that those other things, which they do not believe or fail to see, might possess greater authority if the belief existed that they had already been promised before they came to pass.

6, 9. If they suspect this to be the case, they should turn their attention to the writings of our Jewish opponents.[12] There they can read for themselves either those facts which we have recalled or numerous other ones which we have not mentioned and are almost too many to be counted. These prophecies have been foretold of Christ, the one in whom we believe, and of the Church to which we cling, from the time of faith's laborious beginnings right up until the eternal happiness of the kingdom. But when they do peruse the texts in question they show no amazement that those Jews who possess the writings fail to understand them, because their powers of understanding are darkened through hostility. For those same prophets had warned beforehand that the Jewish people would not understand, that the other prophecies had to be fulfilled in a hidden way, and that in the just judgment of God a fitting punishment would be imposed on this same people. Yet the one whom they crucified and gave gall and vinegar to drink, although hanging on the cross for their sake so as to lead them from darkness into light, exclaimed, *Father forgive them, for they do not know what they are doing* (Lk 23:34). However, because of those others, whom for more hidden reasons he would abandon, he had foretold long before, through the prophet, *For food they offered me gall and gave me vinegar to drink. May their table become a trap for*

---

12. See *Expositions of the Psalms* 56, 9: "A Jew carries the book which is the foundation of faith for a Christian" (trans. Boulding); *The City of God* XVIII, 46; *Answer to Faustus, a Manichean* XIII, 11.

them, an occasion of vengeance and a stumbling-block. May their eyes grow dim so that they are unable to see, may their back be always bent. (Ps 68:22-24) Despite such compelling proofs in support of what we believe, they go around with impaired vision so that, while one group of people brings the prophecies to fulfillment, this results in the other group's being condemned.

Therefore it has come about instead that they would not be destroyed, lest this same sect be completely obliterated, but that, having been scattered throughout the world, they would bring these prophecies which tell of God's grace to us. The outcome of this is both a more robust refutation of unbelievers and a widespread source of good to us. You must take to heart this very point I am making, as has been prophesied: *Do not slay them, lest they forget your law; disperse them by your power* (Ps 58:12). The reason, therefore, they are not slain does not lie in their forgetfulness of what they have read and heard. For, were they to forget completely the sacred scriptures, although they might not understand them, they would be slain by reason of that Jewish ritual itself because, being totally ignorant of the law and prophets, their Jewishness would be of no advantage to them. Consequently they have not been slain but dispersed, and, although they do not possess the faith which could save them, yet the memories they cling to are a source of help to us.[13] In their discourse they oppose us, with their books they support us. In their hearts they are hostile to us, yet they bear witness by their writings.

7, 10. Even were we to suppose that no prior prophetic witnesses existed pertaining to Christ and the Church, what person would not be immediately impelled to believe that the divine splendor had indeed burst forth upon humanity, when he sees how false gods are now abandoned and their images smashed, their temples destroyed or put to another use,[14] and the empty rituals for so long part of human habit discontinued, while the one true God is invoked by the whole human race? And all this took place through one man who was mocked, arrested, bound, scourged, beaten, insulted, crucified, scorned and put to death!

Those disciples he chose to proclaim his teaching were simple and uneducated persons and fishermen and tax-collectors. They proclaimed his resurrection and ascension into heaven, which they declared they had seen for themselves and, filled with the Holy Spirit, they gave voice to this gospel in all manner of languages which they had never learned. The crowd that heard them

---

13. See *Expositions of the Psalms* 58, serm. 1, 22; *Answer to Faustus, a Manichean* XIII, 10.

14. The law distinguished between idols and temples. The former had to be destroyed, but buildings for worship could be retained and used for other purposes. See the *Theodosian Code* 16, 19, 18 (399) and 16, 10, 19 (408). In Hippo, for example, the temple of the Phoenician Dea Celestis was transformed into the Christian Basilica Honoriana. See Sermon 162, 1-2; Letter 232, 2.

partly believed, while the remainder, refusing to believe, resisted stubbornly. These disciples thus fought to death for the truth, declining to repay evil with evil, and were victorious by dying rather than by killing.

As you see, the world has been transformed by this religion. To this gospel human hearts have likewise turned: the hearts of men and women, of people great and small, of learned and ignorant, of wise and foolish, of powerful and weak, those of noble and those of common birth, those of exalted and those of lowly estate. Spread throughout the world, such has been the manner of the Church's growth that no sect or any kind of anti-Christian error arises which does not have glorying in the name of Christ as its aim and aspiration.[15] Indeed, unless adverse movements of this sort exercised a healthy restraint they would not be permitted to spring up in the world.[16]

How could that crucified one possibly have accomplished so much, if not for the fact that God had assumed human nature, even supposing he had not foretold any of these future events through the prophets? But since so wonderful a mystery of love had its own earlier prophets and heralds who prophesied in God's name that he was to come,[17] and he did come as foretold, who then could be so deranged as to assert that the apostles lied about Christ? For they proclaimed that he had indeed come, just as the prophets had earlier foretold that he would. Nor did the prophets remain silent about the future as far as the apostles were concerned, for they had this to say about the apostles: *No speech, no word of theirs goes unheard; their sound has gone forth through all the earth and their words to the ends of the world* (Ps 18:4-5). Without a doubt we see this prophecy fulfilled in the world, even if we did not see Christ in the flesh. What person, therefore, unless mentally blinded through some astonishing ailment, or so coarse and unfeeling, could refuse to believe in those sacred writings which predicted that the whole world would one day believe?

8, 11. As for you, my dear people, let this faith be nurtured and increase within you, a faith which you already have, or have only lately, embraced. For just as those temporal events long since foretold have come to pass, so likewise will those promises of eternity come to fulfillment. Do not allow yourselves to be misled either by arrogant pagans or deceitful Jews or erroneous heretics or even ill-disposed Christians within the Church itself, who as enemies are all the more harmful because they come from within. The divine prophecies in this regard are not silent, for fear that those who are weak in faith should be unduly disturbed, for in the Song of Songs Christ the bridegroom addresses his bride the Church in these words: *As a lily among the thorns, so is my beloved among daughters* (Sg 2:2). He does not say "among strangers" but *among daughters.*

---

15. See Letter 118, 12; *Faith and the Creed* 21.
16. See 1 Cor 11:19; *True Religion* 6, 10.
17. See 1 Tm 3:16.

He who has ears to hear should hear (Mt 13:9); and, while the net which was cast into the sea collects fish of every kind, as the holy gospel relates, and is being hauled to the shore, in other words to the end of the world, people should separate themselves from the bad fish in their hearts, not in their body. This they do by changing their wicked ways and not tearing asunder the holy nets.[18] If it appears that those who have been tried and tested intermingle at present with the wicked, the reason is that, when the separation takes place on the shore, it is not punishment they shall receive but everlasting life.[19]

---

18. The implicit exhortation to remain within the unity of the Church may be a sign of the continuing effects of the Donatist controversy.

19. See Mt 13:47-49.

Demonic Divination

Translation by Edmund Hill, O.P.

Notes by Michael Fiedrowicz

Introduction

1. Occasion, Composition, Form

Human beings have at all times felt a need to explore the future. All the peoples and cultures of antiquity had their prophecies and oracles, their seers and prophets.[1] Augustine found himself having to deal with this phenomenon when, one morning during an Easter octave between 406 and 411, he met with a number of lay Christians in Hippo, his episcopal city.[2]

An event that had occurred some years earlier was still troubling people's minds. In 391 Bishop Theophilus of Alexandria had ordered the destruction of that city's temple of Serapis, which was regarded as one of the wonders of the world. Next to its very extensive grounds there was a colossal statue of Serapis, god of the Nile, which was the main attraction at the temple. But what was now being debated was not so much the destruction of this pagan sanctuary as a sensational prophecy of the event by a pagan priest. The discussion of the subject in Hippo had not ended when the congregation gathered in the Church for the liturgy, and the small group was unable to continue the conversation with Augustine.

It was only a year later that Augustine got around to reconstructing the discussion from memory. He now added personal thoughts which he had not brought into the original conversation.

The work thus has two parts: in the first six chapters (1, 1-2, 6) he repeats from memory, and in dialogue form, his original conversation. The thesis that was being debated was that pagan prophecies must have some element of good since almighty God allows them. The conversation broke off with the statement that the being in whom these prophecies originate must be more closely studied. Now, in the remaining eight chapters Augustine writes a treatise on the demons, their nature, and their resultant capacity for prophesying (3, 7-10, 14). The work thus combines a dialogue and a treatise.

The work is divided as follows:

1. Introduction (1, 1)
2. Discussion (1, 2-2, 6)
3. The natural advantage demons have (3, 7-5, 9)

---

1. See R. L. Fox, *Pagans and Christians in the Mediterranean World from the Second Century A.D. to the Conversion of Constantine* (London 1988) 168-261.
2. For details see K. Kühn, "Augustins Schrift *De divinatione daemonum*," *Augustiniana* 47 (1997) 291-337.

4. The fallibility of all demonic prophecy (6, 10-8, 12)
5. Apologetical conclusion (9, 13-10, 14)

2. Historical Background

With ever-increasing clarity the successors of Emperor Constantine championed an anti-pagan religious policy. Numerous measures taken against every form of superstition, against pagan sacrifices, against viewing the entrails of sacrificed animals in order to ascertain the present and the future, as well as the order to close or even destroy temples—all these measures were meant to drive paganism increasingly from the public scene and to intensify the Christianization of the empire. This anti-pagan legislation reached its high point in Augustine's time under Emperors Theodosius and Honorius.

Nevertheless, the retreat of paganism was a slow process and by no means without resistance from its adherents, who continued to cling to forms of idolatry, astrology, miraculous cures, and, above all, fortune-telling. Coming to grips with this "legacy of paganism"[3] was one of Augustine's daily tasks as bishop of Hippo, as countless references in his writings show.

In this conflict between paganism and Christianity oracles played an important role. Prophecies of an apocalyptic kind multiplied as the intellectual atmosphere heated up due not only to the constant tightening of civil anti-pagan laws at the end of the fourth and the beginning of the fifth centuries but also to the crises Rome endured as a result of barbarian onslaughts. For a long time now, both the pagan and the Christian camps had used oracles as a propaganda tool in the ideological struggle. For example, in the period before the last great persecution of Christians under Emperor Diocletian at the beginning of the fourth century, prophecies were used to incite radical action against followers of the new religion.[4]

In his *Philosophy from Oracles* (*De philosophia ex oraculis*), composed before 305, Porphyry tried to prove that the worship of Jesus as God was due to a misunderstanding by his disciples. Using various pagan oracular statements having to do with Christ, this Neoplatonic adversary of Christians sought to reduce Jesus to the status of a wise and religious man, similar to many others, and

---

3. F. van der Meer, *Augustine the Bishop: Church and Society at the Dawn of the Middle Ages*, trans. B. Battershaw and G. R. Lamb (New York: Harper Torchbooks, 1965) 46 (= title of Chapter 4 of Part 1).
4. See Arnobius, *Against the Nations* I, 26; Lactantius, *The Deaths of Persecutors* 11; Eusebius, *Preparation for the Gospel* IV, 1, 3. See P. De Labriolle, *La réaction païenne: Étude sur la polémique antichrétienne du Ie au Ve siècle* (Paris 1958) 318-323.

to relativize his claim to exclusivity.[5] As late as the second half of the fourth century a Roman senator named Flavian circulated an oracle prophesying that Christianity would end in 394, three hundred and sixty-five years after its start. Augustine's detailed refutation not only of this prophecy but of similar pagan oracles shows the influence this form of anti-Christian propaganda must obviously have exerted.[6]

Yet the Christian side also used the pagan tradition of oracles in order to confirm its own message through these supposed voices in the enemy camp. In the interests of apologetics, such texts were often composed by Christians themselves under a pagan name.[7] As a result, there were Christian interpolations in the *Sybilline Oracles*.[8] More than that, as can be seen from the *Tübingen Theosophy,* which a Christian hand compiled at the end of the fifth century, there were in circulation, in the middle or toward the end of the fourth century, oracles meant to justify the suppression of pagan cults: in these oracles Apollo or Artemis announced the decline of the cults and prophesied the victory of the Christian religion.[9]

The use of oracles, which had a very ancient tradition behind it, thus became a frequently used weapon in the political and ideological struggle between paganism and Christianity. An echo of this tense atmosphere can also be detected in Augustine's *Demonic Divination*.

Paganism, which was increasingly forced on the defensive, tried to play its last card, as it were, toward the end of the fourth century, for the purpose of justifying its own form of worship. There was an appeal to the trustworthiness of pagan oracles, whose truth claims were seemingly confirmed by a higher divinity. Even the destruction of the Egyptian temple of Serapis was turned, on the basis of its being foretold by a pagan seer, into an argument in favor of the pagan gods, who, in spite of everything, manifested their existence and power in that prophecy.

---

5. Augustine, *The City of God* XIX, 23. See F. Culdaut, "Un oracle d'Hécate dans la *Cité de Dieu* de Saint Augustin: 'Les dieux ont proclamé que le Christ fut un homme très pieux' (XIX, 23, 3)," *Revue des études augustiniennes* 38 (1992) 271-89; R. L. Wilken, *The Christians as the Romans Saw Them* (New Haven-London 1984), title of Chapter 6, "Philosophy from Oracles."

6. See *The City of God* XVIII, 54; G. Folliet, in Bibliothèque Augustinienne 36, 774-775, note complémentaire 59; H. Chadwick, "Oracles of the End in the Conflict of Paganism and Christianity in the Fourth Century," in E. Lucchesi and H. Saffrey, eds., *Antiquité païenne et chrétienne. Mémorial A.-J. Festugière* (Geneva 1985) 125-129.

7. See W. Speyer, *Die literarische Fälschung im heidnischen und christlichen Altertum* (Munich 1971) 246-252.

8. See Augustine, *The City of God* XVIII, 23. See H. W. Parke, *Sibylli and Sibylline Prophecy in Classical Antiquity* (London 1992).

9. See P. Battifol, "Oracula Hellenica," *Revue Biblique* 25 (1916) 177-199, esp. 194-199.

Surprisingly, the Christian Augustine, too, now used this argument. When recording the original meeting later on, he represented the fact of the oracle in this way: "By making their objections [those on the opposite side] really seemed to be looking for the answers that should be given to the pagans."[10] He evidently wanted to make it clear that the arguments proposed did not correspond completely to Christian thought. It may be assumed that the faithful who had gathered around the bishop of Hippo had only recently abjured paganism, since after 399 the civil laws prevented them from practicing pagan worship. As their objections against Augustine reveal, they seem not to have by any means completely condemned the religion of their past.[11] They still assigned to paganism an authentic religious meaning, at least for the pre-Christian period. Their line of argument came to this—that a religion must be regarded as good as long as it can be practiced without hindrance.

3. Augustine's Interpretation of Pagan Prophecies

Since "what seemed to be their [the pagans'] astonishing and extensive knowledge,"[12] that is, the knowledge enabling them to foretell the future, evidently did not leave Christians unimpressed, Augustine subjected the phenomenon to an intensive analysis. Foreknowledge of the future was one of the questions that interested him throughout his life. He himself had engaged in such practices when he was young and had only gradually freed himself from them.[13] In his sermons he spoke again and again of the practice of prophesying even among Christians.[14]

Four hundred years earlier, in his work *De divinatione* (*On Foretelling the Future*),[15] Cicero had denied any foreknowledge of the future not only to human beings but even to God. The bishop of Hippo, for his part, hardly tried to prove the unreality of the forms of *divinatio* practiced by both pagans and Christians. His purpose was rather to show that the prophecies given by pagan "gods" were deceptive, malicious, and false, and, in addition, unacceptable in the light of the Christian faith. Thus the rejection of pagan prophecy became at the same time a radical critique of pagan religion.

---

10. *Demonic Divination* 1, 1.
11. See L.-J. van der Lof, "Les interlocuteurs d'Augustin dans le *De divinatione daemonum*," *Revue des études augustiniennes* 13 (1967) 25-30.
12. *Demonic Divination* 1, 1.
13. *Confessions* IV, 3.4-6.
14. See M. M. Getty, *The Life of the North Africans as Revealed in the Sermons of Saint Augustine* (Washington: Catholic University, 1931) 139-148.
15. Augustine occasionally cites this work in his *City of God*; see M. Testard, *Saint Augustin et Cicéron* 1 (Paris 1958) 213.

Despite what the title *Demonic Divination* might lead us to expect, Augustine was not composing a systematic monograph on the phenomenon of pagan prophecy. Nor did he offer any reflections of a fundamental kind on the nature of demons. He followed the biblical and Christian tradition, which understood the pagan gods to be demons and identified the demons in turn with the fallen angels.[16] This was to adopt a position of firm opposition to ancient demonology.

In the Greek world it was especially Plato who regarded the *daimones* as beings intermediate between the realm of the divine and the realm of humanity. "Everything that is demonic lies between God and what is mortal. And what is its function? To interpret and convey to the gods what comes from human beings and to human beings what come from the gods: from the former, prayers and sacrifices, from the latter, commands and repayment for sacrifices."[17] The more strongly the philosophy of the imperial age stressed the transcendence of the divine over the earthly, the more did human beings feel the need to bridge that abyss by falling back on a series of intermediate divinities. To this end, Neo-Pythagoreanism and Middle Platonism developed an extensive demonology.

In the second century A.D., Alcinous, a Middle Platonist, represented demons as created divinities: "From them come prophecies, oracles, dreams, predictions, and other divinatory practices which human beings have adopted."[18] Plutarch likewise wrote of the prophetic abilities of the demons,[19] as did Apuleius, a Middle Platonist, whose work *The Daimon of Socrates* (*De deo Socratis*) was known to Augustine and often cited in *The City of God*.[20] Neoplatonism produced a synthesis of ancient demonology. In the second half of the third century Porphyry distinguished between good and bad demons.[21] His *Philosophy from Oracles* attempted to show the accord between Neoplatonic philosophy and the various oracular traditions. Augustine came to grips, especially in *The City of God*, with the anti-Christian bent of this defense of traditional religion and contemporary philosophy.[22]

---

16. See Augustine, *The City of God* IX, 23. See S. Lyonnet, J. Daniélou, C. Guillaumont, and F. Vandenbroucke, "Démons," *Dictionnaire de spiritualité* 3, 141-238; E. Schweizer and A. Kallis, "Geister (Dämonen)," in *Reallexikon für Antike und Christentum* 9, 688-761.
17. Plato, *Symposium* 202e. See the comprehensive discussion in Augustine, *The City of God* IX (CCL 47, 249-71). See G. Bardy, in Bibliothèque Augustinienne 34, 612-614, note complémentaire 71.
18. Alcinous, *Didaskalikos* 15, 2.
19. Plutarch, *De defectu oraculorum* 38, 431c.
20. Apuleius, *De Deo Socratis* 15-16. See H. Hagendahl, *Augustine and the Latin Classics* 2 (Göteburg 1967) 694.
21. Porphyry, *Epistula ad Marcellam* 21.
22. See *The City of God* XIX, 23. See J. J. O'Meara, *Porphyry's Philosophy from Oracles in Augustine* (Paris: Études Augustiniennes, 1959).

In *Demonic Divination* Augustine set out to show, in particular, that pagan prophecies were nothing wonderful and that the phenomenon reflected, in principle, what was already known about the nature of demons. According to the unanimous view of Greco-Roman philosophy, popular pagan beliefs, Judaism, and Christian theologians, the demons owed their divinatory abilities to their possession of subtle material bodies. In virtue of these bodies they dwelt chiefly in the air, in which they moved about with enormous speed and were therefore ahead of everything that happened. So too, Augustine attributed not only the foretelling of the future but also many other wonderful acts of demons to their nature, that is, to their keen perceptive faculties, their swift movements, and their exceptionally long experience of life. Since these sensational phenomena have a natural explanation, it is an error for human beings to think the demons worthy of worship as gods and to be ready to serve them.[23]

In the name of human dignity and freedom Augustine urgently warned his readers against superstitious practices that amounted to demonolatry and ultimately led to a diabolical perversion of religious activity.[24] Since the demons, being fallen angels, are ruled by a passionate determination to do evil,[25] they cannot be objects of veneration, because "the supremely important thing in religion is to model oneself on the object of one's worship."[26]

So too, the existence of pagan prophecies was not to be misunderstood as a sign of divine approval, which was the mistake of Augustine's partners in the dialogue. God in his omnipotence permits many things even though they are contrary to his will.[27] Although the demons may be deceiving themselves with their prophecies or aiming to deceive human beings, God allows them occasionally to predict what is true. In these cases the demons could be announcing divine decrees which they had learned from angels and prophets.

It was not at all surprising that the demon Serapis made known to one of his worshipers the coming destruction of his temple.[28] Augustine asked: "Why should this not happen, since this is not an assault on the truth but an assertion of it?"[29]

Augustine thought of this truth—the superiority of the only God over all pagan divinities—as having been foretold long ago by the biblical prophets and as being empirically confirmed in his own time by the inexorable decline of paganism.[30] In his view, the prediction of the destruction of the temple of Serapis was only a desperate attempt of the demon resident there to assert a truth which

23. See *Demonic Divination* 3, 7.
24. See *The City of God* VIII, 18-22.
25. See ibid. VIII, 8-9.
26. Ibid. VIII, 17 (trans. Bettenson 324).
27. See *Demonic Divination* 1, 2-3, 5.
28. Ibid. 6, 10-11.
29. Ibid. 8, 12.
30. See ibid. 8, 12-10, 14.

he probably knew from the biblical prophets but about which he had long kept silent, and to bring it before the people at the last moment as his own prophecy, "in order to advertise that his so-called divinity, though now he was beating a hasty retreat, was indeed in full flight."[31]

It was with this prospect of the inexorable decline of paganism that Augustine ended his little work. Its occasion—the phenomenon of pagan prophecies—had given him the opportunity of strengthening the Christians of his day in their faith in the superior reliability of the biblical prophets and of confirming them in their exclusive worship of the true God.

---

31. Ibid. 6, 11.

Demonic Divination

The Occasion that Produced this Little Book; that God Permits Things to Happen Does not Mean that They Must Be Good

1, 1. One day during the holy days of the Easter octave I had several of the brethren with me, Christian laymen,[1] and we had sat down together in the usual place, when a discussion started about the Christian religion as against the claims of the pagans, and what seemed to be their astonishing and extensive knowledge. Having recorded it and given it the finishing touches, I decided it should be committed to writing, without mentioning the names of those who were taking the opposite side, though they were Christians and, by making their objections, really seemed to be looking for the answers that should be given to the pagans.

When the question was raised about the divination of demons, then, and it was stated that someone or other[2] had foretold the demolition of the temple of Serapis, which took place in Alexandria,[3] I replied that it was not surprising if demons had been able both to know and to predict that the destruction of this temple and its idol was imminent, just like the many other things they are permitted to know and foretell.[4]

2. "So then," came the rejoinder, "such kinds of divination are not wrong and don't displease God; otherwise, being omnipotent and just, he would not permit such practices if they were wrong and unjust." I answered: "Simply because the absolutely just and omnipotent God permits these practices, it should not be taken to mean that they are themselves just. After all, many other manifestly unjust things are done, like murders, adulteries, thefts, robberies with violence and so on, which undoubtedly displease the just God precisely because they are unjust; and yet the same God, though almighty, permits them to happen as he thinks fit for some definite reasons of his own. This certainly does not mean,

---

1. There were almost certainly no women present.
2. It can be inferred from the *Life of Aedesius* by Eunapius that this person was an Egyptian priest named Antonius.
3. As a result of the prohibition of pagan worship in Egypt on June 16, 391 (*Codex Theodosianus* 16, 10, 11), the temple of Serapis was destroyed in that same year. See A. D. Nock, "Augustine and a Prophecy of the Destruction of the Serapeum," *Vigiliae Christianae* 3 (1949) 56.
4. In *The City of God* II, 23, Augustine likewise insists that the capacity of the demons to predict the future has been given to them only by divine decree.

however, that they go unpunished; they are permitted for the damnation of those who do these things that displease the Just One."

3. Against this it was argued: "It is indeed beyond all doubt that God is almighty and just, but these human sins which are offences against human society are no concern of his while they are being committed,[5] and that is exactly why they can be, which certainly would not be possible if the Almighty had not allowed it. But in no way at all can he be supposed to turn a blind eye to these matters that concern religion and worship, and thus they could not have happened unless he approved of them, and that is why they ought not to be thought of as being wrong or evil."

To this too I had an answer: "So then, these things do displease him right now, when temples and idols are being demolished, and gentile sacrifices are being punished, if ever they are offered? I mean, just as you are saying that these things could not have been done unless they pleased God, and that is why they must be assumed to be good, since they please the Just One, so too it can be said that they could not have been forbidden, done away with, punished, unless they had displeased God. And thus, if they were at that time being rightly practiced, because they were shown to have pleased the just God through his allowing them to be practiced, so now for the same reason they are being wrongly practiced, because they are shown to displease God through his either commanding or permitting them to be done away with."

God's Allowing Pagan Sacrifices Does not Mean He Approves of Them or Lets Them Go Unpunished

2, 4. Against this someone said: "These things are indeed unjust now, but not evil; and the reason they are unjust is that they are done in breach of the laws which prohibit them, while the reason they are not evil is that, if they were, they would surely never have met with God's approval. Consequently, if they had never met with his approval they would never have been done, because they would not have been allowed by the one who is almighty and who would certainly not have turned a blind eye to such goings-on, seeing that they are so serious that they would have flouted the very religion by which God is worshiped, had it been wrong or evil to do them."

At this point I myself said: "If the reason they are not wrong or evil is that they are shown to have met with God's approval by his allowing them to be done, almighty though he is, then how will it be good for the practice of them to be forbidden and done away with? But if it were not good to do away with what God approves of, being almighty he would not allow it, because this too is flouting

---

5. The implication is, however, that God will punish their perpetrators with eternal damnation.

the religion by which God is worshiped, if things he approves of are done away with by human beings. If, on the other hand, almighty though he is, he permits this, as something wrong or evil, to be done, then we do not have to think those things are good just because the Almighty permitted them to be practiced."

5. Against this someone argued: "I grant you that it is not right to practice these things now; yes, and furthermore, that the reason they are no longer practiced is that they now meet with the Almighty's disapproval. But still he *did* approve of them when they were being practiced. We, I mean to say, just don't know why he approved of them then nor why they meet with his disapproval now. All the same it is quite certain that they could not have been practiced then unless the Almighty had approved of them and that they would not have ceased now unless they had met with the Almighty's disapproval."

To this I said in my turn: "Why then are such things still being practiced privately[6] and are either going continually unnoticed or being punished on discovery, if the Almighty allows none of these things unless they meet with the approval of his justice, since what is unjust cannot please the Just One?"

Against this came the reply: "No, such things are not now being practiced at all. You see," this person said, "those sacred rites which were prescribed in the pontifical books[7] are not being practiced, and they are in fact the ones that used to be performed with every justification in those days; they are the ones that demonstrably met with God's approval then, since their performance was allowed by the Almighty and the Just One. As for any of the forbidden sacrifices being offered nowadays secretly and unlawfully, they are not to be compared with anything contained in the pontifical books but rather to be counted among those nocturnal practices which are all certainly forbidden and condemned as illicit by the pontifical books themselves."

Here I replied: "So why then does God permit even these things to go on, if he doesn't turn a blind eye to any malpractices committed against religion? It is particularly such activities as these, after all, that he *does* care about, as even those who attach great importance to the pontifical books are obliged to concede, because they naturally maintain that things forbidden by these books are forbidden by God. So how is it then that they are forbidden by God, if not because they meet with his displeasure? For, by forbidding them, of course, he shows not only that they meet with his displeasure but also, to such an extent does he care about them, that he is not in the least prepared to turn a blind eye to

---

6. See *The City of God* IV, 1: "...the false gods whom they used to worship openly and still worship secretly..." (trans. Bettenson).

7. The authors of antiquity used this term, "pontifical books," for the most widely varying books of laws and regulations, which can be identified only with difficulty today. The title does not necessarily refer to the books of the old pagan Collegium pontificals, which laid down rites for Roman augurs and for the religious ceremonies connected with the various tutelary gods of Rome.

them. From this it is to be gathered that God may both, as just, disapprove of something and yet, as omnipotent, permit its being done."

6. At this point there was general agreement that there is no reason for thinking something has been done justly and well simply because the Almighty still allows it to be done, though it meets with his displeasure.[8] The others admitted as well that evils perpetrated against the religious worship of God can also meet with the displeasure of God as just and still be permitted by him as almighty in virtue of his mysterious judgment.

But it was agreed that there was another matter now to be discussed: Where do demons, or any of those beings whom the pagans call gods, get their divinations from? For what had to be looked into was not whether these had to be regarded as good because the Almighty permitted them but whether, precisely because they are so remarkably extensive, they would seem to be attributable to nothing less than the power of God. To this point I promised that I would be giving a reply later on, because at the moment it was already high time for us to go out to the people.[9] Nor, when I found time to write, did I put off sewing up the discussion we had had so far, and stitching onto it what follows.

Why It Is Easy for Demons to Divine the Future

3, 7. The nature of demons is such that the sensitivity of their airy bodies[10] easily surpasses that of earthy bodies, and, because of the superior mobility of these airy bodies, they also incomparably outclass in speed not only the most fleet-footed of men or beasts but even the flight of birds. So, endowed in virtue of their airy bodies with these two advantages, namely keen sensitivity and rapid movement, they come to know of many things and predict or announce them to the astonishment of human beings dependent on the sluggish responses of a sense apparatus made largely of earth. Demons also have such a very prolonged lifespan that they gain a much more extensive experience of things than we human beings can come by, given the shortness of our life.

---

8. Here the CSEL text reads: "...simply because God still allows it to be done, when he takes care to have these things forbidden."

9. I.e., to church, to preach and to celebrate the liturgy.

10. The generally held view of the time was that demons had bodies, albeit made of air, while our bodies, while containing all four of the traditional elements, fire, air, water and earth, were primarily of earth, the coarsest of these elements. What was true of the demons was also true of the angels, unless they were conceded bodies of the finest, most subtle of these elements, fire. See, among other places, *The Literal Meaning of Genesis* III, 9, 14; XI, 13, 17. For this idea in the Platonic, Stoic and Neoplatonic traditions see Plato, *Timaeus* 41a; Diogenes Laertius, *The Lives and Opinions of the Philosophers* VII, 147; Plotinus, *Enneads* III, 5, 6; IV, 4, 43; Plutarch, *The Enfeeblement of Oracles* 12-13, 416c-417c; Apuleius, *The Daimon of Socrates* 7-8.

By means of these efficacious powers with which nature has equipped airy bodies, demons not only foretell many future events but also perform many wonders. Since human beings are unable to say and do such things, some people consider demons to be masters worthy of their service and of being paid divine honors.[11] It is above all the vice of curiosity that instigates this attitude, thanks to a love of a false, earthly felicity and of a time-bound superiority.[12]

Others, however, rid themselves of these cravings and do not allow themselves to be led astray and taken captive by them but instead seek and love something that always abides the same, in order by participating in it to find blessedness.[13] The first thing they bear in mind is that, just because demons outclass them in the keener sensitivity of their airy bodies,[14] that is no reason for ranking them above themselves. After all, among creatures with earthy bodies they don't think animals are to be ranked above themselves just because they have much sharper sense perceptions of many things; they don't kowtow to a keen-scented terrier because it has such a supremely sharp sense of smell that it tracks down the wild animal hiding in its lair and shows some man or other the way to its capture in virtue, obviously, not of any more farsighted intelligence but of a more acute bodily sense; or to a vulture because it flies to some cast-out carcass from an unimaginably long distance; or to a fish-eagle, because, so they say, it is able to see a fish swimming under the waves and, dropping like a stone onto the water, to grab its prey with outstretched feet and talons; or to the many other kinds of animal which, as they graze, move around among many plants that are dangerous to their health and do not touch any that might harm them, while human beings have only learned the hard way by bitter experience to avoid them, and go in dread of any number of harmless plants of which they have had no experience.

From all this it is easy to work out how much keener the senses must be in airy bodies and also to appreciate that no sensible person will regard that as a reason for ranking demons, who are equipped with such bodies, above good human beings. Let me make the same point also about rapid bodily movement, for, as regards this ability, human beings are outclassed not only by birds but by any

---

11. See *The City of God* II, 24.

12. The connection between curiosity and these other goals calls for some explanation. The key may be found in 1 Jn 2:16 (*the lust of the flesh and the lust of the eyes and the pride of life*). What Augustine means by "curiosity" is much the same as what John means by *the lust of the eyes*—a misdirected thirst for knowledge. Briefly, what the people Augustine had in mind were curiously seeking was magical powers.

13. Were he to expand on this theme, Augustine would say that they seek this good—i.e., God—by the virtue of which the vice of *curiositas* is the evil parody, namely *studiositas*, an eager quest for the only truth that is worthwhile. See *The Trinity* X, 1, 3 for this contrast and IV, 9, 13 for the vice of curiosity entangling people (especially Neoplatonic philosophers like Porphyry) in magic rites and the cult of demons.

14. Since air is the finer element.

number of quadrupeds too, which make us look in comparison as if we were made of lead; and still that is no reason for us to reckon these kinds of animals higher in the scale than ourselves, seeing that by the power of reason, not by bodily strength, we can dominate them to the extent of catching them, taming them, and training them for our own use and convenience in any way we wish.[15]

Comparison with the Marvels even Bad Human Beings Perform, Which nonetheless Do not Entitle Them to Greater Respect than the Good and Just

4, 7. Coming now to that third power of demons, their having learned from their very long experience how to know things in advance and make accurate forecasts, people who are wide awake and quick to distinguish that sort of thing from the truth revealed by the truest light[16] treat it with a shrug of the shoulders. Upright youngsters, after all, do not reckon that bad old men are better than they are themselves just because they have had much more experience and are thus, you could say, more learned. Nor do they think that doctors or sailors or farmers,[17] whom they can see to be of a crooked disposition and wicked in their behavior, are to be esteemed above themselves just because they make forecasts about matters of health in the first case, storms in the second, orchards and fruit in the third—forecasts of such accuracy that they may appear to one with no experience of such things to be divining.

8. As for the fact that demons not only predict certain future events but also perform certain marvels, thanks of course to the superiority of their bodies, why should sensible people not shrug this off too? For a great many[18] wicked and abandoned characters do such things with their bodies and can by various skills make such amazing contraptions that those who are unfamiliar with them and have not ever seen them will scarcely believe it when they are told about them. How many marvelous things have been done by tightrope dancers and other skilled circus performers, how many by clever craftsmen and especially the inventors of mechanical contrivances![19] Does that mean that they are better than good people whose only talent is a holy piety?

---

15. On these examples from the world of beasts see *The City of God* VIII, 15.
16. I.e., from the truth of inspired prophecy.
17. Augustine uses the same examples in *The Trinity* IV, 17, 22.
18. Reading *plerique* with the CSEL text instead of *plerumque* with the Maurist edition ("for wicked and abandoned characters *frequently*...").
19. Such persons, according to the standards of the time, were ipso facto regarded as "wicked and abandoned characters." The "inventors of mechanical contrivances," just *mechanici* in the Latin, were probably the persons who were responsible for special effects in the theaters, such as the always-needed *deus ex machina*.

Why have I mentioned all this? Simply to draw your attention, dear reader, who can, I trust, consider these matters without any obstinate and futile passion for argument, to a helpful comparison: there are some human beings who with the coarser material at their disposal, whether of their own bodies or of earth and water, stone and wood and various metals, can do such amazing things that those who lack any such ability are frequently so dumbfounded that they treat these people as divine in comparison with themselves, when some of them at least lead better lives than some of those who have more prodigious skills. So just ask yourself how much more prodigious and amazing must be the things demons can do with the faculties and facilities provided by the finest, nimblest kind of body there is, namely an airy one, though, for all that, they are perverse and unclean spirits, their wills twisted and warped especially by the arrogance of pride and the malice of envy. It would take too long now, though, to demonstrate the potentialities of the element of air, which enable demonic bodies invisibly to get to work on a great many visible bodies, moving, changing, twisting and turning them as they please; and in any case I think even a moment's superficial reflection will make it clear.

How Demons Succeed in Forecasting Future Events

5, 9. This being so, the first thing to realize, seeing that we are discussing demonic divination, is that demons for the most part forecast what they themselves are going to do.[20] They often receive the power, you see, to cause epidemics and to render the air itself a carrier of disease by tainting it,[21] and also to induce crooked characters and those who set their hearts on earthly advantages and commodities to acts of wrongdoing: they are assured by the morals of such people that they are going to give in to inducements of that sort. They have in fact at their disposal marvelous and invisible means of persuasion;[22] the fine, rarified nature of their bodies enables them to penetrate the bodies of human beings unperceived, unfelt, and to mix themselves into their thoughts, whether they are asleep or awake, through visions intruded into their imaginations.[23]

At other times, though, they foretell in advance not what they are about to do themselves but future events of which they have foreknowledge through natural

---

20. The same thought is found in *The Literal Meaning of Genesis* II, 17, 37.
21. See also *Expositions of the Psalms* 130, 7. See also Tatian, *Address to the Greeks* 16, 3; 18, 3; Tertullian, *Apology* 22, 4; Minucius Felix, *Octavius* 27, 2; Lactantius, *Divine Institutes* II, 14, 14.
22. For what follows see also *The City of God* X, 32.
23. For the involvement of demons (and angels) in what Augustine there refers to as "spiritual vision," that is, what we "see" in our memories and imaginations, see *The Literal Meaning of Genesis* XII, 13, 27-23, 49. See also Tertullian, *Apology* 22, 6; Lactantius, *Divine Institutes* II, 16, 5.

signs, signs beyond the reach of human senses.[24] Just because a doctor, after all, can foresee what someone ignorant of his art is unable to, that is no reason for now treating him as divine. So when, from the disturbed or the normalized temperature of the human body, he can foresee future states of bad or good health, why be surprised if demons likewise, from the state and condition of the air, perceptible to them but imperceptible to us, can predict future storms? Sometimes they also find it the easiest thing in the world to gain a thorough knowledge of people's plans when they have only been hatched in their thoughts, and before they are stated out loud in words, because they can read the signs by which "body language" gives away the mind's intentions,[25] and from this source of information too they forecast many future events, which amazes others who have no previous knowledge of these plans. Just as a person's being deeply stirred in spirit will be revealed by the expression on his face, so that other people will be able to tell from the outside what is going on inside him, so in a similar way it should not be thought incredible if even calmer thoughts betray themselves through slight indications of "body language," which can be observed by the keen sensitivity of demons but not by the duller senses of human beings.[26]

Demonic Predictions, unlike Genuine Prophecy, Can Be both Mistaken and Deliberately Misleading

6, 10. Thanks to this capacity and others of the same sort demons do foretell many things, but far removed indeed from this is the loftiness of genuine prophecy which God makes through his holy angels and prophets,[27] because, if they foretell anything of what God is planning to do, they listen to it in order to foretell it, and, when they foretell what they hear from that source, they neither deceive nor are themselves deceived, because angelic and prophetic oracles are totally truthful. Now, that demons should overhear and predict any matters of that kind strikes some people as shocking—as though there were anything shocking about bad as well as good angels not hushing up what is uttered precisely in order for it to come to the knowledge of mankind. For even among ourselves in our human society we observe the commandments about the good life being sung equally by the just and by the depraved, and we know perfectly

---

24. See Tertullian, *Apology* 22, 10.
25. In *Revisions* II, 30 Augustine criticizes the excessive certainty of this statement. He makes the point that it is exceedingly difficult, if not impossible, to know whether this knowledge possessed by demons is based on physical signs of human thoughts or is acquired in a different, spiritual way.
26. See Letter 9, 3.
27. See *The City of God* XXI, 6.

well that this does not hinder but rather helps to spread knowledge and love of the truth more widely, when even those who contradict it by their depraved morals publicly tell whatever they have learned about it.

In their other predictions, however, demons frequently both deceive and are deceived. They are deceived, for example, because, when they foretell what they are themselves planning to do, an unexpected order comes from above which upsets all their plans. It's as if any Tom, Dick or Harry under higher authority were planning something which they were sure their superiors would not forbid, and promised they would do it, and then those who had the last say in such matters suddenly decided in view of some higher plan to cancel the whole project and all its preparations. They are also deceived sometimes when they have prior knowledge of things through natural causes, like doctors or sailors or farmers,[28] but of course far more acutely and accurately, given the finer tuning and precision of an airy body's sensitivity, and then these too are suddenly and unexpectedly altered by angels dutifully carrying out some other arrangement of God Most High which was unknown to the demons.

It's as if some accident were to cause the death of a sick person who had been promised by the doctor, reading the genuine signs of improved health, that he was going to live; or as if some sailor, making a genuine weather forecast, had predicted that the gale was going to blow for a long time, which Christ the Lord, in a boat with his disciples, commanded to be quiet, *and there came a great calm* (Mk 4:39); or as if a husbandman, well versed of course in the nature of the soil and the numbers[29] of the seeds, were to predict that a particular vine would bear fruit that year, only to see it struck by lightning in an unforeseen thunderstorm or grubbed up on the orders of some Mister Big.[30] In the same way many events, which demons have prior knowledge of and then predict by foreseeing them in their more immediate and usual causes, can be canceled or changed by remoter and more hidden causes.

As for their deliberately deceiving us, well, it is their métier, the work of that envious attitude which makes them take pleasure in leading human beings astray.[31] But in order not to see their authority with their worshipers undermined, they arrange for their mistakes and their lies to be blamed on their soothsayers and the interpreters of their signals.[32]

---

28. Cicero uses the same examples in *On Divination* 1, 24.
29. I.e., the hidden powers of the seeds. Augustine is thinking of the text of Wis 11:20: *You have disposed all things in measure and number and weight.*
30. This is an allusion to the civil laws against the overproduction of wine. See Suetonius, *Domitian* 7 and 17.
31. There is a similar thought in *Order* II, 9, 27; *Teaching Christianity* II, 23, 35; *Answer to Faustus* XXII, 17.
32. Like the priests of Apollo who interpreted the unintelligible utterances of the oracle at Delphi.

11. What is so surprising, then, when the overthrow of the temples and their idols is already in the offing, as foretold so long before by the prophets of God Most High, if the demon Serapis[33] gives a hint of it to one of his devotees in order to advertise that his so-called divinity, though now he was beating a hasty retreat, was indeed in full flight?

Reasons why Demons Are Allowed to Predict What Had already Been Foretold by the Prophets

7, 11. These creatures are, you see, indeed being put to flight, or being tied up and dragged away and exiled from their traditional places, so that God's will may be put into effect in the affairs which they used to lord it over and for which they used to be worshiped. It was he who foretold so long ago that this was going to take place among all nations and who gave instructions for it to be carried out by his faithful people. And why, I ask you, should a demon not be allowed to predict this event, since he already knew that it was hanging over him? The prediction was in any case born out by the prophets who had written about these things,[34] and clear-sighted people would be given by it some idea of how vigilantly they had to be on their guard against the deceitfulness of demons and to shun their worship. It would show them for how long a stretch of time the demons had first of all kept quiet in their own temples about these future events which they must have known had been foretold by the prophets and how, later on, when the fulfillment of them was drawing near, they decided to "predict" them themselves lest they should be thought to have been ignorant of them and to have been outmaneuvered.

So, to show how long ago it had all been foretold and written down, let me pass over other prophecies for the moment and mention what the prophet Zephaniah says: *The Lord will prevail against them and will banish all the gods of the nations of the earth; and they shall worship him, each from his own place, all the islands of the nations* (Zep 2:11). Now, perhaps the demons who were worshiped in the temples of the gentiles did not believe that these things were going to take place, and that is why they declined to publicize them through their soothsayers and their temple dervishes. This is how their own poet brings Juno on the scene, as not altogether believing what Jupiter has said about the death of Tumus. Juno, by the way, is proclaimed by these people as an airy power; and this is how she speaks in Virgil:

---

33. On Serapis see *The City of God* XVIII, 5. Porphyry made Serapis the leader of the evil demons; see *Philosophy Derived from Oracles* 147.
34. See Justin, *First Apology* 54, 2; Tertullian, *Apology* 22, 9.

Now to a grievous end a guiltless man
Is doomed, or I, the truth eluding me,
Do drift and stray; ah, would that baseless fears
Were playing with me; that thou, who hast the power,
Wouldst bend and turn what sorely has begun
To kinder termination![35]

So then, perhaps the demons, that is the airy powers, doubted whether the things they knew the prophets had predicted could happen to them and for that reason refused to repeat their prediction—and that's enough to show what kind of beings they are. Or perhaps they knew very well that it was all certainly going to happen[36] and for that reason hushed it up in their temples, lest intelligent people should then and there start abandoning them with scorn, because the very prophets who forbade their worship were testifying to the eventual overthrow of their temples and idols.

Now, however, when the time has come that has seen fulfilled what was foretold by the prophets of the one God, who says that these are false gods and forbids their worship with all the force at his command, why should they too not be allowed to predict what they have learned? Like this they would give themselves away even more clearly, as either not having believed it earlier on or as having been afraid to announce it to their worshipers, and finally, with nothing else left to them to do, as having decided to parade their powers of divination in the very places where they are now shown up as having so long been false pretenders to divinity.

The One True God of Israel Has never Been Attacked or Denied by the Oracles of Pagan Gods

8, 12. As for what their remaining worshipers say, that these things were foreknown and are to be found in some books of their own "prophets,"[37] well, if they were there in their temples such a long time beforehand, they ought to have been brought to the attention of their congregations if they were true, just as ours are, when they are recited not only in our churches but also from the most ancient and well-known texts in the synagogues of the Jews, where they provide an even more effective testimony against all our enemies. Still, the predictions they

---

35. *Aeneid* X, 630-632.
36. See Mt 8:29; Rv 12:12.
37. In *Asclepius* 24-26 (*Corpus Hermeticum* II, ed. Nock), a hermetic work from the end of the third century A. D., Hermes announces the decline of the old worship of the gods in Egypt. On later oracles see J. Doignon, "*Oracles, prophéties, 'ont dit' sur la chute de Rome* (395-410). Les réactions de Jérome et Augustin," *Revue des études augustiniennes* 36 (1990) 120-146.

occasionally dredge up from these books "off the record" ought not to trouble us; it just means that some demon or other has had his arm twisted to give out to his worshipers what he has learned from the utterances of the prophets or the oracles of angels. And why should this not happen, since this is not an assault on the truth but an assertion of it? The one thing, after all, that had to be demanded of them[38] is something they have never put about in the past and will never attempt to put about in the future (except perhaps in some forgery), and that is that their gods have dared to predict or to say anything through their soothsayers against the God of Israel.

About this God their most learned authors,[39] who could have read and come to know all these works, spent more time inquiring who God might be than even attempting to deny his existence. On the other hand this God, who none dared deny is the true God (and even if they had denied it, they would not only have been subjected to the appropriate penalty but would also have been convicted and convinced of their error by his undeniable works)—this God, then, who none of them, as I said, dared deny is the true God, through his own soothsayers, that is the prophets, first declared those others to be false gods who were to be totally abandoned, then openly and publicly foretold that their temples and idols and sacred rites would be overthrown, openly and authoritatively commanded it to be done, and openly saw to it that it really and truly was done.

Could any of these people then be quite so silly as not to choose to worship the God whose worship is not forbidden by the gods they used to worship? When they do start to worship him, there is assuredly no doubt at all that they are not going to worship any more those whose worship is forbidden by the one they now worship.

The Conversion of the Gentiles Foretold by the Prophets

9, 13. A little earlier, though, I mentioned his prophets as having predicted that the gentiles were going to worship him once the false gods they used previously to worship had been banished and put out of bounds, and I will now repeat what I quoted: *The Lord, it says, will prevail against them and will banish all the gods of the nations of the earth; and they shall worship him, each from his own place, all the islands of the nations.* And not only the islands but all the nations as also including all the islands, seeing that elsewhere he does not name the islands but the whole wide world, saying: *All the ends of the earth will be reminded and*

---

38. I.e., if they were to be effective opponents of the truth. This is presumably what he means us to understand.

39. He means the great philosophers of the past, above all Pythagoras and Plato among the Greeks, and chiefly Cicero, their Latin filter (so to say) among the Romans; then, nearer his own time, Plotinus and the Neoplatonists; and doubtless the Stoics too, but definitely not the Epicureans.

*converted to the Lord; and all the families of the nations will worship in his pres-
ence, since the kingdom is the Lord's and he himself will lord it over the nations*
(Ps 22:27-28). That all this has been fulfilled through Christ is plain enough,
both from several other texts and from this very psalm which I have just quoted.
He himself, you see, was speaking about his future passion in it through the
prophet a little earlier on, where he said: *They have dug my hands and my feet,
they have counted all my bones; but they gazed at me and inspected me, they
divided my garments among them, and over my vesture they cast lots* (Ps
22:16-18); then shortly after that he brings in what I just quoted: *All the ends of
the earth will be reminded and converted to the Lord*, and so forth.

As a matter of fact, though, the testimony I first presented, where it says, *The
Lord will prevail against them and will banish all the gods of the nations of the
earth*, clearly shows, by saying *will prevail*, that this too was foretold: that the
pagans were first going to assail the Church and persecute the Christian name as
much as they were able, in order if possible to wipe it altogether from the face of
the earth; and, because he was going to overcome them through the patience of
the martyrs and stupendous miracles, and because of the consequent conversion
of whole peoples to the faith, it therefore says, *The Lord will prevail against
them*.

After all, it wouldn't say *he will prevail against them* unless they were going
to oppose him with their assaults. So you also have the prophecy made in the
psalm: *Why did the nations roar, and peoples meditate vain things? The kings of
the earth took their stand, and the princes were gathered together, against the
Lord and against his Christ.* And a little later he says: *The Lord said to me, You
are my son, today have I begotten you; ask of me, and I will give you the nations
for your inheritance, and for your possession the ends of the earth.* (Ps 2:7-8)
There you are, that's where the other psalm also gets it from, the one I introduced
above as saying: *All the ends of the earth will be reminded and converted to the
Lord.*

These and similar prophetic documents show that what we now see being
fulfilled through Christ was predicted: that it was going to come about that the
God of Israel, whom we understand to be the one true God, would be worshiped
not just in that one nation which was called Israel but in all nations; and that he
would cast out the false gods of the gentiles both from their temples and from the
hearts of their worshipers.

The Mockery of the Few Remaining Educated Pagans May Be safely Ignored

10, 14. Let these people go off now and still have the nerve to continue
defending their former futile vanities against the Christian religion and against

the true worship of God, so that they may perish with a bang. That too, you see, is what is foretold about them in the psalm, where the prophet says: *You have taken your seat upon the throne, you who judge with equity. You have rebuked the nations, and the godless man has perished. You have blotted out their name for ever, and for age after age. Their memory has perished with a bang, and the Lord abides for ever.* (Ps 9:4-7) So then, it is necessary for all these things to be fulfilled, nor ought we to let it trouble us that the few of them who are left still have the nerve to make a parade of their empty, boastful doctrines and to make fun of Christians as so many ignoramuses, while we can see the things foretold about them being fulfilled. It is precisely this so-called ignorance and foolishness of Christians, seen by the humble and the holy and the diligent students of it as the one true supreme wisdom—it is, I am saying, precisely this so-called foolishness of Christians that has reduced them to this tiny minority, since as the apostle says, *God has made foolish the wisdom of this world.* Then he adds a wonderful thing, if anyone can understand it, and continues like this: *For, since in the wisdom of God the world did not come to know God through wisdom, it pleased God through the foolishness of the preaching to save those who believe, since the Jews indeed are asking for signs, and the Greeks looking for wisdom. We, however, are preaching Christ crucified, to the Jews indeed a stumbling block, to the Greeks foolishness, but to those who have been called, Jews and Greeks, Christ, God's power and God's wisdom, since the folly of God is wiser than men, and the weakness of God is stronger than men.* (1 Cor 1:20-25)

Let them make fun, then, as much as ever they can, of our ignorance and our foolishness and brag about their learning and their wisdom. What I do know is that this year there are fewer of these people left to make fun of us than there were last year. From the time, you see, that *the nations roared and peoples meditated vain things against the Lord and against his Christ,* when the blood of the saints was being shed by them and the Church being ravaged, until the present time and beyond, they are growing fewer and fewer every day. We, however, are enabled to stand up to their insults and their proud derision with the utmost firmness and confidence by the oracles of our God, which on this point too we rejoice to see being fulfilled. This, you see, is how he addresses us through the prophet: *Listen to me, you that have knowledge of judgment, my people, in whose heart is my law; do not dread the insults of men, nor let yourselves be overwhelmed by their slander, nor think it a great matter that they now despise you. For like a garment, so will they be worn out by time, and eaten away by moth like wool, but my justice abides for ever.* (Is 51:7-8) All the same, let them read these words of mine if they would deign to do so, and, when their objections reach me, I shall reply as best I can with the help of the Lord.

Faith and Works

Translation by Ray Kearney

Notes by Michael Fiedrowicz

Introduction

1. Occasion and Historical Background

In his *Revisions* Augustine tells us why he composed his *Faith and Works*: "Meanwhile, brothers who, though laymen, used to occupy themselves zealously with the divine sayings sent me several pieces of writing in which they tried to separate Christian faith from good works; this they did in order to persuade people that they could not reach eternal life without faith, but could do so without good works. As an answer to them I wrote the book *Faith and Works*. In it I speak not only about how those reborn by the grace of Christ must live but also about the kind of people who are to be admitted to the sacrament of rebirth."[1]

Evidence both internal and external allows us to date the composition to 413.[2] In that same year Augustine had begun his monumental work, *The City of God*. This fact shows how important and urgent it must have seemed to the very busy bishop of Hippo that he give a detailed answer to the question addressed to him.

The historical background of the consultation can be reconstructed with some likelihood from Augustine's answer. It is probable that in a North African community and in connection with a concrete case the question arose of whether divorced and remarried spouses could be admitted to baptism if they were determined to continue living with the new marital partner. The ecclesial authority that was first consulted must have said yes. This tolerance was then extended to all candidates for baptism who were living in such unions and preferred to renounce baptism rather than break off their relationship, which resembled an ongoing adultery. Pastoral practice tended to side with sinners rather than submit to the seemingly rigorous position of Church authority.

In order to justify this generous baptismal practice and, in addition, to give legitimacy to an optimism about salvation that assured all Christians of eternal blessedness solely on the basis of their faith, those concerned searched sacred scripture for relevant passages and produced an extensive dossier. This document fell into the hands of devout laypersons who forwarded it to the bishop of Hippo for his assessment. Since Augustine recognized the dogmatic and pastoral importance of this explosive question he did not delay in giving his opinion in detail.

Beginning in the seventeenth century scholars speculated about who it was

---

1. *Revisions* II, 38.
2. See *Faith and Works* 14, 21; Letter 205, 4, 18; *Eight Questions of Dulcitius* 1, 2.

that took the positions discussed in the present work. But neither Jerome[3] nor a small group of Latin writers (Jerome, Ambrose, Ambrosiaster, possibly Cyprian)[4] could be clearly shown to hold the views challenged by Augustine.[5] The problems raised point not so much to concrete adversaries as to a particular mentality that was held by not a few catechumens, catechists, and baptized persons at that time.

Despite the best of intentions this secularized mentality threatened to promote a laxism which Augustine decisively opposed.[6] In the final analysis he was dealing with a phenomenon that has manifested itself in all periods of Christianity and in a variety of forms, namely, an attack on ecclesial standards, which were rejected in the name of a supposed "spirit of mercy." Beyond that, there was a radical error arising from "human compassion." Those who adopted this attitude thought that God in his mercy demands faith alone as a condition for salvation and therefore that every baptized Christian is saved by his faith, even if he has lived a sinful life on earth.

But to Augustine's mind the eschatological aspect of the problem was only secondary, at least in the present work. The pastoral aspect took precedence for him.

2. Augustine's Answer

At first sight, *Faith and Works* seems not only complex but confusing. Given the countless citations of scripture that are alleged and refuted, the reader can easily lose sight of the basic idea amid the complicated meanderings of the discussion. Briefly put, the thesis, which is worked out in exceptional detail and with often wearisome persistence, is this: Only a faith that is active in love has the promise of everlasting life.

Augustine was at pains to develop three arguments behind the baptismal practice which he was opposing:[7]

1) In permitting access to baptism even for scandalous and hardened sinners it was argued that the Church had never challenged the mingling of good and wicked persons.

2) Proof was sought in the scriptures that since the time of the apostles the rule was first to administer baptism and only later on to call for a change in way of life.

---

3. This was the thesis of J. Garnier (PL 48, 244D).
4. This was the thesis of J. Turmel, *Histoire des dogmes* IV (Paris 1935) 292.
5. See H. De Lavalette, "L'interprétation du Psaume 1, 5 chez les Pères miséricordieux latins," *Recherches de science religieuse* 48 (1960) 544-563.
6. See A. Gaudel, in Bibliothèque Augustinienne 9, 388-391, note complémentaire 40.
7. See *Faith and Works* 27, 49.

3) Eternal salvation is guaranteed solely by the faith received in baptism.

In the opening chapter (1,1) Augustine sketches briefly the adversarial view of an unconditional access to baptism, the idea behind it of an undoubted certainty of salvation for every baptized believer, and, finally, the resultant catechetical practice, which was restricted to dogmatic truths, since good works were irrelevant to salvation.

In his first argument in response (1,1-6,8) Augustine grants that the Church is a community in which the good and the wicked live intermingled. But the toleration of the wicked in the Church, something the Bible itself calls for, must not lead to a state of affairs which puts "the Church's discipline to sleep."[8] Neither, of course, must the Church go to the opposite extreme, which is rigorism.

In a second step (6,9-13,20) Augustine refutes the thesis that candidates for baptism are simply to be instructed in the faith and that only after baptism are they also to be instructed in the principles of a Christian way of life. He calls attention to the fact that faith is a matter not simply of the intellect but also of a concrete manner of life. Therefore candidates for baptism must also receive instruction in morality. It is the practice of the Church (he says) to deny baptism to persons not prepared to repent of their sins and to accept the duties that flow from the teachings of the faith. Therefore those whose lives or professions are not in harmony with the Christian faith cannot be admitted to baptism. This constant practice of the Church is based on the teachings of scripture.[9]

The section 14,21-16,30 is devoted to the third and most important question. Augustine knew how to avoid being trapped in the dilemma constructed by his adversaries: Is it faith that rescues or is it the works of the law? Instead, he replaces these alternatives by another pair, contrasting *dead faith* and the *faith that works through love* (Gal 5:6). It is the unambiguous teaching of the scripture that justification comes only through a faith that shows its vitality in the works of love and not through a faith that is unaccompanied by works.

In order to refute the erroneous idea that at the last judgment every human being will be purified and redeemed, and this through *a kind of fire* (*quasi per ignem*) that obliterates their sins, Augustine had to devote careful study to 1 Cor 3:11-15, since his opponents appealed to it.[10] The disagreement was not with those who claimed a purification after death but with the supposedly "merciful" who saw in this purification a way of rescuing even sinners who still had only a "dead" faith. In Augustine's view, the proponents of a justification by faith alone were mistaken in their interpretation of what the apostle said. When Paul claimed that human beings were justified by faith and not by observance of the

---

8. Ibid.
9. See J. H. S. Burleigh, "St. Augustine on Baptism," *Reformed Theological Review* 15 (1956) 69-75.
10. *Faith and Works* 16, 27.

law, he was speaking of works that preceded justification, not of those that followed upon it. Therefore only those believers whose faith is alive in works of love can hope for eternal blessedness.

It is on the basis of this Pauline teaching that 1 Cor 3:11-15 is to be properly interpreted. When the apostle speaks of the various kinds of material with which the faithful build on the foundation of Christ, his contrast between "wood" and "gold" does not refer to the alternative of "faith without works—faith with works." He is speaking rather of the varying quality of the works themselves. "Wood" and "gold" symbolize the different kinds of intention—self-centered and pure—from which works flow. Purifying fire is a symbol of the suffering that cleanses human beings of their still imperfect motivations for action.

In the next, less clearly structured section (17, 31-21, 38), the opposition between a dead faith and a living faith continues to be the main idea, but the emphasis is now chiefly on its pastoral implications. Augustine is convinced that while some local churches may have grown negligent in their practice, the universal Church has always refused baptism to hardened sinners. He then discusses a series of other scriptural passages that touch on the basic theme of *Faith and Works*.

3. Importance of the Work

In *Faith and Works* Augustine did not simply take a position on a pastoral question. Rather he reflected on the dogmatic problem of the kind of faith needed for salvation. The distinction between dead faith and living faith made it clear that authentic faith must leave its mark on the believer's entire way of life. At the same time, this faith gives human life its deepest meaning, because it makes everlasting life possible for the baptized.

Augustine dealt with this same subject on several subsequent occasions. In about 420 Consentius posed similar questions to him; in response Augustine referred the questioner to his book *Faith and Works*, which contained the answers.[11] A short time later, in 421/22, he returned to the subject in his *Enchiridion* (18, 67-69). When he received another question on the same subject from Dulcitius, he cited in response numerous passages of his treatise on *Faith and Works*.[12] Finally, in 425/26, Augustine distinguished in *The City of God* (XXI, 17-22) six kinds of laxism regarding the conditions for salvation as represented by the "compassionate Christians" with whom he had dealt in his *Faith and Works*, twenty years earlier.

---

11. Letter 205, 3, 18.
12. *Eight Questions of Dulcitius* 1, 1-13.

The present treatise already contains both the main ideas in the Augustinian position and the biblical basis for them. But Augustine's reaction to the "theology of compassion" was by no means the manifestation simply of his personal views. What he was doing was recalling the traditional teaching of the Church on faith and works and bringing it to bear once again on a pastoral practice that had lost its bearings. His theological merit consisted not least in basing ecclesiastical discipline on the dogmatic truths about faith.

But that is not the only standpoint from which *Faith and Deeds* is important. In addition, it is a valuable witness to the practice, especially in the North African Church, of instructing catechumens and administering baptism. In Augustine's discussion of these matters laxism and rigorism can be perceived as the two dangers confronting ecclesiastical authorities at that period. Of interest to the history of dogma are the references to a teaching on purgatory;[13] these would play a role in discussions of the subject in later centuries. Augustine's remarks on various kinds of sins and the corresponding punishments for them became influential in the history of the sacrament of penance.[14] What he had to say about the situation of those living in irregular marriages found a place in canon law.[15]

---

13. *Faith and Works* 16, 29. See J. Ntedika, *L'évolution de la doctrine du purgatoire chez Saint Augustin* (Paris: Études Augustiniennes, 1966); J. Gnilka, *Ist 1 Kor. 3, 10-15 ein Schriftzeugnis für das Fegefeuer? Eine exegetisch-historische Untersuchung* (Düsseldorf 1955).

14. See *Faith and Works* 3, 4; 19, 34; 26, 48. See L. M. J. Verheijen, "Eléments d'un commentaire de la Règle de Saint Augustin," *Augustiniana* 22 (1972) 5-34, esp. 30-34.

15. See M.-F. Berrouard, "Saint Augustin et l'indissolubilité du Mariage. Évolution de sa pensée," *Recherches Augustiniennes* 5 (1968) 139-55, esp. 147-149 on *Faith and Works* 19, 35.

Faith and Works

1, 1. There are certain people who hold the view that absolutely everyone should be admitted to the waters of rebirth in our Lord Jesus Christ.[1] They make no exception even for those who refuse to change a sinful and evil way of life, notorious for its crimes and perversions, and openly declare their intention to go on living in the same way. If, for example, someone has a mistress, it should not be insisted that he first leave her and then come to baptism, but, even while he is still with her and admits or even proclaims that he intends to stay with her, he should be received and baptized. He should not be prevented from being united to the body of Christ, even if he continues to be united to the body of a prostitute.[2] He should be taught how evil this is afterwards and should be instructed about the need for moral reform after he has already been baptized. In their view it is perverse and absurd to teach how a Christian should live first and then baptize. They hold that the sacrament of baptism should come first and that the teaching about life and morality should follow after that. If anyone chooses to accept this teaching and live according to it, he will benefit, but if he refuses, he will still have the Christian faith. Without this he will perish eternally, but with it, whatever sordid crimes he continues with, he will be saved in the manner of one who passes through fire, as he will have built on the foundation, which is Christ, though not with gold and silver and precious stones but with wood and grass and straw,[3] that is to say, not with sinless and chaste conduct but with wicked and impure.

2. They seem to be impelled to this argument because they are concerned that men who have divorced their wives and remarried, or women who have divorced their husbands and remarried, are not admitted to baptism, because Christ testifies unmistakably that these are not marriages but adultery.[4] Although they cannot say something is not adultery, when the Truth declares with no uncertainty that it is adultery, at the same time they would like those they see held by ties of that kind to be approved for the reception of baptism. They reason that, if they are not accepted for baptism, they would choose to live, or

---

1. The conditions set by the Church for baptism at this period are described in J. H. S. Burleigh, "St. Augustine on Baptism," *Reformed Theological Review* 15 (1956) 65-80.
2. See 1 Cor 6:15. Augustine describes the same error in *Expositions of the Psalms* 80, 20; *Eight Questions of Dulcitius* 1; *The City of God* XXI, 17-22.
3. See 1 Cor 3:11-15.
4. See Mt 19:9.

even die, without any sacrament rather than break that adulterous bond and be set free. A certain human compassion moves them to take up their cause, to the extent of holding that not only they but all criminals and flagrant sinners should be accepted for baptism without being checked by any prohibition or corrected by any instruction or changed at all by repentance. They figure that, if this does not happen, they will perish eternally, but, if it does, even those who persist in those evils will be saved after passing through fire.

2, 3. In reply to them, the first thing I say is that those statements of scripture that point to the present intermingling of good and bad persons in the Church, or foretell that it is going to occur in the future, should not be taken by anyone as reason for holding that strict and careful discipline should be entirely relaxed or abandoned. If they think that, they have not been taught by those writings but have been deluded by their own presumptions. Because the Lord's servant Moses patiently endured that mingling among the first people, it does not follow that he did not punish many of them even with the sword, just as the priest Phinehas also struck down with the avenging steel the adulterers who were discovered together.[5] This certainly symbolized that in these times, when in the Church's public discipline the sword is no longer to be seen, the same result has to be achieved through demotion[6] and excommunication. Similarly, because the holy apostle, although saddened, is most tolerant of the false brothers,[7] even allowing some of them to preach Christ despite being motivated by the devil's proddings of envy,[8] it does not follow that he thinks *the one who had his father's wife* should be spared. He commands that in the presence of the assembled Church he be handed over to *Satan for the destruction of the body, so that the spirit will be saved on the day of the Lord Jesus* (1 Cor 5:1.5). Nor does it follow that he himself did not hand others over to *Satan, for them to learn not to blaspheme* (1 Tm 1:20), or that there was no point in his saying: *I wrote to you in a letter not to associate with adulterers, and certainly not with the adulterers of this world or the avaricious or robbers or servants of idols; otherwise you deserve to depart from this world. Now I have written to you that, if any brother is declared to be either an adulterer or a slave to idols or given to cursing or a drunkard or a robber, then do not associate with him and do not even take food with him. How am I to be the judge of those who are outside? Are you not the judges of those within? God will be the judge of those who are on the outside. Remove the evil from yourselves.* (1 Cor 5:9-13) In this passage some interpret the words *from yourselves* as meaning that people individually should remove evil from themselves—in other words, should be good persons. Whichever way

---

5. See Nm 25:7-8.
6. Demotion was a punishment established for the clergy.
7. See 2 Cor 11:26.
8. See Phil 1:15-18.

it is interpreted, however, whether as meaning that evil persons should be censured with the Church's severity and be excommunicated or that individuals should remove evil from themselves by opposing it and correcting it,[9] in the passage we have quoted there is no ambiguity in the part where he commands them not to associate with those brothers who are named, that is to say, known and notorious, for one of the sins mentioned there.

3, 3. He shows clearly in what spirit, and with what love, that merciful severity should be exercised, not only in the passage where he says, *So that the spirit will be saved in the day of the Lord Jesus* (1 Cor 5:5), but also in another place, where he says, *If anyone does not listen to what we say in our letters, note who it is and do not associate with him, so that he might be ashamed, not intending to regard them as enemies, but correcting them as a brother* (1 Thes 3:14-15).

4. The Lord himself was a unique example of tolerance—who even put up with a devil among the twelve apostles until the passion and who said, *Let both grow until the harvest, lest perhaps setting out to gather the darnel you also pull out the wheat at the same time* (Mt 13:29-30), and who also foretold, as an analogy of the Church, that the nets would hold good and bad fish right up to the shore, that is until the end of the world. From these statements and anything else he may have said, explicitly or in parables, about the intermingling of the good and the bad, it still does not follow that he thought the Church's discipline should be put aside. Rather he warned that it should be exercised, when he said, *Attend to yourselves; if your brother offends against you, go and correct him in private. If he listens to you, you will have won your brother. If, however, he does not listen, take one or two others with you, so that everything said may be confirmed by the word of two or three witnesses. If he does not listen to them, speak to the Church. If, however, he does not listen to the Church, treat him as you do pagans and tax collectors.* (Mt 18:15-17) He then added the terrifying threat of that severity, also saying there, *Whatever you loose on earth will be considered loosed also in heaven, and whatever you bind on earth will be considered bound also in heaven* (Mt 18:18). He also forbids us to give what is holy to dogs.[10] The apostle does not contradict the Lord by saying, *Reprimand sinners in the presence of everyone, so that the others will be afraid* (1 Tm 5:20), even though the Lord says, *Correct him in private.* Both procedures are necessary, according to the needs of the different illnesses of those we undertake to correct and care for (and certainly not to lose); different ones have to be cured in different ways. That is the reasoning that justifies maintaining some pretence and tolerating bad

---

9. For this interpretation of the Pauline text see *Answer to the Letter of Parmenian* III, 2, 15.
10. See Mt 7:6.

persons in the Church, and it is also the reasoning that justifies reprimanding them, punishing them, refusing to accept them and excommunicating them.[11]

4, 5. Those who do not take a middle position go wrong. When they rush head-long in one direction, they do not notice other statements of divine authority that could cause them to desist from their purpose and settle in the truth and moderation that is guided from both directions. This applies not only in the question presently under discussion but in many others as well. On reading the passages in the divine writings that teach that we must only worship one God, some have concluded that the Father is both identical with the Son and also identical with the Holy Spirit;[12] others, seemingly afflicted by an opposite disease, attend to the writings that speak of the Trinity, and—unable to understand how there is only one God, since the Father is not the Son, nor the Son the Father, and the Holy Spirit is neither the Father nor the Son—they have thought it necessary to assert that there is a plurality of substances.[13] Some, noticing how the scriptures praise holy virginity, have condemned marriage;[14] others have latched onto the texts that extol chaste marriage and have made virginity and marriage equal.[15] Some have read, *Brothers, it is good not to eat meat or drink wine* (Rom 14:21), and similar texts, and have thought that God's creatures and the food they sought was unclean;[16] others have read, *Everything created by God is good and nothing should be rejected that is taken with thanksgiving* (1 Tm 4:4), and have lapsed into greed and drunkenness.[17] They have not have been able to rid themselves of their faults unless opposite ones, just as bad or even worse, replace them.

6. It is the same in the case at hand. Some attend to the severe command-ments—which warn us to reprimand troublemakers and not to give holy things to dogs and to treat anyone in contempt of the Church as a pagan and to cut off from union with the body any member that causes scandal—and then upset the peace of the Church by trying to separate out the darnel before it is time;[18] and, blinded by this error, they themselves become separated from Christ's unity instead. This is the point of our argument against the schism of Donatus.[19] It is not addressed to those who know that Caecilian was not arraigned on truthful

---

11. For different ways that the Church had of dealing with sinners see sections 34 and 48.

12. This is probably an allusion to Sabellius; see *The Trinity* VII, 4, 9.

13. This was the position of the subordinationists, especially the Arians; see ibid. V, 3, 4; V, 6, 7.

14. The reference is to the Manicheans; see *Answer to the Two Letters of the Pelagians* III, 9, 25; *The Catholic Way of Life* I, 35, 78-80. Augustine is also thinking of the Priscillianists; see *Heresies* 70, 2.

15. Jovinian is meant here; see *The Merits and Forgiveness of Sins* III, 7, 13.

16. Thus the Manicheans; see *The Catholic Way of Life* I, 33.

17. The reference is once again to Jovinian; see Jerome, *Against Jovinian* I, 3.

18. See Mt 18:18.

19. The schism began 311-312 during the persecution of Christians under Emperor Diocletian and was not healed until the Conference of Carthage in 411, thanks to Augustine's authoritative influence.

charges but on lying ones, and who still do not abandon their pernicious opinion in mortifying shame,[20] but to those to whom we have said: "Even if those on whose account you are not in the Church were sinners, you should have stayed in the Church and put up with the ones you could not reform or expel." At the other extreme, there are those who see that the intermingling of good and bad persons in the Church was announced or predicted, and they learn the commandments of tolerance and then become reckless. (We are so reassured by those commandments that, even though we see there is darnel in the Church, neither our faith nor our charity is so impeded that we ourselves leave the Church because we perceive the darnel in the Church.) They conclude that the Church's discipline should be dismantled, ascribing a certain perverted security to the authorities, whereby their only role is to say what has to be avoided or what has to be done but not be concerned about anything anyone actually does.

5, 7. In our judgment sound teaching requires that we be guided by both strands of evidence in what we think and do. Then we shall not only tolerate dogs in the Church for the sake of peace in the Church but shall also not give what is holy to dogs when the peace of the Church is not at risk. When, therefore, we find evil persons in the Church, either through the negligence of those in authority or because of some understandable necessity or through some secret infiltration, and we cannot correct or restrain them with ecclesiastical discipline, let us recall those parables and divine pronouncements, or unmistakable examples, from scripture, where it is revealed and foretold that there will be evil persons in the Church mingling with the good right until the end of the world and the judgment day, and that they will not be detrimental to unity and to the participation in the sacraments of the good persons who do not approve of what they do. Then there will not arise in our hearts the unholy and destructive presumption that would lead us to conclude that we have to cut ourselves off from those people to avoid being tainted by their sins and try to take others with us as our pure and holy disciples, separating them from the unified body as though from an assembly of sinners. On the other hand, those who rule the Church have the power to discipline sinners and criminals, provided it does not compromise peace in the Church. Once again, therefore, to prevent us from falling asleep through indolence or lethargy, we have to be prodded with the prongs of those commandments that relate to strict enforcement. Then, with him as our leader and teacher, we shall direct our steps in the path of the Lord under the guidance of both

---

20. In 311-312 seventy bishops of Numidia met in Carthage and deposed Caecilian, bishop of that city, on the grounds that his ordination was invalid because among his consecrators were *traditores* ("traitors" or "handers-over"), that is, men who had handed over or surrendered the sacred scriptures to the pagan authorities during the persecution. Donatus later became the leader of this opposition movement.

strands of evidence; we shall neither be benumbed in the name of patience nor rage in the guise of being diligent.

6, 8. We must see now what follows if in accordance with sound doctrine we observe this moderation. In other words, should people be accepted for baptism without any concern to see that something holy is not given to dogs, to the extent of not even thinking that notorious adulterers, who announce their intention of continuing in that sin, should be barred from such a holy sacrament? There is no question that they would not be accepted if they announced that, during the actual days when those who are about to receive that grace have submitted their names and are being purified by continence, fasting and exorcisms, they were going to sleep with their true and legitimate wives and that they would not observe abstinence in this matter for those few sacred days, even though this would not be wrong at other times. So, if a married person who refuses to conform is not admitted to those sacred rites, how is it that an adulterer who refuses to reform is admitted to them?

9. "Baptize him first," they say, "and then teach him about leading a good life and morality." This is what is done with someone who may be near death. After stating his belief in very few words, which nevertheless includes everything, he receives the sacrament, so that if he departs from this life he will leave it freed from the guilt of all his past sins. On the other hand, if a person in good health requests it, and there is time for him to be instructed, could we find any better time for him to be told how he ought to reform and live as one of the faithful than then, when his mind is held attentive and uplifted by that religion and he is asking for the sacrament of saving faith? Have we so forgotten ourselves that we do not even recall how anxiously we applied ourselves when our catechists were telling us what we had to do, at the time when we were applying for the sacraments of that font and for that reason were even called applicants?[21] Do we not notice others, who flock every year to the waters of rebirth—what they are like during those days when they are being catechized and exorcised and examined, how alert they are in their meetings, how keenly they listen, how carefully they consider everything? If that is not the time to tell them how to live in a manner befitting that great sacrament which they desire to receive, when will that time be? Will it be rather after they have received it, when they still have those serious sins even after baptism and have become not new persons but old sinners? In other words, will you be so astoundingly perverse as first to say to them, "Put on

---

21. This section is an important document on the catechumenate in North Africa in the fourth century. The catechumens who decided to be baptized had to enter their names on a list before Lent. These seekers of baptism were now called *competentes* or *electi*. During Lent they underwent an intense preparation of an ascetical as well as of a catechetical kind; this meant fasting, continence for the married, a private confession of sins, and exorcisms. See W. Harmless, "Catechumens, Catechumenate," in A. D. Fitzgerald, ed., *Augustine through the Ages* (Grand Rapids 1999) 145-149.

the new person," and after they have put on the new person then to say to them, "Put off the old person"? The apostle maintains the appropriate order when he says, *Put off the old person and put on the new* (Col 3:10); and the Lord himself proclaims, *No one sews new cloth on an old garment, and no one puts new wine in old wineskins* (Mt 9:16-17). What is all that time for, when they hold the status and title of catechumen, if it is not for them to hear what a Christian should believe and what kind of life a Christian should lead, so that, when they have proved themselves, they may then eat from the Lord's table and drink from his cup? This is because all *who eat and drink unworthily, eat and drink judgment for themselves* (1 Cor 11:29). This has been the practice for as long as the Church has had the sound rule that those coming to receive Christ's name are given the status of catechumen, and it is carried out even more strictly and carefully in these times, when those who have submitted their names to receive baptism are called candidates.

7, 10. "What if a virgin unknowingly married someone else's husband?" they say. If she never becomes aware of it, she will never be an adulteress because of it. If she becomes aware of it, she then begins to be an adulteress, because she is knowingly sleeping with someone else's husband. It is the same as with property law, where it is right to say that people hold possession in good faith as long as they do not know that they are in possession of property that belongs to someone else. Once they know this, if they do not vacate the other person's property, they are then held to be in bad faith and are rightly called unjust. Far be it from us, therefore, to feel such grief when scandals are corrected (with a sensitivity clearly not humane and clearly futile) as though marriages were being broken up, especially when this takes place *in the city of our God, on his holy mountain* (Ps 47:2), that is, in the Church. There marriage is esteemed not only as a bond but also as a sacrament,[22] and it is not lawful for a man to give his wife to another.[23] It is said that in the Roman republic, as it then was, Cato did this not only without blame but even with approval.[24]

There is no need to discuss this at any length here, since those we are replying to do not dare to claim that this is not sinful or deny that it is adultery. They do not want to be shown to be openly contradicting the Lord himself and the holy gospel. They do, however, hold the view that persons like that should first of all be admitted to receiving the sacrament of baptism and to the Lord's table, even if they explicitly refuse to be corrected. They hold in fact that they should not be

---

22. When Augustine speaks of marriage as a sacrament, what he has in mind primarily is a "transcendent significance found in human relationships." See D. G. Hunter, "Marriage," in Fitzgerald 535-537, esp. 536.

23. The indissolubility of marriage is for Augustine a visible sign of the invisible unity of Christ with the Church; see *Marriage and Desire* I, 10; *The Excellence of Marriage* 7, 7.

24. See Plutarch, *Cato minor* 25.

given any warning at all in this regard but should be taught about it afterwards. Their reasoning is that, if they agree to obey the commandment and correct their guilt, they will be counted among the wheat, but, even if they reject it, they will be tolerated as darnel. They think they make it sufficiently clear that they are not justifying those sins or acting as though they are not sins at all or merely minor ones. Could there be any hope for a Christian who held that adultery was not a sin at all or merely a minor one?

11. They think that they derive the order to be followed in correcting or instructing in these matters from sacred scripture. They say that this is what the apostles did, and they offer in evidence certain passages from their writings, where they are found to have first imparted the doctrines to be believed and afterwards conveyed the moral commandments. They want the inference to be that those being baptized should only be taught what is required for belief and later, when they have already been baptized, be given the commandments to reform their lives. It is as though they read some letters of the apostles that were written to those being baptized and that discuss belief and different ones that were written to those already baptized and that contain the commands about avoiding evil and adopting good ways of living. Since it is agreed that they gave the writings to those who were already baptized Christians, why do they contain both texts together, namely those relating to belief and those relating to living a good life? Perhaps they now think we should give neither of them to those being baptized and give both to those who have been baptized? If it is absurd to say this, then they should admit that in their letters the apostles put their whole teaching, complete in both respects, but generally taught belief first and followed it with what related to living a good life for the reason that, in the actual individual, belief must come first in order for the good life to follow. If anyone seems to have acted well, he should not be said to have acted rightly unless he has acted out of the duty which has God as its object. If certain foolish and ill-informed persons believed that the apostles' letters were given to the catechumens, surely they would likewise admit that, along with the things that had to be believed, the moral precepts, consonant with that belief, were also imparted to persons not yet baptized. Otherwise their arguments might force us to conclude that they want the first sections of the apostles' letters, where they speak about belief, to be read to the catechumens, and the later sections, where it is laid down how Christians should live, to be read to the faithful.[25] If this is a very stupid thing to say, and therefore there is no text to support this view in the letters of the apostles, why would we think that those being baptized should be instructed only about belief and that those who have been baptized should be instructed

---

25. The term "faithful" (*fidelis*) was reserved to the baptized, whereas "Christian" (*Christianus*) had a broader scope and included catechumens.

about morality, simply because they command faith in the first section of their writings and afterwards urge the faithful to live well as a consequence? Although one must come first and the other second, sound and responsible teaching usually requires that both be preached in the context of a single discourse, whether it is to catechumens or to the faithful, whether to those being baptized or those already baptized, whether as instruction or reminder, whether to inform or to confirm. When in fact they cite in evidence certain passages in the letters of Peter and in the letters of John, let them add also those of Paul and the other apostles. In drawing attention, as they do, to the fact that faith is spoken about first and morals afterwards, this has to be understood in the manner that I believe I have made clear.

8, 12. "In the Acts of the Apostles," they say, "when Peter addressed those who were baptized after hearing the word, three thousand on one day, all he preached to them was faith, to believe in Christ. When they said, *What must we do?* he answered, *You must repent, and every one of you must be baptized in the name of the Lord Jesus Christ for the forgiveness of sins, and you will receive the gift of the Holy Spirit.* (Acts 2:37-39) Why then do they not notice that he said, *You must repent?* There is the elimination of the old life, so that those being baptized may put on the new life. What can repentance achieve, since repentance is for works that are dead, for someone who continues in adultery and other crimes in which the love of this world is entangled?

13. "He only wanted them to repent of their unbelief, because they did not believe in Christ," they say. What astonishing presumption! (I do not wish to speak more harshly.) When they hear the words, *You must repent,* they say it only refers to acts of unbelief, although what the gospel teaching conveys is that there must be a change from the old life to a new one. This certainly includes what the apostle says in that regard, *Anyone who stole must no longer steal* (Eph 4:28), and the rest, where he expands on what it means to put off the old person and put on the new. If they chose to pay careful attention to them, they could take warning from Peter's own words. He said, *You must repent, and every one of you must be baptized in the name of the Lord Jesus Christ for the forgiveness of sins, and you will receive the gift of the Holy Spirit. For this is the promise made to us and our children and to all who are far away, to all whom the Lord our God calls.* (Acts 2:38-39) The writer immediately went on to say: *And he said many other things in support of this, and said: Tear yourselves away from this depraved world. They listened avidly and accepted what he said and believed and were baptized; and on that day three thousand souls were added to their number.* (Acts 2:38-41) Is there anyone who does not understand that, with the *many other things* that the writer omitted for reasons of brevity, Peter's purpose was to persuade them to tear themselves away from this depraved world, given that the actual statement Peter was arguing for in saying *many things* is included in summary form. The summary is stated with the words, *Tear yourselves away*

from this depraved world, and it was in support of this objective that Peter said *many things*. Included there was the condemnation of dead works, the sins committed by those who are attached to this world, and the commendation of a good life accepted and lived out by those who tear themselves away from this depraved world. So now, if they like, let them try to assert that those who merely believe in Christ, though they persist in whatever sins they please, even to the point of open adultery, are tearing themselves away from this depraved world. If, however, it is wrong to say this, then let those who are to be baptized be told not only what they have to believe but also how they must tear themselves away from this depraved world. That requires that they be told how believers have to live.

9, 14. They say that that eunuch whom Philip baptized said nothing other than *I believe Jesus Christ is the Son of God* (Acts 8:37-38) and, on making this declaration, was immediately baptized. Are we content then for people only to give this answer and then be baptized straightaway? Is there nothing the catechist need say and nothing the believer need acknowledge about the Holy Spirit, nothing about the holy Church, nothing about the forgiveness of sins, nothing about the resurrection of the dead, nothing even about the Lord Jesus Christ himself except that he is the Son of God, nothing about his suffering, his death on the cross, his burial, his rising on the third day, his ascension and his sitting at the right hand of the Father? If it was thought that when the eunuch answered, *I believe Jesus Christ is the Son of God*, this was enough for him to be baptized immediately and then go away, why do we not follow this example? Why do we not imitate this and do away with all the rest that we consider it necessary to make explicit by asking questions, even when baptizing under the pressure of limited time, so that the one being baptized may respond to them all,[26] even if there is no time to commit them to memory? It may be, however, that scripture was silent and left to be understood everything else that Philip did with that eunuch he was baptizing. It may be that with the words, *Philip baptized him* (Acts 8:38), it was implied that everything was carried out that we know from a continuous tradition has to be carried out, even if for the sake of brevity it is not all mentioned in scripture. If so, then in the same way, from the fact that it is written that Philip preached the gospel of the Lord to the eunuch, there can be no doubt at all that the teaching included an account of those things that relate to the life and morality of anyone who believes in the Lord Jesus. That is what it means to preach the gospel of Christ: saying not only what has to be believed about Christ but also what commandments have to be kept by anyone who comes to the unity of the body of Christ. It means saying everything that has to be believed

---

26. During the ceremonies of baptism the candidates performed the *redditio symboli* ("the giving back of the creed"), that is, they recited the creed before the assembled community; see Sermon 58, 1.

about Christ, not only whose son he is, his origin with respect to his divinity and with respect to his flesh, the things he suffered and why, the power of his resurrection, the gift of the Spirit that he promised and gave to the faithful, but also what kind of members he looks for to be their head, to establish as his members and cherish and set free and lead to eternal life and honor. When these things are said, sometimes more briefly and compressed, sometimes more extensively and in richer detail, then Christ's gospel is preached. Nothing is passed over that relates to belief, but also nothing that relates to the morality of believers.

10, 15. This can also be inferred from their account of what the apostle Paul said: *I claimed to know nothing while I was with you except Jesus Christ, and him crucified* (1 Cor 2:2). Those people think this means that at first they were not told of anything else they had to believe, and after they were baptized they then learned whatever relates to life and morality. They say this was enough, and more than enough, for the apostle who told them that they might have *many tutors in Christ, but only one father, because it was he who had given them life in Christ Jesus through the gospel* (1 Cor 4:15). Therefore, if he who gave them life through the gospel, even though he gives thanks that he did not baptize anyone among them except Crispus and Gaius and the family of Stephenas,[27] did not teach them anything other than Christ crucified, what then? Suppose someone says that, when they were being given life through the gospel, they were not even told that Christ rose from the dead? How then do we explain that he told them: *I passed it on to you in the beginning that Christ died as the scriptures had foretold, and that he was buried, and that he rose again on the third day as the scriptures had foretold* (1 Cor 15:3-4), if he only taught that he was crucified? If, however, this is not how they understand it, but they maintain that this too relates to Christ crucified, then they should realize that in learning Christ crucified people learn many things, and especially that our former selves were crucified with him, to destroy this sinful body and free us from the slavery of sin.[28] This is why he also says about himself, *Far be it from me to boast except in the cross of our Lord Jesus Christ, through whom the world has been crucified to me and I to the world* (Gal 6:14).

They should take notice, therefore, and see how Christ crucified is taught and learned, and be aware that it relates to his cross that in his body we too are crucified to the world, understanding by this the suppression of evil desires. It follows that it is not possible for open adultery to be condoned in those who are transformed in the cross of Christ. The apostle Peter also gives a warning concerning the sacrament of the cross, that is to say, the sacrament of Christ's passion, that those who are made holy by it should desist from sin. He says, *As Christ suffered*

---

27. Cf. 1 Cor 1:14.16.
28. See Rom 6:6.

in the flesh, you too must arm yourselves with the same thought, that anyone who has died in the flesh ceases to sin, in order to live the rest of this bodily life no longer by human desires but by the will of the Lord God (1 Pt 4:1-2), and the rest that follows. He is showing us that the one who belongs to Christ crucified, that is, to Christ who suffered through the flesh, is the one in whose body carnal desires have been crucified and who leads a good life through the gospel.

16. Can they think that even those two commandments, in which the Lord says the whole of the law and the prophets is contained, support this opinion of theirs? That is how they mention them, since the first commandment is said to be: *Love the Lord your God with your whole heart and your whole soul and your whole mind. The second is similar: Love your neighbor as yourself.* (Mt 22:37-39) Do they then think that the first commandment, where love of God is commanded, is for those who are being baptized, but that the second, which is clearly about social morality, is for those who have been baptized? Do they forget the text: *If you do not love your brother whom you see, how can you love God whom you do not see?* (1 Jn 4:20) and that other text in John's same letter: *Anyone who loves the world does not have the love of the Father* (1 Jn 2:15)? Do all the excesses of immorality relate to anything other than love of this world? It follows that there is no way the first commandment, which they think concerns those who are being baptized, is able to be kept without good morals. I do not want to delay by saying more. On careful consideration, those two commandments are found to be so interrelated that it is not possible for a person either to have love of God without loving his neighbor or to have love of his neighbor without loving God. What we have said about these two commandments is sufficient for our present purpose.

11, 17. On the other hand, the people of Israel were first of all led through the Red Sea, which is a symbol of baptism, and afterwards received the law, from which they learned how they should live. Why then do we even hand on the creed to those who are being baptized and insist on their repeating it? Nothing like that was done in the case of those people when God freed them from the Egyptians by leading them through the Red Sea. If they are right to interpret this as being signified by the previous mysteries of smearing the doorposts with the blood of a lamb and of the unleavened bread of sincerity and truth,[29] why do they not also understand the other as a consequence, namely that the actual separation from the Egyptians symbolizes the separation from sin that is proclaimed by those being baptized? Relevant to this is what Peter said: *You must repent, and every one of you must be baptized in the name of the Lord Jesus Christ* (Acts 2:38), as though to say: "Leave Egypt and pass through the Red Sea." Hence in the letter entitled *To the Hebrews*, when the initiation of those being baptized is

---

29. See Ex 12:7-27.

recounted, it mentions repentance for works that are dead. It says this: *Therefore let us leave behind the basic teaching about Christ and look to its full development, not laying again the foundation of repentance for works that are dead and of faith in God, and of the teaching about baptism and the laying on of hands and the resurrection of the dead and eternal judgment* (Heb 6:1-2). In scripture, therefore, there is enough clear evidence to show that all these matters have a place in the instruction of neophytes. What is repentance for works that are dead, however, if it is not for those works that have to be put to death in order for us to live? If this does not include adultery and fornication, is there anything at all to be counted as works that are dead? It is not enough to profess the abandonment of things of that kind, unless also all past sins, which are following in pursuit as it were, are destroyed by the washing of rebirth, just as it was not enough for the Israelites to leave Egypt, unless that hostile army pursuing them perished in the waters of that same sea that opened up for the people of God to pass through to freedom. If anyone, therefore, openly refuses to change from his state of adultery, how will he be led through the Red Sea, since he still refuses to leave Egypt? They then fail to notice that in that law, which was given to that people after the crossing of the Red Sea, the first commandment is this: *You must not have other gods besides me. You must not make yourself idols or any image of anything in the sky above or on the earth below or in the waters beneath the earth. You must not worship them or be their servants* (Ex 20:3-5), and the rest concerning that commandment. Therefore let them contradict their own statement, if they like, and assert that there should be no preaching about the worship of one God and guarding against idolatry to those who are yet to be baptized but only to those who have already been baptized; but let them not say now that those who are going to receive baptism should only be informed about belief, which is belief in God, and, after receiving the sacrament, then be instructed concerning moral conduct, taking this to be the second commandment, which deals with loving one's neighbor. The law the people received after crossing the Red Sea, the same as after baptism, contains both elements. There was no such division of the commandments, with the people being taught about guarding against idolatry before crossing that sea and, after crossing it, being told they had to honor their father and mother, not commit adultery, not kill, and the rest of the commandments for good and sinless human living.[30]

12, 18. Suppose someone comes and asks for the sacred washing but declares that he will not give up the sacrifices to idols, except perhaps afterwards, when it suits him. Suppose he continues to demand baptism and insists on being made a temple of the living God, even though he is not only a worshiper of idols but even belongs to some forbidden priesthood of that kind. I ask those people to tell me if

---

30. See Ex 20:12-17.

they think someone like that should even be made a catechumen. No doubt they will protest that this must not happen, and there is no reason to think they are not sincere. Let them explain, therefore, in terms of the evidence from scripture, which they think has to be interpreted like that, how it is that they dare to contradict and insist on rejecting this person, who is protesting and saying: "I have learned Christ crucified and I reverence him. I believe Jesus Christ is the Son of God. Do not put me off any longer; you ask for nothing more. The apostle did not want those to whom he gave life to know anything then except Christ crucified. After the eunuch answered that he believed Jesus Christ was the Son of God, Philip did not put it off but baptized him immediately. Why do you forbid me to participate in the worship of idols and refuse to admit me to Christ's sacrament before I give that up? That is something I learned as a child, and I am held to it by the heavy weight of custom. I shall do that when I can, at an opportune time. But even if I do not do it, do not let me come to the end of this life without Christ's sacrament, lest God demand my soul from your hands." What answer do they think they should give to this? Will they agree that the person should be received? That is unthinkable; I cannot believe they would go so far. What will they answer, then, to the one who says this, and who adds that at least nothing should be said to him about giving up idolatry, just as those first people were told nothing about it before the crossing of the Red Sea, since these things are contained in the law, which they received after they had already been liberated from Egypt? They will surely say to this person, "When you receive baptism you will be a temple of God." But the apostle says, *What is there in common between the temple of God and idols?* (2 Cor 6:16) Why then do they fail to see that similarly we have to say, "When you receive baptism, you will be united with the body of Christ. You cannot be united with the body of Christ and also be united with the body of a prostitute"?[31] This is what the apostle says, and in another place he also says, *Make no mistake. Neither fornicators nor the servants of idols* and the others he lists there *will possess the kingdom of God.* (1 Cor 6:9-10) Why, therefore, do we refuse to admit to baptism those who serve idols but think adulterers should be admitted, when he says to these and other sinners, *Some of you were like this, but you have been washed clean, you have been made holy, you have been made just in the name of the Lord Jesus Christ and in the spirit of our God* (1 Cor 6:11)? When, therefore, I have the authority to forbid both, what reason do I have to allow someone coming to baptism to continue to be an adulterer but not to continue to be a servant of idols, since I hear it said to one no less than to the other, *Some of you were like this, but you have been washed clean*? Those opponents are moved to this view because they think salvation is assured, although by passing through fire, for those who believe in Christ and receive his

---

31. See 1 Cor 6:15.

sacrament, that is, become baptized, even if they are so unconcerned about reforming their conduct that they live in sin. For this reason, with God's help, I will now see what is the correct view to take according to scripture.

13, 19. I am still dealing at present with the question at issue, when they take the view that those who have been baptized should be admonished about the morality appropriate for living as a Christian but that those who have yet to be baptized should only be taught to have belief. Apart from everything else I have said, if that were the case John the Baptist would not have said to those who came to him for his baptism, *You brood of vipers, who taught you to flee from the wrath to come? Produce the fruits appropriate to repentance* (Mt 3:7-8), and so on. This is certainly not a warning about faith but about good works. Hence, when the soldiers asked, *What shall we do?* he did not say, "For the present believe and be baptized, and afterwards you will be told what you should do." On the contrary, as the precursor who was clearing the way for the Lord to come into their hearts, he warned them beforehand and told them beforehand, *Do not be violent, do not lay false charges, be satisfied with your pay.* Similarly, when the tax collectors asked what they should do, he said: *Do not demand more than the law stipulates.* (Lk 3:12-14) With these brief accounts, as there was no need for him to insert the entire catechism, the evangelist gave sufficient indication that anyone catechizing someone before baptism has the duty to teach and advise about morals. If their reply to John had been, "We will not produce the fruits appropriate to repentance, we will lay false charges, we will be violent, we will demand what is not our due," and after this declaration he still baptized them, even then, as far as concerns the question presently at issue, it could not be said that, when someone is to be baptized, there is no time to talk to him about how he should lead a good life.

20. Leaving aside other considerations, let them recall what the Lord himself answered when the rich man asked him what good thing he should do to obtain eternal life. *If you want to attain eternal life,* he said, *keep the commandments. Which commandments?* the man said, and the Lord then listed the command-ments of the law, *Do not kill, do not commit adultery*, and the rest. When he answered that he had done this since he was a young man, the Lord added also the commandment of perfection: that, having sold everything he owned and given alms to the poor, he would have treasure in heaven and should follow the Lord.[32] They should notice that he was not told to believe and be baptized, which those people think is all the help anyone needs to come to eternal life. Rather, he was told the moral commandments that have been given to mankind, even though they certainly cannot be preserved and obeyed without faith. At the same time, just because the Lord seems to be silent here about imparting belief, we do

---

32. See Mt 19:16-21.

not insist and do not argue that those who desire to attain life should only be told the moral commandments. As I said before, the two are connected, because there cannot be love of God in someone who does not love his neighbor, and there cannot be love of his neighbor in someone who does not love God. We sometimes find that scripture mentions one without the other, whichever one it may be, instead of the full doctrine, so that even from this we understand that there cannot be one without the other. Anyone who believes in God must do what God commands, and anyone who does what God commands, because God commands it, must believe in God.

14, 21. We must look now at what has to be expunged from the hearts of religious people, so that they will not forfeit salvation because of a false sense of security, thinking that all they need do to obtain it is to have faith, while neglecting to live a good life and stay on God's path by performing good works. Even in the time of the apostles there were some people who failed to understand certain rather obscure statements of the apostle Paul and thought that he said, *Let us do evil, for good to come of it* (Rom 3:8), *because he had said, The law came into the world so that sin would be abundant, but where sin was abundant, grace was even more abundant* (Rom 5:20). The explanation of this is that those who received the law and proudly relied on their own strength, and did not have the correct belief and did not pray for God's help to conquer their evil inclinations, became burdened with additional and more serious sins in that they also violated the law. Driven by this great guilt they fled to faith, and with it they won merciful forgiveness and *help from the Lord who made heaven and earth* (Ps 120:2). Then, with love poured into their hearts through the Holy Spirit,[33] they did with love the things that were commanded contrary to the desires of this world. This was in accordance with what was foretold in the Psalm: *Their weaknesses increased, but afterwards they raced on* (Ps 15:4). Therefore, when the apostle says that he considers we are made just through faith without the works of the law,[34] he does not mean that works of justice should be disdained once faith is accepted and professed but that everyone should know that he can be made just through faith even if he did not perform the works of the law before. They do not come beforehand, before the person is made just, but they follow afterwards, when the person has been made just.

There is no need to go into further explanation of this in the present work, especially as I have published a lengthy book on the subject entitled *The Letter and the Spirit*. Since this opinion had already sprung up at that time, other letters of the apostles—those of Peter, John, James and Jude—oppose it directly, strongly insisting that faith without works brings no benefit. Paul himself also

33. See Rom 5:5.
34. See Rom 4.

stipulated that it had to be not just any faith whereby one believes in God but that full faith of the gospel that brings salvation, the one whose works come from love. *And the faith that works through love* (Gal 5:6), he said. Hence he asserts that that faith which some think is sufficient for salvation is entirely worthless, saying this: *If I have all faith, so as to move mountains, but do not have love, I am nothing* (1 Cor 13:2). When, however, believing love is at work, without doubt there is then a good life, for *love is the fulfilment of the law* (Rom 13:10).

22. Clearly this is why in his second letter Peter remarked that there were some passages in the letters of the apostle Paul that were difficult to understand, and people misinterpreted them, and other scriptures too, for their own destruction, although that apostle held the same views as the other apostles concerning eternal salvation, which is granted only to those who lead good lives. He was commending holiness of life and conduct and proclaiming that this world will pass away, but we look forward to new heavens and a new earth, which will be given to the good to inhabit. He wanted them to see from this how they ought to live in order to become worthy of that dwelling place, as he knew that some wicked persons had taken advantage of certain less clear passages of the apostle Paul in order to have no concern for living a good life, being assured of salvation because that comes from faith. So Peter says this: *As all these things will pass away, what kind of persons should you be, living holy and devout lives, looking forward to and hastening the coming of the day of the Lord, when the lights in the sky will be extinguished and the elements consumed by a burning fire! We look forward to new heavens and a new earth as he promised, in which justice will dwell. Therefore, dear friends, while you are waiting for this, do enough to be found in peace with him, unstained and untarnished, and value the suffering of our Lord as salvation, as our dear brother Paul wrote to you according to the wisdom granted to him, speaking about these things in all his letters. There are some things in them that are difficult to understand, that the unlearned and vacillating distort to their own destruction, as they do with the rest of scripture. You, therefore, my dearest friends, being forewarned, take care not to be led astray by the error of the misguided and lapse from your own steadfastness; but grow in the grace and understanding of our Lord and savior Jesus Christ. To him be glory both now and in eternity.* (2 Pt 3:11-18)

23. James is so strongly opposed to those who hold that faith without works has any value for salvation that he even compares them to devils, saying, *You believe there is one God? You do well. The devils believe this too, and are terrified.* (Jas 2:19) Could he have said anything more succinctly, with greater truth or more emphatically, since we read in the gospel that the devils said this when they acknowledged that Christ was the Son of God, and they were rebuked[35] for

---

35. See Mk 1:24-25.

the same thing as was praised in the case of Peter's declaration of faith?[36] *What does anyone gain, my brothers*, says James, *if he says he has faith, but does not have works? Is it possible for faith to save him?* (Jas 2:14) He also says, *Faith without works is dead* (Jas 2:20). So great, therefore, is the mistake of those who promise themselves everlasting life from a faith that is dead!

15, 24. We should pay careful attention to the way that statement of the apostle Paul, certainly difficult to understand, should be interpreted. His words are: *No one can lay any foundation except the one that has been laid, which is Christ Jesus. If anyone builds on that foundation with gold, silver, precious stones, wood, grass or straw, his work will become evident. The day will make it known, because it will be revealed with fire, and the fire will test the quality of everyone's work. If the edifice anyone has built on it survives, he will receive a reward. If anyone's work burns, he will suffer loss, but he himself will be safe, though as someone who has passed through fire.* (1 Cor 3:11-15) They take the interpretation of this to be that those who add good works to faith, which is faith in Christ, are seen as building on this foundation with gold, silver and precious stones; but those who perform evil works, even though they have the same faith, are seen as building with wood, grass and straw. As a consequence they think that through certain punishments with fire they can be purified in order to receive salvation because of the merits of the foundation.

25. If this is so, we have to admit they are acting with commendable charity in trying to have everyone admitted to baptism indiscriminately, not only adulterers and adulteresses who cling to their false marriages in defiance of the Lord but also public prostitutes who continue in their corrupt profession. In no church, not even the most lax, has it been the practice to admit these unless they are first freed from that past prostitution. By that reasoning, however, I cannot see at all why they are not accepted regardless. Who would not prefer that they be purified by fire, certainly one of some longer duration, because they laid the foundation, even though they piled wood and grass and straw on it, rather than that they perish eternally?

In that case, however, those other texts, which are not obscure or ambiguous, will not be true, namely, *If I have all faith, so as to move mountains, but do not have love, I am nothing* (1 Cor 13:2), and, *What does anyone gain, my brothers, if he says he has faith, but does not have works? Is it possible for faith to save him?* (Jas 2:14) Also untrue will be that text: *Make no mistake. Neither fornicators nor the servants of idols nor adulterers nor catamites nor sodomites nor thieves nor the avaricious nor drunkards nor slanderers nor swindlers will possess the kingdom of God.* (1 Cor 6:9-10) Untrue too will be that other: *The deeds of the flesh are unmistakable. They are fornication, impurity, obscenity,*

---

36. See Mt 16:16-17.

idolatry, witchcraft, enmities, arguments, jealousy, hatred, quarrels, heresies, envy, drunkenness, gluttony, and suchlike. I warn you, as I have warned you before, that those who act like that will not possess the kingdom of God. (Gal 5:19-21) These texts will not be true, for, if they only believe and are baptized, even though they continue with those sins, they will be saved through fire, and so those who have been baptized in Christ, even those who do those things, will possess the kingdom of God.

But it is meaningless to say, *Some of you were like this, but you have been washed clean* (1 Cor 6:11), when they are still the same even after they have been washed. Peter's words will also seem pointless: *You too, in a similar state, are now saved by baptism, which is not the removal of physical dirt, but the questioning of a good conscience* (1 Pt 3:21). There is no point to it, if in fact baptism also saves those who have evil consciences, filled with every crime and atrocity and not changing at all by repenting of those evils, if they too will be saved, even though by passing through fire, because of the foundation that was set in place in that baptism. I do not see either why the Lord said, *If you want to enter into life, keep the commandments* (Mt 19:17), and listed those that relate to good conduct,[37] if even without keeping them one can enter into life merely through the faith that *without works is dead* (Jas 2:17). How then will those words be true that he will say to those he is going to put to his left: *Go into eternal fire, which was prepared for the devil and his angels* (Mt 25:41)? He does not condemn them because they did not believe in him but because they did not perform good works. Without doubt the reason why he said he was going to separate out all the nations that mingled under the care of the same shepherds was to prevent anyone from promising himself eternal life from the faith that without works is dead. In this way it would be clear that those who would say to him, *Lord, when did we see you suffering these things and fail to assist you?* (Mt 25:44) were those who believed in him but were not concerned about performing good works, thinking that eternal life would be attained through a faith that was itself dead. On the other hand, might it be perhaps that those who will go into eternal fire are those who did not perform works of mercy, while those who robbed others or who were merciless towards themselves by desecrating the temple of God within themselves will not go there? As if works of compassion could be worth anything without love,[38] when the apostle says, *If I distribute everything I have to the poor, but do not have love, it does me no good* (1 Cor 13:3), or anyone could love his neighbor as himself, if he did not love himself! *He who loves sin*, it says, *hates his own soul* (Ps 10:6).

---

37. See Mt 19:18-19.
38. See *Enchiridion* 19, 70.

One cannot say here, as some have deceived themselves by saying, that it is the fire that is said to be eternal, not the actual punishment. They think that those to whom they promise salvation through fire because of a faith that is dead will pass through a fire that lasts forever. In other words, the actual fire lasts forever, but their burning, that is, the action of the fire, does not last forever for them.[39] The Lord, being Lord, foresaw this, and he concluded by saying: *So they will go into everlasting burning, but the just will go into everlasting life* (Mt 25:46). Therefore the burning will be everlasting, like the fire. The Truth has said that those who go there will be those he pronounces to have been lacking not in faith but in good works.

26. If all these, as well as innumerable other unambiguous passages to be found in scripture, are untrue, then it is possible that that interpretation of the wood and grass and straw is true, namely that those who will be saved through fire are those who only had faith in Christ but neglected to do good deeds. If, however, these texts are both true and unambiguous, then there is no doubt that we have to look for another interpretation of that statement of the apostle, and it has to be counted among those certain difficult passages that Peter says are in his writings and that people should not misinterpret to their own destruction. They should not go against the clearest evidence of scripture and cause the worst of sinners to feel assured of obtaining salvation, even though they cling stubbornly to their sins and make no change through reform or repentance.

16, 27. At this point I might be asked my opinion about that statement of the apostle Paul and how I think it should be interpreted. I confess that on this matter I prefer to listen to those who are more perceptive and more learned, who explain it in such a way that everything I have cited above, and anything else I have not cited, remains true and unshaken. In those passages scripture testifies in the clearest terms that faith achieves nothing, unless it is faith as the apostle defines it, namely, the faith that *works through love* (Gal 5:6), and that without works it cannot bring salvation, whether through fire or without fire. If it saves through fire, it certainly saves. What it says, however, is explicit and unconditional: *What does anyone gain if he says he has faith, but does not have works? Is it possible for faith to save him?* (Jas 2:14) Just the same I shall also say, as briefly as I can, what my own opinion is concerning that particular statement of Paul that is difficult to understand, provided the main thing kept in mind with regard to my declared position is that I have said that on this matter I prefer to listen to my betters.

The foundation for the building of the wise architect is Christ. This needs no elaboration, as it has been stated explicitly: *No one can lay any foundation except the one that has been laid, which is Christ Jesus* (1 Cor 3:11). If, however,

---

39. See *The City of God* XXI, 23-27.

it is Christ, undoubtedly it is Christ's faith; as the same apostle says, Christ dwells *in our hearts through faith* (Eph 3:17). Then, if it is Christ's faith, it is certainly the faith defined by the apostle, the faith *that works through love.* That faith which the devils have, since even they believe and are terrified and declare that Jesus is the Son of God,[40] cannot be taken as the foundation. Why not? Simply because it is not the faith that works through love but one that is extorted by fear. Therefore, when Christ's faith, the faith of Christian grace, that is, the faith that works through love, is set as the foundation, that faith does not allow anyone to perish. If I try to elaborate too precisely what it means to build on this foundation with gold, silver and precious stones, or with wood, grass and straw, I fear the explanation itself may become too difficult to understand. Nevertheless, with whatever assistance God grants, I shall attempt to explain what I think, both briefly and, as best I can, clearly.

The man who asked the good master what he had to do to obtain eternal life was told that, if he wanted to have life, he had to keep the commandments. When he asked which commandments, he was told, *Do not kill, do not commit adultery, do not steal, do not commit perjury, honor your father and mother* and *love your neighbor as yourself.* (Mt 19:18-19) If he did this with faith in Christ, there is no doubt that he would have the faith that works through love. He would not love his neighbor as himself unless he had acquired the love of God, since without that he would not love himself. Then, if he did what the Lord also went on to say, *If you wish to be perfect, go and sell everything you have, and give to the poor, and you will have treasure in heaven; and come and follow me* (Mt 19:21), he would be building on that foundation with gold, silver and precious stones. He would be thinking only of *the things that concern God, how to please God* (1 Cor 7:32-33), and these thoughts, in my view, are the gold, silver and precious stones. On the other hand, he might be preoccupied by certain material concerns about his riches, even though he made many charitable contributions from them and did not attempt to increase them by any fraud or theft, nor lapse into any crime or corruption for fear of losing them in whole or part; otherwise by doing that he would already be detaching himself from the stability of that foundation. This might happen, as I say, because of carnal attachment to those possessions, which would make him sad to be without them. In that case he would be building on that foundation with wood, grass and straw, especially if he had a wife and on her account his thoughts were about *worldly things, how to please his wife* (1 Cor 7:32-33). Since, therefore, these things that are loved with a carnal attachment are not lost without sorrow, it follows that those who have them in such a way as to have the faith that works through love as the foundation, and do not give them priority over this for any reason or motive, come to salva-

---

40. See Jas 2:19.

tion through a certain fire of sorrow if they undergo the pain of losing them. The less one loves those things, and the more one possesses them as though not possessing them, the more one is protected from such great sorrow and loss. On the other hand, those who commit murder, adultery, fornication, idolatry and anything like that, in order to acquire or keep those possessions, will not be saved by fire because of that foundation but will not have the foundation and will suffer torment in eternal fire.

28. In their desire to show the value of merely believing, they quote the apostle, who says, *If the one who does not believe leaves, let him go; in these circumstances a brother is not bound* (1 Cor 7:15), that is to say, because of Christ's faith it is not wrong even to leave a legitimate wife if she refuses to stay with a Christian husband because he is a Christian. They fail to observe that it is right to divorce her like that, if she says to her husband, "I will not be your wife unless you load me even with stolen wealth, or unless even as a Christian you indulge in the excesses you have made customary in our home," or if there is anything else criminal or sinful that she has experienced with her husband and derived pleasure from, whether by sexual gratification or by living more comfortably or even by having more fashionable clothes.[41] In that case, if the husband whose wife says this to him has truly repented of works that are dead when he has come to be baptized and has the foundation of the faith that works through love, then without doubt he will be bound more by love of divine grace than by love of his wife's body, and he will resolutely cut off the limb that incites him to sin. Any sadness of heart he suffers through this loss because of the physical attraction to his wife, that is, any pain this causes him, constitutes the fire through which he will be saved as the straw burns. On the other hand, if he was already living with his wife in the manner of someone not married, not because of physical desire but out of compassion, hoping perhaps to save her, and granting the marital right only when asked for it but not claiming it, then he will certainly feel no physical sadness when such a marriage is terminated, since his thoughts in her regard will only have been for *the things that concern God, how to please God.* As a result, inasmuch as by thinking like that he built with gold, silver and precious stones, his was not a structure of straw and it would not be consumed by any fire.

29. Whether people suffer these things only in this life or something of the kind also happens subsequent to certain judgments after this life, I do not think that interpretation of the passage is far from being the true explanation. Even if there is a better interpretation that I have not thought of, if we hold to this one we are not forced to say to the unjust and the rebellious, the criminals and the impure, the parricides and matricides, the murderers, the fornicators, those who

---

41. See *Adulterous Marriages* I, 13, 14.

practice homosexuality, the kidnappers, the liars and the perjurers, and those guilty of anything else that *is opposed to the sound teaching, which is based on the gospel of the glory of the blessed God* (1 Tm 1:10-11): "If you merely believe in Christ and receive his baptism, even though you do not change that evil way of life, you will be saved."

30. That Canaanite woman does not even impose this on us, in that the Lord gave her what she asked for, because he first said, *It is not good to take the children's bread and give it to the dogs.* When he praised her, it was because he who sees into our hearts saw that she was changed. Hence he did not say, "Dog, great is your faith!" but, *Woman, great is your faith!* (Mt 15:26.28) He changed the word because he saw that her attitude was changed and knew that that reprimand had borne fruit. I wonder, though, if he would have praised her for a faith without works, in other words, not a faith that could now work through love but a faith that was lifeless, which James did not hesitate to say was not the faith of Christians but the faith of devils. In the end, if they refuse to believe that the Canaanite woman changed her immoral life when Christ answered her with contempt and criticism, then, whenever they find people who merely believe and, instead of at least concealing a sordid way of life, even flaunt it and refuse to change it, let them cure their children, if they can, just as the Canaanite woman's daughter was cured. Let them not, however, join them to the body of Christ while they are still united with the body of a prostitute. There is certainly nothing absurd in their understanding that anyone who refuses to believe in Christ right up to the end of his life sins against the Holy Spirit and is guilty of the everlasting sin for which there is no forgiveness,[42] but only if he has a proper understanding of what it is to believe in Christ. This does not consist in having the faith of the devils, which is rightly branded as dead, but the faith that works through love.

17, 31. In these circumstances, when we refuse to accept people like that for baptism, we are not trying to uproot the darnel before the due time but are refusing to sow more darnel, as the devil does. We are not barring those who want to come to Christ but are persuading them not to want to come to Christ on their own terms. We are not prohibiting belief in Christ but are making it clear that those who say that what he called adultery is not adultery, or that those who believe that adulterers can be part of his body are refusing to believe in Christ. He says through the apostle that they do not possess the kingdom of God and are *opposed to the sound teaching, which is based on the gospel of the glory of the blessed God.* Hence they must not be counted among those who came to the wedding feast but among those who refused to come.[43] When they dare openly to contradict Christ's own teaching and to oppose the holy gospel, it is not that they

---

42. See Mt 12:31-32.
43. See Mt 22:1-14.

are barred from coming but that they scorn to come. On the other hand, those who at least reject the world verbally, even if not in their actions, do in fact come and are sown among the wheat, and gathered on to the threshing floor, and joined to the sheep, and caught in the nets, and mingle with the guests. Once inside, whether they are concealed or in the open, there is then reason for tolerating them, if there is no possibility of reforming them, and it should not be assumed that they will be expelled. In no way, however, must we interpret the scripture which says that *those they found, the good and the bad* (Mt 22:10), were brought to the marriage feast as saying that those who declared they were going to continue in their wickedness were brought there. Otherwise it would be the very servants of the father of the house who sowed the darnel, and those words, *The enemy who sowed them is the devil* (Mt 13:39), would not be true. Since, however, it is not possible for those words to be untrue, *the servants* brought *the good and the bad* either because they were not known as such, or because they became known as such only after they were brought along and admitted, or because the words *good* and *bad* are used in a certain human way of speaking in which it is customary to give praise or blame even to those who do not yet believe. This also explains the advice the Lord gives to the disciples he first sends to preach the gospel, that *whenever they come into any city* they should look for *someone there who is worthy*, and stay with that person until they leave (Mt 10:11). Who will that worthy person be, obviously, other than someone who is held in good repute by his fellow citizens? And who will be unworthy other than someone who is known to them as bad? Persons of both kinds come to Christ's faith, and in this sense the good and the bad are brought along, because even those bad persons do not refuse to repent for works that are dead. If, however, they do refuse, it is not that they wish to enter and are excluded but that they themselves turn away from the entrance by their own open rejection of it.

32. Since those people have refused to accept what he wanted to invest, it follows that the servant who refused to invest the Lord's talent will also be saved and will not be condemned as slothful.[44] This parable was given to us because of them. They refuse to undertake the duty of administrators in the Church, offering the flimsy excuse that they do not want to keep an account of the sins of others. They listen but do nothing; in other words, they receive but give nothing in return. The faithful and diligent administrator, on the other hand, well prepared to invest and very keen for the Lord's profit, says to the adulterer: "If you want to be baptized, do not be an adulterer; if you want to be baptized, believe Christ, who says that what you do is adultery; if you want to be joined to the body of Christ, do not be united to the body of a prostitute." If he answers, "I will not submit to that, I will not do it," then he does not want to receive the Lord's real

44. See Mt 25:14-30.

money but wants to bring his own adulterous money into the Lord's treasury instead. If, however, he declared that he would conform but did not do so, and afterwards there was no way he could be corrected, there would be found a way to deal with him, so that, if he did no good for himself, he would do no harm to others. As a result, if he was a bad fish in the Lord's good nets, he would not draw the Lord's fish into his own evil nets; in other words, even if he led an evil life in the Church, he would not introduce evil doctrine there. When people like that defend their conduct, or those who openly declare that they are going to continue to act like that are accepted for baptism, what is being preached seems to be nothing other than that adulterers and fornicators will possess the kingdom of God, even if they persist in their wickedness right up to the end of this life, and that they will achieve eternal life and salvation by the power of the faith that lacks works and is dead. These are the bad nets, against which the fishermen must be especially on their guard, at least if the fishermen in that gospel parable stand for the bishops and lower-ranking ministers of the Church, because he said, *Come, and I will make you fishers of men.* (Mt 4:19). Good and bad fish can both be caught in good nets, but good fish cannot be caught in bad nets. This is because with good teaching there can be both the good person, who listens and acts, and the bad person, who listens but does not act; whereas with bad teaching the one who thinks it is true but does not act on it is bad, but the one who acts on it is worse.

18, 33. It is quite amazing that the brothers who think differently from this also say that, when wicked persons who publicly announce that they intend to continue with their crimes are refused baptism, this is a new doctrine. Of course, they ought to give up that pernicious view in any case, whether it is old or new. They must be living in some foreign country. The practice is that prostitutes and actors and public sinners of any other kind are not allowed to come to the Christian sacraments without first breaking away or freeing themselves from those attachments. No doubt their view would be followed and all these would be admitted if the holy Church did not maintain its ancient and strongly-established custom, derived as it is from that transparent truth. From this it knows for certain *that those who do those things will not possess the kingdom of God* (Gal 5:21), and, unless they repent of those dead deeds, they are not allowed to receive baptism; and, if they obtain it by deception and do not reform and repent even afterwards, then it is impossible for them to be saved. Drunkards and avaricious persons and slanderers,[45] however, and those guilty of any other damnable sins that cannot be pursued with criminal charges, are at least strongly condemned in the commandments and the catechetical instructions, and anyone like that who proceeds to baptism appears to do so with a reformed attitude. Perhaps they

---

45. See 1 Cor 6:10.

notice that through negligence it is customary in some places to admit adulterers, whom God's law condemns but the human law does not, that is to say, men who take other men's wives as their own or women who take other women's husbands as their own. In that case they should try to correct this and bring it into line with those right practices, namely, by also excluding them. They must not try to corrupt those correct practices because of these perversions. They must not think that the candidates should not even be instructed about moral reform and consequently judge it proper that even those engaged in those public immoralities and crimes, that is to say, prostitutes, pimps, gladiators, and the like, should be received even while they persist with those evils. Those who act more strongly are consistent when they condemn, wherever they appear, all those evils that the apostle lists, when he concludes *that those who do those things will not possess the kingdom of God*, and they do not admit to the reception of baptism those who resist and declare that they will continue in those sins.

19, 34. Those who hold the view that all the other sins are easily compensated for by almsgiving still do not doubt that there are three sins that are fatal and need to be punished by excommunication[46] until such time as they are healed by humble repentance.[47] These three are impurity,[48] idolatry[49] and murder. It is not necessary to ask questions now about the status of that opinion and whether it should be amended or accepted. We do not wish to prolong the task we have undertaken because of this question, as it is not necessary for that purpose. It is sufficient to observe that, if all those sins are impediments to the reception of the sacrament of baptism, one of them is adultery; and if only these three constitute impediments, adultery is also one of these; and it is this that gave rise to the discussion.

35. Because the conduct of bad Christians, even those who were previously the worst, does not seem to have included this evil of men's marrying other men's wives or women's marrying other women's husbands, this is perhaps the reason why that negligence crept into some churches, and, in catechizing the candidates, these sins were not asked about or challenged, and as a result it came to be defended. Even so, provided we do not cause it to become common by our negligence, such conduct is still not common among the baptized. It is probably this kind of negligence, as it is in some cases, or inexperience or ignorance, as it

---

46. On the practice of excommunication, which, among other things, excluded the person from the eucharist, see A. D. Fitzgerald, "Penance," in Fitzgerald 640-646, esp. 643-644.
47. The reference is to public penance, as mentioned in Letter 153, 3, 6-8; *Miscellany of Eighty-three Questions* 26; Sermon 352, 3, 8-9; 392, 3.
48. This included concubinage, adultery, incest and rape.
49. The reference is to apostasy through participation in idolatrous practices such as Augustine often complains of in his sermons. See M. D. Madden, *The Pagan Divinities and Their Worship as Depicted in the Works of Saint Augustine Exclusive of the City of God* (Washington 1930).

is in others, that the Lord was referring to with the word *sleep,*when he said, *While people were asleep, however, an enemy came and sowed darnel among it* (Mt 13:25). We have to believe that those evils were not apparent in the conduct of any Christians, however bad, since blessed Cyprian does not mention them at all in his letter about the lapsed,[50] even though he mentions many sins, deploring and condemning them, which he rightly says so aroused God's anger that he allowed his Church to be scourged by intolerable persecution. This is despite the fact that he is not silent about such conduct and asserts that it is a type of that same immorality, when he asserts that to be united in the bond of marriage with unbelievers is nothing other than to make the members of Christ's body prostitutes for pagans. In our times these things are no longer regarded as sinful,[51] because nothing to that effect is actually commanded in the New Testament, and therefore it is either taken to be allowed or left as uncertain. It is like that uncertainty as to whether Herod married his brother's wife after he died or while he was still alive,[52] and as a consequence it is also unclear what it was that John told him was forbidden.[53] There is reason for uncertainty also about concubines, as to whether they should be accepted for baptism, if they declare they will not give themselves to anyone else even if they are sent away by the one to whom they are subject. It seems that someone who divorces a wife caught in adultery and marries again should not be equated with those who divorce and remarry for reasons other than adultery;[54] and in the actual divine utterances there is a similar uncertainty as to whether such a person, who is certainly allowed to divorce the adulteress, is nevertheless to be regarded as an adulterer if he remarries, especially as the fault in that case would, in my view, be a venial one.[55] For these reasons the immoralities about which there is no question constitute an absolute impediment to baptism, unless they are corrected by a change of heart and repentance, and in the doubtful cases every effort should be made to discourage such unions. What need is there to put oneself at such risk? If, however, such unions have already been contracted, I am not sure whether the parties to them should also be refused baptism.

20, 36. As far as relates to the sound teaching of truth, therefore, in order to avoid giving deadly sin a perilous security, or even attributing to it some perni-

---

50. *The Lapsed*, written c. 251. The letter refers to Christians who had abjured their faith during the persecution under the Emperor Decius (249-250).

51. But many ecclesiastical writers did in fact regard this as a sin. See Tertullian, *To His Wife* II, 1-3; Cyprian, *The Lapsed* 5, 6; Ambrose, *Abraham* I, 9, 84; Jerome, *Against Jovinian* I, 10.

52. See Josephus, *Jewish Antiquities* 18, 7.

53. See Mt 14:3-4.

54. See Mt 5:32.

55. In this more nuanced attitude Augustine differed from that which was current in his time. On the problem see M. F. Berrouard, "Saint Augustin et l'indissolubilité du mariage. Evolution de sa pensée," *Recherches Augustiniennes* 5 (1968) 139-155; A.-M. La Bonnardière, "Adulterium," in C. Mayer, ed., *Augustinus-Lexikon* I, 126-137.

cious official status, the procedure is for those being baptized to accept belief in God the Father and the Son and the Holy Spirit with the ceremony in which the creed is conveyed, and to show repentance for works that are dead, and to have confidence that in baptism they will receive forgiveness for all sins that are entirely in the past. The result is not that sinning becomes lawful but that having sinned is rendered harmless; it is remission for sin that has been committed, not permission for sin to be committed. Then it can truly be said also in a spiritual sense: *See, you have been cured; sin no more* (Jn 5:14). When the Lord said this he was referring to physical health, because he knew that the person he healed had incurred that physical illness because of his sins. I am amazed that those people think they can say, *See, you have been cured*, to someone who comes to be baptized as an adulterer and, after being baptized, goes away still an adulterer. If adultery is good health, what would be a serious terminal disease?

21, 37. "But," they say, "among the three thousand whom the apostles baptized on one day, among those many thousands of believers in whom the apostle accomplished *the gospel from Jerusalem to Illyricum* (Rom 15:19), there must have been some men who were living with other men's wives and women who were living with other women's husbands. With them the apostles should have set the rule to be followed in the Church from then on, as to whether they should be refused baptism if they had not set right those adulteries." As if one could not use a similar argument against them by saying that they do not find any mention of someone like that being received! Was it possible, however, for the crimes of every individual to be listed? The list would be infinite; and that general rule, stated briefly by Peter in his address to those being baptized, is more than adequate: *Tear yourself away from this depraved world.* Does anyone doubt that adultery, and those who choose to remain in that sinful state, are part of the depravity of this world? In the same way one could say that, among the many thousands from many nations who believed at that time, it would have been possible to find public prostitutes, whom no church accepts for baptism unless they are first freed from that sordidness, and the apostles should have set the precedent for accepting or rejecting these. Nevertheless, from certain lesser things we can draw conclusions about the more important. If the tax collectors who came for John's baptism were forbidden to demand more than the law allowed them,[56] I would be astounded if adultery could be allowed for those who come for Christ's baptism.

38. They have also invoked the fact that the Israelites committed many serious wrongs and shed the blood of the prophets, but they did not deserve total destruction for those deeds but only for their lack of faith in refusing to believe in Christ. They fail to see that their sin was not only this, that they did not believe in

---

56. See Lk 3:13.

Christ, but that it was also that they killed Christ. One of these was a sin of unbelief, but the other a sin of inhumanity. One, therefore, was a sin against right belief, the other a sin against right conduct. The person who has belief in Christ avoids both sins. This is not the belief without works that is dead, which even the devils have, but the belief of grace *that works through love.*

39. This is the faith about which it is said: *The kingdom of heaven is within you* (Lk 17:21). It is won by those who are energetic in their belief, attaining the spirit of love, in which *the law is fulfilled* (Rom 13:10) and without which the letter of the law even made them guilty of transgression. We must not think it is said that *the kingdom of heaven falls to force and those who use force win it* (Mt 11:12) because even wicked persons reach the kingdom of heaven merely by believing, while living evil lives. On the contrary, it is because the guilt of that transgression comes from the law commanding in isolation, that is, the letter without the spirit, and it is absolved by believing, and the Holy Spirit is won by the force of the prayers of faith. Then, *with love poured into our hearts* (Rom 5:5) through that Holy Spirit, the law is accomplished not through fear of punishment but through love of what is right.

22, 40. In no way, therefore, must an unwary mind make the mistake of thinking that it has come to know God if it acknowledges God in the manner of the devils with a faith that is dead, that is, one that lacks good works, and as a result feels confident of obtaining eternal life, because the Lord says, *This, however, is eternal life, to know you, the one true God, and Jesus Christ whom you sent* (Jn 17:3). That other text must also be kept in mind: *This is how we know him, by keeping his commandments. Anyone who claims to know him, but does not keep his commandments, is a liar and does not have the truth.* (1 Jn 2:3-4) In case anyone might think that his commandments only relate to believing, further on John himself disclosed what he would say, when he said, *This is his commandment, that we should believe in the name of his son Jesus Christ and that we should love one another* (1 Jn 3:23). No one has actually dared to say this, especially since he said, not wishing to dissipate the consideration with a large list, that *the whole of the law and the prophets are derived from those two*[57] (Mt 22:40). It is true that God's commandments can rightly be said to relate only to faith, provided that this is understood not as a dead faith but as a living one that works through love.

41. What achieves good, therefore, is believing in God with a right faith, worshiping God, knowing God. We then have his assistance to lead good lives, and, if we sin, we will win his forgiveness not by persisting fearlessly with the deeds he abhors but by abandoning them and saying to him, *I said, Lord, have pity on me; heal my soul, because I have sinned against you* (Ps 40:5). Those

---

57. See Mt 22:40.

who do not believe in him do not have anyone to whom they can say this, and those who are strangers to the grace of the mediator, because they are so far from him, say it in vain. This is why the Book of Wisdom has those words: *And even if we have sinned, we belong to you* (Wis 15:2a). I do not know how that ruinous sense of security interprets this. We have a good and powerful master who both wants to and is able to heal the sins of those who repent, but by no means one who does not dare to destroy those who persist with wickedness. Finally, after saying, *We belong to you*, it adds, *We acknowledge your power* (Wis 15:2b), and that is certainly a power from which the sinner is unable to withdraw or hide. Therefore it then goes on to say, *We will not sin, however, because we know that we have been made yours* (Wis 15:2c). Could anyone properly contemplate dwelling with God, which is where all who are called by his predetermining will are destined to have their home, and not try to live in a way that is appropriate for that dwelling place? Therefore, when John also says, *I have written this to you, so that you might not sin, but if anyone does sin, we have an advocate with the Father, the just Jesus Christ, and he is the sacrifice that takes away our sins* (1 Jn 2:1-2), it is not so that we might sin with security but so that we might dissociate ourselves from any sin we may have committed and not despair of obtaining pardon through that advocate, whom unbelievers do not have.

23, 42. These words do not hold a promise of any easier lot for those who choose to believe in God while persisting with gross immorality. Still less do those words of the apostle where he says, *Those who sin without the law will perish without the law; but those who sin under the law will be judged according to the law* (Rom 2:12), as though in this text there were some difference between perishing and being judged, when in fact the different words mean the same thing. Scripture often uses the word "judgment" to mean also eternal damnation, as when the Lord says in the gospel, *The hour will come when everyone who is in the grave will hear his voice; and those who did good will rise again to life, but those who did evil, to judgment* (Jn 5:28-29). Here too he does not speak of one thing for those who have believed and another for those who have not believed but of one thing for *those who did good* and another for *those who did evil*. A good life and the faith *that works through love* cannot be separated; rather, to have that faith is in itself to lead a good life. We see, therefore, that the Lord spoke of rising again to eternal damnation as rising again to judgment. He divided everyone who would rise again (and this undoubtedly includes those who do not believe at all, since they do not remain in the grave either) into two classes, declaring that one will rise again to the resurrection of eternal life and the other to the resurrection of judgment.

43. They may say that this should not be understood as referring to those who do not believe at all but to those who are saved through fire because they believed, even though they lived badly. They would have it that the word *judgment* refers to a passing punishment they suffer. To say this is quite insolent, as

the Lord separated into two classes, *life* and *judgment*, absolutely everyone who rises again, and this undoubtedly includes also those who do not believe. Although he did not state it, he meant the judgment to be understood as being everlasting, the same as the life. (He did not say they would rise again to *eternal* life, although he certainly did not intend it to be understood any other way.) If this is what they say, then let them consider what their answer will be when he says, *Anyone who does not believe is already judged* (Jn 3:18). There is no doubt that here they understand judgment as meaning eternal punishment, unless they are going to be so bold as to say that even unbelievers will be saved through fire, because, he says, *Anyone who does not believe is already judged,* that is to say, already destined for judgment. This is no great benefit to promise to those who believe and lead wicked lives, when even those unbelievers will not have to be cast off but only judged. If they do not dare to say this, then neither should they dare to promise something milder to those of whom it is said: *They will be judged according to the law*, since it is now established that as a rule the word *judgment* is also used to mean eternal damnation. What now? Do we find that those who knowingly sin, far from being better off, are worse off? This includes especially those who have received the law; for, as Scripture says, *Where there is no law there is no transgression* (Rom 4:15). Hence there is also the text: *I would not have known of carnal desires, if the law did not say, Do not have carnal desires. Because of the commandment, therefore, sin has taken the opportunity to cause all kinds of carnal desires in me* (Rom 7:7-8), and many other things that the same apostle says on this subject. Through our Lord Jesus Christ the grace of the Holy Spirit frees us from this heavier guilt. *By pouring love into our hearts* (Rom 5:5) it gives us the delight in goodness with which we may overcome the unruliness of carnal desire. All this, therefore, confirms that, when it is said, *Those who sin under the law will be judged according to the law*, we must not understand this as being not only something less harsh than it is for those who sin without the law and perish without the law but even as something more severe. In this text judgment does not mean a passing punishment but the one by which even unbelievers will be judged.

44. There are some who use this statement to promise salvation through fire to those who believe but live wicked lives, and they say to them, *Those who sin without the law will perish without the law; but those who sin under the law will be judged according to the law*, as though what was said was, "They will not perish but will be saved through fire." They cannot have noticed that, when the apostle said this about those who sinned without the law and those who sinned under the law, he was speaking about Jews and gentiles, with the intention of showing that both, and not just the gentiles, needed to be redeemed by Christ's grace. This is evident from the whole of the letter to the Romans. So now, if they please, let them not promise redemption by Christ's grace and salvation through fire even to Jews who sin under the law, because it is said of them, *They will be*

judged according to the law. If they said this, they would be contradicting themselves, since they say they are guilty of the worst crime of unbelief. If, therefore, they do not say this, why then, as far as concerns believing in Christ, do they transfer what was said about those who sin without the law and those who sin under the law to make it refer to believers and unbelievers, when the discussion was about Jews and gentiles, so that both would be invited to receive Christ's grace?

24, 44. It does not say, "Those who sin without belief will perish without belief, but those who sin in faith will be judged by faith," but the words are *without the law* and *under the law.* It is quite clear from this that it was a question about Jews and gentiles, not about good and bad Christians.

45. If they do choose to take *law* there to mean "faith," unhelpful and silly as that may be, they can still read the unambiguous statement of the apostle Peter. He was speaking of those who had taken the words of Scripture, *We who belong to the New Testament are not children of slaves, but children of the free woman, with the freedom with which Christ set us free* (Gal 4:31-5:1), as an opportunity for the flesh and an excuse for sinning, and thought that living in freedom meant they could consider themselves licensed to do whatever they liked, as though they were assured even of redemption to that extent. They were overlooking the text, *You have been called to freedom, my brothers, but do not turn that freedom into an opportunity for the flesh* (Gal 5:13). Hence Peter himself also says, *You are free, but your freedom is not an excuse for wickedness* (1 Pt 2:16), and it is about those people that he says in his second letter: *They are springs that are dry, and mists driven by whirlwinds, for whom the dark underworld is reserved. With their high-flown, empty talk they use the enticements of carnal impurity to lure back those who have only just escaped. Set in their errors they promise them freedom, although they themselves are slaves to corruption, since anyone who is dominated by something becomes a slave to it. If any have escaped from the defilement of the world by coming to know our Lord and savior Jesus Christ, and have become ensnared and overcome by it again, then their last condition has become worse than their first. It would have been better for them not to have known the way of goodness than to know it and then turn back again from the holy commandment entrusted to them. The proverb truly applies to them, The dog returns to its vomit, and, and the sow that has been washed wallows in the mud.* (2 Pt 2:17-22)

In the face of this clear revelation of the truth, how can they still promise that those who know the way of goodness, which is the Lord Christ, yet live sinful lives, will be better off than those who have not known him at all, when it is openly stated: *It would have been better for them not to have known the way of goodness than to know it and then turn back again from the holy commandment entrusted to them?*

25, 46. The *holy commandment* in that passage should not be understood as being the one that commands us to believe in God (although if we understand the faith of those who believe to be the faith *that works through love*, then that commandment includes everything), but it states explicitly what it means by *holy commandment,* namely, the one in which we are commanded to distance ourselves from the defilement of this world and live chastely. These are his words: *If any have escaped from the defilement of the world by coming to know our Lord and savior Jesus Christ, and have become ensnared and overcome by it again, then their last condition has become worse than their first.* He does not say "escaped from ignorance of God" or "escaped from the world's unbelief," or anything like that, but *the defilement of the world,* and this certainly includes all the uncleanness of open immorality. Speaking about them earlier he said, *Though they dine with you, they have eyes only for adultery and constant sinning* (2 Pt 2:13-14). Therefore he also calls them *springs that are dry,* in other words, *springs* because they have come to know the Lord Christ, and *dry* because they do not live appropriately. Speaking of people like this, the apostle Jude also says, *They contaminate the meals you share in love, shamelessly feeding themselves, clouds without water* (Jude 12), and the rest. Where Peter says, *Though they eat with you, they have eyes only for adultery,* Jude says, *They contaminate the meals you share in love,* because they mix with the good people in the sacramental meals and the care of the common people. Where Peter speaks of *springs that are dry,* Jude says, *clouds without water,* and James, *faith that is dead.*

47. Therefore those who live wicked, corrupt lives must not be promised a passing punishment in fire. They have known the right way, and, as the infallible scripture testifies, it would have been better for them if they had not known it. The Lord says of them too, *And the last state of that person will be worse than the first* (Mt 12:45), because, by not allowing the Holy Spirit to dwell in them for their purification, they cause the unclean spirits to return to them in even greater numbers. Perhaps those of whom we are speaking should be thought to be better because they did not return to sordid adultery, inasmuch as they never left it; they did not soil themselves again after being cleaned but refused to be cleaned. They do not even condescend at least to vomit up their previous impurities in order to approach baptism with a lightened conscience and then like dogs go back and swallow them again, but with their coarse minds they stubbornly try to keep their wickedness unaltered even in the actual sacred washing. They do not even hide it with false promises but flaunt it with insolent public declarations. They do not look back as they leave Sodom, like Lot's wife,[58] but they absolutely refuse to leave Sodom; in fact they try to enter into union with Christ taking Sodom with them. The apostle Paul says, *I was once a blasphemer, and persecuted and did*

---

58. See Gn 19:26.

harm; but I found mercy, because in my unbelief I acted in ignorance (1 Tm 1:13). Those people are told: "On the contrary, you will obtain mercy if you live sinfully even with belief and knowledge." It would be too lengthy a task, almost unending, to try to gather together all the evidence from scripture where it is made clear that those who knowingly lead evil and sinful lives not only have no better case than those who do so in ignorance but by that very fact have a worse one. So this will suffice.

26, 48. With the help of the Lord our God, therefore, let us take special care not to give people a false sense of security by telling them that by being baptized in Christ, no matter how they live in that faith, they will obtain eternal salvation. We must not make Christians in the way the Jews made converts, as the Lord said to them, *Wretched scribes and Pharisees, you travel over sea and land to make a single convert; and when you have converted him you make him twice as much a child of hell as you are yourselves* (Mt 23:15). Rather, we must hold to the saving doctrine of our divine master in both respects, requiring a Christian life to be consistent with holy baptism and not promising eternal life to anyone who is lacking in either way. He who said, *Anyone who is not born again from the Holy Spirit will not enter into the kingdom of heaven* (Jn 3:5), also said, *Unless your goodness exceeds that of the scribes and Pharisees, you will not enter into the kingdom of heaven* (Mt 5:20). He also said of them, *The scribes and Pharisees occupy the chair of Moses. Do what they say, but do not do what they do, for they say but do not do.* (Mt 23:2-3) Their goodness, therefore, consists in saying and not doing, and he wanted our goodness to exceed theirs by being one of saying and doing; no one will enter into the kingdom of heaven without that. It is not that during this life anyone ought to be so proud as even to dare think to himself, let alone boast to others, that he is sinless. If, however,[59] there were not some sins so serious as even to deserve to be punished with excommunication, the apostle would not have said, *When you, and I with you in spirit, have come together, that person is to be handed over to Satan for the destruction of the body, so that on the day of the Lord Jesus his spirit will be saved* (1 Cor 5:4-5). That is why he also says, *Lest I grieve for the many who sinned in the past and have not repented for the impurity and fornication they committed* (2 Cor 12:21). Similarly, if there were not some sins that had to be cured, not by the humility of doing the penance imposed in the Church on those who are officially called penitents but by certain healing effects of corrective advice,[60] the Lord himself would not have said, *Correct him in private; if he listens to you, you have won your brother* (Mt 18:15). Finally, if we did not have

---

59. Here again Augustine describes the threefold distinction of sins and corresponding penances that he had discussed in sections 4 and 34.
60. It is difficult to determine what concrete form this practice took. On the debate over the question see J. Pegon, in Bibliothèque Augustinienne 8, 505-507, note complémentaire 16.

some sins always with us in this life, he would not have put the daily remedy in the prayer he taught us to say: *Forgive us our trespasses, as we forgive those who trespass against us* (Mt 6:12).

27, 49. I think I have now explained well enough my thoughts on the whole of that view. It raised three questions.

One was about good and bad persons being mixed together in the Church, like the wheat and the darnel. On that point we must be careful not to think that the reason those parables were given to us, whether this one or the one about the unclean animals in the ark[61] or any others of similar import, is to put the Church's discipline to sleep. This was described in the person of that woman in the text: *She manages her household strictly* (Prv 31:17). Rather, they were given to us to prevent reckless insanity, instead of stringent care, from going so far as to presume to separate the good from the bad, as it might seem, by means of unholy schisms. In these parables and pronouncements the good are not being advised to be slothful and overlook things they should prohibit but to be patient and, while keeping intact the teaching of the truth, to be tolerant of anything they are unable to correct. In addition, because it is written that even the unclean animals went into the ark with Noah, that is no reason why those in authority should not forbid it when impure persons want to come to baptism while still being dancers, though this is certainly less harmful than if they were adulterers. By the symbolism of this historical event it was foretold that through reasonable toler-ance, and not because of the corruption of doctrine or the decay of discipline, there would be unclean persons in the Church. The unclean animals did not break into the ark and enter as they liked, but, leaving its structure intact, they entered through the one single door that the builder had constructed.

The second question concerns their view that those who are being baptized should only be presented with belief and should be taught about morality after-wards when they are already baptized. It has been shown well enough, if I am not mistaken, that the needs of the inquirer are better served if the punishment the Lord threatens for those who live badly is not concealed at the time when all who are asking for the sacrament of the faithful as a group are listening more atten-tively and more earnestly to everything that is said. This will prevent it from happening that, in baptism itself, to which they come to be absolved of the guilt of all their sins, they incur the guilt of the worst of crimes.

The third question is the one where most harm can be done. Because it has not been given sufficient consideration and not been examined in the light of the divine writings, that whole view has arisen that promises to those who live crim-inal and corrupt lives, even if they continue to live like that and do nothing else except believe in Christ and receive his sacrament, that they will attain salvation

---

61. See Gn 7:8-9.

and eternal life, despite the fact that this contradicts the Lord's clearest teaching. In reply to the one who desired eternal life he said, *If you want to enter into life, keep the commandments* (Mt 19:17), and he stated which commandments.[62] They are the ones where the sins are forbidden by which in some strange way eternal salvation is promised in virtue of a faith that lacks works and is dead.

I believe I have discussed these three questions sufficiently and have shown that bad persons must be tolerated in the Church, but without any neglect of the Church's discipline; that those who seek baptism must be catechized so that they not only hear and accept what they must believe but also how they must live; that eternal life must be promised for those who believe, but that no one must be allowed to think that he can attain it through the dead faith that without works is unable to bring salvation but only through that faith of grace *that works through love*. What follows from this is not that faithful administrators should be blamed for negligence or sloth but that some should be condemned for their obstinacy in refusing to accept the Lord's money and forcing the Lord's servants to invest their own adulterous currency. They refuse to allow that at least those whom Saint Cyprian names[63] as renouncing the world only in words and not in deeds are bad, when they refuse to renounce the works of the devil even verbally and openly declare that they are going to remain in adultery.

If there is something they generally say that perhaps I have not touched on in this discussion, it is because I considered it needed no answer, either because it was not relevant to the question at issue or because it was so flimsy that anyone at all could easily refute it.

---

62. See Mt 19:19.
63. See *The Lapsed* 27.

The Enchiridion on Faith, Hope, and Charity

Translation by Bruce Harbert

Notes by Bruce Harbert and Michael Fiedrowicz

Introduction

1. Occasion and Addressee

From the days of his priesthood to the end of his life Augustine was constantly being asked, by Christians and non-Christians alike, to answer their pressing questions about time and eternity, God and the world. The bishop of Hippo devoted himself tirelessly to this intellectual apostolate. The result was that in addition to his numerous doctrinal and theological writings he produced a number of longer or shorter treatises. The present work, too, owes its origin to the request of a friend. In his *Revisions* Augustine has this to say on the matter: "I also wrote a book on *Faith, Hope, and Charity*, because the person to whom it is dedicated asked me for a short work he might always have at hand—what the Greeks call a 'little handbook' (*enchiridion*). In it, I think, I very carefully summarized the way in which God ought to be worshiped and what the divine scripture really defines as true wisdom for human beings."[1]

Nothing further is known about the Laurence to whom the work is addressed. One of the earliest manuscripts describes him as *primus notariorum urbis*, that is, a government official.[2] To his brother, Dulcitius, an imperial official who had come to Africa to implement the anti-Donatist laws, Augustine dedicated a short book, *Eight Questions of Dulcitius,* in response to various queries. Like this brother, Laurence was not a theologian. But, if we may judge by the questions he proposed to Augustine, he was an educated Christian with a strong interest in theological matters.

Here, as so often, the author knew how to adapt himself to his addressee and to make his very carefully composed work persuasive and easily understandable. The warm, personal words at the beginning and end of the work suggest a relationship of genuine friendship between Laurence and Augustine.

2. Title and Date

The title *Enchiridion* goes back to Laurence himself: "What you are asking from me is a handbook (*enchiridion*), one that can be carried in the hand, not one to burden bookshelves."[3] Augustine leaves it to his addressee to use, and describe, the comprehensive and complex work as a "handbook" in the sense of

---

1. *Revisions* II, 63.
2. See CCL 46, 27.
3. *Enchiridion* 1, 6; see 1, 4.

a "compendium."[4] He himself prefers the title *Faith, Hope, and Charity*, which is inspired by 1 Cor 13:13.[5] That is how he cites the work in *Eight Questions of Dulcitius*,[6] in a letter to Darius,[7] and in the *Revisions*.[8] The *Indiculus* of Possidius also attests to this title.[9]

Some of the references just given, as well as a mention of Jerome,[10] who died 419/20, allow the work to be dated to around 421.

The work thus bears the marks of the period of Augustine's maturity. *The Trinity* had already been published, as had the lengthy commentary on Genesis. *The City of God* had largely been completed. During this phase of his life the Pelagian controversy was particularly intense and was forcing Augustine to think deeply about the fall, grace, and predestination. Thus he was able to bring to the explanation of Christian truths in *Faith, Hope, and Charity* his many years of episcopal experience as proclaimer and defender of the faith.

In comparison with other writings of Augustine the personal element is kept in the background. Also missing are directly polemical emphases such as are found in many of the bishop's works of controversy. But under the smooth surface of the positive presentation the currents of life and experience that determined Augustine's lifelong searching and thought are clearly discernible.

Thus his tireless wrestling with the truth is as perceptible in his expositions as is the echo of the theological controversies that throughout his life refused to leave him at peace. How else is the lengthy excursus on the problem of evil to be explained, with its unmistakable reminder of the struggles with Manichean dualism? Why is the absolutely unmerited character of divine grace emphasized on almost every page if not because the still current dispute with the Pelagians was keeping the author on tenterhooks? Even when Augustine does not name his opponents, it is clear which erroneous doctrines he has in mind.

Yet Augustine was not intending to write a work against heresies. Laurence had asked him for a clear compendium. What concretely did he have in mind when he asked his question? How did Augustine try to respond to his petitioner's desire?

---

4. See ibid. 33, 122.
5. See ibid.
6. *Eight Questions of Dulcitius* 1, 10.
7. Letter 231, 7.
8. *Revisions* II, 63.
9. *Indiculus* X³, 30 (*Miscellanea Agostiniana* II, 180).
10. *Enchiridion* 23, 87.

3. Intention and Content of the Work

Augustine is probably citing Laurence's letter when he says that the latter had asked for an explanation of "what we should seek above all, what we should chiefly seek to avoid because of the various heresies there are, to what extent reason comes to the support of religion, what lies outside the scope of reason and belongs to faith alone, what should be held first and last, what the whole body of doctrine amounts to, and what is a sure and suitable foundation of Catholic faith."[11]

This list of intelligent questions on the relationship of faith to reason and of orthodoxy to heresy, on the hierarchy of truths, and on the specific element of what is Catholic is confirmation that Augustine's recognition of Laurence's education (*eruditio*)[12] was not an empty compliment. The modern reader might perhaps wish that in his answers Augustine had more closely followed the list. But he thought another approach to be more meaningful.

Right at the beginning Augustine tries to direct his friend's intellectual impulse to the proper goal, which is true wisdom. What true wisdom consists in is given in a text from Job: *Behold, piety is wisdom* (28:28). As Augustine transposes wisdom, the supreme ideal of life in antiquity, into a Christian frame of reference, it consists ultimately in the worship of God.[13] But the worship of God, in its turn, takes the form of faith, hope, and charity.

The meaning Augustine gives to these three divine virtues can be seen in what he says in *Teaching Christianity*: A person does not need sacred scripture in order to be a Christian, provided only that he bases his life on faith, hope, and charity.[14] It is through a detailed exegesis of this Pauline triad (1 Cor 13:13) that Augustine promises to answer all of Laurence's questions.[15]

Even before beginning his detailed explanation, Augustine takes up the questions, at least briefly, and seeks to answer them as succinctly as he can. Here is a short formula of Christian doctrine: "beginning with faith and ending with vision." It is also true that "the sure and proper foundation of the Catholic faith is Christ."[16]

The connecting thread in the ensuing detailed explanation of the triad faith, hope, and charity is provided by the confession of faith or creed (*symbolum*) and the Lord's Prayer (*oratio dominica*).

As a result, principles of division of various kinds overlap in the *Handbook*. While in faith, hope, and charity we deal with the subjective act of response to

---

11. Ibid. 1, 4.
12. See ibid. 1, 1.
13. See ibid. 1, 2.
14. *Teaching Christianity* I, 39, 43.
15. *Enchiridion* 1, 3.
16. Ibid. 1, 5.

the divine self-communication in revelation, the concrete content of this revelation is given in the creed and the Lord's Prayer. Augustine is convinced that the creed and the Lord's Prayer are the Christian's real "handbooks": "What text is there that takes a shorter time to hear or to read? What is there that is easier to commit to memory?"[17]

In the choice of points of references for his instruction Augustine was following ancient ecclesial tradition. The exposition of the content of the faith in close connection with the creed and the explanation of the Lord's Prayer had long been customary in catechetical instruction. Augustine assigns the creed as the dogmatic point of reference for faith, while hope is given its direction in the petitions of the Lord's Prayer.

Augustine is convinced that faith and prayer are inseparably interdependent: "In order to pray, let us believe; and, in order that the very faith by which we pray may not fail, let us pray."[18]

As previously in *Faith and the Creed*, the western form of the creed is explained.[19] The creed used at Hippo can be extensively reconstructed on the basis of Sermon 215.

Whereas in his earlier *Faith and the Creed* Augustine had followed the catechetical method and explained the articles one after the other, in the present work he allows himself greater freedom in explaining the several points.

Since in that earlier work he had explained quite extensively the articles on the Trinity and the incarnation, he dwells on them here only briefly, as if he wanted not to repeat himself unnecessarily so that he might deal in greater detail with the other contents of the faith. Not a few digressions disrupt the usual pattern of the baptismal catechesis, allowing him to go more fully into individual questions (*quaestiones*). The desire to comment on the text takes second place here to the interest in a synthesis of Christian doctrine.

In the setting of Christian initiation the Lord's Prayer, too, functioned as a synthesis. It was regarded as a summary (*breviarium*) of the gospel in regard to the basic ideas of Jesus' preaching and of the Christian faith and life. Augustine considered the *oratio dominica* to be the model and norm of all Christian prayer.[20] In the present work the Lord's Prayer structures the treatment of hope.

On the other hand, Augustine's comments on charity are not based on any fundamental text.

---

17. Ibid. 2, 7.
18. Sermon 115, 1 (trans. Hill 4, 198).
19. See C. Eichenseer, *Das Symbolum Apostolicum beim Heiligen Augustinus, mit Berücksichtigung des dogmengeschichtlichen Zusammenhanges* (St. Ottilien 1960).
20. See Letter 130, 22.

4. *Structure*

While faith, hope, and charity determine the structure of the *Enchiridion*, the space given to each of the three is not equal. The main focus is on the presentation of the content of faith, while hope and charity are discussed only in the short concluding sections. Here, then, is the structure.[21]

Prologue (1, 1-2, 8)
I. Faith (3, 9-29, 113)
    1. Faith in God as creator (3, 9-7, 22)
    2. Faith in Christ as redeemer (8, 23-14, 55)
    3. Faith in the Holy Spirit and in the Church (15, 56-16, 63)
    4. Faith in the forgiveness of sins (17, 64-22, 83)
    5. Faith in the resurrection of the flesh and everlasting life (23, 84-29, 113)
II. Hope (30, 114-116)
III. Charity (31, 117-32, 121)
Epilogue (33, 122)

The perspective of the *Enchiridion* is thus that of the history of salvation. As seen by Christian revelation, the destiny of the entire human race is determined by three basic coordinates: the mysteries of creation, the fall, and redemption. True wisdom consists in acknowledging the constitutive relationship between God and human beings, finding in Christ the true mediator between creator and creation, and uniting oneself to this mediator through the Church.[22]

5. *Theological Importance*

In form and extent the work goes far beyond Laurence's questions. As so often, Augustine was here inspired by particular questions put to him but in his reflections did not limit himself to the path sketched out for him by these questions. Instead he placed the particular subject matters in larger settings, extended the formulation of the questions, and broadened their perspectives. Laurence had looked for a concise practical manual, but Augustine's composition became a complex *summa* of Christian teaching on faith and life. Again, Augustine does not build this *summa* out of parts already existing in a complete form so that they needed only a finishing synthesis. Rather the composition of *Faith, Hope, and*

---

21. See L. Alici, Introduction to *Sant'Agostino, Manuale sulla Fede, Speranza e Carità* (Rome 1995) 453. J. Rivière gives a different division in his Introduction in Bibliothèque Augustinienne 9, 85-87.
22. See É. Lamirande, "L'Église dans l'*Enchiridion* de saint Augustin. Quelques questions aux théologiens," *Église* et *Théologie* 10 (1979) 195-206.

Charity became an effort at the deeper understanding of the faith (*intellectus fidei*) that had been such a concern of his ever since the months spent at Cassiciacum. In the *Enchiridion*, however, Christ takes a more important place than before as a *fundamentum fidei*. The anti-heretical tendency is likewise clearer.[23]

Augustine once expressed his self-understanding as a theological writer in the fine statement that he wanted to be among those "who, as they advance, write and, as they write, advance" (*proficiendo scribunt et scribendo proficiunt*).[24] Since Laurence himself had asked about the relationship between faith and reason, Augustine now draws him into the living flow of his own thinking about the mystery of faith.

If, on the one hand, Augustine thus strove for a rational elucidation of the truths of faith, on the other he sought to maintain constant contact with the Bible and especially with the writings of Paul. This last remark about Paul applies especially to the doctrine of grace and its connected problems, as well as to the treatment of hope.[25]

Not without good reason has it been said that "perhaps nowhere else has Augustine better summed up his teaching and better explained his method" than in the present work.[26] As a "handbook of authentic Augustinianism,"[27] the treatise is a precious reflection of the world of Augustinian thought. The classical themes of Christian dogma and moral teaching find expression in it. On the one hand, it deals with creation, the original condition of humanity, angels and demons, the person of Christ and his redemptive sacrifice, justification, Church, the sacraments of baptism and penance, judgment, purgatory, and resurrection; on the other, with the theory of the virtues and sin, of prayer and good works. In addition, Augustine focuses especially on questions that occupied him during the Pelagian controversy: the problem of evil, the nature and consequences of the fall, the necessity of grace, the mystery of predestination, and the conditions for salvation. Timelessly valid ideas are combined with many personal insights of Augustine that remain theologically debatable. Despite this last caveat, the *Enchiridion* can be regarded as a "comprehensive theology of redemption."[28]

It is true that in the history of theology before Augustine there were attempts to provide a systematic presentation of the truths of faith. The first effort to go beyond the creed and bring the truths of faith together in a theological synthesis

---

23. See *Enchiridion* 1, 5.
24. Letter 143, 2.
25. See B. Studer, "Augustine and the Pauline Theme of Hope," in idem, *Dominus Salvator. Studien zur Christologie und Exegese der Kirchenväter* (Rome 1992) 499-533, esp. 518-532.
26. F. Cayré, *Précis de Patrologie* I (Paris 1938³) 634.
27. E. Portalié, "Augustin," *Dictionnaire de théologie catholique* I, 2302.
28. Rivière, in Bibliothèque Augustinienne 9, 85.

was that of Origen in his *First Principles* (220/30). In the period from 304 to 311 Lactantius, acting as an apologist, composed his *Divine Instructions* as well as an *Epitome* or short summary of that work. Around 350, Cyril of Jerusalem preached eighteen catecheses in which he explained the requirements of the Christian faith and, in connection with the baptismal creed, set forth the entire Christian faith. In 386 Gregory of Nyssa composed his *Great Catechetical Discourse.*

In *The Christian Combat*, an earlier work written in 396 and intended for simple people, Augustine himself had presented the rule of faith (*regula fidei*) and the precepts of morality (*praecepta vitae*) or, in other words, Christian theory and practice.[29]

Nevertheless, of all these doctrinal summaries from the patristic period the *Enchiridion* was the most influential in the subsequent history of theology.[30] In his *Sentences* Peter Lombard cites it no fewer than eighty times.[31] Thomas Aquinas, the greatest theologian of the Middle Ages, modeled his *Summa Theologiae* on Augustine's *Enchiridion*. The Synod of Lavaur (1368), the entire focus of which was on catechesis, referred expressly to Augustine when it described the triad of faith, hope, and charity as the whole way to God.[32] In the modern period, the Jansenists thought that a translation of the work was the best way to spread Augustinian teaching and promote their own views. In Protestant textbooks on the history of dogma that were produced at the beginning of the twentieth century an analysis of the *Enchiridion* became the basis of a summary review of Augustine's teaching.[33] These Protestant works regarded a number of Augustinian themes (merit, almsgiving, sacramental piety, offering of Masses for the souls of the deceased, veneration of the saints, the ascetic ideal of life) as an expression of "popular Catholicism."

In any case, the *Enchiridion* accurately reflects the faith of the Church at that time. Augustine did not intend either an original work or a personal theological system. As a bishop of the *catholica* he professed its creed. His sole concern was to understand this faith of the Church more fully, to make it intelligible to the faithful, and to defend it against every kind of distortion. The relevance of *Faith, Hope, and Charity* is due not least to the fact that not a few of its themes—

---

29. See *Revisions* II, 3.
30. See A. Grillmeier, "Vom Symbolum zur Summa," in idem, *Mit ihm und in ihm. Christologische Forschungen und Perspektiven* (Freiburg 1975) 585-636, esp. 624-625; idem, "Patristische Vorbilder frühscholastischer Systematik. Zugleich ein Beitrag zur Geschichte des Augustinismus," *Studia Patristica* VI (Berlin 1962) 390-408, esp. 396.
31. See the Quaracchi edition (1916) 1049.
32. See J. D. Mansi, *Sanctorum conciliorum nova et amplissima collectio* (Florence 1759-1927) 26, 486.
33. See A. v. Harnack, *Lehrbuch der Dogmengeschichte* III (Tübingen 1910⁴; repr. 1990) 220-36; R. Seeberg, *Lehrbuch der Dogmengeschichte* II (Leipzig 1923³ = Darmstadt 1965⁶) 550-67.

worship of God, faith, human creatureliness, freedom through submission to God, the impossibility of self-redemption, the divinity of Christ, and the shattering of world-immanent expectations by Christian hope—contradict the secular mentality of the modern age.

The Enchiridion on Faith, Hope, and Charity

Prologue

The Beauty of Wisdom

1,1. My dearest son Laurence, it would be impossible to say how much your learning delights me, and how much I desire that you should be wise[1]—not one of those of whom scripture says, *Where is the one who is wise? Where is the scribe? Where is the debater of this age? Has not God made foolish the wisdom of the world?* (1 Cor 1:20) but rather one of those of whom it is written, *The multitude of the wise is the salvation of the world* (Wis 6:24). This is the kind of person the apostle wants people to be when he says to them, *I want you to be wise in what is good and guileless in what is evil* (Rom 16:19).[2]

Wisdom Is the Same as Piety

2. Now, for human beings, wisdom is the same as piety.[3] You can read this in the book of the holy man Job. There we find that Wisdom herself said to a man, *Behold, piety is wisdom* (Jb 28:28). If you ask what kind of piety she was speaking of in that place, you will find that the Greek expresses it more clearly as *theosebeia*, which is reverence toward God. There is another word for piety in Greek, *eusebeia*, which means good reverence, although this chiefly signifies the worship of God. But no word is more suitable to explain what human wisdom is than the one that expressly denotes worship of God. You ask me to speak briefly about great matters. Do you wish me to find an even more concise expression than this? Perhaps this is exactly what you wish me to explain briefly and to sum up in a few words: how God is to be worshiped.

---

1. *Scientia*, for Augustine, is the rational knowledge of temporal and mutable realities, whereas *sapientia* refers to the contemplation of eternal and immutable realities; see *The Trinity* XII, 12, 17; XIV, 1, 3.
2. Some manuscripts add: "Just as nobody can be the cause of his own existence, so nobody can cause his own wisdom, but wisdom comes from the enlightenment of the one of whom it is written: *All wisdom is from God* (Sir 1:1)."
3. In contrast to "the wisdom of this world," which in ancient philosophy reached, at best, an intellectual relationship with God, authentic wisdom is the same as *pietas*, which is based on faith, hope and love; see *True Religion* 5, 8; *Confessions* V, 5, 8; VIII, 1, 2; *The Spirit and the Letter* 11, 18; *The Trinity* XII, 14, 22; Letter 167, 3, 11.

God Is to Be Worshiped with Faith, Hope, and Charity

3. If I answer that God is to be worshiped with faith, hope and love, you will certainly say that this is a shorter answer than you wish for, and then you will ask for a brief explanation of the objects of each of these three, that is, what we should believe, what we should hope for, and what we should love. When I have done this, you will have an answer to all the questions you put in your letter: if you have a copy of it at hand, you can easily turn to them and read them again; if not, let me help you to remember them.

The Origin of the Handbook

4. You write that you wish me to make a book for you to keep, what is known as a handbook, never to be let out of your hands, containing an exposition of what you have asked about, namely, what we should seek above all, what we should chiefly avoid because of the various heresies there are, to what extent reason comes to the support of religion, what lies outside the scope of reason and belongs to faith alone, what should be held first and last, what the whole body of doctrine amounts to, and what is a sure and suitable foundation of Catholic faith.[4]

Without a doubt you will know all these things for which you are looking if you take care to know what should be believed, hoped for, and loved. These are the most important things, or rather the only things, that are to be followed in religion: anybody who denies these things is either a total stranger to the name of Christ or else a heretic. These are the truths we should defend by reason, whether we know them from our bodily senses or have discovered them with the understanding of our minds. But the things that we have not discovered through sense experience, and have been and are unable to reach with our minds, must be believed in without any doubt on the evidence of the witnesses by whom those writings that have already gained the name of sacred scripture were compiled: they were able to see these things, or even to foresee them, either physically or in their minds with divine help.

Beginning with Faith and Ending with Vision

5. When a mind is filled with the beginning of that faith which works through love,[5] it progresses by a good life even toward vision, in which holy and perfect hearts know that unspeakable beauty, the full vision of which is the highest

---

4. It is highly probable that here Augustine is citing Laurence's letter.
5. See Gal 5:6.

happiness. This is without doubt what you are seeking, what we must hold first and last, beginning with faith and ending with vision. This is what the whole body of doctrine amounts to. The sure and proper foundation of the Catholic faith is Christ, as the apostle says, *For no one can lay any foundation other than the one that has been laid; that foundation is Jesus Christ* (1 Cor 3:11). Nor is the fact that this may be thought something we hold in common with some heretics any reason for denying that this is the true foundation of the Catholic faith. For, if we consider carefully the things that concern Christ, Christ is found only in name among some heretics who wish to be called Christians,[6] but in truth he is not to be found among them. To demonstrate this would take too long, since it would involve mentioning all the heresies that have been or are or may have been under the name of Christian, and explaining how this is true in each case: such an argument would take up so many books that it would seem endless.[7]

Your Heart Must Be Set on Fire with Great Love

6. But what you are asking from me is a handbook, one that can be carried in the hand, not one to burden bookshelves. So let us return to the three things by which we have said God must be worshiped, faith, hope, and charity: it is easy to say what must be believed, what hoped, what loved. But to defend this against the criticism of those who hold a different opinion demands fuller and more laborious teaching: for this it is necessary not that your hand be filled with a brief handbook but that your heart be set on fire with great love.

The Creed and the Lord's Prayer

2, 7. Think of the creed and the Lord's Prayer. What text is there that takes a shorter time to hear or to read?[8] What is there that is easier to commit to memory? Because the human race was oppressed with great misery on account of sin, and stood in need of the divine mercy, the prophet foretold the time of God's grace and said, *Then everyone who calls on the name of the Lord shall be saved* (Jl 2:32).[9] That is the reason for the prayer. But when the apostle quoted this testimony of the prophet in order actually to proclaim God's grace, he immediately added, *But how are they to call on one in whom they have not believed?* (Rom 10:14) That is why we have the creed. Notice that the three things we mentioned earlier are contained in these two: faith believes, hope and

---

6. See Letter 118, 12; *Faith and the Creed* 21.
7. Some years later (around 428) Augustine wrote a work entitled *Heresies*, in which he listed eighty-eight heresies.
8. See *Faith and the Creed* 1.
9. See Acts 2:21; Rom 10:13.

charity pray. But hope and charity cannot be without faith, and so faith prays as well. That is why Paul said, *But how are they to call on one in whom they have not believed?*

Charity Cannot Exist without Hope nor Hope without Charity, nor Can Either Exist without Faith

8. What is there that we can hope for without believing in it? To be sure, we can believe in things for which we do not hope. Who among the faithful does not believe in the punishments of the wicked, but without hoping for them? Anybody who believes they are destined for him, and in his mind runs away from them in horror, is more rightly said to fear them than to hope for them. One writer has written to distinguish the two, "Give hope to the fearful."[10] Another, though a better poet, speaks inaccurately when he says, "Had I been able to hope for this one sorrow."[11] Some teachers of grammar use this line as an example to illustrate the improper use of words and comment that "he said 'hope' instead of 'fear.' " So there is faith in good things and bad, for both good and bad things are believed, and both in good faith, not bad. There is also faith in past realities, in present ones, and in future ones. We believe that Christ died, which is now in the past; we believe that he sits at the right hand of the Father, which is in the present; we believe that he will come in judgment, which is in the future. There is also faith in things that concern us, and in things that concern others; everybody believes that he had a beginning, that he has not always existed, and that the same is true of other people and other things. We have also many religious beliefs not only concerning other humans but also concerning angels.

But hope is only for good things, only for things that are in the future and concern the one who is said to have hope in them. For these reasons it has been necessary to make a rational distinction between faith and hope and to give them different names. The fact that we do not see either the things we believe in or those we hope for makes not seeing a feature that faith and hope have in common. In the Letter to the Hebrews, on whose testimony distinguished defenders of Catholic faith and discipline have relied, faith is said to be *the conviction of things not seen* (Heb 11:1).[12] However, if a person asserts that he

---

10. See Lucan, *Civil War* 2, 15.
11. Virgil, *Aeneid*, 4, 419.
12. Note that Augustine does not attribute the Letter to the Hebrews to St. Paul. By the time he wrote the *Enchiridion* he had come to regard it as anonymous. It was not universally regarded as part of the New Testament canon in his day, whence his appeal in this sentence to other writers to justify his use of it as an authority. See A.-M. La Bonnardière, "L'Épitre aux Hébreux dans l'oeuvre de Saint Augustin," *Revue des études augustiniennes* 3 (1957) 137-162.

has believed (that is, he has found faith) not in words, not in witnesses, not in arguments of any kind, but in the evidence of things actually present to him, we do not think him so absurd that it would be right to criticize his expression and say to him, "You have seen, and therefore you have not believed"; so it may be thought inconsistent that something that is believed is not necessarily unseen. But it is better to follow the teaching of the divine words in reserving the term "faith" for faith in things that are not seen.[13] The apostle also speaks of hope, saying, *Now hope that is seen is not hope. For who hopes for what is seen? But if we hope for what we do not see, we wait for it with patience.* (Rom 8:24-25) So when we believe that good things await us in the future, this is nothing other than to hope for them.[14] And now what should I say about love? Without it faith has no value. But hope cannot exist without love. The apostle James says, *Even the demons believe—and shudder* (Jas 2:19), yet they do not hope or love but rather fear that which we hope for and love, believing that it will come about. That is why the apostle Paul approves and recommends *the faith that works through love* (Gal 5:6), which cannot exist without hope. So love cannot exist without hope nor hope without love, nor can either exist without faith.

Faith in God the Creator

The Cause of Created Things Is the Goodness of the Creator

3, 9. Since, therefore, we are considering what ought to be believed in the sphere of religion, we do not need to inquire into the nature of things as did those whom the Greeks call *physikoi*,[15] nor need we fear that the Christian is ignorant of something they have discovered or think they have discovered concerning the properties and number of the elements, the movement and order and phases of the stars, the shape of the heavens, the kinds of animals, fruits, stones, springs, rivers, and mountains and their natures, the measurement of time and space, the indications of imminent storms and hundreds of other such things.[16] This is because they themselves have not discovered everything, powerful as they are of

---

13. See Augustine's treatise on this subject, *Faith in the Unseen.*
14. Augustine relates Christian hope to the eternal happiness which the faithful on earth possess "in hope" but not yet "in reality." But this hope already brings happiness here on earth; see *The City of God* XIX, 4-5.
15. The reference is to the natural philosophers of Ionia.
16. Augustine relativizes the importance of investigation into and knowledge of the natural sciences for Christians, since the primary question for them concerns God and everlasting life; see *Enchiridion* 5, 16; *Confessions* V, 4, 7; Letter 11, 2; 118, 2, 11.13; *Teaching Christianity* II, 29, 46.

intellect, eager in study, and abundantly gifted with leisure: some matters they investigate with the power of human speculation, others on the basis of facts and experience, and, in those matters which they boast of having discovered, much is a matter of opinion rather than of knowledge. For a Christian it is enough to believe that the cause of created things, whether in heaven or on earth, visible or invisible, is nothing other than the goodness of the creator who is the one true God, and that there is nothing that is not either himself or from him,[17] and that he is a Trinity, that is, a Father, the Son begotten from the Father, and a Holy Spirit who proceeds from the same Father[18] and is one and the same Spirit of Father and Son.

3, 10. By this Trinity, supremely, equally, and unchangeably good, all things have been created: they are not supremely, equally, or unchangeably good, but even when they are considered individually, each one of them is good; and at the same time all things are very good, since in all these things consists the wonderful beauty of the universe.

Evil Is the Removal of Good

11. In this universe even that which is called evil, well ordered and kept in its place, sets the good in higher relief, so that good things are more pleasing and praiseworthy than evil ones. Nor would Almighty God, "to whom," as even the pagans confess, "belongs supreme power,"[19] since he is supremely good, in any way allow anything evil to exist among his works were he not so omnipotent and good that he can bring good even out of evil.[20] For what else is that which is called evil but a removal of good?[21] In the bodies of animals, to be afflicted with diseases and wounds is nothing other than to be deprived of health: the aim of treatment is not to make the evils which were in the body, such as diseases and wounds, move from where they were to somewhere else, but rather that they

---

17. The emphasis on both the goodness of God and his exclusive creative activity is directed against Manichean dualism.
18. See *Faith and the Creed* 19. The present Western version of the Nicene-Constantinopolitan Creed, widely familiar through its use at the Sunday eucharist, says that the Holy Spirit proceeds "from the Father and the Son," although its original form, as approved by the Council of Constantinople in 381, spoke only of the procession of the Spirit "from the Father." The Western doctrine of the double procession of the Spirit was developed by Augustine and by subsequent thinkers influenced by him. See *The Trinity* IV, 20, 29; XV, 17, 27; XV, 26, 45. It is worth noting that here, although Augustine speaks of the "Spirit of Father and Son," he follows the pre-Augustinian pattern in speaking only of a procession "from the Father."
19. Virgil, *Aeneid* X, 100.
20. Augustine's theodicy is based primarily on this argument; see *Enchiridion* 8, 27; 28, 104.
21. It was in opposition to the Manichean idea of the substantiality of evil that Augustine developed the definition of evil as *privatio boni*, "the removal of good." See *Free Will* III, 13, 36; *The City of God* XIV, 11; *The Nature of the Good* 3, 23.

should cease to exist, since a wound or a disease is not in itself a substance but a defect in the substance of flesh. The flesh itself is the substance, a good thing to which those evil things, those removals of the good, known as health, occur. In the same way all evils that affect the mind are removals of natural goods: when they are cured they are not moved to somewhere else, but, when they are no longer in the mind once it has been restored to health, they will be nowhere.

Corruption Cannot Consume Good without Consuming the Thing Itself

4, 12. So all things are good, since the maker of all things is supremely good. But since they are not supremely and unchangeably good like their creator, in them goodness can be decreased and increased. For good to be decreased is evil, even though, however much it is decreased, some of it must remain for the thing to exist at all, if it does still exist. Nor can the good that makes it a thing entirely cease to be, however small the thing is and of whatever kind, unless the thing itself ceases to be as well. Rightly is a thing highly esteemed that is not corrupted; furthermore, if it is incorruptible, completely incapable of corruption, it is worthy of still higher esteem. But when it is corrupted, its corruption is an evil because it deprives it of some good. If it did not deprive it of good, it would not harm it; but it does harm it, and therefore it takes away good. So, for as long as a thing is corrupted, there still remains in it some good that can be removed, and so if in a being there remains something that cannot be corrupted, such a thing will be incorruptible and will arrive at this state, which is so good, by way of corruption. But if it never ceases to be corrupted, it will never cease to contain some good that corruption can remove from it. If corruption totally consumes it, no good will remain in it, for it will have ceased to exist. So corruption cannot consume good without consuming the thing itself. Therefore every thing is good, a great good if it cannot be corrupted, a small one if it can: but it cannot be denied, except by fools and the inexpert, that it is good. If it is consumed by corruption, then corruption itself will no longer exist, since there will be no thing for it to exist in.

Good and Evil People

13. From this it follows that, if there were nothing good, there would be nothing that could be called bad. But good that is without any evil is wholly good, while good that has evil in it is a contaminated or corrupt good. Nor can there ever be any evil where there is no good. This leads to a surprising conclusion, which is that, since every being insofar as it exists is good, when we speak of a contaminated thing as evil, we are saying nothing other than that something

good is bad, and that only what is good is bad, since every being is a good thing, nor would there be any evil thing if the very thing that is evil were not a being. So only something good can be evil. When this is said it seems absurd, and yet this line of thinking leads inevitably to this conclusion. We must beware lest we incur the censure of the prophecy in which we read, *Woe to those who call evil good and good evil, who say darkness for light and light for darkness, who say bitter for sweet and sweet for bitter!* (Is 5:20) And the Lord himself says, *The evil person out of the evil treasure of the heart produces evil* (Lk 6:45). But what is an evil man if not an evil being, since a man is a being? Moreover, if a man is something good because he is a being, what is an evil man but an evil good? But when we make a distinction we find that he is not an evil being because he is a man, nor is he a good being because he is wicked, but he is a good being because he is a man and an evil being because he is wicked. So whoever says, "It is evil to be a man" or "It is good to be wicked," incurs the censure of the prophet, *Woe to those who call evil good and good evil*, for he speaks ill of God's work, which is the man, and praises the man's vice, which is that man's iniquity. So every being, even if it is corrupt, insofar as it is a being is good and insofar as it is corrupt is evil.

Two Contraries Cannot Exist Simultaneously in One Thing

14. So, with regard to those two opposites that are called good and evil, the rule of the logicians fails according to which they say that two contraries cannot exist simultaneously in one thing. For no air is simultaneously dark and light, no food or drink is simultaneously sweet and sour, no body is simultaneously black and white in the same place, or ugly and beautiful in the same place. We find this to be true in many, indeed in almost all contraries, that they cannot coexist in one thing simultaneously. But, while nobody doubts that good and evil are contraries, not only can they exist simultaneously, but evils cannot exist at all without goods, and they can only exist in goods, although goods can exist without evils. For a man or an angel is capable of not being unjust, but someone who is unjust can only be either a man or an angel: that he is a man or an angel is a good, while that he is unjust is an evil. And these two contraries coexist in such a way that evil would be quite unable to exist if there were no good for it to exist in, since not only would corruption have nowhere to be, but it would have nowhere to arise from if there were nothing to be corrupted, since only a good thing can be corrupted, corruption being the extermination of good. So evils have arisen out of goods, and they only exist within things that are in some way good. There was nowhere else for any evil being to arise from. If there were, it would plainly be good insofar as it was a being, and either it would be that great good which is an incorruptible being or else corruptible nature would in no way exist were it not in

some way a good, which corruption was able to spoil by corrupting what was good.

The Tree and the Fruits

15. But, while we have said that evils arise out of goods, we should not be thought to be contradicting the saying of the Lord: *A good tree cannot bear bad fruit* (Mt 7:18). For, as Truth has said, grapes cannot be gathered from thorns, because grapes cannot grow from thorns; but we see that both vines and thorn bushes can grow from good soil. In the same way an evil will, like an evil tree, cannot make good fruits, that is, good works, but from the good nature of man both a good and an evil will can arise.[22] Nor was there anything at all for an evil will to arise from at the beginning except the good nature of angels and men. The Lord demonstrates this most clearly in the place where he was speaking about the tree and the fruits. He says, *Either make the tree good, and its fruit good; or make the tree bad, and its fruit bad* (Mt 12:33). Here he warns us with sufficient clarity that evil fruits cannot grow from a good tree or good fruits from an evil tree, but that from the earth itself, to which he was speaking, both kinds of tree can grow.[23]

5, 16. This being so, although we love the line of Virgil that says, "Happy was he who was able to know the causes of things,"[24] it does not seem to us to have anything to do with the pursuit of happiness if we know the causes of the great movements of physical objects in the world,[25] which are hidden away in the most secret extremities of the natural universe:

> Whence come the tremblings of the earth,
> what power causes the deep seas to swell and break their bounds
> and then to subside into themselves again?[26]

and suchlike. But we must know the causes of good and evil things insofar as it is allowed to man to know them in this life which is so full of errors and troubles,[27]

---

22. See Mt 7:16. By "will" here Augustine does not mean the capacity for willing but the concrete act of the will by which one deliberately consents to good or evil.
23. In using this image Augustine's intention is to emphasize, in opposition to the Manicheans, that human nature is good in itself and that the direction given to the moral life depends on the free decision of the will; see *Proceedings with Felix the Manichean* 2, 4.
24. *Georgics* II, 490. Virgil was speaking of the Greek philosopher Epicurus.
25. On the use of Virgil see M. G. St. A. Jackson, "*Confessions* V, 4, 7 and Its Classical Background," in *Congresso internazionale su S. Agostino nel XVI centenario della conversione*, Roma, 15-20 settembre 1986 (Rome 1987) 413-417.
26. *Georgics* II, 479-480.
27. This is an echo of Cicero, *Hortensius*, frag. 107 (ed. Grilli); see Augustine, *Answer to Julian* IV, 15, 78.

in order that he may avoid those same errors and troubles. What we must do, surely, is make our way toward that happiness where we shall not be disturbed by any trouble or deceived by any error. If we were obliged to know the causes of the movements of physical objects, there would be nothing more necessary for us to know than the causes of our own health; but since we seek out physicians in our ignorance of them, who cannot see with what great patience we should bear our ignorance of the secrets of the heavens and the earth?

Error: One Takes Something False to Be True

17. For, although we should beware of error with all possible care, not only in great matters but also in lesser ones, and although the only possible cause of error is ignorance, it does not follow that anybody who is ignorant of something is thereby in error but only a person who thinks he knows what he does not know: he takes something false to be true, and that is exactly what error consists in.[28] What is most important is what a person is in error about. For in a single matter one who knows is rightly preferred to one who does not know and one who is not in error to one who is. But in different matters, that is, when one person knows some things and another others, one knowing useful things and another useless or even harmful things, with regard to these latter things, who would not put the one who does not know them above the one who does? For there are some things of which ignorance is better than knowledge.

Also, there have been times when to err has been advantageous to some people, but only on paths we travel with our feet, not on the path of the moral life. It has happened to me myself that I lost my way[29] at a crossroads and so did not pass through a place where I would have been ambushed by an armed band of Donatists[30] had they discovered me traveling there, and so it happened that I arrived at my destination by a circuitous route, and when I discovered they had laid an ambush I was glad that I had lost my way and gave thanks for this to God. Who would hesitate to set a traveler who lost his way like that above a robber who did not lose his way? Perhaps that is why in the works of the same supreme poet some unhappy lover says: "How I saw, how I perished, how my evil error took me away!"[31] Since there is also a good kind of error which not only does me no harm but even brings me some good.

---

28. See Cicero, *Academica* II, 66.
29. In Latin, "to be mistaken" and "to lose one's way" are expressed by the same verb, *errare*.
30. The Donatists were a rigoristic sect named after their early leader, Donatus, which denied the validity of sacraments conferred by those who had lapsed from the Catholic faith in times of persecution. Augustine spent much effort in controversy with them. They were associated with a rural terrorist movement, by one of whose cells Augustine was threatened in the episode that he describes here; see Possidius, *Life of St. Augustine* 12.
31. Virgil, *Eclogues* 8, 41.

But if we consider the truth more carefully, it seems that to err is nothing other than to think true what is false and to think false what is true, to think what is certain uncertain or what is uncertain certain, whether it is false or true, and this is an ugliness and deformity in the mind equal to the beauty and suitability we perceive in the words *yes, yes; no, no* (Mt 5:37) when a person speaks or gives assent. Indeed, this is certainly one reason why the life we lead is a miserable one, that from time to time error is necessary to preserve life. Far otherwise is that life in which Truth itself is the life of our soul, in which nobody deceives or is deceived. But here men deceive and are deceived, and they are more to be pitied when they deceive by lying than when they themselves are deceived by putting trust in liars. So much does our rational nature flee falsehood and avoid error as much as it can, that even those who love to deceive are unwilling to be deceived. For a liar does not think he is in error himself but rather that he is causing another who believes him to err. And indeed in that respect he is not in error, but rather concealing the truth, if he himself knows what is true, but he is deceived in thinking that his lie does him no harm, since sin is always more harmful to the person who commits it than to the one who suffers it.

Lying

6, 18. But here a very difficult and complicated question arises, about which I have already written a large book[32] when obliged to reply to the question whether it was ever the duty of a just man to lie. For there are some people who have gone so far as to claim that it is sometimes a good and religious thing to commit perjury and to speak falsely about things that concern the worship of God and even the very nature of God himself.[33]

My view, however, is that all lying is sin, but that it is very significant with what intention and about what matters a person lies. For a person who lies with the intention of helping somebody does not sin in the same way as one who lies with the intention of doing harm, nor does a person who sends a traveler on a different route by lying do as much harm as one who by lying deceives another and leads him to take an evil path in life.

Certainly nobody is to be judged a liar who says something false while believing it to be true, since as far as he is concerned he is not deceiving but deceived. Nor is a person to be accused of lying, but rather of rashness, who

---

32. I.e., Lying. On this work and on lying in general see B. Ramsey, "Mendacio, De/Contra mendacium," in A. D. Fitzgerald, ed., *Augustine Through the Ages* (Grand Rapids 1999) 555-557.

33. This is an allusion to the Priscillianists, who adopted Gnostic and Manichean positions and, in order to disguise these views, followed the maxim: "Swear, perjure yourself, do not betray the secret!" See *Heresies* 70, 1; Letter 237, 3; *Against Lying* 2.

considers true false things in which he has placed his belief too incautiously: on the contrary, insofar as the person himself is concerned, the person who deserves the title of liar more is the one who says something true which he believes to be false. For, as far as his mind is concerned, since he does not believe what he says, he does not speak the truth, although what he says may be discovered to be true; nor is a person at all free from the sin of lying who unknowingly speaks the truth with his mouth while his conscious will is to tell a lie.

If we do not consider the subject matter about which a person is speaking but only the intention of the speaker, a person who unknowingly tells an untruth because he believes it to be true is better than one who knowingly has the disposition of a liar and does not know that what he is saying is true. In the former person the mind and the words are consistent, while the other, whatever the nature of what he says in itself, has one thought hidden in his breast and another ready on his tongue,[34] and this is the evil proper to the liar.

But with regard to the words that are spoken, it is very important to consider the subject matter about which a person is deceived or lies, so that, while to be deceived is a lesser evil than to lie insofar as a person's will is concerned, it is very much more tolerable to lie in matters not concerned with religion than to be deceived in matters in which, without faith or knowledge, it is impossible to worship God. To illustrate this by examples, let us compare the case of a person who lies by announcing that somebody is dead with that of one who mistakenly believes that Christ will die again,[35] however long this death may be delayed: is it not far better to lie in the former way than to be deceived in the latter, and a much lesser evil to lead a person into the former error than to be led by someone else into the latter?

Every Error Is in Itself an Evil

19. In some matters we are deceived by a great evil, in others by a little one, in others by no evil at all, and in some matters we are even deceived by some good. A man is deceived by a great evil when he does not believe what leads to eternal life or believes something that leads to eternal death, but he is deceived by a small one when, taking the false to be true, he falls into some temporal difficulties such as a faithful person can turn to good use by his patience—for example, when somebody, thinking a person to be good who is in fact evil, suffers some evil from him.

---

34. This is an echo of Sallust, *The Catilinian Conspiracy* 10.
35. The example is a reminder of a doctrine attributed to Origen that was condemned at the synod of Constantinople in 543, namely, that in the future world Christ will be crucified once again for the sake of the demons.

But someone who believes an evil person to be good without suffering any evil from him is not deceived by any evil, and so he does not bring on himself the scorn of the prophet who says, *Woe to those who call evil good* (Is 5:20). These words should be understood as spoken about the things that make people evil, not about people themselves. So a person who says that adultery is good rightly comes under the censure of these words of the prophet; but a person who calls somebody good, thinking him to be chaste and not knowing that he is an adulterer, is not deceived by false doctrine concerning what is good and evil but concerning secrets of human behavior, calling a person good whom he believes to be that which he knows to be good, and calling an adulterer evil and a chaste person good, but calling this person good without knowing that he is an adulterer and not chaste. Furthermore, if a person escapes danger through an error, as I said earlier had happened to me when I was on a journey, even something good comes to that person by reason of his error.

But when I say that in some cases it is not evil or is even in some way good to be deceived, I am not saying that error itself is not an evil or is in some way good, but I am speaking about the evil that is avoided or the good that is arrived at by way of error, that is, the evil that does not happen or the advantage that comes about because of the error. For error in itself in an important matter is a great evil and in a small matter a small evil, but it is always an evil. For who without error can deny that it is evil to take the false for true or to deny the truth as false, or to consider uncertain what is certain or certain what is uncertain? It is one thing to believe that an evil man is good, which is an error, and another to suffer no evil from the evil of that error, when an evil man who is thought to be good does no harm. Similarly, it is one thing to think a particular way is the right way when it is not, and another to receive some good, such as escaping an ambush of evil men, from that error which is in itself evil.

Not Every Error Is a Sin

7, 20. I really do not know about other errors such as these: when a person thinks well of an evil person, not knowing what he is like, or when similar things happen regarding what we perceive through our bodily senses, so that we perceive things spiritually as if we were perceiving them physically or physically as if we were perceiving them spiritually (like the apostle Peter, when he thought he was seeing a vision when he was suddenly freed from bondage and imprisonment by an angel),[36] or when with regard to physical things we think something is smooth when in fact it is rough, or sweet when it is bitter or sweetly perfumed when it has a foul smell, or when we mistake the noise of a chariot passing for thunder, or when we mistake

---

36. See Acts 12:9.

one person for another very like him, as happens often in the case of twins (so that Virgil says, "And the error was pleasing to their parents"[37]), I do not know whether these and other similar occurrences are also to be called sins.

Nor have I undertaken at this moment to unravel the complicated question which tormented the Academics,[38] those sharpest of intellects, that is, whether a wise man should agree to anything, for fear of falling into error by taking the false as true since, as they assert, everything is either hidden or uncertain. For this reason I wrote three books soon after my conversion, to remove from my path the obstacle which their arguments put before me, as it were, on the threshold, and indeed it was necessary to remove that despair of finding the truth which their arguments seemed to foster.[39] According to them, then, every error is thought to be sin, which they claim can only be avoided by the avoidance of all assent.[40] They say that anybody who assents to an uncertainty is in error, that there is nothing certain in human sight because the true and the false are so similar as to be indistinguishable, even if what is seen does happen to be true: these are their arguments, most ingenious but most shameless.

For us, however, *the righteous person lives by faith* (Hb 2:4; Rom 1:17; Gal 3:11; Heb 10:38). But if assent is taken away, faith is taken away, since nothing can be believed without assent. And those things that we must believe in order to come to the blessed life which can only be eternal are true, although we cannot see them. But I do not know whether we should speak with those who not only do not know that they will live eternally but do not even know that they are alive now: indeed, they claim not to know what they cannot but know. Nor can anybody be ignorant that he is alive, inasmuch as if he is not alive he is unable even to be ignorant of anything, since not only knowledge but also ignorance belongs to the living. Clearly, by not acknowledging that they are alive they seem to be taking care to avoid error, but their error itself proves that they are alive, since nobody who is not alive can err. Hence, just as it is not only true but certain that we are alive, so many other things are true and certain, and to deny this is properly known not as wisdom but as insanity.

---

37. Virgil, *Aeneid X*, 392.
38. A philosophical school named after the Academy, a building in Athens. The Academics were noted for their skepticism and called for an *epoché*, that is, the holding back of one's judgment; see Cicero, *Academica* II, 21, 67-68.
39. See *Answer to the Skeptics*.
40. Looking back on the period when he was a skeptic, Augustine says in *Confessions* VI, 4, 6: "I was hanging back from any assent…and nearly died by hanging instead" (trans. Boulding).

Error, though not always a Sin, Is always an Evil

21. But as for things concerning which, as far as gaining the kingdom of God is concerned, it does not matter whether we believe them or not, nor whether they are true or false, to err about such things, that is, to think one thing rather than another, should not be considered a sin, or if it is, the tiniest and least serious of sins. In the last analysis, whatever it is and however important, it has nothing to do with the path we take to God, which is the path of faith working through love.[41] The pleasing error of the parents concerning their twins did not take them away from this path; nor did the apostle Peter leave this path when, thinking he was seeing a vision, he mistook one thing for another, so that the bodily images with which he thought he was surrounded prevented him from recognizing the bodily images by which he was in fact surrounded until the angel by whom he had been freed left him;[42] nor was the patriarch Jacob straying from this path when he believed that his son had been killed by a beast when he was in fact alive.[43] In these and similar mistakes we are deceived without damage to our faith in God, and we err without straying from the path that leads to him.

These errors, even if they are not sins, are nonetheless to be counted among the evils of this life, which is so subject to vanity that false things are here taken for true, the true is rejected as false, and what is uncertain is taken as certain. For, although these things do not belong to that true and certain faith by which we move toward eternal happiness, they do belong to the misery in which we are still living now: we would not be deceived in any way in the perceptions of our minds or of our senses if we were already enjoying that true and perfect happiness.

To Use Words for Deception, and not for What They Were Instituted, Is a Sin

22. To go further, however, every lie must be called a sin because a person, not only when he himself knows what is true but also when he errs and is deceived, being human, must say what is in his mind, whether it is true or he only thinks it true when it is false. But everyone who lies speaks contrary to what is in his mind, with the intention of deceiving.[44] Words were surely instituted not so that people could deceive each other with them but so that each person could

---

41. See Gal 5:6.
42. See Acts 12:9.
43. See Gn 37:33.
44. In Augustine's view, the intention to deceive is the decisive element in the definition of a lie; see *Lying* 3, 1; *Against Lying* 12, 26; *True Religion* 33, 61; *Teaching Christianity* I, 36, 40.

make his thoughts known to another. So, to use words for deception, and not for what they were instituted, is a sin.

Nor should it be thought that any lie is not sinful because we can sometimes do a person good by lying. We can also do good by stealing, if a poor person to whom we secretly give what we have stolen feels a benefit and the rich person from whom we have secretly stolen is not aware of any loss: this would not lead anybody to say that such a theft was not sinful. We can also do good by adultery, if it seems that a woman will die from lack of love unless this is granted to her, and that if she lives she will be cleansed of her sin by penitence: this will not be thought a reason for denying that such adultery is sinful. But if we rightly love chastity, what is wrong with truth if for the good of another we will violate it by lying although we would not violate chastity by committing adultery? It cannot be denied that people who lie only for the salvation of others have made great progress in goodness; but it is the good will of those who have made such progress, not their lying, that is rightly praised and even rewarded with temporal gifts. It is enough to excuse their lying without praising it as well, especially in the case of the heirs of the new covenant, to whom these words are addressed: *Let your word be yes, yes or no, no: anything more than this comes from the evil one* (Mt 5:37). Because of this evil one, since he never ceases to insinuate himself into our mortal affairs, the coheirs of Christ[45] say, *Forgive us our trespasses* (Mt 6:12).

Faith in Christ the Redeemer

Causes of Good and Evil

8, 23. Having treated these matters with the brevity that a book like this demands, since we must know the causes of good and evil insofar as is necessary to enable us to travel along the road that leads us to the kingdom where there will be life without death, truth without error, happiness without anxiety, we must in no way doubt that the only cause of the good things that come our way is the goodness of God, while the cause of our evils is the will of a changeable good falling away from the unchangeable good, first the will of an angel, then the will of a human being.

---

45. See Rom 8:17.

Ignorance and Desire

24. This is the first evil that affected the rational creation, the first privation of good. Then there came even upon those who did not wish it ignorance of what should be done and desire for harmful things, together with their companions' error and suffering: when these two evils are felt to be near at hand, the movement of the mind fleeing them is called fear. Further, when the mind gains the things it desires, however harmful and empty they may be, since it does not realize their true nature because of its error, it is either overcome with a sick pleasure or inflated with an empty joy. These are, as it were, the sources of sickness, sources not of abundance but of deprivation, from which all the unhappiness of rational nature flows.

Death of the Body

25. However, this nature, in the midst of all its evils, has not been able to lose the appetite for happiness. Rather, these evils are common to both human beings and angels who have been condemned for their malice by the Lord's justice. But man has also his own special penalty, since he has been punished with the death of the body as well. God had threatened him with the punishment of death if he sinned, bestowing free will on him while still ruling him by his authority and terrifying him with the thought of death, and placing him in the bliss of paradise as if in the shadow of life, from which he was to rise to better things if he preserved his state of justice.

Adam's Sin

26. After his sin he became an exile from this place and bound also his progeny, which by his sin he had damaged within himself as though at its root,[46] by the penalty of death and condemnation. As a result, any offspring born of him and the wife through whom he had sinned, who had been condemned together with him, born through the concupiscence of the flesh which was their punishment, carrying within it a disobedience similar to that which they had showed, would contract original sin,[47] which would drag it through various errors and pains to that final punishment with the deserter angels, his corruptors, masters, and accomplices. *Therefore, sin came into the world through one man, and*

---

46. Augustine thinks of the whole human race as contained within Adam, since all come from his seed. Therefore, in hurting himself, Adam hurt his descendents.
47. This term is sometimes misunderstood. "Original" derives from the Latin *origo*, meaning "origin." Original sin belongs to us by reason of our origin. See P. Rigby, "Original Sin," in Fitzgerald 607-614.

death came through sin, and so it spread to all: in him all have sinned (Rom 5:12).[48] When he used the word *world* in that text, the apostle was of course referring to the whole human race.

God Judged It Better to Bring Good out of Evil than to Allow Nothing Evil to Exist

27. So that was how things stood. The condemned mass[49] of the whole human race lay prostrate in evil, or rather was wallowing in evil and hurtling from evil to evil and, in common with those of the angels who had sinned, was paying the penalty most justly deserved by their disloyal desertion. The deeds the evil do willingly as a result of their blind and untamed concupiscence, together with their punishments, which are plain for all to see and which they suffer against their will, belong to God's just anger. But this does not mean that the goodness of the creator failed or that he ceased to bestow on the angels their life and vital powers, without which they would die, or to give form and life to the seeds of men, born though they are from corrupt and condemned stock, or to control the growth of their limbs through time and space, to give life to their senses or to feed them. He judged it better to bring good out of evil than to allow nothing evil to exist.

And if he had willed no reformation of man to bring him to a better condition, as in the case of the wicked angels, would it not have been just that the being that has deserted God—which by the evil use of its power has trampled under foot and transgressed the command of its creator that it could very easily have kept, which has impaired the image of its maker within itself by proudly turning away from his light, which by the evil use of free choice has broken away from healthy obedience to his laws—should be eternally deserted by him and pay the eternal penalty that it has deserved? It plainly would be so, if the one who is just were not also so merciful, showing his unmerited mercy the more clearly in choosing rather to set free the unworthy.

---

48. Augustine's text was different from that of modern editions. This is how he would have translated it. Augustine takes the Latin translation, *in quo omnes peccaverunt*, to be a relative clause that he refers to Adam. See G. Bonner, "Augustine on Romans 5, 12," *Studia Evangelica* 5 (1968) 244-247.

49. This expression goes back to a Pauline image (see Rom 9:20-21) which originally referred to the situation of the Jews in relation to justification by God. In Augustine's thought, the idea of the *massa damnata* is simply a consequence of the guilt stemming from Adam and affecting the whole human race. See P. Fredriksen, "Massa," in Fitzgerald 545-547.

The Angels

9, 28. So, after some angels in wicked pride had deserted God and been cast down into the deep darkness of the air,[50] the remaining angels stayed in eternal happiness with God. There was not one fallen and condemned angel who had engendered the others, so that the original evil might bind them in the chains of harmful succession and drag them all to their deserved punishment, but after the one who became the devil was exalted with his companions in wickedness and was laid low with them because of this exaltation,[51] the rest remained with the Lord in loyal obedience and also received what the others did not have, a sure knowledge to make them secure concerning their own everlasting stability, from which they were never to fall.

The Promise Made to the Saints

29. So it pleased God, the maker and governor of all things, that, since it was not the whole company of angels that had perished by deserting God, those who had perished should remain in perpetual perdition, while those who had perse-vered with God when the others deserted should have the joy of knowing that their future happiness was assured. As for the other part of the rational creation, that is, humankind, since they had totally perished by reason of their sins and punishments, both original and each person's own, some of them were to be restored to fill the gap left in the company of the angels by the devil's fall.[52] For this is the promise made to the saints when they rise again, that they will be equal to the angels of God.[53]

So, the Jerusalem that is above, our mother, the city of God,[54] will not be cheated of the due number of her citizens, or perhaps will reign with an even greater number. For we do not know the number either of holy men and women or of the impure demons into whose place will succeed the children of that holy mother who appeared barren on earth, to live unendingly in the peace from

---

50. The air directly above the earth was regarded as the dwelling place of demons, who from that base carried on their pernicious activity among human beings; see *Exposition of the Psalms* 148, 9; *The City of God* VIII, 15; *The Christian Combat* 3, 3; *The Literal Meaning of Genesis* III, 10, 14; *Letter* 103, 2, 20.
51. See *The City of God* XIV, 13. See also D. J. McQueen, "*Contemptus Dei.* St. Augustine on the Disorder of Pride in Society and its Remedies," *Recherches Augustiniennes* 9 (1973) 227-293, esp. 238-240.
52. This doctrine was already to be found in Origen, *Homilies on Ezekiel* 13, 2. See also *The City of God* XXII, 1. On the subject see E. Lamirande, *L'Église céleste selon Saint Augustin* (Paris: Études Augustiniennes 1963) 144-147. On the continuance of the idea see Gregory the Great, *Homilies on the Gospels* 21, 2; 34, 11; Anselm of Canterbury, *Cur deus homo?* 1, 16-18.
53. See Lk 20:36.
54. See Gal 4:26.

which they fell. But the number that there will be of those citizens, either now or in the future, is in the contemplation of the maker who calls into existence the things that do not exist[55] and arranges *all things by measure and number and weight* (Wis 11:20).

By Grace You Have Been Saved through Faith

30. But can this part of the human race to which God promises freedom and an eternal kingdom be rewarded for its works? Certainly not! What good can one who is ruined do, except insofar as he is set free from his ruin? Can he perhaps do good by the free choice of his own will? This too must not be thought, for it was by evil use of his power of free choice that man ruined both that power and himself.[56] Just as a person who kills himself is alive when he does so, but by doing so becomes no longer alive, nor is he able to revive himself once he has killed himself, so, when sin is committed by free choice, sin is the victor and free choice also is lost, *for people are slaves to whatever masters them* (2 Pt 2:19)—this is certainly the opinion of the apostle Peter. And as it is correct, I ask what freedom can be enjoyed by one bound to slavery except when he takes pleasure in sin? One who gladly does the will of his master is serving freely, and in this way one who is a slave of sin is free to sin. So, he will not be free to act justly unless he is freed from sin and begins to be a slave of justice.

This is a true freedom because of the joy he finds in doing good, and a faithful slavery because he is doing as he has been told. But how will a person who has been sold into slavery and is bound by it find freedom to do good unless he is redeemed by the one who said, *If the Son makes you free, you will be free indeed* (Jn 8:36)? Before this begins to take place in a person, how can anybody who is not yet free to do good boast of his free choice as shown in a good deed, unless he is puffed up with empty pride, against which the apostle warns when he says, *By grace you have been saved through faith* (Eph 2:8)?

We Are Truly Free when God Makes Us

31. And lest such people claim that faith at least is their own achievement, not realizing that this has been given them by God, as the same apostle said in

---

55. See Rom 4:17.
56. For an accurate understanding of this passage one must attend to Augustine's distinction between free will and freedom. In his *Answer to the Two Letters of the Pelagians* I, 2, 5 he stresses the point that even sinners never lose freedom of the will, since they do evil not by necessity but freely. What they do lose is the freedom that man had in paradise. This freedom, that is, the power given to the first man of being able not to sin (*posse non peccare*), was lost through original sin.

another place that he received mercy so that he might be faithful,[57] here too he went on to add, *And this is not your own doing; it is the gift of God, not the result of works, so that no one may boast.*[58] Lest his readers might think the faithful would be lacking in good works, he further added, *For we are what he has made us, created in Christ Jesus for good works, which God prepared beforehand to be our way of life.*[59] We are truly made free when God makes us, that is, forms and creates us, not that we may be men, which he has already done, but that we may be good men: this he does now by his grace, that we may be a new creation in Christ, according to the saying, *Create a pure heart in me, O God* (Ps 51:10). For it could not be said that God had not already created his heart, as far as the nature of a human heart is concerned.

Give What You Command; Command What You Will

32. Also, so that nobody, although not boasting of his works, might boast of the freedom of his will, as if he had earned as a reward the very freedom to do good works,[60] let him hear the same proclaimer of grace saying, *For it is God who is at work in you, enabling you both to will and to work for his good pleasure* (Phil 2:13), and in another place, *So it comes not from the one who wills or runs, but from God who shows mercy* (Rom 9:16). Since there is no doubt whatever that a man, if he is already old enough to have the use of reason, cannot believe, hope, or love unless he wills to do so, nor can he win the reward of God's high vocation unless he runs for it willingly, how can it depend not on human will or exertion but on the God who shows mercy unless the will itself is prepared by the Lord,[61] as it is written?

Alternatively, if the words, *So it comes not from the one who wills or runs, but from God who shows mercy*, are written because it depends both on human will and on God's mercy, so that we should understand the text, *So it comes not from the one who wills or runs, but from God who shows mercy,* as if it said that human will alone is not enough without God's mercy, then God's mercy is not enough without human will. Consequently, if it is right to say, *So it comes not from the one who wills or runs, but from God who shows mercy*, because it is not done by human will alone, why is it not right also to say the opposite, "It depends not on God who shows mercy but on human will," since it is not done by God's mercy alone? Further, since no Christian will dare to say, "It depends not on God's

57. See 1 Cor 7:25.
58. See Eph 2:8-9.
59. See Eph 2:10.
60. See *The Grace of Christ and Original Sin* I, 31, 34; *Answer to the Two Letters of the Pelagians* IV, 6, 12-14.
61. See Prv 8:35 LXX.

mercy but on human will," for fear of openly contradicting the apostle, it remains for us to recognize that the words, *So it comes not from the one who wills or runs, but from God who shows mercy*, are said truly, that all may be given to God, who makes the good will of man ready for his help and helps the will he has made ready.[62]

For the good will of man precedes many of God's gifts but not all of them, and it is itself one of the gifts that it does not precede. For in sacred scripture we read both *His mercy shall go before me* (Ps 59:10) and *His mercy shall follow me* (Ps 23:6): it goes before the unwilling, that they may will, and it follows the willing, that they may not will in vain. For why are we commanded to pray for our enemies,[63] although they plainly have not the will to live holy lives, if not in order that God may be at work in them, enabling them to will? And why are we commanded to ask that we may receive,[64] if not in order that he who has given us the will may give us that which our will desires? Let us pray, then, for our enemies, that his mercy may go before them as it has also gone before us: let us also pray for ourselves, that his mercy may follow us.

The Grace of God through our Lord Jesus Christ

10, 33. So the human race was justly held in condemnation, and all its members were children of wrath. Of this wrath it is written: *For all our days have come to an end, and in your wrath we have ceased to be; our years will make designs like a spider* (Ps 90:9). And Job says of it: *A mortal, born of woman, few of days and full of wrath* (Jb 14:1). And the Lord Jesus said of this wrath: *Whoever believes in the Son has eternal life; whoever disobeys the Son will not see life, but God's wrath endures over him* (Jn 3:36). He does not say that God's wrath will come to him but that *God's wrath endures over him*. In fact, every human being is born with this wrath, which is why the apostle says, *For we were by nature children of wrath, like everyone else* (Eph 2:3).

Since human beings were in this wrath because of original sin, which became more serious and damaging as they added more or worse sins, there was need for a mediator, that is, a reconciler, to appease this wrath by the offering of a unique sacrifice, of which all the sacrifices of the law and the prophets were shadows.[65] Hence the apostle says, *For if while we were enemies, we were reconciled to God through the death of his Son, much more surely, having been reconciled in his blood, will we be saved through him from the wrath of God* (Rom 5:10). When

---

62. Augustine is referring to what later theology called prevenient and subsequent grace.
63. See Mt 5:44.
64. See Mt 7:7.
65. This point is taken up in greater detail in *The City of God* X, 5-6; *Answer to Faustus, a Manichean* XX, 18. 21; XXII, 17.

God is said to be angry, this does not mean that his mind was disturbed like the mind of a person who is angry, but his vengeance, which is nothing but just, is, by an extension of meaning, called his anger. So our reconciliation with God by a mediator and our reception of the Holy Spirit to make us children of the one to whom we were enemies—*for all who are led by the Spirit of God are children of God* (Rom 8:14): this is the grace of God through our Lord Jesus Christ.

Jesus Born of Mary

34. About this mediator it would take a long time to say as much as deserves to be said, although in fact no man can say what deserves to be said. For who can find suitable words to explain this one truth, that *the Word became flesh and lived among us* (Jn 1:14), that we may believe in the only Son of God the almighty Father, born of the Holy Spirit and the Virgin Mary? Yet we can say that, when the Word became flesh, flesh was taken by the Godhead; the Godhead was not changed into flesh. In this text by *flesh* we must understand "man," a part standing for the whole, as when it is said, *For no flesh*—that is, no man—*will be justified by the works of the law* (Rom 3:20). For it is not right to say that in that taking anything was lacking that belongs to human nature; but in this case we mean a human nature entirely free from every entanglement of sin, not of the sort that is born to the two sexes through the concupiscence of the flesh with bondage to sin, whose guilt is washed away in rebirth, but of the sort that could only be born from a virgin, conceived not by desire but by the faith of his mother. But if her virginity were impaired by his birth he would not then be born of a virgin, and the whole Church would be wrong—which God forbid—in acknowledging him as born of the virgin Mary, the Church which in imitation of his mother daily brings his members to birth and remains a virgin. Read, if you will, the letter on the virginity of holy Mary that I wrote to the illustrious Volusianus, whom I name with respect and affection.[66]

Son of God and Son of Man

35. So Christ Jesus, the Son of God, is God and man: God before all worlds, man in our world: God because he is the Word of God—for *the Word was God* (Jn 1:1)—and man because a rational soul and flesh were joined to the Word in one person. Therefore, insofar as he is God, he and the Father are one,[67] and insofar as he is man, the Father is greater than he.[68] But since he is the only Son of

---

66. See Letter 137, written in 411-412.
67. See Jn 10:30.
68. See Jn 14:28.

God, by nature and not by grace, he became also the Son of Man that he might be full of grace as well; he, one and the same, is both, one Christ from both natures since, though he was in the form of God, he did not regard what he was by nature, that is, being equal to God, as something to be grasped. But he emptied himself, taking the form of a servant, not losing or diminishing the form of God.[69] And through this he was both made less and remained equal, one and the same person in each case, as has been said. But he is different as regards the Word and as regards man: as regards the Word he is equal, as regards man lesser; one and the same person is Son of Man and Son of God; there are not two sons of God, divine and human, but one Son of God, God without beginning, man from a certain beginning in time, our Lord Jesus Christ.[70]

The Word is Full of Grace

11, 36. Here the grace of God is made clearly and abundantly plain. For what did human nature in Christ the man do to deserve being assumed in a unique way into the unity of the person of the one Son of God? What good will, what care for carrying out good intentions, what good works went before, that that man might be worthy to be one person with God? Was he human before, and was the unique benefit of being worthy of God offered to him alone? Certainly from the moment when he began to be human he began to be nothing other than the Son, the only Son, of God, and because of God the Word, which on assuming him became flesh, he was certainly God, so that, just as any human being is one person, that is, a rational soul and flesh, so Christ is one person, Word and man.[71] Whence can human nature have received such great glory, which is without doubt a free gift, given without preceding merit?[72] Surely, to those who consider the matter soberly and with faith, that great grace which is God's alone is here plainly shown, that men may understand that they are both freed from their sins and justified by the very grace which made Christ the man unable to have any sin. So

---

69. See Phil 2:6-7.
70. The remarks on the unity of Christ call to mind the christological confession of faith (*Libellus emendationis*) signed by the monk Leporius a few years earlier (418-419). There the monk distanced himself from erroneous views that would later turn poisonous in Nestorianism. Augustine's influence on the formulations of the *Libellus* is unmistakable; see Letter 219. See B. Daley, "Christology," in Fitzgerald 164-169, esp. 166.
71. The same analogy, formulated in a similar way, is to be found in the *Quicumque* (Pseudo-Athanasian) Creed, which was composed by an unknown Latin author in the second half of the fifth century in southern Gaul.
72. In the free assumption of human nature in the incarnation Augustine sees the prototype of grace; see sections 12, 40; 28, 108. This theme also served as an argument in the Pelagian controversy; see *Rebuke and Grace* 11, 30; *The Predestination of the Saints* 15, 30-31; *The Gift of Perseverance* 24, 67; *Unfinished Work in Answer to Julian* I, 138-140; IV, 84.

it was that the angel greeted his mother when he announced to her this future birth, saying, *Hail, full of grace* (Lk 1:28), and a little later, *You have found grace with God* (Lk 1:30). Now she was indeed said to be full of grace and to have found grace with God in order that she might be the mother of her Lord, or rather of the Lord of all. But about Christ himself the evangelist John, having said, *And the Word became flesh and lived among us, and we have seen*, continues, *his glory, glory as of a Father's only Son, full of grace and truth* (Jn 1:14). When he says that *the Word became flesh*, he means that the Word is full of grace, and when he speaks of the *glory as of a Father's only Son*, he means that he is full of truth. The truth is that he who is the only Son of God by nature, not by grace, took man to himself by grace into such a unity of person that he was also Son of Man.

Born of the Holy Spirit

37. For the same Jesus Christ, God's only-begotten, that is, only Son, our Lord, was born of the Holy Spirit and of the Virgin Mary. We know also that the Holy Spirit is a gift of God, a gift equal to the giver, and so the Holy Spirit is also God, no less than the Father and the Son. And by the fact that the human birth of Christ is from the Holy Spirit, what else is manifested but grace itself? For when the virgin asked the angel how what he had told her would come about, seeing that she knew no man, the angel replied, *The Holy Spirit will come upon you, and the power of the Most High will overshadow you; therefore the child to be born will be holy; he will be called Son of God* (Lk 1:35). And when Joseph wanted to put her away on suspicion that she was an adulteress, knowing that it was not by him that she had become pregnant, the reply he received from the angel was, *Do not be afraid to take Mary as your wife, for the child conceived in her is from the Holy Spirit* (Mt 1:20): that is, what you suspect is from another man is from the Holy Spirit.

The Holy Spirit Is not Father

12, 38. But are we to say that the Holy Spirit is the father of Christ the man in such a way that, while God the Father begot the Word, the Holy Spirit begot the man, and that the one Christ is from these two substances, both Son of God the Father according to his nature as Word and Son of the Holy Spirit according to his humanity, since the Holy Spirit begot him of the virgin mother like a father? Who will dare to say this? There is no need to show by argument how many other absurdities would follow from this, since this is already so absurd that none of the faithful would be able to bear listening to it. So we acknowledge our Lord Jesus Christ, who is God from God but was born as man of the Holy Spirit and of the Virgin Mary, to be in both his substances,[73] the divine and the human, the only Son of God the almighty Father, from whom the Holy Spirit proceeds.[74] How then can we say that Christ was born of the Holy Spirit if the Holy Spirit did not beget him? Is it because he made him, since, insofar as our Lord Jesus Christ is God, *All things were made through him* (Jn 1:3); but insofar as he is human, he too was made, as the apostle says, *He was made from the seed of David according to the flesh* (Rom 1:3)?

But since that creature whom the virgin conceived and bore, although he belongs only to the person of the Son, was made by the whole Trinity—since the operations of the Trinity are inseparable—why was only the Holy Spirit named in connection with his making? Must the whole Trinity be understood to operate whenever one of them is named in connection with a particular deed? It must, as can be demonstrated by examples. But we must not delay too long over this matter, for our question concerns how it is that we say that he was born of the Holy Spirit[75] when he is in no way the son of the Holy Spirit. Similarly, the fact that God made this world does not justify our calling it God's Son, or saying that it was born of God, but we can rightly speak of it as made or created or established or instituted by him, or other similar and suitable expressions. So in this case, while we acknowledge that he was born of the Holy Spirit and of the virgin Mary, it is hard to explain how he is not the son of the Holy Spirit and *is* the son of the virgin Mary; without doubt the Holy Spirit's relationship to him is not that of a father, while the virgin's relationship to him *is* that of a mother.

The Meaning of Sonship

39. So it should not be conceded that anything that is born of another thing is inevitably to be called its son. I do not wish to mention the fact that a hair, a louse, and a tapeworm are born from a person in a different way from a son, and that none of these is a son.[76] I do not wish to mention them because it is not suitable to compare them to something so great, but certainly nobody can rightly speak of those who are born of water and the spirit as sons of water,[77] yet they are clearly called sons of God the Father and of Mother Church. So it was in a similar way that he was born of the Holy Spirit, the Son of God the Father, not of the Holy

---

73. Augustine uses the term "substance" where theology since the Council of Chalcedon (451) has usually used the term "nature." However, "substance" was regularly used in this sense by Latin theologians from Tertullian to Leo the Great.
74. Augustine once more speaks of the Holy Spirit as proceeding only from the Father. See section 9.
75. See Mt 1:20.
76. Augustine shared the ancient persuasion that certain lower organisms sprang spontaneously from inanimate matter.
77. See Jn 3:5.

Spirit. For what we said about hair and other things is valuable only to show that not everything that is born of someone can also be called that person's son, just as not everybody who is called a person's son was necessarily born from that person, as is the case with those who are adopted. And people are called "sons of hell"[78] not because they were born from there but because they are being prepared to go there, just as the sons of the kingdom are being prepared for the kingdom.[79]

The Gift of God

40. So, just as a thing can be born from somebody without being that person's son, and not everybody who is called a son is born of the person whose son he is called, clearly the manner in which Christ was born of the Holy Spirit not as a son and of the virgin Mary as a son shows us the grace of God by which a man without any preceding merits, at the very beginning of his natural existence, was joined to the Word of God in so great a personal unity that the Son of God was Son of Man and the Son of Man Son of God, and thus in the assumption of human nature grace itself, which cannot allow any sin, became in some way natural to that man. It was right that this grace should be signified by mention of the Holy Spirit because his mode of being God is such that he is also called the Gift of God: to say enough about that, if it were possible, would demand a truly lengthy discussion.[80]

Jesus Was Called Sin

13, 41. His begetting or conception, then, was not due to the pleasure of carnal concupiscence,[81] and so he contracted no sin from his origin, and by God's grace he was joined and united in a wonderful and indescribable way in unity of person to the unbegotten Word of the Father, who is God's Son not by grace but by nature, with the result that he himself committed no sin, and yet because he came in the likeness of sinful flesh[82] he too was called sin[83] and was destined to be sacrificed for the washing away of sins.[84] In the old law, in fact, sacrifices for

---

78. See Mt 23:15.
79. See Mt 8:12.
80. Augustine discusses this question at length in *The Trinity*.
81. Augustine seems here to leave open the possibility that the transmission of original sin is due to the pleasure of intercourse. He disowned this view in *Marriage and Desire*.
82. See Rom 8:3.
83. See 2 Cor 5:21.
84. Augustine is dealing here with the objective aspect of redemption, that is, the reconciliation of humanity with God through the sacrifice of the cross. The subjective aspect of redemption, that is, the conversion of the sinful human being, is discussed in section 108.

sins were called sins.[85] He was the true sacrifice for sins, of which they were shadows.[86] So the apostle, after saying, *We entreat you on behalf of Christ, be reconciled to God*, immediately added: *For our sake he made him to be sin who knew no sin, so that in him we might become the righteousness of God* (2 Cor 5:20-21). He did not say, as some lying manuscripts would have it, "He who had known no sin made sin for us," as if Christ himself had sinned for us, but he said that the God to whom we were to be reconciled *for our sake made him to be sin who knew no sin*, that is, to be a sacrifice for sins through which we might be reconciled. So he was sin that we might be righteousness, not our own righteousness but God's, and not in ourselves but in him, just as he revealed sin, not his own but ours, not in himself but in us, in the likeness of sinful flesh in which he was crucified, so that since there was no sin in him he might in some way die to sin when he died to the flesh in which was the likeness of sin, and, although he had never lived the old life of sin, he might signify by his resurrection the restoration of our life to newness from the old death by which we were dead in sin.

The Great Mystery of Baptism

42. This is the great mystery of baptism which is celebrated among us, that all who share in that grace may die to sin, just as he is said to have died to sin because he died to the flesh, that is, to the likeness of sin, and that they might have life by being reborn from the font, whatever their physical age, just as he had life when he rose from the grave.

43. For just as nobody is to be forbidden baptism, from a newborn baby to a decrepit old man, so there is nobody who does not die to sin in baptism. But babies die only to original sin, while older people die to all those sins that by evil living they have added to the sin they have brought with them from birth.

The Use of the Singular and the Plural

44. But they are also usually said to die to sin, although doubtless they die not to one sin but to all the many sins that they have committed on their own account up till then, whether by thought, word, or deed, since the plural is often signified by the singular, as when Virgil says, "And they fill the womb with an armed soldier,"[87] although they did this with a number of soldiers. And we read in our own scriptures: *Pray to the Lord to take away the serpent from us* (Nm 21:7): he

---

85. See Lv 6:23; Nm 8:8; Hos 4:8.
86. See section 33.
87. See *Aeneid* II, 20. Virgil is speaking here of the Greek soldiers inside the wooden horse by which they gained entrance to the city of Troy.

does not say "serpents," although many serpents were plaguing the people to lead them to say this. And there are countless similar instances. But when the one original sin is signified by a plural, when we say that infants are baptized for the remission of sins, rather than the remission of sin, this is the opposite figure of speech, which uses a plural to signify a singular. For example, after the death of Herod come the words: *For those who were seeking the child's life are dead* (Mt 2:20), not "is dead." And in Exodus it says: *They have made for themselves gods of gold* (Ex 32:31), when they had made a single golden calf, about which they said, *These are your gods, O Israel, who brought you up out of the land of Egypt* (Ex 32:4), again using the plural for the singular.

In Adam's Sin There Are Many Sins

45. However, even in the one sin which came into the world through one man and passed to all men, because of which even infants are baptized,[88] we can understand there to be many sins, if the one sin is divided into its component parts. For there is pride there, by which the man preferred to be in his own power rather than God's, and sacrilege because he did not believe God, and murder because he cast himself down to death, and spiritual fornication because the integrity of a human mind was corrupted by the persuasion of the serpent, and theft because a forbidden food was wrongfully taken, and avarice because he sought more than should have been sufficient for him, and all the other sins that can be discerned in this one crime by a person who considers carefully.

A Person's Rebirth

46. It is said, and not without probability, that infants are also liable for the sins of their parents, not only those of the first humans but also those of the people from whom they were born.[89] The divine judgment, *I shall punish children for the iniquity of their parents* (Ex 20:5; Dt 5:9), certainly applies to them until they begin to belong to the new covenant by regeneration. This covenant was prophesied when it was said through Ezekiel that children would not receive the sins of their parents, nor would it be any longer said in Israel: *The parents have eaten sour grapes, and the children's teeth are set on edge* (Ez 18:2). So the purpose of each person's rebirth is that whatever there is in him of sin that he was born with may be done away with. For sins that are committed later through evil

---

88. Important for this subject is *The Merits and Forgiveness of Sins and the Baptism of Infants* III, 4, 7.
89. See A.-M. Dubarle, "La pluralité des péchés héréditaires dans la tradition augustinienne," *Revue des études augustiniennes* 3 (1957) 113-136.

action can be healed also with penitence,[90] as we see happening even after baptism. This shows that regeneration was only introduced because of a fault in our generation which is such that even one who was conceived in legitimate matrimony says, *I was born guilty, a sinner when my mother conceived me* (Ps 51:5). He did not here say "in iniquity" or "in sin," though he could rightly have said that, but he preferred to speak of iniquities and sins, because even in that one sin which passed to all men, and which is so great that by it human nature was changed and came under the necessity of death, there are found to be several sins, as I have shown;[91] and there are the other sins of parents which, although they cannot make such a change to human nature, nonetheless bind the children with guilt unless the free grace and mercy of God comes to their help.

The Sins of Ancestors

47. But there would be good cause for discussing the sins of other parents, the ancestors of each of us from Adam down to our own fathers. We might ask whether each person who is born is implicated in the evil actions and the many faults found in his origins, so that the later one is born the worse one's situation is, and whether the reason why God threatens descendants to the third and fourth generation about the sins of their parents is that in his mercy he tempers his anger regarding the sins of ancestors so that it extends no further than that, so that those on whom the grace of regeneration is not conferred are not too heavily burdened in their eternal damnation as they would be if they incurred guilt by reason of their origin for the sins of all their ancestors from the beginning of the human race and had to pay the just penalty for them. I am not so rash as to say whether or not any other statement about so great a matter can be found in holy scripture after more careful search and discussion.

The One Mediator between God and Humanity

14, 48. That one great sin, which was committed in a place and state of life of such happiness with the result that the whole human race was condemned originally and, so to say, at root in one man, is not undone and washed away except by the one mediator between God and humanity, the man Christ Jesus,[92] who alone was able to be born in such a way that he had no need to be reborn.

---

90. See section 65.
91. See section 45.
92. See 1 Tm 2:5.

Jesus' Example

49. Those who were baptized with the baptism of John, with which Jesus too was baptized, were not reborn, but, by a kind of preparatory ministry of the one who said, *Prepare the way of the Lord* (Mt 3:3; Lk 3:4; Is 40:3), they were made ready for him through whom alone they could be reborn. For his baptism is not in water alone, as John's was, but also in the Holy Spirit,[93] so that whoever believes in Christ is reborn in that Spirit by which Christ was born and so needed no rebirth. That is why the Father's voice was heard over him when he was baptized: *Today I have begotten you* (Ps 2:7; Heb 1:5; 5:5),[94] speaking not of the one day in time when he was baptized but of the day of changeless eternity, to show that that man belonged to the person of the only Son: a day that neither begins with the end of yesterday nor ends with the beginning of tomorrow is always "today." So he willed to be baptized in water by John, not that any sin might be washed away from him, but to show his great humility.[95] Baptism found nothing in him to wash away, just as death found nothing in him to punish, so that the devil might be overcome and conquered not by power and violence but by truth and justice, and, since he had most wickedly killed Christ, who had committed no sin to deserve his death, so that he might fully deserve to lose those he justly held captive because of their sin.[96] So he accepted both baptism and death out of firm purpose, not driven by pitiable necessity but moved by his merciful will, so that one man might take away the sin of the world just as one man brought sin into the world, that is, to the entire human race.

Rebirth in Christ

50. There is this difference: that one man brought one sin into the world, but the other one took away not only that one sin but all the other sins that he found had been added to it. That is why the apostle says: *And the free gift is not like the effect of the one man's sin. For the judgment following one trespass brought condemnation, but the free gift following many trespasses brings justification.* (Rom 5:16) This is because that one sin which comes to men from their origin,

---

93. See Mt 3:11; Mk 1:8.
94. See Mt 3:17. Augustine himself points out that this addition from Ps 2:7 is not found in the earliest Greek manuscripts but is present in most of the later manuscripts; see *Agreement among the Evangelists* II, 14, 31. In the Greek ecclesiastical writers this reading is attested from the second century on.
95. See Mt 3:15.
96. This argument is based on the conviction that the devil was given the power to punish human beings. Since Christ was sinless, death as punishment for sin could not touch him. The slaying of Christ was therefore a misuse of the power loaned to the devil. In just punishment for that misuse, the devil lost this power over sinful humanity. See J. Rivière, *Le dogme de la Rédemption chez St. Augustin* (3 ed. Paris 1931) 118, 320-338.

even if it is their only sin, makes them subject to condemnation, while grace *following many trespasses* justifies a person who has committed many sins of his own in addition to that one which he has contracted from his origins in common with everybody else.

51. But what he says a little later, *Just as one man's trespass led to condemnation for all, so one man's act of righteousness leads to justification and life for all* (Rom 5:18), shows plainly enough that there is nobody born from Adam who is not under condemnation, and that nobody is freed from that condemnation except by being reborn in Christ.

Baptized into Christ's Death

52. When he considered he had said enough for that place in his letter concerning the punishment that came from one man and the grace that comes from one man, he went on to commend the great mystery of holy baptism in the cross of Christ, so that we might understand that baptism in Christ is nothing other than an image of the death of Christ, and that the death of Christ on the cross is nothing other than an image of the forgiveness of sins, so that just as he suffered a true death, in us there is a true forgiveness of sins,[97] and just as his resurrection was true, so also is our justification true.[98] For he says, *What then are we to say? Should we continue in sin in order that grace may abound?* (Rom 6:1) having said earlier, *For where sin increased, grace abounded all the more* (Rom 5:20). So he asked himself the question whether it is right to persist in sin in order to receive an abundance of grace. But he replied, *By no means!* and continued, *How can we who died to sin go on living in it?* (Rom 6:2) Then, to show that we are dead to sin, he said, *Do you not know that all of us who have been baptized into Christ Jesus were baptized into his death?* (Rom 6:3) So, if the fact that we have been baptized into the death of Christ shows that we are dead to sin, clearly infants who are baptized into Christ also die to sin,[99] since they are baptized into his death, for no exception is made when he says, *All of us who have been baptized into Christ Jesus were baptized into his death* (Rom

---

97. Julian of Eclanum reproached Augustine for holding that baptism does not bestow the forgiveness of all sins but only erases them, so that the roots of sin remain, somewhat as the roots of one's hair remain after a haircut. In contrast, Augustine always emphasized the real nature of the removal of sin; see *Answer to the Two Letters of the Pelagians* I, 13, 26-27; *Expositions of the Psalms* 31, sermon 2, 9.

98. Augustine sees the positive effect of justification in the fact that human beings become just and children of God and obtain a participation in the divine nature; see *The Spirit and the Letter* 26, 45; Sermon 166, 4.

99. In the North African Church of Augustine's time infant baptism was common; see sections 66 and 97. During the Pelagian controversy the Church's practice of infant baptism became a principal argument for the existence of original sin. See R. Fairweather, "St. Augustine's Interpretation of Infant Baptism," *Augustinus Magister* II (Paris 1954) 897-903.

6:3). He spoke in this way to prove that we are dead to sin. But what is the sin to which infants die when they are reborn if not one they have contracted by being born? So what follows also applies to them: *Therefore we have been buried with him by baptism into death, so that, just as Christ was raised from the dead by the glory of the Father, so we too might walk in newness of life. For if we have been united with him in a death like his, we shall certainly be united with him in a resurrection like his. We know that our old self was crucified with him so that the body of sin might be destroyed and we might no longer be enslaved to sin. For whoever has died is justified from sin. But if we have died with Christ, we believe that we shall also live with him. We know that Christ, being raised from the dead, will never die again; death no longer has dominion over him. The death he died, he died to sin, once for all; but the life he lives, he lives to God. So you also must consider yourselves dead to sin and alive to God in Christ Jesus.* (Rom 6:4-11) At this point he had begun to prove that we are not to continue in sin that grace may abound, saying, *How can we who died to sin go on living in it?* (Rom 6:2) and, in order to show that we are dead to sin, adding, *Do you not know that all of us who have been baptized into Christ Jesus were baptized into his death?* (Rom 6:3) So, he ended that whole passage just as he had begun it: he spoke of the death of Christ in such a way as to indicate that Christ too was dead to sin. To what sin? Surely to the flesh, in which there was not sin but the likeness of sin,[100] which is why the flesh is called sin. So, to those who have been baptized in the death of Christ, in which not only adults but also infants are baptized, he says, *So you also* (that is, like Christ) *must consider yourselves dead to sin and alive to God in Christ Jesus* (Rom 6:11).

The Mysteries of Christ

53. So, whatever took place in Christ's crucifixion, his burial, his resurrection on the third day, his ascension into heaven and his sitting at the right hand of the Father was done in such a way that Christians might live within these mysteries, which are historical facts and not merely mystical utterances.[101] It was because of his cross that Paul said, *And those who belong to Christ Jesus have crucified the flesh with its passions and desires* (Gal 5:24); because of his burial that he said, *We have been buried with him by baptism into death*; because of his resurrection that he said, *So that, just as Christ was raised from the dead by the glory of the Father, so we too might walk in newness of life* (Rom 6:4); and because of his ascension into heaven and sitting at the right hand of the Father that he said, *So, if you have been raised with Christ, seek the things that are above, where*

---

100. See Rom 8:3.
101. See *Faith and the Creed* 5, 11 – 7, 14.

Christ is seated at the right hand of God. Set your mind on things that are above, not on things that are on earth, for you have died, and your life is hidden with Christ in God. (Col 3:1-3)

To Judge the Living and the Dead

54. But what we profess about Christ concerning the future, that he will come from heaven and judge the living and the dead, has nothing to do with our life as we lead it here, since it does not belong among the things that he has done but among the things that are to be done at the end of the world. It was concerning this that the apostle went on to say, *When Christ who is your life is revealed, then you also will be revealed with him in glory* (Col 3:4).

55. But there are two ways in which we can understand his future judging of the living and the dead: by the living we can understand those whom his coming will find here not yet dead but still living in this flesh of ours, and by the dead those who have left the body or will do so before he comes; or else we can understand the living to signify the just and the dead the unjust, since the just will be judged as well.[102] For sometimes the day of judgment is spoken of as something evil, for example, *And those who have done evil, to the resurrection of condemnation* (Jn 5:29), and sometimes as something good, as when scripture says, *Save me, O God, by your name, and judge me by your might* (Ps 54:1). It is by God's judgment that the good and the evil are separated, so that the good, who are to be delivered from evil, not lost with the evil, may be set at God's right hand. That is why he cries, *Judge me, O God*, and then, as if to explain what he has said, *and defend my cause against an ungodly people* (Ps 43:1).

Faith in the Holy Spirit and the Church

The Holy Church

15, 56. When we have said about Jesus the only Son of God, our Lord, what is appropriate in a brief confession of faith, we add, as you know, that we believe also in the Holy Spirit, to complete that Trinity which is God. Then we mention the holy Church, whence we may understand that the rational part of creation which belongs to the free city of Jerusalem[103] must be mentioned after the

---

102. See ibid. 8, 15. There is a full discussion of the final judgment in *The City of God* XX, 1-5.18-24.27-30.
103. See Gal 4:26.

creator, that is, the supreme Trinity, for what has been said about Christ the man concerns the one person of God's only Son. Therefore due order in the profession of faith required that the Church should be named after the Trinity, like a house after the one who lives in it, a temple after its god and a city after its founder. Here the whole Church should be understood to be meant,[104] not only the part that is on pilgrimage on earth, praising the name of the Lord from the rising of the sun to its setting and singing a new song after its old captivity, but also that part which has remained with God in heaven ever since its foundation and has never suffered any fall into evil.[105] This part is found among the holy angels and continues in blessedness, giving generous help as it should to its comrades who are on pilgrimage, since they will together form one company in eternity, which is one already by the bond of charity, established to worship the one God.

So neither the whole Church nor any part of it desires to be worshiped instead of God, nor does anybody want to be a god to those who belong to the temple of God which is built of those made into gods by the uncreated God.[106] So the Holy Spirit, if he were a creature and not the creator, would certainly be a rational creature—for rational creatures are the highest of creatures—and so would not be placed before the Church in the rule of faith,[107] since he would also be a member of the Church in that part of it which is in heaven and would have no temple but would be himself a temple. But he has a temple, of which the apostle says, *Do you not know that your body is a temple of the Holy Spirit within you, which you have from God?* (1 Cor 6:19) Of the body he says elsewhere, *Do you not know that your bodies are members of Christ?* (1 Cor 6:15) How then can he not be God, since he has a temple, or be less than Christ, since Christ's members are his temple? Nor is his temple different from the temple of God, since the same apostle says, *Do you not know that you are God's temple?* and to prove this added, *and that God's Spirit dwells in you?* (1 Cor 3:16) So God dwells in his temple, not only the Holy Spirit but also the Father and the Son. The Son also said of his body, through which he became head of the Church that is among men, *so that he might come to have first place in everything* (Col 1:18), *Destroy this temple, and in three days I will raise it up* (Jn 2:19). For the temple of God, that is, of the whole supreme Trinity, is the holy Church, that is, the whole Church, in heaven and on earth.

---

104. See sections 57 and 61-62.
105. See E. Lamirande, *L'Église céleste selon Saint Augustin*; idem, "L'Église dans l'*Enchiridion* de Saint Augustin. Quelques questions aux théologiens," *Église et Théologie* 10 (1979) 195-206.
106. See Gn 3:5; Ps 81:6; Jn 10:34-35.
107. I.e., the creed, which was anciently known as the Canon or Rule of Faith.

The Church in Heaven

57. But what can we say of the part of the Church that is in heaven? Only that nobody in it is evil, and that nobody has fallen from there or will fall in the future, since *God did not spare the angels when they sinned,* as the apostle Peter writes, *but cast them into hell and committed them to prisons of deepest darkness to be kept until the judgment* (2 Pt 2:4).

The Angels

58. But what that highest and most blessed society is like, and what the differences are in rank there according to which all are called angels as if by their common name, as we read in the Letter to the Hebrews, *But to which of the angels has he ever said, Sit at my right hand?* (Heb 1:13)—which means that they are all called angels—and yet there are archangels there as well, let those who are able tell us, provided they can prove the truth of what they say. Let them say whether these archangels are also called powers, so that scripture says, *Praise him, all his angels; praise him, all his powers!* (Ps 148:2) as if that were the same as saying, "Praise him, all his angels; praise him, all his archangels." And let them explain the difference among the four words the apostle seems to use to refer to that entire heavenly society when he says, *Whether thrones or dominions or rulers or powers* (Col 1:16). I confess that I am ignorant of these things.[108] Nor am I certain whether the sun and the moon and all the stars belong to that same society, although some people think that there exist shining bodies that do not lack sense or intelligence.[109]

The Bodies of Angels

59. Furthermore, who can explain the nature of the bodies with which angels have appeared to humans, so that they can not only be seen but also touched,[110] and they sometimes present visions not to people's physical eyes but to their

---

108. See *Answer to the Priscillianists* 11, 14.

109. Ever since Hellenistic times the stars were regarded as divine beings that played a mediating role between human beings and the supreme divinity. Passages from both the Jewish and the Christian scriptures (Is 14:12; Rv 1:20; 12:1-4) led to the idea of an equivalence between the stars and the angels. See A. Scott, *Origen and the Life of the Stars. A History of an Idea* (Oxford 1991). In his *Answer to the Priscillianists* 11, 14, Augustine takes up the question as to whether stars, sun and moon "have rational souls within their remarkable bodies." There he inclines to the view that spiritual beings dwell in and guide the stars.

110. Because of their manifestations angels were assigned a kind of corporeality. Augustine often discusses the problem; see *Free Will* III, 11, 33; Letter 95, 8; Sermon 362, 17, 20; *The Trinity* III, 1, 4-5.

spiritual eyes or to their minds, or they say something not outwardly to the ear but inwardly to a person's soul, being themselves also within the soul, as it is written in the book of the prophets, *The angel who talked in me said to me* (Zec 1:9) (for he did not say "who spoke to me" but *in me*), or they appear to people during sleep and speak with them as in dreams (for we read in the gospel, *Behold, an angel of the Lord appeared to him in a dream and said* [Mt 1:20])? These are the means by which angels indicate that they do not have bodies that can be felt: they raise the very difficult question of how the patriarchs washed their feet[111] and how Jacob wrestled with an angel whose presence was so solidly tangible.[112] When such questions are asked, and each person tries to answer them as best he can, our minds are given useful exercise, if moderation is observed in the discussion and the error is avoided of those who think they know what they do not know. What need is there to affirm or deny these and similar opinions, or to define them with care, when no harm is done by being in ignorance of them?

Putting Our Hope In God

16, 60. It is more necessary to judge and recognize when Satan *disguises himself as an angel of light* (2 Cor 11:14), lest he seduce us into some harm by his deceit. For when bodily sense deceives us, but without moving the mind from that true and right way of thinking which enables a person to live faithfully, there is no danger to our religious way of life; also, when he makes himself appear good and does or says things appropriate to good angels, even if he is believed to be good, this mistake brings no harm or danger to Christian faith. But when by these means he begins to gain control of what does not belong to him, then there is need for great vigilance in order to recognize him and refuse to follow him. But how many people are able to escape all his deadly tricks without the guidance and protection of God? This very difficulty is useful in ensuring that a person does not put hope in himself or in somebody else but rather in God, the hope of all who belong to him: surely none of the faithful doubts that this profits us more.

The Pilgrim Church

61. So this Church, which exists among the holy angels and powers of God, will be known to us as it is when we are joined with it at the end to share in unending blessedness. But this Church, which is wandering on earth in separation from the other, is better known to us because we are within it, and because it

---

111. See Gn 18:4; 19:2.
112. See Gn 32:24-25.

is composed of human beings like ourselves. It has been redeemed from all sin by the blood of the mediator who has no sin, and of him it is said, *If God is for us, who is against us? He who did not withhold his own Son, but gave him up for all of us.* (Rom 8:31-32) Christ did not die for the angels, but the redemption and liberation from evil of any human being by his death benefits the angels, since such a person in a sense returns into good relations with them after the enmity caused between men and the holy angels by sins,[113] and by the redemption of men the losses caused by the fall of the angels are made good.[114]

Reconciliation on Earth and in Heaven

62. The holy angels, taught by God, the eternal contemplation of whose truth is the source of their blessedness, know how large a number of members of the human race is required to complete that city. That is why the apostle says, *To renew all things in Christ, things in heaven and things on earth* (Eph 1:10). Things in heaven are made new when the loss caused by the fall of angels from heaven is made good from among men; and things on earth are restored when men themselves, predestined to eternal life, are freed from their old corruption and made new. And thus, through the unique sacrifice in which the mediator was immolated, which the many sacrifices of the old law prefigured, things in heaven are reconciled with things on earth, and things on earth with things in heaven. For, as the same apostle says, *For in him all the fullness of God was pleased to dwell, and through him God was pleased to reconcile to himself all things, whether on earth or in heaven, by making peace through the blood of his cross* (Col 1:19-20).

Peace through the Blood of the Cross

63. This peace, as it is written,[115] surpasses all understanding, and we can only know it by coming to it. How do things in heaven receive peace, if not with us, that is, by being reconciled with us? Peace is always there, both among all the intelligent creatures and between them and their creator.[116] This peace surpasses all understanding, as has been said, but that means *our* understanding, not that of those who always see the face of the Father. But we, however great our human understanding, know in part and see *in a mirror, dimly* (1 Cor 13:9.12). But when we are equal to the angels of God,[117] then we shall see face to face as they

---

113. See Eph 2:14-16; Col 1:20.
114. See section 28.
115. See Phil 4:7.
116. See *The City of God* XXII, 29.
117. See Lk 20:36.

do, and we shall be as much at peace with them as they are with us, for we shall love them as much as we are loved by them. So we shall know their peace, since our own peace will be like theirs and as great, nor will it then surpass our understanding. But the peace of God, which is offered to us in that place, will without doubt surpass both our understanding and theirs. From him every rational creature that is blessed receives its blessedness, but he does not receive his blessedness from them. So it is better to understand the words of scripture, *the peace of God, which surpasses all understanding* (Phil 4:7), as not excluding from that *all* even the understanding of the holy angels but only that of God, for not even his peace surpasses his understanding.

Faith in the Forgiveness of Sins

The Forgiveness of Sins

17, 64. Even now, however, the angels are in concord with us when our sins are forgiven. So in our confession of faith the forgiveness of sins comes next in order after the mention of the holy Church. It is because of this that the Church on earth stands,[118] because of this that what was lost is found and does not perish.[119] With the exception of the gift of baptism, which has been given to us against original sin, so that what was contracted through birth might be taken away through rebirth—and it also takes away actual sins which it finds to have been committed whether in the heart or the mouth or in deed[120]—with the exception of this great forgiveness, the beginning of man's regeneration in which all guilt whether inborn or acquired is removed, the rest of our life once we have come to the age when we can use our reason, however rich it may be in fruits of justice, is not lived without forgiveness of sins, since God's children, for as long as they live this mortal life, are in conflict with death. And although it is truly said of them: *For all who are led by the Spirit of God are children of God* (Rom 8:14), they are moved by God's Spirit and they journey toward God as children of God in such a way that, like children of men, they fall back on themselves under certain human impulses even in their spirit, especially since it is weighed down by the corruptible body, and so they sin.[121] But there are differences of

---

118. This trenchant remark must have been aimed at Donatism, which would accept only a "Church of saints."
119. See Lk 15:32.
120. Augustine again responds to the Pelagian objection that in his view baptism is without effect; see *Answer to the Two Letters of the Pelagians* II, 13, 26; *Answer to Julian* VI, 13, 40.
121. In opposition to the optimism of the Pelagians, who believed in the possibility of a life without sin, Augustine insisted that in fact no one can live without sin; see *Faith and the Creed* 10, 21;

degree, since, although every crime is a sin, not every sin is a crime. Hence we say that the lives of holy men, for as long as they live in this death,[122] can be found to be without crime, but the great apostle says, *If we say that we have no sin, we deceive ourselves, and the truth is not in us* (1 Jn 1:8).

Special Times of Penance

65. But we should not despair of God's mercy for the forgiveness of actual crimes, however great, in the holy Church for those who do penance,[123] each in a way appropriate to his sin. But in works of penance, when a sin has been committed of such a kind that he who committed it is also cut off from the body of Christ,[124] time should not be measured so much as sorrow, since God does not despise a broken and contrite heart.[125] But because the sorrow of one heart is usually hidden from another and does not become known to others either by words or by any other signs, although it is known to him to whom it is said, *My sighing is not hidden from you* (Ps 38:9), times of penance are rightly established by those who govern the Church, so that satisfaction may be made also to the Church, in which sins themselves are forgiven. Indeed, outside the Church they are not forgiven,[126] for it is the Church that has received the Holy Spirit as her own as a pledge[127] without which no sins are forgiven, in such a way that those to whom they are forgiven receive eternal life.

The Future Judgment

66. The forgiveness of sins in this life is chiefly because of the future judgment. The words of scripture, *A heavy yoke is upon the sons of Adam from the day they come forth from their mother's womb till the day they are buried in the mother of all* (Sir 40:1), are so true that we see even infants tormented by various evils after the washing of rebirth: from this we should understand that everything that is done in the sacraments of salvation is concerned more with the hope of good things to come than with retaining or gaining good things in the present. Many sins are pardoned here and not avenged with any punishment, but their

---

The Deeds of Pelagius 11, 23. See also E. TeSelle, "Pelagius, Pelagianism," in Fitzgerald 633-640, esp. 634-636.

122. Augustine sees this life as a death in comparison with the life to come.

123. See A. D. Fitzgerald, "Penance," in Fitzgerald 640-646 for a systematic survey of the subject.

124. In the early Christian centuries, sinners would do public penance for a period before being readmitted to the communion of the Church.

125. See Ps 51:17.

126. The statement is a reminder of the principle that "outside the Church there is no salvation"; see *Baptism* IV, 17, 24; Sermon 71, 20, 33.

127. See 2 Cor 1:22.

penalties are reserved for the future—and it is not in vain that the day when the judge of the living and the dead will come has as its proper name the Day of Judgment—just as on the contrary there are some sins that are punished here, and if they are forgiven they will certainly do no harm in the world to come. That is why the apostle says concerning certain temporal punishments imposed on those who sin in this life, to those whose sins are forgiven and not reserved for the final judgment, *But if we judged ourselves, we would not be judged by the Lord. But when we are judged by the Lord, we are disciplined so that we may not be condemned along with this world.* (1 Cor 11:31-32)

Faith and Good Works

18, 67. There are some who believe that also those who are baptized with Christ's cleansing and do not desert his name nor are cut off from him by any heresy or schism, however great the sins in which they live without washing them away with penitence or redeeming them with acts of charity, but persisting in them most tenaciously until the last day of this life, will be saved by fire, although because of the greatness of their sins and wickednesses this will be after they have been punished with a fire that lasts for a long time, but not for eternity.[128] But it seems to me that people who believe this, Catholic though they are, are deceived by a certain humane good will. When we consult holy scripture, it gives us a different reply. I have written a book about this question, with the title *Faith and Works*,[129] where I have demonstrated as best I might with God's help how, according to the holy scriptures, the faith that saves is the one the apostle Paul described plainly enough when he said, *For in Christ Jesus neither circumcision nor uncircumcision counts for anything; the only thing that counts is faith working through love* (Gal 5:6). But if faith works evil rather than good, without a doubt, as the apostle James says, it *is dead in itself* (Jas 2:17), and he also says, *If a person says he has faith, but does not have works, will faith be able to save him?* (Jas 2:14)

Furthermore, if a wicked man will be saved purely by fire, and this is how we are to understand the words of blessed Paul, *He will be saved, but only as through fire* (1 Cor 3:15), then faith will be able to save without works, and the words of his fellow apostle James will be untrue. Also Paul's own words will be false when he says, *Do you not know that wrongdoers will not inherit the kingdom of God? Do not be deceived! Fornicators, idolaters, adulterers, male prostitutes, sodomites, thieves, the greedy, drunkards, revilers, robbers—none*

---

128. On several occasions Augustine rejects this thesis, which rests on a misunderstanding of divine mercy; see sections 70, 75, 112; as well as *Faith and Works* 14, 21; 26, 48; *The City of God* XXI, 17-22; *Eight Questions of Dulcitius* 1, 10-13.
129. See esp. *Faith and Works* 13.

of these will inherit the kingdom of God. (1 Cor 6:9-10) If those who persist in these sins will nonetheless be saved because of faith in Christ, how is it that they will not be in the kingdom of God?

Saved by Fire

68. But since these utterances of the apostles, most plain and clear as they are, cannot be false, the obscure saying about those who build on the foundation that is Christ not with gold, silver, or precious stones, but with wood, clay, and straw[130]—for it is of these that it is said that they will be saved by fire, since by virtue of their foundation they will not perish—must be understood in a way that does not contradict those plain statements.

By wood, clay, and straw we can reasonably understand desires for worldly things, although they are granted to us as lawful, so strong that they cannot be lost without mental agony. And since such agony burns us, if Christ's foundation is in our heart, that is, in such a way that nothing is put before him, and a person on fire with this agony would rather be deprived of the things he so loves than be deprived of Christ, he is saved by fire. But if in the time of temptation he prefers to hold on to such temporal, worldly things rather than to Christ, he does not have Christ in his foundation, since he gives these the first place, and nothing in a building comes before the foundation.

The fire of which the apostle speaks in that place must be understood to be of such a kind that both pass through it—those who build on this foundation with gold, silver and precious stones, and those who build with wood, clay, and straw—for after those words he added, *The fire will test what sort of work each has done. If what has been built on the foundation survives, the builder will receive a reward. If the work is burned up, the builder will suffer loss; the builder will be saved, but only as through fire.* (1 Cor 3:13-15) So fire will test the work not only of one of the groups but of both. The test of tribulation is one kind of fire, of which scripture speaks openly in another place: *The kiln tests the potter's vessels, and the trial of tribulation the just man* (Sir 27:6).

This fire has in this intermediate life the effect the apostle spoke of if it comes to two of the faithful, one thinking of the things of God and how he may please God,[131] that is, building on the foundation that is Christ with gold, silver, and precious stones, while the other thinks of the things of the world, how he may please his wife,[132] that is, building on the same foundation with wood, clay, and straw. For the work of the former is not burnt up, since he did not love things

---

130. See 1 Cor 3:12.
131. See 1 Cor 7:32.
132. See 1 Cor 7:33.

whose loss causes him pain. But the work of the latter is burnt up, since the loss of things we possess with love never happens without pain; but since, given the choice, he would rather lose them than Christ, nor does he desert Christ out of fear of losing them, although he is grieved by their loss, he is saved, but as if by fire, for the pain of losing things he loves burns him, but without ruining or consuming him, since he has the protection of a foundation that is firm and without decay.

Purifying Fire

69. Nor is it beyond belief that something of the same kind could happen also after this life, and it can be asked if it is the case, whether or not an answer can be found, that some of the faithful are saved by a purifying fire[133] more or less quickly, depending on whether they have loved perishable good things more or less; but this does not apply to those of whom it is said that they will not possess the kingdom of God[134] unless those sins are forgiven them and they do suitable penance. By "suitable" I mean that they should not be sterile in works of charity, to which holy scripture attaches so much importance that the Lord says he will consider only the fruitfulness in such works of those on his right and the sterility in them of those on his left when he says to the former, *Come, you that are blessed by my Father, inherit the kingdom* (Mt 25:34), and to the latter, *Depart into the eternal fire* (Mt 25:41).

Works of Charity

19, 70. Certainly nobody should think that those unmentionable crimes whose perpetrators will not possess the kingdom of God should be committed every day and expiated every day by works of charity.[135] We should amend our lives and do good works to beg God's mercy for our past sins, not try to buy him in some way so as always to be able to do such things with impunity. He has never given anybody freedom to sin, although in his mercy he cancels the sins we have already committed, provided we do not neglect to make appropriate satisfaction.

---

133. *Purgatorium*: Augustine's teaching in this section shows the doctrine of purgatory at an early stage in its development.
134. See 1 Cor 6:10.
135. Some appealed to Dn 4:24 (*Make up for your sins by almsgiving*) to argue the thesis that almsgiving by itself guaranteed eternal salvation; see *The City of God* XXI, 22.

The Lord's Prayer

71. As for the daily brief and unimportant sins without which it is impossible to lead this life, the daily prayer of the faithful makes satisfaction for them. For they have the right to say, *Our Father in heaven*, since they have already been reborn as children of a heavenly Father by water and the Holy Spirit.[136] This prayer entirely cancels tiny daily sins. It also cancels those from which the faithful turn away by penance and reform, even though they have lived wickedly, provided that, as they truthfully pray, *Forgive us our sins*—for they have no lack of sins to be forgiven—they are also speaking the truth when they say, *as we forgive those who sin against us*, that is, provided what they say is what they do, for to forgive a person who asks for pardon is itself a work of charity.

Giving Alms

72. And so the Lord's words, *Give alms, and everything is clean for you* (Lk 11:41), apply to any work of mercy that benefits somebody. Not only somebody who offers food to the hungry, drink to the thirsty, clothing to the naked, hospitality to the traveler, asylum to the refugee, a visit to the sick or the prisoner, redemption to the captive, support to the weak, guidance to the blind, comfort to the sorrowful, medicine to the unwell, a path to the wanderer, advice to the uncertain, or whatever is necessary to a person in need, but also one who offers pardon to the sinner, is giving alms. And one who uses the whip to correct somebody over whom he has power, or disciplines him in some way, and yet puts away from his heart that person's sin by which he has been hurt or offended, or prays that it may be forgiven him, is giving alms not only through forgiveness and prayer but also in reproof and correction by some punishment, for thus he is showing mercy. Many good things are offered to people unwilling to accept them when what is good for them is being considered rather than what they desire, because they prove to be their own enemies, while their true friends are rather those whom they consider enemies, mistakenly repaying them evil for good, whereas a Christian should not repay evil even for evil. So there are many kinds of alms, and when we do them we receive help for the forgiveness of our sins.

Loving Your Enemies and Willing Them Good

73. But there is no almsdeed greater than forgiving from our heart a sin that somebody has committed against us. It is a lesser thing to be kind or even

---

136. See Jn 3:5.

generous to a person who has done you no harm. Much greater, a sign of the most generous goodness, is to love your enemy also and to will good, and when possible to do good, to a person who wills you ill and does it if he can: when you do this you are listening to the voice of Jesus saying, *Love your enemies, do good to those who hate you, and pray for those who persecute you* (Mt 5:44). But this is a characteristic of perfect children of God, which each one of the faithful must strive for, training his human spirit in such love by prayer to God and discipline and struggle within himself, and, since this great virtue is not possessed by as many people as those whose prayers we believe are heard when the prayer is made, *Forgive us our debts as we also forgive our debtors* (Mt 6:12), without a doubt the words of this promise are fulfilled when a person who has not yet progressed so far as to love his enemy nevertheless forgives from his heart one who has sinned against him and asks for forgiveness, since he himself also desires the forgiveness he asks for when he prays and says, *As we also forgive our debtors*, that is, forgive our debts when we ask as we forgive our debtors when they ask us.

Forgiveness from the Heart

74. A person who pleads with one against whom he has sinned, if he is moved by his own sin to make his plea, should no longer be thought of as an enemy whom it is as difficult to forgive as it was when he was behaving as an enemy. But anybody who refuses to forgive from his heart one who asks forgiveness and repents of his sin should not think that the Lord forgives his sins, since the Truth cannot lie. What hearer or reader of the gospel does not know who said, *I am the truth?* (Jn 14:6) When he had taught us his prayer, he strongly emphasized the thought it contains by saying, *For if you forgive others their sins, your heavenly Father will also forgive you; but if you do not forgive others, neither will your Father forgive your sins* (Mt 6:14-15). Anybody who does not wake up on hearing such a clap of thunder is not asleep but dead; and yet he is able to raise even the dead to life.

Not just Almsgiving

20, 75. Certainly those who live very wickedly, and take no care to correct their lives or morals, and yet never cease to give alms in the midst of their very sins and crimes, take comfort in vain from the Lord's words, *Give alms, and everything is clean for you* (Lk 11:41): they do not understand how widely these words apply. It is true that in the gospel is written: *While he was speaking, a Pharisee invited him to dine with him; so he went in and took his place at the table. The Pharisee was amazed to see that he did not first wash before dinner.*

Then the Lord said to him, Now, you Pharisees clean the outside of the cup and of the dish, but inside you are full of greed and wickedness. You fools! Did not the one who made the outside make the inside also? But for the rest, give alms and see, everything is clean for you. (Lk 11:37-41) Are we to understand this to mean that all things are clean to the Pharisees who have no faith in Christ, even though they have not believed in him or been reborn by water and the Holy Spirit, provided only they give alms in the way they think right? All are unclean who are not purified by faith in Christ, of which it is written, *In cleansing their hearts by faith* (Acts 15:9), and the apostle says, *But to the corrupt and unbelieving nothing is pure. Their very minds and consciences are corrupted.* (Ti 1:15) So how can all things be pure to the Pharisees if they give alms without faith? How can they have faith if they have refused to believe in Christ and to be reborn in his grace? But still the words they heard are certainly true: *Give alms, and everything is clean for you* (Lk 11:41).

Almsgiving Is a Work of Mercy

76. A person who wishes to give alms as they should be given must begin from himself and give them first to himself. Almsgiving is a work of mercy, and the saying is very true: *Have mercy on your soul and please God* (Eccl 30:24). We are reborn in order to please God, who is rightly displeased with the sin we have contracted by our birth. These are the first alms we gave ourselves, for by the mercy of the merciful God we searched for ourselves in our misery, acknowledging as just his judgment which brought us to misery, of which the apostle says, *The judgment following one trespass brought condemnation* (Rom 5:16), and giving thanks to his great love, of which the same preacher of grace himself says, *But God proves his love for us in that while we still were sinners Christ died for us* (Rom 5:8). Thus we also, judging rightly of our misery, and loving God with the love he has given us, lead holy and upright lives. The Pharisees, having neglected the justice and the love of God, used to tithe the tiniest items of their produce for the alms they gave,[137] and so they did not begin from themselves when giving alms or show mercy first to themselves. Because of this order of love it is said: *You shall love your neighbor as yourself* (Lk 10:27). So, after rebuking those who washed themselves outside but were full of greed and wickedness within, he taught them to purify themselves within by giving alms of the kind that a man should give himself first of all; he said, *But for the rest, give alms and see, everything is clean for you* (Lk 11:37-41). Then, to show what he was urging them to do and what they did not care to do, that they might not think he knew nothing of their almsgiving, he said, *Woe to you Pharisees*, as if to say: "I

---

137. See Lk 11:42.

have exhorted you to give alms that will make everything clean for you, *but woe to you, for you tithe mint and rue and herbs of all kinds* (Lk 11:42); for I know about these alms of yours, so do not think I was exhorting you about those, *and you neglect justice and the love of God*, the alms by which you could be cleansed from every inner defilement, so that the physical objects that you wash might also be clean to you." This is what *everything* means, both inner and outer things, as we read elsewhere: *First clean the inside, and the outside also will be clean* (Mt 23:26). But he did not wish to be thought to have rejected alms that come from the fruits of the earth, and so he said, *It is these you ought to have practiced*, that is, justice and the love of God, *without neglecting the others* (Lk 11:42), that is, alms from the fruits of the earth.

God's Mercy Shall Go before Me

77. So let not people deceive themselves who think that by almsgiving, however generous, from their produce or any financial wealth they may own, they can purchase for themselves impunity to continue in great crimes and wicked sins. Not only do they commit such deeds but they love them so much that they wish to continue in them forever, provided they can do so with impunity. But a person who loves wickedness hates his own soul,[138] and one who hates his soul is not merciful to it, but cruel. By loving it by the world's standards he hates it according to God's standards. If he wished to give it alms that would make everything clean for it, he would hate it by the world's standards and love it by God's. Nobody gives alms of any kind without receiving what he gives from the one who lacks nothing. That is why it is said: *His mercy shall go before me* (Ps 59:10).

Trivial and Serious Sins

21, 78. To distinguish between trivial and serious sins is a matter for divine, not human, judgment. We see that some have been pardoned and permitted even by the apostles, such as what the venerable Paul says to husbands and wives: *Do not deprive one another except perhaps by agreement for a set time, to devote yourselves to prayer, and then come together again, so that Satan may not tempt you because of your lack of self-control* (1 Cor 7:5). It might have been thought that this is not a sin, that is, to have intercourse with one's spouse otherwise than for the purpose of having children, which is one of the goods of marriage, but even for physical pleasure, in order that incontinent people in their weakness might avoid the deadly evil of fornication or adultery or some other impurity

---

138. See Ps 11:5 LXX.

which it is disgraceful even to speak of. So, as I have said, this might be thought not to be a sin had he not added, *This I say by way of concession, not of command* (1 Cor 7:6). But who could deny that this is a sin when it is acknowledged by the authority of an apostle that a concession is made to those who do it?[139] The case is similar when he says, *When any of you has a grievance against another, do you dare to take it to court before the unrighteous, instead of taking it before the saints?* (1 Cor 6:1) and a little later, *If you have ordinary cases, then, do you appoint as judges those who have no standing in the Church? I say this to your shame. Can it be that there is no one among you wise enough to decide between one believer and another, but a believer goes to court against a believer and before unbelievers at that?* (1 Cor 6:4-6)

Here it might be thought that to go to court against somebody else is not a sin, but only to wish the case to be judged outside the Church, had he not gone on to add: *In fact, to have lawsuits at all with one another is already an offense for you* (1 Cor 6:7). And to prevent anybody from excusing himself with the claim that his grievance is just, and that he is suffering a wrong which he wishes to have removed by judicial sentence, he at once meets such notions or excuses with the words: *Why not rather be wronged? Why not rather be defrauded?* (1 Cor 6:7) in order to recall what the Lord says: *If anyone wants to sue you and take your coat, give your cloak as well* (Mt 5:40), and (in another place): *If anyone takes away your goods, do not ask for them again* (Lk 6:30). Thus he prohibited his followers from entering legal proceedings with others about worldly matters, and this teaching led the apostle to call that an offense. But from the fact that he permits such cases to be judged within the Church, but forbids them outside the Church in fearsome terms, it is plain that here too he is pardoning something allowed as a concession. Because of these and similar sins, and others that may be lesser, offenses in word and thought, the confession the apostle James makes by saying: *For all of us commit many offenses* (Jas 3:2), shows that we must daily and often pray to the Lord and say, *Forgive us our debts*, and not be lying when we go on to say, *as we also forgive our debtors*.

Some Sins Appear Trivial but Are Serious

79. There are also some sins that might be thought very trivial were they not shown in the holy scriptures to be more serious than is thought. Who would think a person who said *you fool* would be *liable to the hell of fire* (Mt 5:22) had not Truth said so? But he at once applied medicine to this wound by adding a

---

139. The interpretation given here of 1 Cor 7:5-6 relies on the Latin word *venia*, which, when understood as "forgiveness," presupposes guilt. Augustine argues similarly, but more fully, in *Marriage and Desire* 1, 14; 24, 27: Paul makes the "concession" in order to give human nature its rights. See E. Clark, ed., *St. Augustine on Marriage and Sexuality* (Washington 1996).

command that brothers should be reconciled, for the next thing he said was: *So when you are offering your gift at the altar, if you remember that your brother has something against you* (Mt 5:23), and so on.[140] Or who would realize how great a sin it is to observe days and months and years and times, like those people who will or will not begin something on certain days or in certain months or years,[141] because they consider certain times favorable or unfavorable according to some empty human teaching, did not the fear of the apostle give us a standard to measure the seriousness of this evil when he says to such people, *I am afraid that my work for you may have been wasted* (Gal 4:10-11)?

Great and Terrible Sins, if They Are Habitual, Seem Trivial

80. We must also recognize that sins, however great and terrible, are thought to be small or non-existent when they become habitual, to such an extent that people think they should not only not be hidden but even be proclaimed and advertised when, as it is written, *the wicked boast of the desires of their heart, and those who do evil are spoken well of* (Ps 10:3). In holy scripture such wickedness is called a cry, as you read in Isaiah the prophet when he speaks of the evil vineyard: *I expected him to do justice, but he did wickedness, I expected righteousness, but heard a cry!* (Is 5:7) and similarly in Genesis: *How great is the cry of Sodom and Gomorrah!* (Gn 18:20) since not only did those sins already go unpunished among them but they were even practiced publicly and almost officially. So in our days many evils, if not the same ones, have come to be openly and habitually practiced, so that we are afraid not only to excommunicate a lay person for them but even to degrade a cleric. So, when a few years ago I was expounding the letter to the Galatians, at the place where the apostle says, *I am afraid that my work for you may have been wasted,*[142] I was compelled to cry out, "Woe on the sins of men, which horrify us only when we are unused to them! But as for habitual sins, to wash away which the blood of the Son of God was shed, although they are so serious that they cause God's kingdom to be entirely closed to those who commit them, we are often compelled to look on and tolerate them, and even to commit some of those we tolerate, and grant, O Lord, that we may not commit all of those that we are unable to forbid!" But I shall consider whether my immoderate sorrow caused me to speak somewhat incautiously.

---

140. Jesus' words continue: *Leave your gift there before the altar, and go first to be reconciled to your brother, and then come and offer your gift* (Mt 5:24).
141. The Roman state recognized certain days as *dies nefasti*, on which business was forbidden for religious reasons.
142. See *Exposition of the Letter to the Galatians* 35.

Two Causes of Sins: Ignorance and Weakness

22, 81. What I shall now say is what I have also often said in several places in my shorter works:[143] there are two reasons why we sin, either because we do not see what we ought to do or because we do not do what we know ought to be done: the first of these evils comes from ignorance, the second from weakness. We should fight against both of them. But we cannot win without divine help not only to see what ought to be done but also in order that we may be healed and that pleasure in doing right may overcome within us the pleasure we take in things which we desire to have or fear to lose, which leads us to sin with knowledge and awareness. In this case we are not only sinners, which we were even when we sinned through ignorance, but also transgressors of the law, when we do not do what we already know should be done, or when we do what we already know should not be done. So we should pray to God not only that he will forgive us if we have sinned, which is why we say, *Forgive us our debts as we also forgive our debtors,* but also that he will guide us so that we do not sin, which is why we say, *And do not bring us to the time of trial* (Mt 6:13). For these things we should pray to him to whom it is said in the psalm: *The Lord is my light and my health* (Ps 27:1), so that his light may take away our ignorance, and his health our weakness.

For Penance We Need God's Mercy

82. Penance itself, when there is a good reason for doing it according to the custom of the Church,[144] is often neglected because of weakness, for shame brings with it a fear of being ill thought of when we care more for the good opinion of others than for the righteousness that leads a person to humiliate himself in penance. So we need God's mercy not only when we do penance but also in order that we may do penance. Otherwise the apostle would not say of certain people, *God may perhaps grant that they will repent* (2 Tm 2:25); and the evangelist tells us that, in order that Peter might weep bitterly, *the Lord turned and looked at him* (Lk 22:61).

---

143. See *Free Will* III, 18, 55; *Miscellany of Eighty-three Questions* 26; *Answer to Faustus, a Manichean* XXII, 78; *The Merits and Forgiveness of Sins* I, 39, 70; II, 17, 26; *Nature and Grace* 67, 81; *Answer to the Two Letters of the Pelagians* I, 3, 7.
144. See section 65.

Sin against the Holy Spirit

83. But anybody who does not believe that sins are forgiven in the Church,[145] with contempt for this great and generous divine gift, and ends his last day obstinate in his opinion, is guilty of the unforgivable sin against the Holy Spirit, in whom Christ forgives sins.[146] I have discussed this difficult question as clearly as I could in a small book I wrote solely for that purpose.[147]

Faith in the Resurrection of the Body and Life Everlasting

The Resurrection of the Body

23, 84. As for the resurrection of the flesh, not that of some who have come back to life and then died again,[148] but resurrection to eternal life like that of the flesh of Christ, I do not know how I can treat this briefly and answer all the questions that are usually raised concerning this matter. But a Christian must in no way doubt that the flesh of all human beings who have been born or are to be born, and have died or will die, will rise again.[149]

85. The first question that arises in this regard concerns aborted fetuses, which have already been born in the wombs of their mothers, but not yet in such a way that they can be reborn.[150] If we say that they will rise again, this may be a tolerable opinion concerning those that are already formed. But as regards unformed fetuses, who would not rather think that they perish entirely like seeds that have not been conceived?[151] But who would dare to deny, even though he may not dare to affirm it, that resurrection will supply anything the fetus lacks in form? Thus that perfection which was destined to come with time will not be lacking, just as the defects that time would have brought will be absent, so that nature will not be deprived of anything fitting and suitable that time would have brought or be defiled with things hostile and contrary to it that time has already

---

145. The reference is probably to the Novatians, whose rigorism completely excluded apostates from forgiveness through the Church.
146. See Jn 20:22.
147. See Sermon 71.
148. The reference is to the raisings from the dead that are reported in the scriptures.
149. See *Faith and the Creed* 10, 23-24.
150. See *The City of God* XXII, 13. See F. Cayré, "Une rétractation de Saint Augustin. Les enfants morts sans baptême," *Année théologique augustinienne* 12 (1952) 131-143.
151. According to ancient biological theories, the female contributed nothing in conception except a receptacle for the growth of the seed contributed by the male.

brought, but what was not yet complete will be completed, and what had been spoiled will be restored.

The Beginning of Life

86. And so a question that can be discussed in great detail among the most learned[152] (and I do not know whether an answer to it can be found by human beings) is when a human being begins to live in the womb, and whether an infant has some kind of hidden life before it begins to move perceptibly. It seems to me to be too presumptuous to say that fetuses that are cut out and removed from the womb, lest by remaining there dead they might also kill their mothers, have never been alive. Now once a person begins to live, from that moment he is already able to die; and I cannot find a reason why a dead person, however death has happened to him, should be excluded from the resurrection of the dead.

Complete Human Bodies at the Resurrection

87. For the same reason it will not be denied that seriously deformed babies that are born and live, however soon they die, will rise again, nor should it be believed that they will rise in the condition in which they were born rather than with their nature healed and rectified. We should not think that the Siamese twins recently born in the East, whom many most trustworthy brethren claim to have seen, and about whom the presbyter Jerome of blessed memory has left us an account in writing,[153] will rise as one double person rather than as two people, which they would have been had they been born as true twins, just as all others born separately who are said to be physically deformed because they have an extra part to their bodies or one missing or some major deformity will be restored to a normal human form by the resurrection, so that each soul will have its own body, and none will be joined together, even though they may have been born joined together, but each will receive his own limbs separately so that all will have complete human bodies.

The Material of the Body Never Perishes

88. Nor does the earthly material from which mortal flesh is created perish in the sight of God, but whatever dust or ashes it may dissolve into, whatever vapors or winds it may vanish into, whatever other bodies or even elements it

---

152. Augustine may be thinking of Porphyry. See A.-J. Festugière, *La révélation d'Hermès Trismégiste* III (Paris 1953) 265-302.
153. Letter 72, 2. See *The City of God* XVI, 8, 2.

may be turned into, by whatever animals or even men it may have been eaten as food and so turned into flesh, in an instant of time it returns to the human soul that first gave it life so that it might become human, grow, and live.

89. The earthly material that becomes a corpse on the departure of the soul, then, will not be restored at the resurrection in such a way that those substances which seep away and are turned into one kind and shape of thing after another, although they return to the body they have left, will necessarily return to the same part of the body as they were in before.[154] Otherwise, if all the hair were to receive back what has been removed by frequent cutting, and the nails all that has been removed so often from them by paring, anybody who thought about it would form a picture of extreme and unsuitable ugliness, and be led to disbelief in the resurrection of the flesh. But as when a statue of somebody made of some destructible metal is melted by fire or ground into dust or molded into a lump, and a craftsman wants to restore it using the same quantity of material, it does not matter for the perfection of the statue which part of the material is used for which part of the statue, so long as all the material of which the statue was originally made is used in the restoration, so God, the wonderful and indescribable craftsman, will remake our flesh with wonderful and indescribable speed from all the material that had constituted it. Nor will it matter for the flesh's restoration whether hair returns to hair and nails to nails, or whether some part of them which had decayed is turned into flesh and other parts of the body, for the providence of the craftsman will ensure that nothing is done that is not suitable.

90. Nor does it follow that those who return to life will be of different heights because they were of different heights when they were alive, or that thin people will rise again as thin as before and fat people as fat as before. But if it is in the plan of the creator that each person retains his or her distinctive and discernible appearance, while all are equal in the other qualities of the body, the matter belonging to each one will be modified so that none of it perishes and any deficiency will be supplied by the one who was able to make what he willed even out of nothing. But if there is a reasonable inequality among the bodies of those who rise, like that of voices in a choir, the bodily material of each person will be transformed and fitted to the company of the angels, with nothing that is unsuitable for them to perceive with their senses.[155] Certainly, there will be nothing indecorous there, but whatever will be will be suitable, and anything unsuitable will find no place there.

91. So the bodies of the saints will rise again with no defect, no deformity, no corruption, burden, or difficulty, and their facility in living will be equal to their felicity. That is why they are called spiritual,[156] although there is no doubt that

---

154. See *The City of God* XXII, 19.
155. Augustine considered that angels had bodies, a view largely abandoned in later theology.
156. See 1 Cor 15:44.

they will be bodies, not spirits. But as we now speak of an ensouled body, which however is a body and not a soul, so then the body will be spiritual, while being a body and not a spirit. And as for the corruption which now weighs down the soul, and the vices which cause the flesh to have desires contrary to the spirit,[157] then it will be not flesh but a body, for there are also said to be heavenly bodies.[158] That is why it is said: *Flesh and blood cannot inherit the kingdom of God*, and the author goes on as if to explain what he has said: *nor does the perishable inherit the imperishable* (1 Cor 15:50). What he previously called *flesh and blood* he subsequently called *corruption*, and what he previously called *the kingdom of God* he subsequently called *incorruption*. But, as for its substance, even then it will be flesh, which is why even after the resurrection the body of Christ is called flesh.[159] But that is why the apostle says, *It is sown a physical body, it is raised a spiritual body* (1 Cor 15:44), because there will be such harmony between flesh and spirit, the spirit giving life without need of any sustenance to the body that will be subject to it, that nothing within us will fight against us, but just as we shall have no external enemies, so we shall not have to suffer ourselves as our own inner enemies.

The Resurrection of the Lost

92. As for those who are not set free by the one mediator between God and man from that mass of perdition which was caused by the first human, they also will rise again, each with his or her own flesh, but in order to be punished with the devil and his angels. Surely there is no need to expend effort in inquiring whether they will rise with the defects and deformities of their bodies and whatever defective and deformed limbs they had formerly. Nor should we weary ourselves by considering their appearance or beauty, since their damnation will be certain and unending. Nor is it of interest to ask how their bodies will be incorruptible if they are capable of suffering, or corruptible if they cannot die, for there is no true life but a happy life, and no true incorruption except where health has no pain to corrupt it. But where an unhappy person is not allowed to die, so to say, death itself does not die, and where perpetual pain causes not death but torment, corruption is not at an end. This is what sacred scripture calls the second death.[160]

---

157. See Wis 9:15; Gal 5:17.
158. See 1 Cor 15:40.
159. See Lk 24:39.
160. See Rv 2:11; 20:6.14.

Punishment in Accord with Guilt

93. But neither the first death, by which the soul is compelled to leave its body, nor the second, by which the soul is not permitted to leave the body under punishment, would have happened to human beings if nobody had sinned.[161] Certainly the gentlest punishment of all will be for those who have added no further sin to the original sin they have contracted;[162] and as for those who have added further sins, the smaller each person's wickedness here, the more bearable will be his damnation there.[163]

The Will of the Almighty

24, 94. And so, while wicked angels and humans remain in eternal punishment, the saints will know more fully the good that grace has conferred on them. Then events themselves will demonstrate more clearly the truth of what is written in the psalm: *I will sing of mercy and of justice; to you, O Lord, I will sing* (Ps 101:1), for nobody is set free except by an undeserved mercy, and nobody is damned except by a judgment he deserves.[164]

95. Then what is hidden now will no longer be hidden, for of two infants one is to be taken up through mercy and the other is to be left because of judgment,[165] and in him the one who is taken up sees what would be due to him by judgment if mercy had not come to his aid, and why he rather than the other was assumed, since they were both on trial in the same court, and why miracles were not performed in the presence of some people who would have done penance if they had been performed there, while they were performed in the presence of some who were not to believe. The Lord says quite plainly, *Woe to you, Chorazin! Woe to you, Bethsaida! For if the deeds of power done in you had been done in Tyre and Sidon, they would have repented long ago in sackcloth and ashes.* (Mt 11:21) Nor was God unjust in not willing to save them, since they could have been saved had they wished.[166] Then will be seen in the clearest light of Wisdom

---

161. See sections 25-26. For the distinction between "first" and "second" deaths see *The City of God* XIII, 12.
162. This is the case with unbaptized small children. See Letter 166, 16-17; *Answer to Julian* V, 11, 44; *The Merits and Forgiveness of Sins* I, 16, 21. On the problem in general see W. Harmless, "Baptism," in Fitzgerald 84-91, esp. 89-90.
163. See sections 110-111.
164. See section 98.
165. See Rom 9:10-13.
166. The variant *vellet* ("had he wished"), instead of *vellent* ("had they wished"), led to raging theological controversies. Whereas the more reliably attested plural (*vellent*) ascribes damnation to the bad will of sinners, the singular form (*vellet*) makes the will of God absolute and thus favored the teaching of the Jansenists. See J. Rivière, in Bibliothèque Augustinienne 9, 402-403, note complémentaire 46.

what the faithful believe before it is seen openly, how sure, unchangeable and most efficacious the will of God is, and how many things he could do but does not will to do, while he wills nothing that he cannot do, and how true are the words that are sung in the psalm: *Our God is in the heavens; he has done whatever he willed* (Ps 115:3). This is not true if there are things that he willed but did not do, or, what would be more unworthy, if what the Almighty willed was prevented from happening by the will of man. So nothing happens unless the Almighty wills it, either by allowing it to happen or by doing it himself.

The Permission of Evil

96. Nor should it be doubted that God does good even when he permits evil things to happen, for he does not permit this except by his just judgment, and clearly everything that is just is good. And so, although evil things, insofar as they are evil, are not good, yet the fact that there are not only good things but evil ones is good.[167] For, if the existence of evil things as well as good were not good, they would by no means be permitted to exist by the almighty Good, for whom without doubt it is as easy to prevent things he does not will to exist as it is to do what he wills. If we do not believe this, the very beginning of our profession of faith is endangered, in which we confess our belief in one God the almighty Father. For the only true reasons why he is called almighty are that he can do whatever he wills, and that the effectiveness of the will of the almighty is not impeded by the will of any creature whatsoever.

The Salvation of All

97. For this reason we must see how it is that we say what the apostle most truthfully said of God: *Who wills everyone to be saved* (1 Tm 2:4). Since not all are saved, but many more are not saved,[168] it seems that what God wills to happen does not happen because a human will frustrates the will of God.[169] When it is asked why not all are saved, the reply usually given is that it is because they themselves do not wish to be saved. This cannot be said of infants, who cannot yet either will or not will. If we thought we could attribute to their own

---

167. See *Free Will* III, 9, 26-28.
168. See section 99. The restrictive view of the number of the redeemed is probably to be understood in light of the relatively small number of baptized and true Christians that Augustine saw in his time.
169. Augustine stresses the point here that the redemptive act performed for the sake of all human beings is not effective in all because of subjective guilt. See *Homilies on the Gospel of John* 32, 4 ("The wellspring does not abandon us if we do not abandon the wellspring"); Sermon 22, 9.

will the babyish movements they make when they are baptized, we should say that they do not wish to be saved, since they resist as much as they can.

The words of the Lord in the gospel make the matter even clearer when he rebukes a wicked city with the words: *How often have I desired to gather your children together as a hen gathers her brood under her wings, and you were not willing!* (Mt 23:37) as if God's will had been overcome by the will of men and the most mighty one were not able to do as he willed because the very weak prevented him by not being willing. Where is that omnipotence that has done whatever it willed in heaven and on earth[170] if he willed to gather together the children of Jerusalem and did not do so? Or was it rather the city that did not want her children to be gathered together by him? But he gathered together the children he willed to gather together despite her unwillingness, for in heaven and on earth he did not will some things and do them and did will others but not do them, but he did everything he willed.

Grace Alone Distinguishes the Redeemed from the Lost

25, 98. Furthermore, who is so irreligious and foolish as to say that God cannot turn to good any of the evil wills of men he wishes, when and where he wishes? When he does this, he does it by mercy, and when he does not do it, it is by judgment that he does not do it, since *he has mercy on whomever he chooses, and he hardens the heart of whomever he chooses* (Rom 9:18). The apostle said this to commend God's grace, having already spoken about the twins in Rebecca's womb about whom, before they had been born or had done anything good or bad (*so that God's purpose of election might continue, not by works but by his call*) she was told, *The elder shall serve the younger* (Rom 9:11-13). For this reason he quoted the other prophecy where it is written: *I have loved Jacob, but I have hated Esau* (Mal 1:2-3; Rom 9:13). But, realizing how this saying could strike those who cannot penetrate with their understanding the depths of this grace, he said, *What then are we to say? Is there injustice on God's part? By no means!*—(Rom 9:14) For it seems unfair that God should love one and hate the other without their deserving it by good or bad deeds. If in this discussion he had intended us to understand that God foreknew their future deeds, either Jacob's good ones or Esau's evil ones, he would by no means have said *not by works* but "by future works" and would have resolved the question in this way, or rather, he would not have raised any question that needed resolution. But now, having replied *by no means!* that is, by no means can there be unfairness with God—he immediately says, to prove that this happens without any unfairness on

170. See Ps 115:3.

God's part, *For he says to Moses, I will have mercy on whom I have mercy, and I will have compassion on whom I have compassion* (Rom 9:15).

Who but a fool could think that God is unfair, whether he passes adverse judgment on one who deserves it or shows mercy to one who is unworthy? Then he adds his own comment and says, *So it comes not from the one who wills or the one who runs but from God who shows mercy* (Rom 9:16). So both those twins were born *by nature children of wrath* (Eph 2:3) not because of any deeds of their own but being bound by the chains of damnation because of their origin in Adam. But he who said, *I will have mercy on whom I have mercy*, loved Jacob with gratuitous mercy but hated Esau because of the judgment he deserved. And since this judgment by rights belonged to both of them, one brother learned from the example of the other that he should not boast of the difference of his merits, as if that saved him from receiving the same sentence in the same trial, but of the generosity of divine grace, since *it comes not from the one who wills or the one who runs but from God who shows mercy*. What I might call the entire face or countenance of the sacred scriptures is found by those who look well at it to warn us in its profound and saving mysteries that *the one who boasts should boast in the Lord* (1 Cor 1:31).

99. Since he has commended the mercy of God by saying that *it comes not from the one who wills or the one who runs but from God who shows mercy*, so that he may commend his justice as well, since when mercy is not shown to a person this is not unfairness but judgment—as there is not any unfairness with God—he at once went on to add, *for the scripture says to Pharaoh, I have raised you up for the very purpose of showing my power in you, so that my name may be proclaimed in all the earth* (Rom 9:17). Having said this, he ends by speaking of both, that is, mercy and judgment, saying, *So then he has mercy on whomever he chooses, and he hardens the heart of whomever he chooses.* That is, he has mercy in his great generosity, and he hardens the heart without any unfairness, so that one who has been set free should not boast of his merits, nor should one who has been damned complain, except of his lack of merits. For grace alone distinguishes the redeemed from the lost, who have been formed into one mass of perdition by a cause common to all which they draw from their origin. But if anybody understands this in such a way as to say, *Why then does he still find fault? For who can resist his will?* (Rom 9:19) as if it did not seem that an evil person should be blamed, since God *has mercy on whomever he chooses, and hardens the heart of whomever he chooses*, we should not be ashamed to give the reply that, as we see, was given by the apostle: *Who are you, a human being, to argue with God? Will what is molded say to the one who molds it, Why have you made me like this? Has the potter no right over the clay, to make out of the same lump one object for honor and another for dishonor?* (Rom 9:20-21) There are some foolish people who think that here the apostle was lost for a reply and crushed the boldness of his opponent because he was at a loss for an explana-

tion.[171] But the words, *Who are you, a human being?* are very weighty, and in such discussions they recall human beings to consider their limitations with a brief phrase which in fact carries within it a very serious explanation, for a person who understands this can find no further reply to make. If he understands, he sees the entire human race condemned in its traitorous root by God's judgment, which is so just that, even if nobody were to be released from that condemnation, nobody would have any right to criticize God's justice. He sees also that it was necessary for those who are set free to be set free in such a way that, from the large number who are not set free but are subjected to a condemnation that is entirely just, it might be clear what the whole multitude deserved and where God's just judgment would lead even those who are freed if they had not the help of his undeserved mercy, so that *every mouth may be silenced* (Rom 3:19) of those who wish to boast of their own merits, and *the one who boasts may boast in the Lord* (1 Cor 1:31).

Good out of Evil

26, 100. These are the great works of the Lord, *sought out according to all his purposes* (Ps 111:2 LXX), and sought out so wisely that when creatures, both angels and humans, had sinned, that is, had done not what *he* willed but what *they* willed, the creator fulfilled what he willed by means of that very will of the creature by which what was against his will was done, making good use even of evil creatures as befits the one who is supremely good, for the damnation of those whom he had justly predestined to punishment and for the salvation of those whom he had mercifully predestined to grace. For as far as they were concerned, they did what God did not will, but as far as the omnipotence of God is concerned, they were in no way able to contravene his will. By the very fact that they acted against his will, his will was done through them. For the great works of the Lord are sought out according to all his purposes in order that even what happens against his will should in a wonderful and inexplicable way not be done despite his will, since it would not happen if he did not permit it, and he does not permit things unwillingly but willingly; nor would he in his goodness allow anything evil to happen were he not able in his omnipotence even to bring good out of evil.

101. But sometimes a human being wishes with a good will something that God does not will, even though God's will is more fully and certainly good (since his will can never be evil), as when a good son wants his father to live, while God in his good will wills that he should die. Again, it can happen that a human wills with an evil will what God wills with his good will, as when a bad

---

171. The reference is probably to the Pelagians; see *The Christian Combat* 11, 12.

son wishes his father to die, and God wills that also. Certainly the former person wills what God does not will while the latter wills what God does will, and yet the devotion of the former is more in harmony with the good will of God, although he wills something different from God, than the disloyalty of the latter, who wills the same as God.

In order to judge whether a person's will is good or bad, we need only know what it befits man to will and what it befits God to will, and to what end each person directs his will. For God fulfills some of his purposes, which of course are good, through the evil wills of evil humans, as when by means of ill-willed Jews, in accordance with the good will of the Father, Christ was killed for us, a good so great that when the apostle Peter did not wish it to happen, he was called Satan by the very one who was on his way to be killed.[172] How good to all appearances were the wills of the faithful believers who did not wish the apostle Paul to go to Jerusalem so that he might avoid the sufferings that the prophet Agabus had predicted![173] And yet God wanted him to undergo those things to proclaim the Christian faith, making him a witness to Christ. And God did fulfill that good will of his through the good wills of Christians but also through the evil wills of Jews, and those who did not will what God willed belonged to God more than those through whose evil wills what he willed was done, for they did the same deed, but they did it with an evil will, while God did it through them with a good will.

102. But however many wills there are, whether of angels or humans, good or evil, willing the same as God or differently, the will of the Almighty is always undefeated: it can never be evil, for even when it commands evils it is just, and clearly what is just is not evil. So almighty God either in his mercy shows mercy to whom he wills or through justice hardens whom he wills, and never does anything unfairly or unwillingly, and does everything that he wills.[174]

The Meaning of 1 Timothy 2:4

27, 103. And so when we hear and read in the sacred scriptures that God wills everyone to be saved, although we are certain that not everybody is saved, we should not for that reason envisage any limitation to the will of almighty God but understand the words of scripture, *who wills everyone to be saved*, as meaning that nobody is saved except those whom he wills to be saved,[175] not because there is nobody whom he does not will to be saved but because nobody is saved except those whom he wills to be saved, and so we should pray him to will, for what he

---

172. See Mt 16:22-23.
173. See Acts 21:10-14.
174. See Ps 115:3.
175. See Letter 217, 6, 19; *Answer to Julian* IV, 8, 42.

wills must necessarily come about. The apostle was speaking about praying to God, and that led him to say those words. We must also understand in a similar way the words of the gospel, *who enlightens everyone who comes* (Jn 1:9), not that there is nobody who is not enlightened, but that nobody is enlightened except by him.[176] Or in any case, *who wills everyone to be saved* is said not because there is nobody whom he does not will to be saved—he who did not will to perform deeds of power in the presence of people who he said would have done penance if he had performed them[177]—but in order that we might understand by *everyone* the whole race of humankind in all its diversity,[178] kings and private citizens, nobles and commoners, important people and humble ones, the learned and the uneducated, the healthy and the weak, the clever, the slow-witted, the foolish, the rich, the poor and those of moderate means, men and women, infants, children, adolescents, young people, middle-aged people, old people, of all languages and customs, skills and professions, with their innumerable variety of desires and thoughts and everything else which makes human beings different from one another. Is there any group out of which God does not will that human beings of all races should be saved through his only Son our Lord, and so does not save them, for the Almighty cannot will in vain anything that he wills?

The apostle had urged that *prayers be made for everyone,* and had added in particular, *for kings and all who are in high positions* (1 Tm 2:1-2), who might be thought to be repelled by the humility of the Christian faith because of the trappings of power and worldly pride. Then, saying, *This is right and is acceptable in the sight of God* (1 Tm 2:3), that is, to pray for such people, he immediately added as a remedy against despair, *who wills everyone to be saved and to come to the knowledge of the truth* (1 Tm 2:4). God has judged it good that he should deign to give salvation to important people through the prayers of the humble, which we see has already been fulfilled.[179] The Lord used the same way of speaking in the gospel when he said to the Pharisees, *You tithe mint and rue and all herbs* (Lk 11:42), since not even the Pharisees tithed all the herbs belonging to others and all the herbs of all the other nations throughout the earth. So just as here *all herbs* means every kind of herb, so there we can understand *everyone* to mean every race of humanity. And it can be understood in any other way,[180] provided we are not compelled to believe that the Almighty willed anything to happen that did not happen; if, as the Truth sings without any ambi-

---

176. Augustine connects the verse with the light of grace and of revelation, whereas John's text has in mind a more comprehensive enlightenment of all human beings by the Word.
177. See Mt 11:21.
178. See *Correction and Grace* 14, 44.
179. Augustine is thinking here of the conversion of the Roman emperor and the intellectual upper class to Christianity.
180. See *Answer to Julian* IV, 8, 44; *Correction and Grace* 15, 47.

guity, *He has done whatever he willed* (Ps 115:3) in heaven and on earth, then plainly whatever he has not done he has not willed to do.

The First Human Being

28, 104. So God would have willed to preserve even the first man in that healthy state in which he had been created, and at the appropriate time after he had had children to bring him to better things without the intervention of death, where he would be unable not only to sin but even to will to sin, had God foreknown that he would have a permanent will to remain without sin as he had been created. But because God foreknew that he would make evil use of his free will, God prepared his design[181] to bring good even out of one who did evil, so that man's evil will might not be made of no effect but nevertheless the Almighty's good will might be fulfilled.

105. It was right that the first man should be made capable of willing both good and evil, not without reward if he willed good nor without punishment if he willed evil. But later his condition will be that he cannot will evil, nor will he for that reason be without free will. The will that is utterly incapable of serving sin will be much more free. For we should not blame the will, or say that it is not a will, or that it is not free, by which we so will to be blessed that we not only do not will to be wretched but are entirely incapable of willing it. Just as our will even now is unable to will unhappiness, so it will forever refuse to will iniquity. But it was necessary to observe the order according to which God willed to show how good the rational creature is even when able not to sin, although it is better when it is not able to sin; similarly, that immortality in which he was able not to die was real, although lesser than the future immortality in which he will be unable to die.

The Mercy of God Has Been Greater since the Fall

106. The former was the immortality that human nature lost through its free choice, while the latter it will receive through grace and, had it not sinned, would have received through merit. However, even then that merit could not have existed without grace, for although sin depended entirely on the freedom of the will, free will was not strong enough to retain man's original justice without divine help and participation in the unchanging good. So just as it is within a person's power to die when he will—for there is nobody who cannot kill himself, for instance by not eating, to say no more—but the will is not enough for remaining alive without the help of nourishment and other things that support

---

181. See Prv 8:35 LXX: *The will is prepared by the Lord.*

life, so man in paradise was able by his will to relinquish justice and so to destroy himself, but his will was not enough to retain the life of justice without the help of the one who had made him. But since that fall the mercy of God has been greater, since the will itself has also to be released from slavery, ruled over as it is by sin and death. Its liberation comes not at all from itself but only through the grace of God which is in the faith of Christ: thus, as it is written, *the will* itself *is prepared by the Lord* (Prv 8:35 LXX), and by the will man gains the other gifts of God through which he comes to an eternal reward.

Eternal Life Is the Reward for Good Works

107. So the apostle gives the name of a free gift of God to eternal life itself, which is certainly a reward for good works, when he says, *For the wages of sin is death, but the free gift of God is eternal life in Christ Jesus our Lord* (Rom 6:23). Wages are due payment for military service, not a gift, and so he said, *The wages of sin is death*, to show that death rightly followed sin, not undeservedly. But grace is not grace unless it is free.[182] Therefore it should be understood that even a person's meritorious good deeds are gifts of God,[183] and when eternal life is given in payment for them, what is that but grace given in return for grace? So man was made upright[184] in order that he might remain in that uprightness not without divine help, or be perverted through his own will. Whichever of these he chose, God's will would be done either by him or certainly concerning him. Hence, because he preferred to do his own will rather than God's, God's will concerning him was done, and God makes out of the mass of perdition that has flowed from his stock some vessels of honor and some of dishonor;[185] the vessels of honor he makes through his mercy, those of dishonor through his justice, so that nobody may boast of humanity, and consequently nobody may boast of himself.

Only God Could Be Mediator

108. For we would not be freed even by the one mediator between God and man himself, the man Christ Jesus, if he were not also God. But when Adam was created, an upright man, there was no need of a mediator. But when sins had separated the human race far from God, it was necessary for us to be reconciled to God for the resurrection of our flesh to eternal life by the mediator who alone

---

182. See Rom 11:6.
183. See Letters 186, 3; 194, 5, 19; *Grace and Free Will* 6, 15; 8, 19-20; Sermons 169, 2, 3; 170, 10.
184. See Eccl 7:29.
185. See Rom 9:21-23.

was born, lived and was killed without sin, so that human pride might be rebuked and healed by the humility of God and man might be shown how far he had wandered from God when he was called back by God incarnate, and an example of obedience might be offered to rebellious man by the man who is God, and, when the only-begotten took the form of a slave that had previously deserved nothing,[186] the fountain of grace might be opened, the resurrection of the flesh promised to the redeemed might be foreshown in the redeemer himself,[187] the devil might be vanquished by the very nature which he was rejoicing to have deceived, and yet man might not boast, lest pride be born again, and anything else concerning the great mystery of the redeemer which can be seen or told by those who have made progress in the faith,[188] or can only be seen, even if it cannot be told.

Between Death and Resurrection

29, 109. As for the time between a person's death and the final resurrection, souls are kept in hidden places of rest or of punishment depending on what each soul deserves because of the lot they won for themselves while they lived in the flesh.[189]

110. Nor should it be denied that the souls of the dead are supported by the piety of their loved ones who are alive, when the sacrifice of the mediator is offered for them or alms are given in the Church.[190] But such things only benefit those who during their lives have deserved that they would later benefit them. For there is a way of living that is neither so good that these things are not necessary after death, nor so bad that they are of no use after death: but there are those whose lives are so good that they do not need them, and also those whose lives are so evil that, after they have passed from this life, even such things cannot help them. Therefore it is here that we accrue all the merit or demerit that can either support a person or weigh him down. But nobody should hope to gain in the sight of the Lord after death what he has neglected here. So the customs of the Church in praying for the dead are not contrary to the mind of the apostle, who said, *For all of us must appear before the judgment seat of Christ, so that each may receive recompense for what has been done in the body, whether good or evil* (2 Cor 5:10); for even the possibility of benefiting from them was won by each person

---

186. See sections 36 and 40.
187. See 1 Cor 15:20; Col 1:18.
188. See F. G. Clancy, "Redemption," in Fitzgerald 702-704.
189. Augustine also discusses this subject in *Confessions* IX, 3, 6; *The Care to be Taken of the Dead* 3, 5; *The Trinity* XV, 25, 45; *The City of God* XII, 9, 2; XIII, 8; Sermon 280, 5.
190. In this section Augustine is giving a summary of his treatise *The Care to be Taken of the Dead*. See A. Rush, *Death and Burial in Christian Antiquity* (Washington 1941) 74-75. On the offering of the sacrifice of the Mass for the deceased see *Confessions* IX, 11, 27.

while living in the body. They are not beneficial to everybody. And why not, if not because of the differences between the life that each person lived in the body? So when sacrifices, whether that of the altar or sacrifices of alms, are offered for all the baptized who are dead, for the truly good they are acts of thanksgiving, for those who are not truly good they are propitiatory, and, as far as the truly evil are concerned, although they are of no help to the dead, they offer some kind of consolation to the living. And when they benefit somebody, they either bring full remission of punishment or at least make the condemnation itself more tolerable.[191]

The Two Cities

111. But after the resurrection, when the universal judgment is over and done with, the two cities[192] will have their boundaries, one of Christ and the other of the devil, one of the good and the other of the wicked, both composed of angels and men. The former will have no will to sin and the latter no ability to do so, nor will either have any possibility of dying; the former will live truly and happily in eternal life, the latter will exist unhappily in eternal death without the possibility of dying, for the condition of both will be without end. But among the former some will rank above others in blessedness while among the latter misery will be more tolerable for some than for others.

Future Punishments Cannot Be Denied

112. Thus it is in vain that some people, or rather most people,[193] feel human sympathy concerning the eternal punishment and the unending, unremitting suffering of the damned, and so do not believe that it will happen. It is not that they argue against holy scripture but that of their own accord they soften what is hard and eliminate the harshness of an opinion concerning the damned which they imagine to be more terrible than true. God, they say, will not forget to be merciful or in his anger shut up his compassion.[194] We read this in a holy psalm, but without any doubt it should be understood with reference to those who are

---

191. In *Expositions of the Psalms* 105, 3, too, Augustine cautiously offers the hypothesis that the divine mercy may alleviate the punishments of some of the damned, without removing them completely.
192. Augustine deals with this subject not only in *The City of God* but often elsewhere; see *True Religion* 27, 50; *The Instruction of Beginners* 19, 31; 20, 36-21, 37; *The Literal Meaning of Genesis* II, 15; *Expositions of the Psalms* 64, 2. See also G. O'Daly, *Augustine's City of God. A Reader's Guide* (Oxford 1999) 53-66.
193. See section 67.
194. See Ps 77:9.

called vessels of mercy,[195] for they too are set free from their misery not because of their own merits but by God's mercy. But if they consider that these words apply to everybody, that does not mean that they must think the damnation of those of whom it is written, *And these will go away into eternal punishment* (Mt 25:46a), can be brought to an end, for otherwise the blessedness of those of whom the opposite is said, *but the righteous into eternal life* (Mt 25:46b), would also be thought destined to end at some time. But let them think, if they so wish, that the pains of the damned are mitigated to an extent at certain intervals of time.[196] This interpretation allows us to understand that the wrath of God, which is damnation—for that is what is meant by the wrath of God, not some disturbance in the divine spirit—remains on them,[197] so that in his anger, that is, with his anger remaining, he still does not shut up his compassion, not by bringing eternal punishment to an end but by giving an alleviation or interruption of torment; for the psalm does not say "to end his anger" or "after his anger" but *in his anger* (Ps 77:9). If that meant nothing more than the least it could possibly mean, to perish from God's kingdom, to be exiled from the city of God, to be cut off from the divine life, to be deprived of that abundant sweetness of God which he has laid up for those who fear him[198] and made perfect for those who hope in him, so great is this punishment that none of the torments that we know can be compared with it if it is eternal, however many centuries they may last.[199]

Perpetual Death of the Damned

113. So that perpetual death of the damned which is separation from the life of God will last forever and will be the same for all, whatever views people may have because of their human feelings concerning varieties of punishment or alleviation or interruption of suffering, just as the eternal life of the saints will remain the same for all, whatever the differences in honor of those who shine with one harmonious light.

---

195. See Rom 9:23.
196. See S. Merkle, "Augustin über die Unterbrechung der Höllenstrafen," in M. Grabmann and J. Mausbach, eds., *Aurelius Augustinus. Die Festschrift der Görres-Gesellschaft zum 1500. Todestag des hl. Augustinus* (Cologne 1930) 197-202.
197. See Jn 3:36.
198. See Ps 31:19.
199. See the extended discussion of this subject in *The City of God* XXI.

Hope

Hope Accompanied by Holy Charity

30, 114. From this confession of the faith, which is contained in short compass in the creed and is like milk for infants[200] when considered according to the flesh, but is food for the strong when spiritually meditated and reflected on, arises the good hope of the faithful which is accompanied by holy charity.[201] But of all those things that must be faithfully believed, the only ones that concern hope are those that are contained in the Lord's Prayer, since, as the word of God attests, *Cursed are those who trust in mere mortals* (Jer 17:5), and consequently anybody who trusts in himself is bound by the chain of this curse. So it is only from the Lord God that we must ask for any good deeds that we hope to do or any reward that we hope to receive for good deeds.

The Seven Petitions of the Lord's Prayer in Matthew

115. It seems that in the gospel of Matthew the Lord's Prayer contains seven petitions, three of which are for eternal gifts and the remaining four for temporal ones, which however are necessary for acquiring the eternal gifts. What we ask for when we say, *Hallowed be your name, your kingdom come, your will be done, on earth as it is in heaven* (Mt 6:9-10)—which some people have not absurdly understood as meaning "in the body and in the spirit"—are certainly gifts that we must keep permanently: they begin here and as we progress they grow in us, but once they are perfect, which is something we must hope for in the next life, they will be possessed forever. But when we say, *Give us this day our daily bread, and forgive us our debts as we also forgive our debtors, and do not bring us to the time of trial, but deliver us from the evil one* (Mt 6:11-13), who cannot see that these petitions concern our needs in the present life? So that eternal life in which we hope to be for ever, the hallowing of God's name, his kingdom and his will will endure perfectly and immortally in our spirit and body. But our daily bread is so called because we need it here in sufficient quantity to meet the needs of body and soul, whether we understand these words spiritually or carnally or in both ways. Also it is here that the forgiveness of sins for which we ask belongs, for it is here that sins are committed: here are the temptations that lure or drive us to sin; here, finally, is the evil from which we desire to be delivered; but there none of those things exist.

---

200. See 1 Cor 3:1-2.
201. See 1 Cor 13:13.

Luke's Five Petitions

116. The evangelist Luke, however, included in the Lord's Prayer not seven but five petitions,[202] not disagreeing with Matthew but showing us by his brevity how Matthew's seven petitions are to be understood. The name of God is hallowed in the spirit, but God's kingdom will come in the resurrection of the flesh. So Luke, to show that the third petition was in a sense a repetition of the two preceding ones, made us understand it better by omitting it. Then he added three others, for daily bread, the forgiveness of sins, and avoidance of tempta- tion. But he did not include Matthew's last petition, *But deliver us from the evil one*, in order to show us its connection with the preceding one which concerns temptation. So he says *But deliver*, not "And deliver," as if to show it is one peti- tion, "Do not do this but that," so that each person may know that he is delivered from evil when he is not led into temptation.

Love

The Primacy of Love

31, 117. Now, as for love, which the apostle says is greater than the other two, that is faith and hope,[203] the greater it is in a person, the better is that person in whom it is. For when we ask whether somebody is a good person, we are not asking what he believes or hopes for but what he loves. For one who rightly loves without doubt rightly believes and hopes, and one who does not love believes in vain, even if the things he believes are true; he hopes in vain, even if the things for which he hopes are those which, according to our teaching, belong to true happiness, unless he also believes and hopes that if he asks he may also be given the ability to love. For although he cannot hope without love, it may be that he does not love that without which he cannot reach that for which he hopes, for instance if he hoped for eternal life—and who does not love that?—and did not love justice, without which nobody comes to eternal life. This is the faith of Christ, which the apostle commends to us, which works through love[204] and asks in love that it may be given what it does not yet have, seeks that it may find and knocks that the door may be opened to it.[205] For faith obtains by prayer what the law commands. Without the gift of God, that is, the Holy Spirit, by whom love is

---

202. See Lk 11:2-4.
203. See 1 Cor 13:13.
204. See Gal 5:6.
205. See Mt 7:7.

poured out in our hearts,[206] the law can command but not help, and moreover it can make a transgressor of one who cannot offer ignorance as an excuse. Where the love of God is absent, there the cupidity of the flesh reigns.

The Four Stages of Humanity

118. When people live according to the flesh, in the deepest darkness of ignorance, with no resistance from the reason, this is the first state of humanity. Then when knowledge of sin comes through the law, if the help of God's Spirit is not yet available, one who wishes to live according to the law is overcome and sins knowingly and becomes a slave of sin—*for people are slaves to whatever masters them* (2 Pt 2:19)—since knowledge of the law causes sin to *work every kind of concupiscence* (Rom 7:8) in humans, piling up transgressions so that what is written is fulfilled: *But law came in, with the result that the trespass multiplied* (Rom 5:20). This is humanity's second state. But if God turns again, so that we can believe that he helps us to obey his commandments, and a person begins to be *led by the Spirit of God* (Rom 8:14), he begins to desire against the flesh with the stronger love of charity, so that although the struggle of man against himself continues, since his sickness has not yet been entirely cured, nonetheless the one *who is righteous lives by faith* (Rom 1:17), and he lives justly insofar as he does not give in to the evil of concupiscence, because that is conquered by delight in justice. This is the third state of humanity, a good that is hoped for, and if a person perseveres religiously in this, peace awaits him at the end, which will be fulfilled after this life in repose of the spirit, and then also in the resurrection of the flesh. The first of these four states is before the law, the second under the law, the third under grace and the fourth in full and perfect peace. And this is how the life of God's people progressed through time, as it pleased God who *disposes all things in measure and number and weight* (Wis 11:21). His people existed first before the law was given, then under the law that was given through Moses, then under the grace that was revealed by the first coming of the mediator. However, grace was not lacking even earlier to those on whom it was right that it should be conferred, although it was veiled and hidden as God's dispositions for that period required. Except through the faith of Christ, not one of the just ones of old could find salvation, nor could he have been prophesied for us through their ministry, sometimes in a more open and sometimes in a more secret manner, had he not also been known to them.

---

206. See Rom 5:5.

The Grace of Regeneration

119. Whenever in any of what we may call those four ages the grace of regeneration has found out a single person, all his previous sins are remitted, and that guilt which he contracted by being born is removed by rebirth, although so true is the saying, *The Spirit blows where it chooses* (Jn 3:8), that some have never known that second state of servitude under the law but begin to receive God's help when they receive his commandment.

No Harm to Those Who Have Received the Sacrament of Regeneration

120. Before a person can be capable of keeping the law, he must live according to the flesh. But, if he has already received the sacrament of regeneration, he will receive no harm if he then passes away from this life, because Christ died and rose again that he might be Lord of the living and the dead,[207] and the kingdom of death will not hold one for whom he, free among the dead, laid down his life.[208]

The End of the Commandment Is Charity

32, 121. So all the divine commandments concern charity, of which the apostle says: *The end of the commandment is charity that comes from a pure heart, a good conscience, and sincere faith* (1 Tm 1:5). Thus charity is the end of every commandment, that is, every commandment concerns charity. But what is done in fear of punishment or for any carnal reason, and not with reference to that charity which the Holy Spirit pours out in our hearts,[209] is not yet being done as it should be done, although it seems to be being done. This charity has to do with God and our neighbor, and *on these two commandments hang all the law and the prophets* (Mt 22:40). Consider also the gospel and the apostles, for that is where we find the sayings, *The end of the commandment is charity*, and *God is love* (1 Jn 4:8). So whatever God commands, such as, *You shall not commit adultery* (Ex 20:14; Dt 5:18), and whatever is not commanded but advised for spiritual reasons, for instance, *It is well for a man not to touch a woman* (1 Cor 7:1), is rightly observed when it is done out of love of God and of one's neighbor because of God, both in this world and in the world to come, of God now through faith and then face-to-face, and of our neighbor now also through faith. For we mortals do not know the hearts of other mortals. But then the Lord *will bring to*

---

207. See Rom 14:9.
208. See Ps 88:5.
209. See Rom 5:5.

light the things now hidden in darkness and will disclose the purposes of the heart. Then each one will receive commendation from God (1 Cor 4:5), because each will praise and love in his neighbor what God has illuminated, so that it may not be hidden from him. As charity grows, cupidity decreases until in this world that greatness is reached than which nothing can be greater, for *no one has greater charity than this, to lay down his life for his friends* (Jn 15:13). But who can say how great charity will be where there is no cupidity to restrain or overcome it? Nobody, surely, for where there is no battling with death,[210] there health will be at its most perfect.

Epilogue

Conclusion

122. But there must come a time for this book to end, and it is for you to see whether or not you should call it a handbook. But I, not thinking it right to spurn your eagerness for Christ, believing good of you and hoping for good from you with the help of our redeemer, and loving you greatly among his members, have done what I can to write this book, *Faith, Hope, and Charity,* for you, and I wish it were as useful as it is long.

---

210. The words translate *contentio mortis*, found in the North African Vulgate translation of 1 Cor 15:54.

Index of Scripture

(prepared by Michael Dolan)

The numbers after the scriptural reference refer to the section of the work

True Religion
(pp. 29-104)

The Advantage of Believing
(pp. 116-148)

Faith and the Creed
(pp. 155-174)

Faith in the Unseen
(pp. 183-194)

Demonic Divination
(pp. 204-217)

Faith and Works
(pp. 226-261)

Enchiridion
(pp. 273-343)

General Index

(prepared by Kathleen Strattan)

Numbers refer only to sections of
the works, not to chapters.

True Religion

(pp. 27-102)

The Advantage of Believing
(pp. 114-146)

Faith and the Creed
(pp. 153-172)

Faith in the Unseen

(pp. 181-192)

Demonic Divination

(pp. 202-215)

Faith and Works

(pp. 224-259)

Church:
    discipline by, 3–4; 6–7; 32; 34; 48; 49
    good and wicked in, 1–8; 31–39; 49
Church unity. *See* unity
commandments
    faith and, 20; 40
    the first, 17
    the holy commandment, 45–46
    to love, 16; 40
    rich man and, 20; 27; 49
compassion
    See also tolerance
    love and, 25
concubines, 35
confession of sin: baptism, preparation for,
    8–9
conscience, 25
continence: baptism, preparation for, 8–9
converts, 48
1 Cor. 3:11-15, 27
Creed, the, 14; 36
Crispus, 15
crucifixion of Christ, 15
cursing, 3; 25
Cyprian, 35; 49

damnation, eternal, 25–27; 42–45; 49
dancers, 49
darnel. *See under* Church: good and wicked in
dead faith, 21–30; 31–38; 40; 46
demons. *See* devils
demotion, 3
devil. *See* Satan
devils: faith of, 22; 27; 30; 38; 40
disciples, 31
    See also individual names
discipline
    See also punishment
    after death, 4
    by the Church, 3–4; 6–7; 32; 34; 48; 49
divorce, 28; 35
    adultery and, 35
    baptism and, 2
Donatists, 6
drunkenness, 3; 25; 33

emnities, 25
envy, 25
    devil as envious, 3
eternal life, 25; 40; 42–43; 48–49
    See also salvation
    rich man and, 20; 27; 49
eternal punishment, 25–27; 42–45; 49
eunuch, baptism of, 14; 18
everlasting life. *See* eternal life

evil
    See also under Church: good and
      wicked in; sin
    and eternal damnation, 42
    Remove the evil from yourselves, 3
excommunication, 3–4; 6; 34; 48
exorcisms: baptism, preparation for, 8–9

faith, 11; 27; 39; 41
    See also Christian faith, the; salvation
    and baptism (*see* baptism)
    in Christ, 14
    *Christ dwells in our hearts through
      faith,* 27
    and the commandments, 20
    of devils, 22; 27; 30; 38; 40
    faith that works through love, 21–30;
      27; 42
    grace and, 38
    intellect and, 9–20
    justification, 27
    and the law, 21–30; 45
    living vs. dead, 21–30; 31–40; 46
    prayers of, 39
    without love, 21; 25
    without works, 21; 40
faithful, the, 11
fasting: baptism, preparation for, 8–9
fear: love and, 39
fire:
    eternal, 25
    purifying, 27
    salvation through, 18; 24–28; 42–44; 47
fishermen, 32
flesh, lusts of. *See* carnal desires
forgiveness of sin:
    at baptism, 36
    ongoing, 41
fornication, 25; 29
    See also adultery
    baptism and, 17–18
foundation, Christ as, 24–28
freedom, 45

Gaius, 15
generosity, 25
gentiles, 44
gladiators, 33
gluttony, 25
God
    See also Trinity; *specific topics*
    believing in, worshiping, knowing, 41
    "gold" and "wood." *See* foundation, Christ
      as
    good, achieving, 41
    good and wicked people. *See under* Church:

Enchiridion

(pp. 271-341)